MONGOLIA

INVESTMENT AND BUSINESS GUIDE

VOLUME 1

STRATEGIC AND PRACTICAL INFORMATION

International Business Publications, USA
Washington DC, USA - Mongolia

MONGOLIA

INVESTMENT AND BUSINESS GUIDE

VOLUME 1 STRATEGIC AND PRACTICAL INFORMATION

UPDATED ANNUALLY

Cover Design: **International Business Publications, USA**

We express our sincere appreciation to all government agencies and international organizations which provided information and other materials for this guide

2013 Updated Reprint International Business Publications, USA
ISBN 1-57751-598-6

This guide provides basic information for starting or/and conducting business in the country. The extraordinary volume of materials covering the topic, prevents us from placing all these materials in this guide. For more detailed information on issues related to any specific investment and business activity in the country, please contact Global Investment Center, USA
Please acquire the list of our business intelligence and marketing reports and other business publications. We constantly update and expand our business intelligence and marketing materials. Please contact the center for the updated list of reports on over 250 countries.

in the USA: **Global Investment Center, USA.**
P.O.Box 15343, Washington, DC 20043
Phone: (202) 546-2103, Fax: (202) 546-3275, E-mail: rusric@erols.com

For additional analytical, marketing and other information please contact Global Investment Center, USA

Printed in the USA

MONGOLIA

INVESTMENT AND BUSINESS GUIDE

VOLUME 1

STRATEGIC AND PRACTICAL INFORMATION

STRATEGIC AND DEVELOPMENT PROFILES

Capital (and largest city)	Ulan Bator 47°55′N 106°53′E47.917°N 106.883°E
Official language(s)	Mongolian
Official script(s)	Mongolian Cyrillic Mongolian script
Ethnic groups	95.35% Mongols 3.86% Kazakhs 0.8% others
Demonym	Mongol, Mongolian
Government	Parliamentary republic
- President	Tsakhiagiin Elbegdorj
- Prime Minister	Norovyn Altankhuyag
Legislature	State Great Khural
Formation	
- Formation of the Xiongnu confederation	209 BC
- Formation of the Mongol Empire	1206
- Independence declared (from Qing Dynasty)	December 29, 1911
Area	
- Total	1,564,115.75 km^2 (19th) 603,909 sq mi
- Water (%)	0.43
Population	
- 2010 census	2,754,685
- Density	1.76/km^2 (236th) 5.03/sq mi
GDP (PPP)	2011 estimate
- Total	$13.264 billion
- Per capita	$4,743
GDP (nominal)	2011 estimate
- Total	$8.506 billion
- Per capita	$3,042
Gini (2005)	33.0 (medium)
HDI	▲0.653 (medium) (100th)
Currency	Tögrög (MNT)
Time zone	(UTC+7 to +8)
Date formats	yyyy.mm.dd (CE)
Drives on the	right
ISO 3166 code	MN
Internet TLD	.mn
Calling code	976

Mongolia literally *Mongol country/nation*) is a landlocked country in East and Central Asia. It is bordered by Russia to the north and the People's Republic of China to the south, east and west. Although Mongolia does not share a border with Kazakhstan, its western-most point is only 38 kilometres (24 mi) from Kazakhstan's eastern tip. Ulaanbaatar, the capital and largest city, is home to about 38% of the population. Mongolia's political system is a parliamentary republic.

The area of what is now Mongolia has been ruled by various nomadic empires, including the Xiongnu, the Xianbei, the Rouran, the Gökturks and others. The Mongol Empire was founded by Genghis Khan in 1206. After the collapse of the Yuan Dynasty, the Mongols returned to their earlier pattern of constant internal conflict and occasional raids on the Chinese borderlands. In the 16th and 17th centuries, Mongolia came under the influence of Tibetan Buddhism. At the end of the 17th century, most of Mongolia had been incorporated into the area ruled by the Qing Dynasty. During the collapse of the Qing Dynasty in 1911, Mongolia declared independence, but had to struggle until 1921 to firmly establish *de facto* independence from the Republic of China, and until 1945 to gain international recognition.

As a consequence, it came under strong Russian and Soviet influence; in 1924, the Mongolian People's Republic was declared, and Mongolian politics began to follow the same patterns as the Soviet politics of the time. After the breakdown of communist regimes in Eastern Europe in late 1989, Mongolia saw its own Democratic Revolution in early 1990, which led to a multi-party system, a new constitution in 1992, and transition to a market economy.

At 1,564,116 square kilometres (603,909 sq mi), Mongolia is the 19th largest and the most sparsely populated independent country in the world, with a population of around 2.9 million people. It is also the world's second-largest landlocked country after Kazakhstan. The country contains very little arable land, as much of its area is covered by steppes, with mountains to the north and west and the Gobi Desert to the south. Approximately 30% of the population are nomadic or semi-nomadic. The predominant religion in Mongolia is Tibetan Buddhism, and the majority of the state's citizens are of the Mongol ethnicity, though Kazakhs, Tuvans, and other minorities also live in the country, especially in the west. About 20% of the population live on less than US$1.25 per day. Analysts have predicted that Mongolia can become one of fastest-growing economies of the 2010s, as well as a key investment target for global mining corporations

STRATEGIC PROFILE

Background: Long a province of China, Mongolia won its independence in 1921 with Soviet backing. A communist regime was installed in 1924. During the early 1990s, the ex-communist Mongolian People's Revolutionary Party (MPRP) gradually yielded its monopoly on power. In 1996, the Democratic Union Coalition (DUC) defeated the MPRP in a national election and has attempted to establish a number of reforms to modernize the economy. However, many former communists retain key posts and implementation has been difficult.

GEOGRAPHY

Location: Northern Asia, between China and Russia

Geographic coordinates: 46 00 N, 105 00 E

Map references: Asia

Area:
total: 1.565 million sq km
land: 1.565 million sq km
water: 0 sq km

Area - comparative: slightly smaller than Alaska

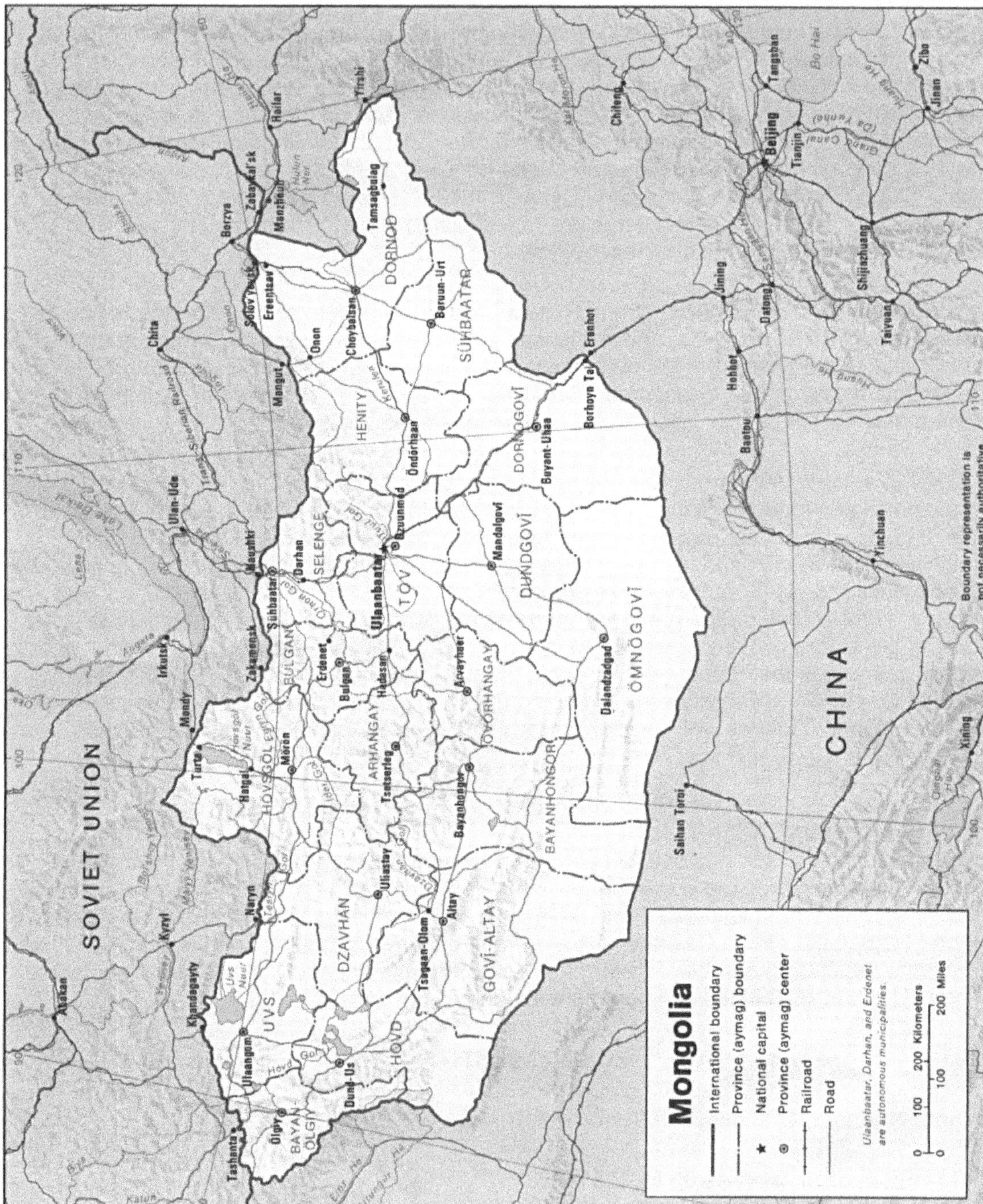

Land boundaries:
total: 8,114 km
border countries: China 4,673 km, Russia 3,441 km

Coastline: 0 km (landlocked)

Maritime claims: none (landlocked)

Climate: desert; continental (large daily and seasonal temperature ranges)

Terrain: vast semidesert and desert plains; mountains in west and southwest; Gobi Desert in southeast

Elevation extremes:
lowest point: Hoh Nuur 518 m *highest point:* Tavan Bogd Uul 4,374 m

Natural resources: oil, coal, copper, molybdenum, tungsten, phosphates, tin, nickel, zinc, wolfram, fluorspar, gold

Land use:
arable land: 1% *permanent crops:* 0% *permanent pastures:* 80%
forests and woodland: 9% *other:* 10%

Irrigated land: 800 sq km
Natural hazards: dust storms can occur in the spring; grassland fires
Environment - current issues: limited natural fresh water resources; policies of the former communist regime promoting rapid urbanization and industrial growth have raised concerns about their negative effects on the environment; the burning of soft coal in power plants and the lack of enforcement of environmental laws have severely polluted the air in Ulaanbaatar; deforestation, overgrazing, the converting of virgin land to agricultural production have increased soil erosion from wind and rain; desertification and mining activities have also had a deleterious effect on the environment

Environment - international agreements:
party to: Biodiversity, Climate Change, Climate Change-Kyoto Protocol, Desertification, Endangered Species, Environmental Modification, Hazardous Wastes, Law of the Sea, Nuclear Test Ban, Ozone Layer Protection, Wetlands
signed, but not ratified: none of the selected agreements

Geography - note: landlocked; strategic location between China and Russia

PEOPLE

Population: 2,650,952

Age structure:
0-14 years: 34% (male 461,719; female 447,426)
15-64 years: 62% (male 816,851; female 816,651)
65 years and over: 4% (male 46,682; female 61,623)

Population growth rate: 1.54%

Birth rate: 21.53 births/1,000 population
Death rate: 6.14 deaths/1,000 population
Net migration rate: 0 migrant(s)/1,000 population

Sex ratio:
at birth: 1.05 male(s)/female
under 15 years: 1.03 male(s)/female
15-64 years: 1 male(s)/female
65 years and over: 0.76 male(s)/female
total population: 1 male(s)/female

Infant mortality rate: 41.22 deaths/1,000 live births

Life expectancy at birth:
total population: 67.25 years
male: 64.98 years
female: 69.64 years

Total fertility rate: 2.4 children born/woman

Nationality:
noun: Mongolian(s)
adjective: Mongolian

Ethnic groups: Mongol 90%, Kazakh 4%, other 6%
Religions: predominantly Tibetan Buddhist, Muslim 4%
note: previously limited religious activity because of communist regime
Languages: Khalkha Mongol 90%, Turkic, Russian

Literacy:
definition: age 15 and over can read and write
total population: 82.9%
male: 88.6%
female: 77.2% (1988 est.)

GOVERNMENT

Country name:
conventional long form: none
conventional short form: Mongolia
local long form: none
local short form: Mongol Uls
former: Outer Mongolia

Data code: MG
Government type: republic
Capital: Ulaanbaatar

Administrative divisions: 18 provinces (aymguud, singular - aymag) and 3 municipalities* (hotuud, singular - hot); Arhangay, Bayanhongor, Bayan-Olgiy, Bulgan, Darhan*, Dornod, Dornogovi, Dundgovi, Dzavhan, Erdenet*, Govi-Altay, Hentiy, Hovd, Hovsgol, Omnogovi, Ovorhangay, Selenge, Suhbaatar, Tov, Ulaanbaatar*, Uvs

Independence: 13 March 1921 (from China)
National holiday: National Day, 11 July (1921)
Constitution: 12 February 1992

Legal system: blend of Russian, Chinese, Turkish, and Western systems of law that combines aspects of a parliamentary and presidential system; constitution ambiguous on judicial review of legislative acts; has not accepted compulsory ICJ jurisdiction

Suffrage: 18 years of age; universal

Executive branch:

chief of state: President Tsakhia ELBEGDORJ (since 18 June 2009)

head of government: Prime Minister Norov ALTANKHUYAG (since 9 August 2012); Deputy Prime Minister Dendev TERBISHDAGVA (since 20 August 2012)

cabinet: Cabinet nominated by the prime minister in consultation with the president and confirmed by the State Great Hural (parliament)

elections: presidential candidates nominated by political parties represented in State Great Hural and elected by popular vote for a four-year term (eligible for a second term); election last held on 24 May 2009 (next to be held by May 2013); following legislative elections, leader of majority party or majority coalition usually elected prime minister by State Great Hural

election results: in elections in May 2009, Tsakhia ELBEGDORJ elected president; percent of vote - Tsakhia ELBEGDORJ 51.2%, Nambar ENKHBAYAR 47.4%, others 1.3%

Legislative branch:

unicameral State Great Hural (76 seats; of which 48 members are directly elected from 26 electoral districts, while 28 members are proportionally elected based on a party's share of the total votes; all serve four-year terms)

elections: last held on 28 June 2012 (next to be held in June 2016)

election results: percent of vote by party - NA; seats by party - DP 31, MPP 25, Justice Coalition 11, others 5, vacant 4

Judicial branch: Supreme Court, serves as appeals court for people's and provincial courts, but to date rarely overturns verdicts of lower courts, judges are nominated by the General Council of Courts for approval by the State Great Hural

Political parties and leaders: Democratic Union Coalition or DUC (includes the MNDP and the MSDP); Independence Party [leader NA]; Mongolian Conservative Party or MCP [JARGALSAIHAN]; Mongolian Democratic New Socialist Party or MDNSP [B. ERDENEBAT, chairman]; Mongolian Democratic Renaissance Party or MDRP [BYAMBASUREN, chairman]; Mongolian National Democratic Party or MNDP [R. AMARJARGAL, chairman; B. DELGERMAA, general secretary]; Mongolian People's Revolutionary Party or MPRP [N. ENKHBAYAR, chairman; L. ENEBISH, general secretary]; Mongolian Republican Party or MRP [B. JARGALSAIHAN]; Mongolian Social Democratic Party or MSDP [Radnaasumbereliyn

GONCHIGDORJ, chairman; N. ALTANKHUYAG, general secretary]; Mongolian United Heritage Party or UHP [B. JAMTSAI] (includes the United Party of Herdsman and Farmers, Independence Party, Traditional United Conservative Party, and Mongolian United Private Property Owners Party); Mongolian United Private Property Owners Party [leader NA]); United Party of Herdsman and Farmers [leader NA]; Traditional United Conservative Party [leader NA]; Workers' Party [leader NA]

International organization participation: AsDB, ASEAN (observer), CCC, ESCAP, FAO, G-77, IAEA, IBRD, ICAO, ICFTU, ICRM, IDA, IFAD, IFC, IFRCS, ILO, IMF, IMO, Intelsat, Interpol, IOC, ISO, ITU, NAM, OPCW, UN, UNCTAD, UNESCO, UNIDO, UPU, WHO, WIPO, WMO, WToO, WTrO

Diplomatic representation in the US:
chief of mission: Ambassador Jalbuugiyn CHOINHOR
chancery: 2833 M Street NW, Washington, DC 20007
telephone: (202) 333-7117
FAX: (202) 298-9227
consulate(s) general: New York

Diplomatic representation from the US:
chief of mission: Ambassador Alphonse F. LA PORTA
embassy: inner north side of the Big Ring, just west of the Selbe Gol, Ulaanbaatar
mailing address: c/o American Embassy Beijing, Micro Region 11, Big Ring Road, C. P. O. 1021, Ulaanbaatar 13; PSC 461, Box 300, FPO AP 96521-0002
telephone: [976] (1) 329095
FAX: [976] (1) 320776

Flag description: three equal, vertical bands of red (hoist side), blue, and red; centered on the hoist-side red band in yellow is the national emblem ("soyombo" - a columnar arrangement of abstract and geometric representation for fire, sun, moon, earth, water, and the yin-yang symbol)

ECONOMY

Mongolia's extensive mineral deposits and attendant growth in mining-sector activities have transformed Mongolia's economy, which traditionally has been dependent on herding and agriculture. Mongolia's copper, gold, coal, molybdenum, fluorspar, uranium, tin, and tungsten deposits, among others, have attracted foreign direct investment. Soviet assistance, at its height one-third of GDP, disappeared almost overnight in 1990 and 1991 at the time of the dismantlement of the USSR.

The following decade saw Mongolia endure both deep recession, because of political inaction and natural disasters, as well as economic growth, because of reform-embracing, free-market economics and extensive privatization of the formerly state-run economy. The country opened a fledgling stock exchange in 1991. Mongolia joined the World Trade Organization in 1997 and seeks to expand its participation in regional economic and trade regimes. Growth averaged nearly 9% per year in 2004-08 largely because of high copper prices globally and new gold production. By late 2008, Mongolia was hit hard by the global financial crisis. Slower global economic growth hurt the country's exports, notably copper, and slashed government revenues. As a result, Mongolia's real economy contracted 1.3% in 2009. In early 2009, the International Monetary Fund reached a $236 million Stand-by Arrangement with Mongolia and the country has largely emerged from the crisis with better regulations and closer supervision.

The banking sector strengthened but weaknesses remain. In October 2009, Mongolia passed long-awaited legislation on an investment agreement to develop the Oyu Tolgoi mine, considered to be among the world's largest untapped copper-gold deposits. Mongolia's ongoing dispute with a foreign investor over Oyu Tolgoi, however, has called into question the attractiveness of Mongolia as a destination for foreign direct investment. Negotiations to develop the massive Tavan Tolgoi coal field also have stalled. The economy has grown more than 10% per year since 2010, largely on the strength of commodity exports to nearby countries and high government spending domestically. Mongolia's economy, however, faces near-term economic risks from the government's loose fiscal and monetary policies, which are contributing to high inflation, and from uncertainties in foreign demand for Mongolian exports.

Trade with China represents more than half of Mongolia's total external trade - China receives more than 90% of Mongolia's exports and is Mongolia's largest supplier. Mongolia has relied on Russia for energy supplies, leaving it vulnerable to price increases; in the first 11 months of 2013, Mongolia purchased 76% of its gasoline and diesel fuel and a substantial amount of electric power from Russia. A drop in foreign direct investment and a decrease in Chinese demand for Mongolia's mineral exports are putting pressure on Mongolia's balance of payments. Remittances from Mongolians working abroad, particularly in South Korea, are significant.

GDP (purchasing power parity):
$17.03 billion (2013 est.)
country comparison to the world: 140
$15.23 billion (2012 est.)
$13.57 billion (2011 est.)
note:data are in 2013 US dollars

GDP (official exchange rate):
$11.14 billion (2013 est.)

GDP - real growth rate:
11.8% (2013 est.)
country comparison to the world: 6
12.3% (2012 est.)
17.5% (2011 est.)

GDP - per capita (PPP):
$5,900 (2013 est.)
country comparison to the world: 152
$5,400 (2012 est.)
$4,900 (2011 est.)
note:data are in 2013 US dollars

GDP - composition, by end use:
household consumption: 58.5%
government consumption: 14.9%
investment in fixed capital: 55.8%
investment in inventories: 0%
exports of goods and services: 50%
imports of goods and services: -79.2%

(2013 est.)

GDP - composition, by sector of origin:
agriculture: 16.5%
industry: 32.6%
services: 50.9% (2013 est.)

Agriculture - products:
wheat, barley, vegetables, forage crops; sheep, goats, cattle, camels, horses

Industries:
construction and construction materials; mining (coal, copper, molybdenum, fluorspar, tin, tungsten, gold); oil; food and beverages; processing of animal products, cashmere and natural fiber manufacturing

Industrial production growth rate:
11% (2013 est.)
country comparison to the world: 10

Labor force:
1.037 million (2011 est.)
country comparison to the world: 141

Labor force - by occupation:
agriculture: 33%
industry: 10.6%
services: 56.4%

Unemployment rate:
9% (2011 est.)
country comparison to the world: 99
13%

Population below poverty line:
29.8% (2011 est.)

Household income or consumption by percentage share:
lowest 10%: 3%
highest 10%: 28.4%

Distribution of family income - Gini index:
36.5
country comparison to the world: 84
32.8 (2002)

Budget:
revenues: $3.462 billion
expenditures: $4.36 billion (2013 est.)

Taxes and other revenues:
31.1% of GDP (2013 est.)
country comparison to the world: 87

Budget surplus (+) or deficit (-):
-8.1% of GDP (2013 est.)
country comparison to the world: 196

Fiscal year:
calendar year

Inflation rate (consumer prices):
8.2% (2013 est.)
country comparison to the world: 196
15% (2012 est.)

Central bank discount rate:
13.25% (31 December 2012)
country comparison to the world: 15
12.25% (31 December 2011 est.)

Commercial bank prime lending rate:
17.5% (31 December 2013 est.)
country comparison to the world: 23
18.2% (31 December 2012 est.)

Stock of narrow money:
$1.219 billion (31 December 2013 est.)
country comparison to the world: 143
$1.318 billion (31 December 2012 est.)

Stock of broad money:
$6.329 billion (31 December 2013 est.)
country comparison to the world: 120
$5.472 billion (31 December 2012 est.)

Stock of domestic credit:
$3.297 billion (31 December 2013 est.)
country comparison to the world: 122
$3.09 billion (31 December 2012 est.)

Market value of publicly traded shares:
$1.293 billion (31 December 2012 est.)
country comparison to the world: 92
$1.579 billion (31 December 2011)
$1.093 billion (31 December 2010 est.)

Current account balance:
-$3.639 billion (2013 est.)
country comparison to the world: 162

-$3.362 billion (2012 est.)

Exports:
$4.294 billion (2013 est.)
country comparison to the world: 117
$4.382 billion (2012 est.)

Exports - commodities:
copper, apparel, livestock, animal products, cashmere, wool, hides, fluorspar, other nonferrous metals, coal, crude oil

Exports - partners:
China 89%, Canada 4.1%

Imports:
$5.696 billion (2013 est.)
country comparison to the world: 121
$5.934 billion (2012 est.)

Imports - commodities:
machinery and equipment, fuel, cars, food products, industrial consumer goods, chemicals, building materials, cigarettes and tobacco, appliances, soap and detergent

Imports - partners:
China 37.5%, Russia 25.6%, US 9.4%, South Korea 6.1%, Japan 4.9%

Debt - external:
$4.954 billion (31 December 2013 est.)
country comparison to the world: 120
$4.669 billion (31 December 2012 est.)

Stock of direct foreign investment - at home:
$1.69 billion (31 December 2013 est.)
country comparison to the world: 101
$4.452 billion (31 December 2012 est.)

Stock of direct foreign investment - abroad:
$NA (31 December 2013 est.)
$44 million (31 December 2012 est.)

Exchange rates:
togrog/tugriks (MNT) per US dollar -
1,444.3 (2013 est.)
1,357.6 (2012 est.)
1,357.1 (2010 est.)
1,442.8
1,170

ENERGY

Electricity - production:
4.48 billion kWh
country comparison to the world: 120

Electricity - consumption:
3.951 billion kWh
country comparison to the world: 124

Electricity - exports:
22 million kWh
country comparison to the world: 88

Electricity - imports:
263 million kWh
country comparison to the world: 83

Electricity - installed generating capacity:
833,200 kW
country comparison to the world: 128

Electricity - from fossil fuels:
99.9% of total installed capacity
country comparison to the world: 45

Electricity - from nuclear fuels:
0% of total installed capacity
country comparison to the world: 133

Electricity - from hydroelectric plants:
0% of total installed capacity
country comparison to the world: 182

Electricity - from other renewable sources:
0.1% of total installed capacity
country comparison to the world: 102

Crude oil - production:
9,935 bbl/day
country comparison to the world: 91

Crude oil - exports:
5,680 bbl/day
country comparison to the world: 64

Crude oil - imports:
0 bbl/day

country comparison to the world: 88

Crude oil - proved reserves:
NA bbl

Refined petroleum products - production:
0 bbl/day
country comparison to the world: 169

Refined petroleum products - consumption:
21,610 bbl/day
country comparison to the world: 125

Refined petroleum products - exports:
0 bbl/day
country comparison to the world: 195

Refined petroleum products - imports:
17,360 bbl/day
country comparison to the world: 109

Natural gas - production:
0 cu m
country comparison to the world: 161

Natural gas - consumption:
0 cu m
country comparison to the world: 167

Natural gas - exports:
0 cu m
country comparison to the world: 142

Natural gas - imports:
0 cu m
country comparison to the world: 91

Natural gas - proved reserves:
0 cu m
country comparison to the world: 165

Carbon dioxide emissions from consumption of energy:
10.21 million Mt

COMMUNICATIONS

Telephones - main lines in use:
176,700
country comparison to the world: 129

Telephones - mobile cellular:
3.375 million
country comparison to the world: 126

Telephone system:
general assessment: network is improving with international direct dialing available in many areas; a fiber-optic network has been installed that is improving broadband and communication services between major urban centers with multiple companies providing inter-city fiber-optic cable services
domestic: very low fixed-line teledensity; there are multiple mobile-cellular providers and subscribership is increasing
international: country code - 976; satellite earth stations - 7

Broadcast media:
following a law passed in 2005, Mongolia's state-run radio and TV provider converted to a public service provider; also available are private radio and TV broadcasters, as well as multi-channel satellite and cable TV providers; more than 100 radio stations, including some 20 via repeaters for the public broadcaster; transmissions of multiple international broadcasters are available

Internet country code:
.mn

Internet hosts:
20,084
country comparison to the world: 118

Internet users:
330,000
country comparison to the world: 125

TRANSPORTATION

Airports:
44
country comparison to the world: 98

Airports - with paved runways:
total: 15
over 3,047 m: 2
2,438 to 3,047 m: 10
1,524 to 2,437 m: 3

Airports - with unpaved runways:
total: 29

over 3,047 m: 2
2,438 to 3,047 m: 2
1,524 to 2,437 m: 24
under 914 m:
1

Heliports:
1

Railways:
total: 1,908 km
country comparison to the world: 73
broad gauge: 1,908 km 1.520-m gauge
note:the railway is 50 percent owned by the Russian State Railway

Roadways:
total: 49,249 km
country comparison to the world: 78
paved: 4,800 km
unpaved: 44,449 km

Waterways:
580 km (the only waterway in operation is Lake Hovsgol) (135 km); Selenge River (270 km) and Orhon River (175 km) are navigable but carry little traffic; lakes and rivers freeze in winter, they are open from May to September)
country comparison to the world: 82

Merchant marine:
total: 57
country comparison to the world: 68
by type: bulk carrier 21, cargo 25, chemical tanker 1, container 2, liquefied gas 2, passenger/cargo 2, roll on/roll off 3, vehicle carrier 1
foreign-owned: 44 (Indonesia 2, Japan 2, North Korea 1, Russia 2, Singapore 3, Ukraine 1, Vietnam 33)

MILITARY

Military branches:
Mongolian Armed Forces (Mongol ulsyn zevsegt huchin): Mongolian Army (includes Mongolian Air and Air Defense, which is to become a separate service in 2015); there is no navy

Military service age and obligation:
18-25 years of age for compulsory and voluntary military service; conscript service obligation is 12 months in land or air defense forces or police; a small portion of Mongolian land forces (2.5 percent) is comprised of contract soldiers; women cannot be deployed overseas for military operations

Manpower available for military service:
males age 16-49: 898,546
females age 16-49: 891,192 (2010 est.)

Manpower fit for military service:
males age 16-49: 726,199
females age 16-49: 756,628 (2010 est.)

Manpower reaching militarily significant age annually:
male: 30,829
female: 29,648 (2010 est.)

Military expenditures:
1.12% of GDP
country comparison to the world: 92
0.99% of GDP
1.12% of GDP

TRANSNATIONAL ISSUES

Disputes - international:
none

Refugees and internally displaced persons:
stateless persons: 220

IMPORTANT INFORMATION FOR UNDERSTANDING MONGOLIA

Official Name: Mongolia

PROFILE

Geography
Area: 1,566,500 sq. km. (604,103 sq. mi.); slightly larger than Alaska (land boundaries 8,114 km.).
Terrain: Almost 90% of land area is pasture or desert, of varying usefulness; 1% arable; 9% forested.
Climate: Continental, with little precipitation and sharp seasonal fluctuations.

People
Nationality: *Noun and adjective*--Mongolian(s).
Population: 2.735 million.
Annual population growth rate: 1.4%.
Health: *Infant mortality rate* (under 1 year)--19.4/1,000 ; 20/1,000 .
Life expectancy--67 yrs. 67.9 yrs..
Ethnic groups: About 95% Mongol (predominantly Khalkha); 5% Turkic (largest group, Kazakh); Buriat.
Language: Mongolian.
Religions: Buddhist Lamaism 50%, Muslim 4% (primarily in the southwest), shamanist and Christian 6%, and none 40%.
Education: *Years compulsory*--9 (provided free by the government). *Literacy*--98%.

Government
Type: Mixed parliamentary/presidential.
Independence: gained in 1921; in 1990, democratic reform begun and shift from dependence on the former Soviet Union declared.
Constitutions: 1960 and February 12, 1992.
Branches: *Executive*--power is divided between a president (elected by a popular election in May 2009) and prime minister (current cabinet nominated by the prime minister was approved in November 2009 following the appointment of a new prime minister; most cabinet members remained in place from the September 2008 government of the previous prime minister, who stepped aside due to health problems). *Legislative*--State Great Hural (parliament; 76 members elected in June 2008). *Judicial*--Constitutional Court is empowered to supervise the implementation of the constitution, makes judgment on the violation of its provisions, and solves disputes. Legal code based on Continental and Russian law. Legal education at Mongolian State University and private universities. Mongolia accepts International Court of Justice jurisdiction.
Political parties : 17 registered political parties.
Suffrage: Universal at 18.
Administrative subdivisions: 21 aimags (provinces) and one city (Ulaanbaatar).

Economy
GDP (est.): 8.25 trillion Mongolian Tugruks/MNT (U.S. $6.8 billion at current exchange rates).
GDP growth : 7%.
Per capita GDP : approx. $2,008.
Natural resources: Coal (thermal and metallurgical), copper, molybdenum, silver, iron, phosphates, tin, nickel, zinc, wolfram, fluorspar, gold, uranium, and petroleum.
Agriculture (15% of 2010 GDP, livelihood for about 40% of population): *Products*--livestock and

byproducts, hay fodder, vegetables.
Industry (31% of 2009 GDP, composed of mining 21.8%, manufacturing 6.4%, and utilities (electricity, gas, and water) 2.4%: *Types*--minerals (primarily copper and gold), animal-derived products, building materials, food/beverage.
Trade: Total turnover of foreign trade for 2010 was $6.2 billion. *Exports*--$2.9 billion (U.S. dollar (USD) figures based on current USD/MNT exchange rate): minerals, livestock, animal products, and textiles. *Markets*--Asian countries (approx. 87.4%), European countries (approx. 4.5%), and countries of American continent (approx. 5.1%). *Imports*--$3.3 billion: machinery and equipment, fuels, food products, industrial consumer goods, chemicals, building equipment, vehicles, textiles. *Suppliers*--91 countries account for 93.2% of total imports, of which European countries (46.5%) and Asian countries (47.3%).
Aid received: From 1991-2009, official development assistance to Mongolia from bilateral and multilateral donors totaled over $4.056 billion. Received $357.47 million in official development assistance in 2009.
Fiscal year: Calendar year.

PEOPLE

Life in sparsely populated Mongolia has become more urbanized. Nearly half of the people live in the capital, Ulaanbaatar, and in other provincial centers. Seminomadic life still predominates in the countryside, but settled agricultural communities are becoming more common. Mongolia's birth rate is estimated at 1.4% (2000 census). About two-thirds of the total population are under age 30, 36% of whom are under 14.

Ethnic Mongols account for about 85% of the population and consist of Khalkha and other groups, all distinguished primarily by dialects of the Mongol language. Mongol is an Altaic language--from the Altaic Mountains of Central Asia, a language family comprising the Turkic, Tungusic, and Mongolic subfamilies--and is related to Turkic (Uzbek, Turkish, and Kazakh), Korean, and, possibly, Japanese. The Khalkha make up 90% of the ethnic Mongol population. The remaining 10% include Durbet Mongols and others in the north and Dariganga Mongols in the east. Turkic speakers (Kazakhs, Turvins, and Khotans) constitute 7% of Mongolia's population, and the rest are Tungusic-speakers, Chinese, and Russians. Most Russians left the country following the withdrawal of economic aid and collapse of the Soviet Union in 1991.

Traditionally, Tibetan Buddhist Lamaism was the predominant religion. However, it was suppressed under the communist regime until 1990, with only one showcase monastery allowed to remain. Since 1990, as liberalization began, Buddhism has enjoyed a resurgence. About 4 million Mongols live outside Mongolia; about 3.4 million live in China, mainly in the Inner Mongolia Autonomous Region; and some 500,000 live in Russia, primarily in Buryatia and Kalmykia.

HISTORY

In 1203 AD, a single Mongolian state was formed based on nomadic tribal groupings under the leadership of Genghis Khan. He and his immediate successors conquered nearly all of Asia and European Russia and sent armies as far as central Europe and Southeast Asia. Genghis Khan's grandson Kublai Khan, who conquered China and established the Yuan dynasty (1279-1368 AD), gained fame in Europe through the writings of Marco Polo.

Although Mongol-led confederations sometimes exercised wide political power over their conquered territories, their strength declined rapidly after the Mongol dynasty in China was overthrown in 1368. The Manchus, a tribal group which conquered China in 1644 and formed the Qing dynasty, were able to bring Mongolia under Manchu control in 1691 as Outer Mongolia when the Khalkha Mongol nobles swore an oath of allegiance to the Manchu emperor. The Mongol rulers of Outer Mongolia enjoyed considerable autonomy under the Manchus, and all Chinese claims to Outer Mongolia following the establishment of the republic have rested on this oath. In 1727, Russia and Manchu China concluded the Treaty of Khiakta, delimiting the border between China and Mongolia that exists in large part today.

Outer Mongolia was a Chinese province (1691-1911), an autonomous state under Russian protection (1912-19), and again a Chinese province (1919-21). As Manchu authority in China waned, and as Russia and Japan confronted each other, Russia gave arms and diplomatic support to nationalists among the Mongol religious leaders and nobles. The Mongols accepted Russian aid and proclaimed their independence of Chinese rule in 1911, shortly after a successful Chinese revolt against the Manchus. By agreements signed in 1913 and 1915, the Russian Government forced the new Chinese Republican Government to accept Mongolian autonomy under continued Chinese control, presumably to discourage other foreign powers from approaching a newly independent Mongolian state that might seek support from as many foreign sources as possible.

The Russian revolution and civil war afforded Chinese warlords an opportunity to re-establish their rule in Outer Mongolia, and Chinese troops were dispatched there in 1919. Following Soviet military victories over White Russian forces in the early 1920s and the occupation of the Mongolian capital Urga in July 1921, Moscow again became the major outside influence on Mongolia. The Mongolian People's Republic was proclaimed on November 25, 1924. Between 1925 and 1928, power under the communist regime was consolidated by the Mongolian Peoples Revolutionary Party (MPRP). The MPRP left gradually undermined rightist elements, seizing control of the party and the government. Several factors characterized the country during this period: Tthe society was basically nomadic and illiterate; there was no industrial proletariat; the aristocracy and the religious establishment shared the country's wealth; there was widespread popular obedience to traditional authorities; the party lacked grassroots support; and the government had little organization or experience.

In an effort at swift socioeconomic reform, the leftist government applied extreme measures which attacked the two most dominant institutions in the country--the aristocracy and the religious establishment. Between 1932 and 1945, their excess zeal, intolerance, and inexperience led to anti-communist uprisings. In the late 1930s, purges directed at the religious institution resulted in the desecration of hundreds of Buddhist institutions and imprisonment of more than 10,000 people.

During World War II, because of a growing Japanese threat over the Mongolian-Manchurian border, the Soviet Union reversed the course of Mongolian socialism in favor of a new policy of economic gradualism and buildup of the national defense. The Soviet-Mongolian army defeated Japanese forces that had invaded eastern Mongolia in the summer of 1939, and a truce was signed setting up a commission to define the Mongolian-Manchurian border in the autumn of that year.

Following the war, the Soviet Union reasserted its influence in Mongolia. Secure in its relations with Moscow, the Mongolian Government shifted to postwar development, focusing on civilian enterprise. International ties were expanded, and Mongolia established relations with North Korea and the new communist governments in eastern Europe. It also increased its participation in communist-sponsored conferences and international organizations. Mongolia became a member of the United Nations in 1961.

In the early 1960s, Mongolia attempted to maintain a neutral position amidst increasingly contentious Sino-Soviet polemics; this orientation changed in the middle of the decade. Mongolia and the Soviet Union signed an agreement in 1966 that introduced largescale Soviet ground forces as part of Moscow's general buildup along the Sino-Soviet frontier.

During the period of Sino-Soviet tensions, relations between Mongolia and China deteriorated. In 1983, Mongolia systematically began expelling some of the 7,000 ethnic Chinese in Mongolia to China. Many of them had lived in Mongolia since the 1950s, when they were sent there to assist in construction projects.

CHRONOLOGY OF MONGOLIAN HISTORY 1921-PRESENT

March 13, 1921: Provisional People's Government declares independence of Mongolia.
May 31, 1924: U.S.S.R. signs agreement with Peking government, referring to Outer Mongolia as an "integral part of the Republic of China," whose "sovereignty" therein the Soviet Union promises to respect.
May-September 16, 1939: Largescale fighting takes place between Japanese and Soviet-Mongolian forces along Khalkhyn Gol on Mongolia-Manchuria border, ending in defeat of the Japanese expeditionary force. Truce negotiated between U.S.S.R. and Japan.
October 6, 1949: Newly established People's Republic of China accepts recognition accorded Mongolia and agrees to establish diplomatic relations.
October 1961: Mongolia becomes a member of the United Nations.
January 27, 1987: Diplomatic relations established with the United States.
December 1989: First popular reform demonstrations. Mongolian Democratic Association organized.
January 1990: Largescale demonstrations demanding democracy held in sub-zero weather.
March 2, 1990: Soviets and Mongolians announce that all Soviet troops will be withdrawn from Mongolia by 1992.
May 1990: Constitution amended to provide for multi-party system and new elections.
July 29, 1990: First democratic elections held.
September 3, 1990: First democratically elected People's Great Hural takes office.
February 12, 1992: New constitution goes into effect.
April 8, 1992: New election law passed.
June 28, 1992: Election for the first unicameral legislature (State Great Hural).
June 6, 1993: First direct presidential election.
June 30, 1996: Election of first noncommunist government.
July 2, 2000: Election of the former communist Mongolian Peoples Revolutionary Party (MPRP); formation of new government by Prime Minister N. Enkhbayar.

GOVERNMENT

Until 1990, the Mongolian Government was modeled on the Soviet system; only the communist party--the MPRP--officially was permitted to function. After some instability during the first two decades of communist rule in Mongolia, there was no significant popular unrest until December 1989. Collectivization of animal husbandry, introduction of agriculture, and the extension of fixed abodes were all carried out without perceptible popular opposition.

The birth of perestroika in the former Soviet Union and the democracy movement in Eastern Europe were mirrored in Mongolia. The dramatic shift toward reform started in early 1990 when the first organized opposition group, the Mongolian Democratic Union, appeared. In the face of extended street protests in sub-zero whether and popular demands for faster reform, the politburo of the MPRP resigned in March 1990. In May, the constitution was amended, deleting reference to the MPRP's role as the guiding force in the country, legalizing opposition parties, creating a standing legislative body, and establishing the office of president.

Mongolia's first multi-party elections for a People's Great Hural were held on July 29, 1990. The MPRP won 85% of the seats. The People's Great Hural first met on September 3 and elected a president (MPRP), vice president (SDP--Social Democrats), prime minister (MPRP), and 50 members to the Baga Hural (small Hural). The vice president also was chairman of the Baga Hural. In November 1991, the People's Great Hural began discussion on a new constitution, which entered into force February 12. In addition to establishing Mongolia as an independent, sovereign republic and guaranteeing a number of rights and freedoms, the new constitution restructured the legislative branch of government, creating a unicameral legislature, the State Great Hural (SGH).

The 1992 constitution provided that the president would be elected by popular vote rather than by the legislature as before. In June 1993, incumbent Punsalmaagiyn Ochirbat won the first popular presidential election running as the candidate of the democratic opposition.

As the supreme government organ, the SGH is empowered to enact and amend laws, determine domestic and foreign policy, ratify international agreements, and declare a state of emergency. The SGH meets semiannually. SGH members elect a chairman and vice chairman who serve 4-year terms. SGH members are popularly elected by district for 4-year terms. In the most recent parliamentary election on June 30, 1996, the opposition, running together under the banner of the Democratic Union, won a landslide victory, taking 50 of 76 seats in the SGH. The first completely noncommunist government was installed in July 1996, headed by Prime Minister M. Enkhsaihan.

The president is the head of state, commander in chief of the armed forces, and head of the national security council. He is popularly elected by a national majority for a 4-year term and limited to two terms. The constitution empowers the president to propose a prime minister, call for the government's dissolution, initiate legislation, veto all or parts of legislation (the SGH can override the veto with a two-thirds majority), and issue decrees, which become effective with the prime minister's signature. In the absence, incapacity, or resignation of the president, the SGH chairman exercises presidential power until inauguration of a newly elected president. In the most recent presidential election on May 18, 1997, the MPRP candidate, N. Bagabandi, was elected with 57% of the vote.

The government, headed by the prime minister, has a 4-year term. The prime minister is nominated by the president and confirmed by the SGH. The prime minister chooses a cabinet, subject to SGH approval. Dissolution of the government occurs upon the prime minister's resignation, simultaneous resignation of half the cabinet, or after an SGH vote for dissolution.

Local hurals are elected by the 18 aimags (provinces) plus the capital, Ulaanbaatar, and cities of Darhan and Erdenet. On the next lower administrative level, they are elected by provincial subdivisions and urban subdistricts in Ulaanbaatar and the municipalities, Darhan and Erdenet.

Political Parties

Mongolian People's Revolutionary Party
Mongolian Social Democratic Party
Mongolian National Democratic Party
Mongolian People's Party
Mongolian Green Party
Mongolian Religious Democratic Party

Party for Mongolia
Mongolian Republican Party
Mongolian Workers' Party
Mongolian Traditional United Party
Mongolian Democratic Renaissance Party
Mongolian Solidarity Party
Mongolian Party for Tradition and Justice
Mongolian Democratic Socialist Party
Mongolian Youth Party
Mongolian Liberal Democratic Party
Mongolian Democratic New Socialist Party
Mongolian Communist Party
Mongolian Rural Development Party
Mongolian Local Development Party
Mongolian Civil Democratic New Liberal Party
Mongolian Citizens' Will Party
Mongolian Democratic Party
Mongolian New Social Democratic Party

LEGAL SYSTEM

The new constitution empowered a General Council of Courts (GCC) to select all judges and protect their rights. The Supreme Court is the highest judicial body. Justices are nominated by the GCC and confirmed by the SGH and president. The court is constitutionally empowered to examine all lower court decisions--excluding specialized court rulings--upon appeal and provide official interpretations on all laws except the constitution.

Specialized civil, criminal, and administrative courts exist at all levels and are not subject to Supreme Court supervision. Local authorities--district and city governors--ensure that these courts abide by presidential decrees and SGH decisions. At the apex of the judicial system is the Constitutional Court, which consists of nine members, including a chairman, appointed for 6-year terms, whose jurisdiction extends solely over the interpretation of the constitution.

Principal Government Officials

Pres., **Tsakhia ELBEGDORJ**
Prime Min., **Norov ALTANKHUYAG**
Dep. Prime Min., **Dendev TERBISHDAGVA**
Min. of Construction & Urban Development, **Tsevelmaa BAYARSAIKHAN**
Min. of Culture, Sports, & Tourism, **Tsedevdamba OYUNGEREL**
Min. of Defense, **Dashdemberal BAT-ERDENE**
Min. of Economic Development, **Nyamjav BATBAYAR**
Min. of Education & Science, **Luvsannyam GANTMUR**
Min. of Energy, **Mishig SONOMPIL**
Min. of Environment, **Sambuu DEMBEREL**
Min. of Finance, **Mendsaikhan ENKHSAIKHAN**
Min. of Food, Agriculture, & Light Industry, **Khaltmaa BATTULGA**
Min. of Foreign Affairs & Trade, **Luvsanvandan BOLD**
Min. of Health, **Natsag UDVAL**
Min. of Justice & Home Affairs, **Khishigdemberel TEMUUJIN**
Min. of Labor, **Yadamsuren SANJMYATAV**
Min. of Mining, **Davaajav GANKHUYAG**

Min. for Population Development & Social Welfare, **Sodnomzundui ERDENE**
Min. of Road & Transportation, **Amarjargal GANSUKH**
Min. & Chief of the Govt. Secretariat, **Chimed SAIKHANBILEG**
Governor, Bank of Mongolia, **Lhanaasuren PUREVDORJ**
Ambassador to the US, **Khasbazar BEKHBAT**
Permanent Representative to the UN, New York, **Od OCH**

Mongolia maintains an embassy in the U.S. at 2833 M Street, NW, Washington, DC, 20007; tel. (202) 333-7117, fax (202) 298-9227.

ECONOMY

Rank	142nd (est.)
Currency	1 tögrög (MNT) = 100 möngö
Fiscal year	Calendar year
Trade organisations	WTO, IMF, World Bank, ADB, SCO (Observer)
	Statistics
GDP growth	17.3% (est.)
GDP per capita	$4,800 (2011, PPP)
GDP by sector	agriculture: 15.8%, industry: 32.6%, services: 51.6% (est.)
Inflation (CPI)	9.5% (est.)
Population below poverty line	39.2% (est.)
Gini coefficient	36.5
Labour force by occupation	agriculture: 33.5%, industry: 11.5%, services: 55%
Unemployment	9.9%
Main industries	construction and construction materials, mining (coal, copper, molybdenum, fluorspar, tin, tungsten, and gold), oil, food and beverages, processing of animal products, cashmere and natural fiber manufacturing
Ease of Doing Business Rank	86th
	External
Exports	$4.78 billion (est.)
Export goods	copper, apparel, livestock, animal products, cashmere, wool, hides, fluorspar, other nonferrous metals, coal, crude oil
Main export partners	China 92.1%, Russia 2%, Canada 1.9%,(est.)
Imports	$6.527 billion (est.)
Import goods	machinery and equipment, fuel, cars, food products, industrial consumer goods, chemicals, building materials, cigarettes & tobacco, soap & detergent
Main import partners	China 30.7%, Russia 24.5%, United States 8.1%, Japan 7.4%, South Korea 5.5%, (est.)
	Public finances
Public debt	$1.9 billion
Revenues	$3.44 billion (est.)
Expenses	$3.496 billion (est.)
Economic aid	$185.94 million
Credit rating	Standard & Poor's: BB- (Domestic) BB- (Foreign) BB (T&C Assessment) Outlook: Stable

Moody's:
B1
Outlook: Stable
Fitch:
B+
Outlook: Stable

Economic activity in Mongolia has traditionally been based on herding and agriculture. Mongolia has extensive mineral deposits; copper, coal, molybdenum, tin, tungsten, and gold account for a large part of industrial production. Soviet assistance, at its height one-third of GDP, disappeared almost overnight in 1990-91 at the time of the dismantlement of the U.S.S.R., leading to a very deep recession. Economic growth returned due to reform embracing free-market economics and extensive privatization of the formerly state-run economy. Severe winters and summer droughts in 2000-2001 and 2001-2002 resulted in massive livestock die-off and anemic GDP growth of 1.1% in 2000 and 1% in 2001. This was compounded by falling prices for Mongolia's primary-sector exports and widespread opposition to privatization. Growth improved to 4% in 2002, 5% in 2003, 10.6% in 2004, 6.2% in 2005 and 7.5% in 2006. Much of the growth was due to high copper prices and new gold production.

Other than agriculture (20.2% of GDP), dominant industries in the composition of GDP are mining 20.4%, trade and service 24.8% and transportation, storage, and communication 12.2%. Mongolia's economy continues to be heavily influenced by its neighbors. For example, Mongolia purchases 80% of its petroleum products from Russia. China is Mongolia's chief export partner and a main source of the "shadow," or "gray" economy. The gray economy is estimated to be at least one-third the size of the official economy. The actual size of this gray--largely cash--economy is difficult to calculate since the money does not pass through the hands of tax authorities or the banking sector. Remittances from Mongolians working abroad, both legally and illegally, constitute a sizeable portion. Money laundering is growing as an accompanying concern. Mongolia settled its large debt to Russia at the end of 2003 on favorable terms. Mongolia, which joined the World Trade Organization in 1997, is the only member of that organization to not be a participant in a regional trade organization. Mongolia seeks to expand its participation and integration into Asian regional economic and trade regimes.

Because of Mongolia's remoteness and natural beauty, the tourism sector has recently shown signs of rapid growth. With spiking international commodity prices, there has been a surge of international interest in investing in Mongolia's minerals sector despite the absence of a policy environment firmly conducive to private investment. How effectively Mongolia mobilizes private international investment around its comparative advantages (mineral wealth, small population, and proximity to China and its burgeoning markets) will ultimately determine its success in sustaining rapid economic growth. Parliament passed a windfall profits tax on copper and gold that took effect in mid-2006, and major amendments to the minerals law allowing the government to take an equity stake in major new mines. It is unknown what effect these laws will have on mining activities in Mongolia, although major potential investors expressed considerable concern about the changes.

Parliament in 2006 passed four new tax laws: personal and corporate income, value-added and excise, intended to reduce the overall tax burden on taxpayers and stimulate the economy. Most provisions of the new laws took effect January 1, 2007. No projections of the economic effects are currently available.

ENVIRONMENT

As a result of rapid urbanization and industrial growth policies under the communist regime, Mongolia's deteriorating environment has become a major concern. The burning of soft coal coupled with thousands of factories in Ulaanbaatar has resulted in severely polluted air. Deforestation, overgrazed pastures, and efforts to increase grain and hay production by plowing up more virgin land has increased soil erosion from wind and rain. Most recently, with the rapid growth of newly privatized herds, overgrazing in selected areas also is a concern.

FOREIGN RELATIONS

In the wake of the international socialist economic system's collapse and the disintegration of the former Soviet Union, Mongolians began to pursue an independent and nonaligned foreign policy. The Prime Minister called for coexistence with all nations, and Mongolia follows a general policy of expanding relations with as many countries as possible.

Due to Mongolia's landlocked position between the new independent states (NIS) of the former Soviet Union and China, it was essential to continue and improve relations with these countries. At the same time, Mongolia is reaching out to advance its regional and global relations.

As part of its aim to establish a more balanced nonaligned foreign policy, Mongolia is seeking active supporters and friends beyond its neighbors and looking to take a more active role in the United Nations and other international organizations. While it is downgrading relations with most of its former east European allies, it is pursuing a more active role in Asian and Northeast Asian affairs. Mongolia is seeking to join APEC and became a full participant in the ASEAN Regional Forum (ARF) in July 1998. Mongolia became a full member of the Pacific Economic Cooperation Council in April 2000.

High-level Mongolian officials and/or parliamentarians have made official visits to countries, including the United States, China, Japan, South Korea, Australia, Nepal, the Philippines, Pakistan, and several west European countries, as well as Russian and the former Soviet Union countries. Mongolia also has established diplomatic relations with a number of other nations, among them Oman, Brunei, and Israel, and in early 2000 opened an embassy in Bangkok, Thailand. An embassy is to be opened in Ottawa, Canada, in late 2000.

Asia

Mongolian relations with China began to improve in the mid-1980s when consular agreements were reached and crossborder trade contacts expanded. In 1989, China and Mongolia exchanged visits of foreign ministers. In May 1990, a Mongolian head of state visited China for the first time in 28 years. The cornerstone of the Mongolian-Chinese relationship is a 1994 Treaty of Friendship and Cooperation, which codifies mutual respect for the independence and territorial integrity of both sides. Today, relations between Mongolia and China are correct. The two foreign ministers exchanged visits in 1997, as did the leaders of the two countries' parliaments. President Jiang Zemin visited Mongolia in July 1999.

Mongolia is expanding relations with Japan and South Korea. Its Prime Minister visited Japan in March 1990 and Prime Minister Obuchi reciprocated with a visit to Mongolia in July 1999. Japan has provided more than $100 million in grants and loans since 1991 and coordinated international assistance to Mongolia. Diplomatic relations were established with South Korea in 1991, and during the Mongolian President's visit, seven agreements and treaties were signed, providing the legal basis for further expanding bilateral relations. Japan is Mongolia's largest bilateral aid donor.

Russia

After the disintegration of the former Soviet Union, Mongolia developed relations with the new independent states. Links with Russia and other republics were essential to contribute to stabilization of the Mongolian economy. The primary difficulties in developing fruitful coordination occurred because the NIS were experiencing the same political and economic restructuring as Mongolia. Despite these difficulties, Mongolia and Russia successfully negotiated both a 1991 Joint Declaration of Cooperation and a bilateral trade agreement. This was followed by a 1993 Treaty of Friendship and Cooperation establishing a new basis of equality in the relationship. President Bagabandi visited Moscow in 1999, and there have been frequent bilateral visits since then.

Europe

Mongolia seeks closer relations with countries in Europe and hopes to receive most-favored-nation status from the European Union (EU). During 1991, Mongolia signed investment promotion and protection agreements with Germany and France and an economic cooperation agreement with the United Kingdom. Germany continued former East German cooperative programs and also provided loans and aid. The Prime Minister has traveled to Germany, France, Belgium, and EU headquarters in Brussels seeking economic cooperation. President Bagabandi visited several European capitals in 1999-2000.

U.S.-MONGOLIAN RELATIONS

The U.S. Government recognized Mongolia in January 1987 and established its first embassy in Ulaanbaatar in June 1988. It formally opened in September 1988. The first U.S. ambassador to Mongolia, Richard L. Williams, was not resident there. Joseph E. Lake, the first resident ambassador, arrived in July 1990. Secretary of State James A. Baker, III visited Mongolia in August 1990, and again in July 1991. Mongolia accredited its first ambassador to the United States in March 1989. Secretary of State Madeline Albright visited Mongolia in May 1998, and Prime Minister Enkhbayar visited Washington in November 2001. Deputy Secretary of State Richard L. Armitage visited Mongolia in January 2004, and President Bagabandi came to Washington for a meeting with President Bush in July 2004. President Bush, Mrs. Bush, and Secretary of State Condoleezza Rice visited Mongolia in November 2005. Defense Secretary Rumsfeld visited in October 2005 and Speaker of the House of Representatives Dennis Hastert visited Mongolia in August 2005. Agriculture Secretary Johanns led a presidential delegation in July 2006 in conjunction with Mongolia's celebration of its 800th anniversary.

The United States has sought to assist Mongolia's movement toward democracy and market-oriented reform and to expand relations with Mongolia primarily in the cultural and economic fields. In 1989 and 1990, a cultural accord, Peace Corps accord, consular convention, and Overseas Private Investment Corporation (OPIC) agreement were signed. A trade agreement was signed in January 1991 and a bilateral investment treaty in 1994. Mongolia was granted permanent normal trade relations (NTR) status and generalized system of preferences (GSP) eligibility in June 1999. In July 2004, the U.S. signed a Trade and Investment Framework Agreement with Mongolia to promote economic reform and more foreign investment.

The U.S. Agency for International Development (USAID) plays a lead role in providing bilateral American assistance to Mongolia. The program emphasizes two main themes: sustainable, private sector-led economic growth; and more effective and accountable governance. Total USAID assistance to Mongolia from 1991 through 2007 was about $170 million, all in grant form. About two-thirds of USAID Mongolia's current budget of $5.6 million a year promotes economic growth, and focuses on macroeconomic policy reform, energy sector commercialization, financial sector reform, strengthening the cashmere and tourism industries, and providing business development services to small and medium enterprises in both rural and urban areas. The other third focuses on judicial sector reform, electoral reform, parliamentary reform, and anti-corruption work.

In most years since 1993, the United States Department of Agriculture has provided food aid to Mongolia under the Food for Progress and 416(b) programs. The monetized proceeds of the food aid ($3.7 million in 2005) are currently used to support programs bolstering entrepreneurship, herder diversification, better veterinary services, and disaster relief. The United States has also supported defense reform and an increased capacity by Mongolia's armed forces to participate in international peacekeeping operations. Mongolia has contributed small numbers of troops to coalition operations in Iraq and Afghanistan since 2003, gaining experience which enabled it to deploy armed peacekeepers to both UN and NATO peacekeeping missions in 2005. With U.S. Department of Defense assistance and cooperation, Mongolia and the U.S. jointly hosted "Khan Quest 06," the Asian region's premier peace-keeping exercise in 2006. "Khan Quest 07" will be hosted on 01-16 August 2007.

The Peace Corps currently has over 100 Volunteers in Mongolia. They are engaged primarily in English teaching and teacher training activities. At the request of the Government of Mongolia, the Peace Corps has developed programs in the areas of public health, small business development, and youth development. In 2005 and 2006 Mongolian Government officials, including President Enkhbayar and Prime Minister Elbegdorj, requested significant increases in the number of Volunteers serving in country. The Peace Corps has responded with a commitment to make modest annual increases until 2010. The program celebrated its 15th anniversary in 2006 with participation by President Enkhbayar.

Principal U.S. Embassy Official
Ambassador--Mark C. Minton

The U.S. Embassy is located in Micro District 11, Big Ring Road, Ulaanbaatar; tel. [976] (1) 329-095 or 329-606, fax 320-776. Consular and commercial information are available at the embassy's web site: http://mongolia.usembassy.gov.

TRAVEL AND BUSINESS INFORMATION

The U.S. Department of State's Consular Information Program provides Consular Information Sheets, Travel Warnings, and Public Announcements. **Consular Information Sheets** exist for all countries and include information on entry requirements, currency regulations, health conditions, areas of instability, crime and security, political disturbances, and the addresses of the U.S. posts in the country.

Travel Warnings are issued when the State Department recommends that Americans avoid travel to a certain country.

Public Announcements are issued as a means to disseminate information quickly about terrorist threats and other relatively short-term conditions overseas which pose significant risks to the security of American travelers. Free copies of this information are available by calling the Bureau of Consular Affairs at 202-647-5225 or via the fax-on-demand system: 202-647-3000. Consular Information Sheets and Travel Warnings also are available on the Consular Affairs Internet home page: http://travel.state.gov. Consular Affairs Tips for Travelers publication series, which contain information on obtaining passports and planning a safe trip abroad are on the internet and hard copies can be purchased from the Superintendent of Documents, U.S. Government Printing Office, telephone: 202-512-1800; fax 202-512-2250.

Emergency information concerning Americans traveling abroad may be obtained from the Office of Overseas Citizens Services at (202) 647-5225. For after-hours emergencies, Sundays and holidays, call 202-647-4000.

Passport information can be obtained by calling the National Passport Information Center's automated system ($.35 per minute) or live operators 8 a.m. to 8 p.m. (EST) Monday-Friday ($1.05 per minute). The number is 1-900-225-5674 (TDD: 1-900-225-7778). Major credit card users (for a flat rate of $4.95) may call 1-888-362-8668 (TDD: 1-888-498-3648). It also is available on the internet.

Travelers can check the latest health information with the U.S. Centers for Disease Control and Prevention in Atlanta, Georgia. A hotline at 877-FYI-TRIP (877-394-8747) and a web site at http://www.cdc.gov/travel/index.htm give the most recent health advisories, immunization recommendations or requirements, and advice on food and drinking water safety for regions and countries. A booklet entitled Health Information for International Travel (HHS publication number CDC-95-8280) is available from the U.S. Government Printing Office, Washington, DC 20402, tel. (202) 512-1800.

Information on travel conditions, visa requirements, currency and customs regulations, legal holidays, and other items of interest to travelers also may be obtained before your departure from a country's embassy and/or consulates in the U.S. (for this country, see "Principal Government Officials" listing in this publication).

U.S. citizens who are long-term visitors or traveling in dangerous areas are encouraged to register at the U.S. embassy upon arrival in a country (see "Principal U.S. Embassy Officials" listing in this publication). This may help family members contact you in case of an emergency.

EU- MONGOLIA RELATIONS

GENERAL FRAMEWORK

Prior to the political reforms of 1990, relations between the EU and Mongolia were extremely limited. Since then, however, these relations have developed fairly rapidly and positively. In January 1991, Mongolia entered into the GSP arrangement. The EU delegate in Beijing was accredited in Mongolia in May 1991, whilst the Mongolian ambassador to the EU presented his credentials in November 1992.

The Trade and Co-operation Agreement was signed on 16.06.1992 and entered into force in March 1993. It is concluded for a period of five years and shall be tacitly renewed. The Agreement includes a commitment to protect human rights. In their trade relations, the two Parties shall accord each other the most-favored-nation treatment. The Agreement doesn't provide the implementation of a trade preferential regime. The adoption of appropriate measures in order to facilitate and to increase the trade is provided. The third meeting of the Joint Committee took place on 25 and 26 April 1996 in Ulaanbatar. The fourth one was held in Brussels on 30 September 1997. The fifth one took place on 19 December 2004 in Ulaanbatar.

Textile agreement: The European Community and Mongolia have concluded an Agreement on trade in Textile Products which has expired on 31.12.97. The textile trade between the EC and Mongolia is now fully liberalized.

TRADE

After China, Switzerland Russia, Korea and Japan, the EU is the sixths biggest trading partner of Mongolia. In 1998 13.4 % of imported goods came from EU-countries, 9.5 % of Mongolia's export went to the EU. The turnover of EU-Mongolia trade amounted to € 115 million in the year 2004. The major EU import commodity from Mongolia is cashmere wool and products (namely imported by Italy and the UK). The major export items from the EU are machinery, agricultural products and chemicals, coming mainly from France and Germany. Statistics on the development of bi-lateral trade see below.

EC ASSISTANCE

In 1992-1993 Mongolia received nearly ECU 8.0 million in technical assistance under the PUD/ALA Program.

Mongolia became eligible for TACIS support in 1994 when a Aid-Co-ordinating Unit was established in Ulaanbatar.

The 1996-2001 TACIS allocation was 26,5 M €.

The budget of the 1998-1999 Action Program amounted to 11 M €. It covered projects in the field of structural and institutional reform (2,8 M €), support to enterprises and financial development (3,1 M €), infrastructure development (1,6 M €) and Small project programs (3,0 M €) (Reserve: 0,5 M €).

The 2004-2001 Action Program (6,0 M €) was adopted by the Commission at the end of 2004 and is under implementation. It was prepared within the framework of the new Indicative Program (IP) for 2004-2003. Two key priority areas of co-operation had been defined in the new regulation (Council Regulation 99/2004 of 29 December 1999): Development of the Rural Economy (2,9 M €) and Support to the Private Sector and Assistance for Economic Development (1,0 M €). Additionally 1,7 M € have been allocated for Small projects programs.

Since 1994 Mongolia has also actively participated in the TACIS Small Project Program (Tempus, Lien, Democracy, City Twinning, Productivity Initiative Program, ESSN, Statistics, and Customs).

In 2004 1,875 M € have been provided in the framework of ECHO, above all for food aid. In the year 2001 1,03 M € have already been provided to fight against the consequences of the last harsh winter ("Dzud").

FUTURE RELATIONS

The EU-Mongolia relationship has been consolidated over the last few years and will increase in the future given the enlargement of the Union to the East. The new TACIS Regulation, which covers the years 2004-2006, sets out the new priorities for the assistance program and takes into consideration the post-enlargement effects, notably the increase in the trade flow, the need for expanded transport networks, new investment opportunities, demands for increased co-operation on environmental protection, cross border co-operation and co-operation in the field of Justice and Home Affairs. These new priorities take into account the changed economical and political environment in the NIS and Mongolia, and the necessity for a greater concentration in cross-sectoral areas of co-operation. The TACIS assistance will target the Political, Economic, Social, Environmental aspects and the Rural economy.

JAPAN MONGOLIA RELATIONS

BASIC DATA

Number of Residents:
Number of Japanese nationals residing in Mongolia: 229 (Nov. 1999)
Number of Mongolian nationals residing in Japan: 349 (Oct. 1999)

BILATERAL RELATIONS

(1) Diplomatic relations between Japan and Mongolia were established in 1972. However, owing to the international situation prevailing at that time, characterized by East-West antagonism as a result of the Cold War, the environment was not particularly conducive to the vigorous development of the relationship between Japan and Mongolia.

(2) Nevertheless, the moves towards democratization and the transformation to a free-market economic system in Mongolia opened up a new phase in the development of relations by Japan and Mongolia on the previously-established foundation. A visit in April 1989 by the then Japanese foreign minister Sousuke Uno, the first foreign minister of a Western industrialized country to pay a visit to Mongolia, was followed in March 1990 by a visit to Japan by the then Prime Minister Sodnom, in August 1991 by a visit to Mongolia by the then Prime Minister Kaifu, the first prime minister of a Western industrialized country to visit to Mongolia, and by visits to Japan in May 1992 and November 1993 by the Mongolian prime minister. These high-level exchanges resulted in the accelerated development of relations between the two countries.

(3) Based on Japan's belief that the success of democratization and of the transformation to a free-market economy in Mongolia would contribute to peace and stability in the East Asian region, from the outset it has given active assistance to newly democratized Mongolia, and since 1991 has continued to be the largest donor of aid.

(4) In February 1997, the 25th anniversary of the establishment of diplomatic relations between the two countries, the then Prime Minister Enkhsaikhan visited Japan, where a joint announcement was made. Then in May 1998, President Bagabandi has paid an official visit to Japan, which was the first one made by a Mongolian President. During the visit, a joint statement was announced. These confirmed the goal of building a comprehensive partnership between the two countries.

(5) High level exchanges at both political and government level were kept at a good pace, which resulted in an official visit made by the Speaker of the Mongolian Parliament, Mr. R. Gonchigdorj in March and a Foreign Ministerial Meeting held in May.
(6) Assistance from Mongolia

(i) Mongolia has been a firm supporter of Japan in the United Nations, other international organizations, international conferences and international committees. In particular Mongolia has maintained a policy of cooperation with Japan in pursuit of the peace and stability of the northeast Asian region. Mongolia has also been a steadfast supporter of Japan's becoming a permanent member of the United Nations Security Council,
(ii) A memory that remains firmly in the minds of many Japanese people is that of the friendship displayed by the Mongolian people at the time of the Great Hanshin-Awagi Earthquake in 1995, when they were quick to provide a special airlift of relief supplies.

ECONOMIC COOPERATION

(1) The economic cooperation and aid extended by Japan to Mongolia has expanded rapidly since 1991, accounting for approximately one-third of total aid for Mongolia by foreign countries and international organizations.

Japan's economic cooperation with Mongolia (million yen)

Fiscal year	1990	1991	1992	1993	1994	1995	1996	1997	1999
Grant aid	494	3,308	3,908	4,535	5,905	5,825	4,803	4,298	29,987
Loan assistance	0	4,836	2,458	3,321	4,753	4,493	5,827	5,046	49,583
Technical cooperation	151	402	681	1,810	2,272	2,337	1,813	1,933	16,108

Initially, economic cooperation was principally in the form of humanitarian aid for the Mongolian people, who were suffering deprivation amid the deteriorating economic situation in Mongolia at that time. Gradually, however, the cooperation came to be focused on the development of infrastructure to assist the gaining of economic self-sufficiency.

(2) In March 1997 the Governments of the two countries held discussions on the policy for medium to long-term assistance for Mongolia by Japan, and it was agreed that the following four should be the priority fields for economic cooperation.

(i) The development of the economic base and prerequisites for fostering the development of the industrial base (The fields of energy, transportation, and communications)
(ii) Intellectual aid and human-resource development for the transformation to a market economy.
(iii) Aid for agriculture and livestock farming.

(iv) Aid for basic living conditions (Education, health and medical care, water supply)
(3) In addition, not only with regard to bilateral relations, but also in the international arena, Japan is actively taking initiatives in aid of Mongolia. Since 1991 a total of seven conferences of countries providing aid to Mongolia have been held, of which six conferences were held jointly with the World Bank in Tokyo. The seventh conference was held in Ulaanbaatar with the Chair of the World Bank in June 1999. It is of note that at the Conference, the Government of Japan expressed its intention to provide the largest ever amount of aid, totaling US$ 320 million, which has been of great assistance to Mongolia's development efforts

VIP VISITS

From Japan to Mongolia

1993.8		Delegation of the House of Councilors
1997.7		Delegation of the House of Representatives
1997.8		Ministry of Health and Welfare Junichiro Koizumi
1999.7		Prime Minister Keizo Obuchi Ministry of Home Affairs Takeshi Noda Deputy Chief Cabinet Secretary Muneo Suzuki Minister of Posts and Telecommunications Seiko Noda
1999.8		Delegation of the House of Councilors
2004.5		Senior State Secretary for Foreign Affairs Tetsuma Esaki

CULTURAL EXCHANGE

Cultural exchange between the two countries has been expanding in recentyears, both at the government and private levels. In 1994 the number of Mongolian students who had enrolled in Japanese schools totaled only 84, but just three years later, in 1998, this had tripled to 308. Japan is also cooperating in the preservation of Mongolia's cultural inheritance, including the one through the surveyingand excavation of relics at Karakorum,the capital of the Mongolianempire in the 13th century. In addition, a Japan Festival was held in Mongolia in 1997, during which a wide variety of cultural events took place, including demonstrations of the tea ceremony and traditional Japanese music, helping to deepen mutual understanding between the peoples of the two countries. Last June a cultural delegation headed by Mrs. Ayako Sono, a famous novelist was dispatched to Mongolia in aiming to study a possibility of how to promote and broaden mutual exchanges in cultural field.

STRATEGIC INFORMATION FOR CONDUCTING BUSINESS

ECONOMIC OVERVIEW

The process of restructuring of the Mongolian economy started in December 1988. Since 1991, the Mongolian Government has been working toward solving fundamental economic problems: to overcome the shock derived from the abrupt end of the Soviet assistance and find new markets following the collapse of the CMEA trading block. Recovering from this crisis and determining the long term economic goals are of vital importance. The Government of Mongolia is working with IMF, IBRD, ADB, and EEC to implement a number of reform measures designed to stabilise the economy; reverse the decline in production and raise the living standard of the population.

Government procurement has been substantially reduced.The price and exchange rate were liberalised; and a new taxation system was created. Bank reserve requirements were increased. The dual exchange rate was abolished and replaced with a unified floating rate. A strong tendency towards macroeconomics stabilisation was evident in the 1994 inflation results. A significant improvement in the supply of key consumer goods, particularly foodstuffs, has been achieved since 1993. In the last year the Government has been concentrating its efforts on the implementatio of the mid-term program of restructuring of the Mongolian economy agreed to with the IMF.

The Mongolian economy has been shifting gradually from an agrarian-industrial economy to an industrial-agrarian-based one. The Mongolian economy expanded into processing of animal husbandry raw materials, garment production, building materials, food, and mining. The diversification of industry proceeded in coal, copper and molybdenum mining, grain and fodder production, consumer goods.

The law on privatisation passed in May 1991 and as subsequently amended, defines procedures and responsibilities for the privatisation process. The privatisation is being implemented in two phases. In the first "small" privatisation phase, the assets of small businesses, enterprises, shops and retail outlets with a total voucher value of Tg 5,9 billion, were auctioned to individuals. In the second big privatisation phase, the assets of large state enterprises with a total voucher value of Tg 13.9 billion are being converted into joint stock companies, with shares for sale in batches at the Mongolian Stock Exchange.

Over 3000 entities (including livestock holdings) with assets worth Tg 3.7 billion and with some 947000 shareholders have been privatised. Certain enterprises are of strategic economic importance and a state interest is retained. Secondary market tradings started in summer 1995

A two-tier banking system replaced the previous monobank in 1991 with the adoption of the Banking Law by Parliament. According to that law the Mongolbank (the Central Bank) is authorised to implement the monetary policy of the Government. Commercial activities of the former State Bank were transferred to commercial banks. The Central Bank has a supervisory role with regard to banking activities and observance of regulations by the commercial banks. Due to the tight policy pursued by the Mongolbank some positive signs appeared in the monetary sector. The slowdown in inflation led to a gradual decrease in nominal interest rates in 1994 and increase of togrog-denominated time deposits.

For up dated exchange rate of national currency (Togrog-Tg) consult the "Homepage of Mongolian Chamber of Commerce and Indusrtry" http://www.mongoliaonline.mn/mcci Central Bank tightened up the regulations on clearing credits. Reserve money increased due to an increased liquid ability of the banks. Foreign currency deposits rose by only 6 % in the year.

MAJOR TRENDS

Following sweeping political changes in 1990, Mongolia embarked on an ambitious program of economic reforms aimed at replacing the centrally planned economy. This goal was pursued against the background of a series of severe external shocks, notably the abrupt termination of the Soviet Union's trade support and foreign aid which comprised 37% of Mongolia's GDP.

In the years immediately after the reform program began, the economy declined. Output decreased, the balance of payments deteriorated, and inflation grew rapidly, reaching almost 400% in 1992. The Mongolian social safety net could not meet the demands placed upon it. Nonetheless, Mongolia remained committed to reform. It has closely followed the recommendations of IMF advisors and has used the IMF's enhanced structural adjustment facility to slow the decline of the economy. In 1993-94, the economy hit bottom and began to rebound. In 1994 Mongolia achieved positive growth for the first time since the reform process began, with growth of 2.4%. Since 1995 the economy has grown by 3-6% a year. Unemployment is about 20% and underemployment is higher. After the June 1996 parliamentary elections the new government accelerated the pace of reform and announced the liberalization of energy prices and its intent to increase the speed of privatization. The Ministry of Finance and central bank were committed to providing a stable macroeconomic environment. Thanks to these efforts, inflation dropped to 17% in 1997, 6% in 1998 and 10% in 1999.

Mongolia's reform government, under the Democratic Coalition, has made important economic progress. Sound macro-economic policies, supported by the donor community, have allowed Mongolia to weather the worst of the Asian financial crisis, despite several drops in world prices of Mongolia's key exports: copper, cashmere, and gold. Gross Domestic Product (GDP) grew by 2.7 percent in 1999, continuing the positive growth trend begun in 1995. Inflation was 10 percent, marking the second year in a row with moderate price increases, compared to hyper-inflationary rates earlier in the decade. Most impressive has been the growth of the private sector. The private sector share is now 72 percent. Private sector value-added grew by 12.7 percent in 1997, 15.0 percent in 1998, and 6 percent in 1999.

The total external trade turnover for 1999 equaled USD $761.4 million, of which USD $335.6 million were in exports and USD $425.8 million in imports. The total trade volume was down 10.3 percent from 1998, particularly imports, reflecting the imposition of a 5 percent import tariff in mid-

1999 as required by IMF conditionality. Exports of textiles and textile articles increased by 58.7 percent or USD $45.7 million. However, mineral product exports declined by 13.2 percent, showing the effects of the gold export tax imposed in late 1998 and the low world price for copper.

New firms are emerging in Mongolia. In 1998 textile and garment exports were larger than mineral exports for the first time in Mongolian history. Due to the relative stability of Mongolia, some American firms have established operations here, using Mongolia as a base for operations in Siberia. The modest trend is expected to continue as firms begin to realize the strategic location of Mongolia. In addition, the informal sector is emerging as a major engine of growth and employment and may account for 13 percent of the GDP.

During the past four years the Mongolian economy has been transformed from a state-owned to a private one. This has been the result of three complementary trends:

- Private enterprises have performed far better than state enterprises in sector after sector, and agriculture, which is an almost entirely private sector, has been the leading growth sector.
- New private companies have been contributing more and more to economic output
- A sustained broad privatization program has shifted significant number of enterprises from state to private ownership.

PRINCIPAL GROWTH SECTORS

Mongolia's long-term growth depends principally on mineral and petroleum extraction, and value-added processing of livestock products (particularly cashmere and meat). While tourism offers some potential, it is limited by the short summer, the cost of travel to Mongolia, and lack of infrastructure (roads, hotels, etc.). For more information, see Chapter 5.

GOVERNMENT ROLE IN THE ECONOMY

Since the beginning of reform in 1990, the role of the government in the economy has been strong. Adjustments in purchase prices for grain and other commodities, wage increases for state workers, difficulty in collecting national taxes, and the decline of world market prices for Mongolia's principal exports (gold, copper, cashmere) have contributed to a decline in official government revenues. The largest state-owned enterprises (such as Erdenet copper concern) have yet to be privatized. However, the private sector now makes up over 70% of GDP and privatizations continue through sealed bid auctions.

INFRASTRUCTURE INVESTMENT

Infrastructure development is the key to Mongolia's economic development. A north-south paved road running from the Russian border to the Chinese border through the capital city is complete from Ulaanbaatar north to the Russian border. The project was financed by the Asian Development Bank. A north-south rail corridor already exists. The country lacks an east-west paved road or rail line. Without transportation infrastructure it is difficult to attract investment in the mining or petroleum sectors. However, the government does not have the resources to undertake these projects.

If the government continues with privatization of major state-owned companies, the national petroleum distribution company, NIC, will be sold within a year. NIC imports petroleum products, mainly from Russia, and distributes and sells them countrywide. A Mongolian-Chinese joint venture company, the Mongolian Refinery Company, plans to construct a refinery 45 km east of Ulaanbaatar. Several gold and coal mines have been privatized through sealed-bid auction. The embassy makes every effort to inform US businesses of these opportunities through International Market Insight (IMI) reporting and the National Trade Data Base.

FOREIGN TRADE

Compared to other countries in transition, Mongolia achieved tangible results in trade liberalization. Mongolia`s accession to the WTO in January 1997 highlights its relative success in pursuing economic reforms and developing a new trade regime in line with international trading principles (The advantages are: becoming a part of global trade regime, full access to information on WTO member countries, benefiting from human resource development in trade field, etc.).

Changes are also underway in Mongolia`s foreign trade geography. Germany, Switzerland, USA, Japan and some other developed countries have increased considerably their share in foreign trade of Mongolia. As of today, nearly 90 per cent of exported goods are in hard currency.

The United States of America and Mongolia signed an Agreement on Transparency in Matters Related to International Trade and Investment today in New York, New York. The agreement, signed by United States Trade Representative Michael Froman and Mongolian Foreign Minister Luvsanvandan Bold, marks an important step in developing and broadening the economic relationship between Mongolia and the United States. The U.S.-Mongolia relationship has seen impressive growth over the past two decades. This bilateral Transparency Agreement adds to the continuing positive momentum in relations and benefits both countries by creating a more transparent and predictable environment for doing business.

The goal of the Transparency Agreement is to make it easier for American and Mongolian firms to do business. The agreement covers transparency in the formation of trade-related laws and regulations, the conduct of fair administrative proceedings, and measures to address bribery and corruption. In addition, it provides for commercial laws and regulations to be published in English, making it easier for international investors to operate in Mongolia.

Month	Exports	Imports	Balance
January 2013	13.2	0.1	13.1
February 2013	18.3	5.8	12.5
March 2013	16.4	0.4	16.0
April 2013	15.7	0.1	15.6
May 2013	131.4	6.0	125.4
June 2013	14.2	0.3	13.9
July 2013	11.9	0.4	11.6
August 2013	10.1	0.8	9.3
September 2013	20.5	5.1	15.4
October 2013	13.6	0.3	13.3
November 2013	5.9	0.2	5.7
December 2013	8.2	0.2	8.0
TOTAL 2013	279.5	19.7	259.8

INVESTMENT ENVIRONMENT

Over the past 20 years, Mongolia has transformed itself from a socialist country to a vibrant multiparty democracy with a booming economy. Mongolia is at the threshold of a major transformation driven by the exploitation of its vast mineral resources. The Mongolian economy has achieved remarkable progress over the last two years and its medium-term prospects are promising. It has emerged as one of the fastest growing economies in the world over the last two years and rising incomes have helped to reduce the poverty rate by 11.3 percentage points during the period. The economy is expected to show double digit growth again in 2013 despite the unfavorable external environment. The medium-term prospects are also promising, given the expected ramp-up of major mineral production including copper, coal, and gold.

The share of mining in GDP today stands at 20 percent, twice the ratio of a decade ago. The economy grew by 12.4 percent in 2012, compared to 6.4 percent GDP growth in 2010. GDP is expected to grow at a double digit rate over the period from 2013 to 2017.

Indicative assessment of economic policies, Mongolia's economic policy stance can be compared with those in other peer countries in the region. This box compares key economic parameters and policy variables between Mongolia and other countries in the East Asia and Pacific countries.

For further information please visit: www.investmongolia.com/en

A member of WTO since 1997, Mongolia acceded to the "Washington Convention on Investment Dispute Settlement of 1965" in 1996, joined the "Seoul Convention on Investment Insurance of 1985" in 1999 and a member of the Multilateral Investment Guarantee Agency (MIGA) of the World Bank Group and investors will thus be eligible for risk insurance through MIGA.Mongolia respectively signed the "Agreement on Mutual Protection and Promotion of Investment" more than 40 countries, "Agreement on Avoidance of Double Taxation" signed with 34 countries.

By the Law on Foreign Investment /passed in 1990 and subsequently revised in 1993, 1998, 2002 and 29 May 2008/ the foreign investor may run any business in all areas of production and all services other than those prohibited by the laws of Mongolia; establish wholly foreign-owned business entities or joint business entities with Mongolian investors. The Constitution of Mongolia protects FDI and the Foreign Investment Law complemented by relevant legislation and regulations, as well as international treaties and agreements to which Mongolia is bound and thus it is prohibits nationalizing and illegally confiscating assets and capital of foreign investors. Foreign investors receive treatment equal to that enjoyed by domestic investors as regards rights to own, utilize and exploit assets and capital. Amendments of 2002 were are aimed to create more favorable legal environment for foreign investment, to improve the legal conditions for potential long-term investors and to bring Mongolian FDI legal environment close to the international. Amendments of 28 May, 2008 were legalized the requirements from the foreign investors to create the minimum of investment in 100 000 USD to attract the interests of its bigiest investors and attribute the quality of foreign investment.

Foreign investors are grantees the following rights:

to own, utilize and dispose of investment assets and to repatriate capital invested in Mongolia;

to manage and to participate in management of economic entities with foreign investment participation;

to assign and transfer their rights and duties to other legal bodies;

to transfer the following revenue, income and profits out of Mongolia

a) Dividends and income associated with shareholders' contributions;

b) Income associated with disposal of assets, bond sales and transfer of ownership rights and liquidation of assets.

Foreign investors are permitted to lease land for up to 60 years and such a lease can be extended for another 40 years.

Foreign investors have a right conclude a Stability Agreement with the Government of Mongolia

Foreign investors have a right implement an investment project without registering a business entity in Mongolia

With the purpose to improve the competitive capacity of the country, to create new workplace, to decrease informal economy and to bring the legal environment close to the international standards, the Parliament of Mongolia amended set of laws on taxes in June 2006. According to those laws, the taxes of business entities has decreased by 5% each and became 10% and 25% that as we consider, is a big concession to investors.

On 5th of March 2008, the Government in its Resolution No.83 has re-approved a list of priority sectors. For instance,

in manufacturing sector production of:

processed oil products or refinery of oil and coal

iron and steel production

processed products in coke furnace

The Mongolian Government is fully committed to create better investment and business climate and eliminate retraining problems as quickly as possible and thus, for instance, in 2001 in the new Special Licensing Law of the government of Mongolia has reduced the number of licenses and permissions that needed to be obtained for business activities from 600 to 82. FIFTA /Foreign Investment and Foreign Trade Agency/ makes foreign investors' registration procedure prompter and quicker and all issues relevant to set up a foreign invested company will be decided in 3 working days.

Since July, 2005, Mongolia became eligible for exporting to the EU market without any duties or quata under the GSP Plus scheme. As a result, there is an opportunity to supply over 7200 product items to all the 27 EU member countries (for instance, copper and copper products, iron and iron products, zync, alluminuim, lead and lead products edible products of animal origin, meat, meat offal or blood products, prepared or preserved meat, textile, knitted or crocheted articles, wool, cashmere, woolen and cashmere products, wool, fine or coarse animal hair, horsehair, yarn just to name a few). In this relation, it is obvious that not only domestic enterprises but also foreign invested industries will benefit and it is with no doubt that their numbers will also grow.

One of the factors in increasing FDI in Mongolia, besides new investors, re-investment made by the excisting investors plays an important role proving that Mongolia has created favorable investment climate that has been noted by the international organizations.

A favorable condition for investment and business created by the Government of Mongolia was also noted by the international organizations, for instance, in the Report of UNICTAD, it highlights the continued growth of FDI in Mongolia whereby the country entered into the list of the leading countries by investment capacity index among 140 countries. In 2005, the two internationally-renowned agencies Moody's and Fitch Rating has assigned long-term foreign currency and local currency rating of BB- to Mongolia.

Mongolia currently enjoying stable economic growth and moderate inflationaccording to a WTO Secretariat report on Mongolia Trade Policy Review made in March, 2005.

Also, in 2005, the Government of Mongolia has successfully completed the Trade policy review by the WTO. The World Bank with the cooperation of International Finance Cooperation has conducted "Doing business 2007" research on business legal framework of 175 countries and Mongolia is included in the leading 45 countries that have a favorable business environment.

The amount of foreign investment in Mongolia is increasing day-by-day as a result of favorable external and internal legal environment of foreign investment.

As a result of the Government effort to create more favorable climate for investment, the foreign investment amount is steadily increasing year by year and its socio-economic influence is becoming more tangible. As the end November, 2008, 9271 companies from 100 countries were registered with total investment of 2,980 billion USD.

RESTRICTIONS ON FOREIGN INVESTMENT

Foreign investors can invest in all sectors of Mongolian economy except cultivation collection and sale of drugs and drug containing herbs, manufacturing of military weapons and guns, pornographic advertisement.
Special autorisation is needed for investment in banking, financial and insurance services, manufacturing and sale of spirits, tobacco products, chemicals and explosives, establishment of hospitals. production and sale of medicines and biochemical's, establishment of schools.

In which sectors to invest?
More than 1400 foreign companies and joint ventures representing 70 countries worldwide have been officially registered to operate in Mongolia. The aggregate amount of the investments total more than 300 million US dollars. Within this total, Chinese, Japanese, Russian and US companies are prevailing.

Trade an food sectors are leading in by the number of foreign investment companies and construction, production of construction materials, mining, food and light industry, processing animal origin raw materials, transportation and agriculture sectors are the areas of most interest to investors.

	Number of Foreign invested companies	FDI

Sectors' name							
	JVC	100% foreign invested	Total amount	Suspended	Million USD	suspended	FDI per company /1000 USD/
Mining	125	59	184	29%	129	6%	701
Light industry	87	56	143	17%	78	13%	545
Processing animal origin raw materials	113	20	133	26%	46	8%	346
Trade, public catering	206	143	349	31%	43	24%	123
Construction, industry of construction materials	174	53	227	27%	38	28%	167
Total amount	705	331	1036		334		
All			1955	26%	489	22%	250
Percentage			53%		68%		
Other sectors			47%		32%		

KEY INDUSTRIAL SECTORS

The process of industrialisation of Mongolia began in early 1940s with construction of a power plant and some semi-processing enterprises of raw materials in Ulaanbaatar. With the membership of the country in CMEA, the process accelerated. The new industrial cities such as Darkhan and Erdenet were founded. The country received financial and technical assistance not only from former Soviet Union, but also from Eastern European countries. Gross industrial output grew significantly throughout the 1980s, averaging about 9 per cent per annum during the first half of the decade, and 5 per cent thereafter.

AGRICULTURE

Although the Mongolian economy has experienced considerable ndustrialisation for the last 3 decades, the agriculture sector remains the backbone of the economy, with about 26 per cent of GNP. Itis employing 95 percent of the rural population and 40 percent of the total labour force.It accounts for about 44 per cent of total ex-ports, mostly livestock products. 80 percent of the land is suitable mainly for ex-tensive animal husbandry. 29.3 million heads of live-stock include: 13.5 mln sheep, 9.1 mln goats, 3.5 mln cattle, 2.8 mln horses and 0.36 mln camels. Around 95 per cent of all livestock is in private possession. Agriculture has important linkages with the rest of the conomy and provides more than 75 per cent of raw materials and other inputs for leather and shoes fac-tories, wool processing mills, milk and bakery plants.

The strategy of the Government is to reduce the dependence of the economy on agriculture, in particular, animal husbandry based on traditional nomadic culture and to move to a more technologically sophisticated industry-based production structure. In this strategy, while agriculture would continue to be an important component of production, the strategic focus will be developing it as an input supplier for higher value-added and growth-leading manufacturing activities.

Crop cultivation began on a significant scale only in 1950s by developing virgin land. Most crop cultivation takes place on large state farms. Although important progress has been made towards diversifying agriculture, and, in particular, attaining self-sufficiency in cereal crops such as wheat, livestock raising continues to be the dominant subsection in agriculture, contributing over 70 per cent of the gross output in the sector. However, agricultural crops which contributed less than 1 per cent of the gross output of the sector in 1940 have improved their share to 30 per cent today. In 1996 the farmers harvested 220140 tonnes of grain and 69840 tonnes of potatoes and vegetables.

Mongolian agriculture produces the highly-valued raw materials such as cashmere, camel wool, horse tail, etc.. Herd quality improvement is sought, particularly, in such a field as colour rationalisation.

MINING

Since the first industrial exploitation of 500 deposits of 40 different minerals have been evaluated and 150 deposits have been worked on. In the 1980s, the mining industry was targeted for expansion. Mining output rose substantially during the ten-year period beginning in 1978. Assistance from CMEA was given for geological surveying activities in Mongolia through the years. Joint Soviet-Mongolian surveying activities were conducted throughout Mongolia.

In the 1970s and 1980s the main activities were focused on industrial minerals, including copper, molybdenum, fluorspar, phosphorites, gold, tin and coal. Today, nearly 200 deposits of coal, ferrous and non-ferrous metals, rare earth metals and precious stones are being mined. Mining is dominated by large-scale development of coal, copper, fluorspar and molybdenum, whereas mining of gold, tin and tungsten is primarily small scale. Mining sector accounts for a significant share of national income, and coal, copper, fluorspar and molybdenum are the most important commodities produced. Copper, molybdenumand fluorspar account for 60 per cent of export revenues of the country. Except for the Mongolian-Russian Joint Venture of copper ore-extraction in Erdenet, the mining sector has limited development, but geological surveys suggest it has an important future in foreign exchange earnings.

Nearly three quarters of the coal production of Mongolia comes from the Baganuur, Nalaykh and Sharyngol mines and is used primarily for production of electric power. Baganuur lignite supplies a thermal power station at the mine site and meets much of the energy requirements of the mining and industrial centres in Bor-Ondor, Darkhan, Erdenet and Ulaanbaatar in northern Mongolia.

Mongolia is one of the leading world producers of fluorspar, and a major producer and exporter of copper and molybdenum among the former centrally planned economies.

Fluorspar deposits being mined in east-central and south-east Mongolia include those at Berkh and Bor-Ondor (Khentiy), Khar-Ayrag (Dornogovi), Urgen (Dornogovi) and Hajuu-Ulaan (Dornogovi). Essentially all fluorspar output was traditionally exported to the former Soviet Union for use in its metallurgical industry.

The copper and molybdenum deposit at Erdenet was initially surveyed by Mongolian and Czechoslovakian scientists in the mid-1960s and subsequently investigated by Soviet and

Mongolian geologists. Joint Soviet-Mongolian development of the deposit proceeded through the 1970s, and in December 1978 the Erdenet mine complex began operations. Several stages of expansion took place at Erdenet boosting concentrate production capacity to 16 million tones per year. Erdenet officials are today seeking advanced recovery technologies for the copper-molybdenum complex, in addition to financial assistance for a metal smelter facility.

Mongolia has a wide variety of mineral resources available for development. Though the minerals industry will continue to be dominated by production of coal, copper, fluorspar and molybdenum, other commodities will also be subject to new or expanded development, including gold, silver, limestone, nickel, phosphate, rare earth metals, tin, tungsten, zealots, lead and zinc. Mongolia will require continued financial and technical investment from external sources to develop its minerals base.

Given the varied geological environment of Mongolia, the long-term prospects for mining in the country are considered favourable. Efforts to attract foreign investors to the mining activities of Mongolia in the years ahead will be influenced by several factors, including the favourability of rules and regulations governing joint minerals development, and the stability of the country which will reassure investors and buyers alike of the guaranteed continuity of production.

Mongolia is uniquely situated to take advantage of minerals trade, both with its two neighbouring nations, Russia and China, and also with the rapidly developing and industrialised nations of the Asia-Pacific region. Located between Russia and China, both large mineral-consuming and producing nations, Mongolia has been and will continue to be a major supplier of minerals to these two large economies, albeit under differing arrangements.

The access of Mongolia to European markets and those of the Asia-Pacific region is also quite favourable. An obvious difficulty is the necessity to tranship ores /concentrates/ metals to these markets either through Russia to Europe or through China to the Asia-Pacific region. However, neither route presents an insurmountable barrier. Considering that Mongolia has been a supplier of ores/concentrates to Russia and Eastern Europe in the past, it has a proven means of access and known markets in that area. Continued and expanded trade with those areas is very likely.

Mongolia reached an agreement with China on the transhipment of goods, including ores/concentrates from Mongolia through China to the port facilities of Tianjin for forwarding to the Asia-Pacific region. Mongolia used this route for shipping tens of thousand tonnes of copper concentrate from the Erdenet mine to Japan. An alternate route through Russia to the port of Nakhodka is also available and already being used by Mongolia for shipping of goods to the Asia-Pacific region.

In the near future, Mongolia's new major external markets will be within the Asia-Pacific region, specifically Japan, Republic of Korea and USA. This does not take into account existing long-term contractual arrangements with Russia. Subsequent, markets within ASEAN and Indochin may present opportunities for Mongolian mineral commodity trade. Reopening and expansion of markets with Russia and Eastern Europe will be dependent on the economic performance and political stability in these areas.

A further factor in determining the nature and extent of the minerals trade from Mongolia will be the development of a proposed copper smelter to refine copper ore produced at Erdenet. The development of a smelter now or in the future would materially facilitate copper trade by increasing the value-added to the Erdenet ore, which is now exported as a concentrate, and would reduce transportation volumes and costs and would produce a more desirable product for most of the world market. A secondary benefit of on-site smelting of Erdenet ore would be the recovery of by-product molybdenum, silver, gold and other metals for sale on the world market.

An internal market for minerals in Mongolia is very small and is primarily for iron and steel. With construction of a metal recovery facility at Darkhan, using scrap metal, domestic demand can be satisfied. Although primarily designed for domestic supply, the Darkhan plant could be expanded for the production of iron and steel for export. Additionally, an iron and steel facility is being discussed with several countries to exploit the iron ore reserves of Tumurtiin Ovoo. Discussions on how to exploit iron ore reserves at Tumurtiin Ovoo are taking place with several countries.

Though the major mining areas are all adjacent to, or connected with, the existing rail system to Russia and China, the poor transportation infrastructure of Mongolia is a main constraint for new minerals' development and trade. However development of new fields may require infrastructure investment either on roads or branch railway lines (up to a maximum of 100 km length).

Mongolian Parliament adopted in December 1994 a new law on Mineral resources which improves the legal environment for mineral exploitation. Other factors that have an impact on decisions to invest will include infrastructure and energy constraints, climate conditions and division of management control
to joint ventures.

Mongolia has many important mining projects and petroleum fields which are available for joint venture and foreign direct investment. Starting 1989, Mongolia has been negotiating with major foreign companies on prospecting for and processing of oil. Several international energy firms are already pursuing investment opportunities in Mongolia, surveying the southern, eastern and south-eastern regions of Mongolia for prospective oil deposits. Western company officials have estimated oil reserves in place at two known fields of Mongolia at 50 million barrels, of which between 10 to 30 per cent can be recovered.

Priority also is given to mining and processing of lead, zinc, silver, molybdenum, gold, copper deposits.

Gold mining is to be increased at least 4 times over the current volume by way of establishing small and medium enterprises of all forms of ownership within the framework of the " Gold project". Placer gold production is profitable.

MANUFACTURING

Mongolia has built a significant capacity in light- and food- industry. The major enterprises of light industry are concentrated in Ulaanbaatar, Darkhan, Erdenet and Choibalsan cities. A number of enterprises have an excess capacity and are monopolist in the sector. The development of Mongolian light industry was designed to add value to the raw materials produced by animal husbandry and to create jobs for the increasing urban population mainly female residents. The developmentof Mongolian light industry began with establishment of wool washing, spinning and animal skin-processing enterprises. Also large state-owned garment factories were built. Military and other uniforms, fur and sheepskin garments have significant share in their products.

During 70s and 80s, the sector extended to the production of shoes, carpet, leather and skin garments. Three big carpet factories are situated in Ulaanbaatar, Erdenet and Choibalsan. The sector used to export its products to the CMEA member countries under fixed prices from bilateral government agreements. Until recently, the large state-owned wool- and skin-processing factories have played an important role in the national economy. In 1992-1993, all state- owned companies of light industry sector were privatised through "yellow" voucher scheme and became share-holding companies.

Wool and Cashmere Processing branch of the sector contributes over 10 per cent to the net industrial production and employs 5 per cent of workers. Only 2 out of 20 previous large state-owned companies remain as state property and the rest became share-holding companies. In recent years, a considerable amount of small and medium capacities have been introduced in the sector. Mongolia produces 20.000 m/t of sheep wool, about 2004 tons of cashmere and 1500 tons of camel wool per year. Encouragement is given to foreign investment in cashmere processing.

Skin and hide processing is traditionally known to Mongolians.Development of the hide and skin processing industry is based on the raw materials of about 8-9 million animals slaughtered yearly in Mongolia. The industry expanded rapidly with the establishment of an integrated leather garment and shoe factory for the production of domestic consumption and export. The whole sector is privatised. There are many small and medium enterprises involved in processing hides and skins and producing leather garments.

Almost all products of food industry are consumed on the domestic market. There are large-scale meat processing and flour plants in Ulaanbaatar, Darhan, Choibalsan and Suhbaatar.

Enterprises are divided into two categories by their size and significance; big enterprises with the production for the consumption of the country or to some extent for export and the local food factories with small production.

In early 1990s the sector suffered lingering stagnation and sharp decline across all areas.The light and food industry sectors of Mongolia have mainly obsolete, outdated equipment and technology except for a few cashmere processing enterprises. In the new business environment, the light and food industries are facing great difficulties concerning quality and cost of their production. Foreign investment is considered an important source for the recovery and further development of the sector.

Nowadays investors from USA, South Korea, Hong-Kong and other countries are establishing joint ventures with Mongolian partners using the existing facilities and skilled workers of the sector. They also are engaged in the production of garments for export using imported inputs.

Foreign investors are attracted by the favourable conditions set forward by Mongolian enactment concerning foreign investment and preferential tariff treatment in USA, EU and Japanese market for products of Mongolian origin. National economic development has been leading to the introduction of new manufacturing industries such as production of construction materials, assembly lines of various types based on imported spare parts, metallurgy in Mongolia.

Increasing demand for steel and iron products led Mongolia to construct its own steel mill in Darkhan city. The operation of this ill started in 1993 with annual capacity of 100.000 tons.

TOURISM AND SERVICE INDUSTRY

Although tourism in our country began to be a recognizable part of our economy 40 years ago, the Government at that time did not give proper attention to its development. Tourism policy was neglected, the material basis of tourism organization was not strengthened and infrastructure therefore remained poor. Training of personnel in the industry does not meet international standards and nothing much has been done to bring services and facilities up to the required level to satisfy sophisticated travellers.

Individual tourism and tourism originating from western countries were not encouraged, despite the fact that nowadays there are many countries which derive much of their income from tourism. We believe that tourism is an important source of foreign exchange and therefore it can become a vital part of the Mongolian economy. An important, but indirect effect of foreign tourism is the generation of foreign investment. After the political and economic changes of 1990, Mongolia opened its borders. The bases for developing tourism in Mongolia are its diverse fauna and flora, its pristine nature, fresh air, pure crystal water, rare animal kingdom, unique historical and cultural traditions, nomadic life style of Mongolian herdsmen. Particularly, in the last few years Mongolia has been more attracting foreign tourists and is becoming one of the fascinating destinations of the world. Since the transition of our country to a market oriented economy around 200 private and public entities involved in tourism have been set up within a few last years . On the one side, companies are becoming very eager to reap the benefits from tourism activity, and on the other side the state organizations are trying to determine the path of legislating and regulating the sector so that the business itself, its customers and the country's economy could all be given equal protection. Because tourism is a specific and efficient sector of the economy the Government of Mongolia has recently approved "Basic Guidelines for the Development of Tourism in 1995-2005". Subsequently, within the framework of the guidelines Programme of actions for 1995-1996 was worked out. Eco tourism has been identified as a main potential for development of the sector in the country. The most serious constraints in the development of tourism were determined as (1) the inappropriate infrastructure and tourism services; and (2) the inadequate human resource capabilities in the sector. Based on the Guidelines, the country has been divided into seven main regions, depending on their potential for attracting foreign tourists. In addition, a gradual approach towards their development has been adopted. The main regions for the development of tourism are as follows:

Ulaanbaatar - the capital of Mongolia, was founded in 1639. The centre of Buddhism in the country has grown to reflect a mix of ancient traditions and modern life style.

Khuvsgul region - Mongolia's alpine area with snow-covered mountains and crystal clear lakes. Lake Khuvsgul is one of the deepest in the world, twin of the famous Baikal Lake in Siberia.

Orkhon Valley - the site of the ancient Karakorum, or throne of the Khans. The famous Erdene Zuu Monastery, the first temple in the country, is still functioning, and has numerios monuments and historical relics.

Gobi Desert - largest and best known desert in Asia. Not a sand desert like the Sahara, it has a rich biodiversity with many fascinating plant and animal species.

Mongolian Steppes - the vast, flat, treeless plains were the site of many ancient battles, and refuge of horse thieves. In some areas, caves lead underground into huge water-filled caverns.

Hentii aimag - the birth place of Chingis Khan. Set amongst beautiful scenery are monuments to the emperor, as well as museums displaying his life history and achievements.

However, an accurate analysis of the tourism potential in these regions, cost and benefits involved has not been undertaken because of lack of basic information and data on the number and status of existing tourist facilities and visitors to the country. The Tourism Policy Department was first established in 1995 within the former Ministry of Trade and Industry with the objective implementing the Guidelines. Now this Department operating within the Ministry of Infrastructure is assigned a large number of responsibilities, including the elabration of regulations and procedures related to tourism activities. Besides, the Department coordinates the participation of the country in the activities of the world and regional tourist organizations. Mongolia became a full member of the World Tourism Organization in 1990. The number of foreign visitors in 1995 exceeded 110 thousand, from which 15% were tourists. Most of the tourists came from Japan, Western Europe & USA.

INFRASTRUCTURE. ENERGY SUPPLY

The industrialisation of the country led to the foundation of the present network of energy supply. Mongolia has developed energy production based on coal burning thermal power plants. There are 6 major thermal power plants of different capacity; three of them are situated in Ulaanbaatar with capacity of 21MW, 134MW and 560MW, and the others in Darkhan, Choibalsan and Erdenet cities with capacities of 48MW, 48MW and 36MW respectively.

The main economic region of Mongolia, and the region along the Trans-Mongolian Railroad and its spurs are connected with high power transmission lines. This network is known as Central Energy System (CES) which also is linked to the Buryat Energy System of the Russian Federation through 220KW line. The CES network consists of 1044 km of 220KV, 2100 km of 110KV and 2950 km of 35KV transmission lines, and covers the territory of Selenge, Bulgan, Darhan-Uul, Orkhon, Tov, Ovorkhangai, Arkhangai, Dornogovi and Govisumber aimags. The CES provides power supply to one third of the territory and half of the population of the country.

The headquarters of the CES is located in Ulaanbaata and responsible for import/export of electricity and its distribution. The CES is under the direct supervision of the Ministry of Agriculture and Industry. The towns and settlements beyond the CES network have their own small power stations or diesel generators.

During periods of power shortage, especially in winter, the CES buys electricity from Russia and distributes among its consumers. Thanks to the considerable Government investment, and the financial and technical assistance from the donor countries and international organizations, the power supply of the country is being improved.

There is a proposal that a hydropower station of 250 MW capacity on the river Egiin Gol will be constructed with a soft loan from the Asian Development Bank (ADB). Also other smaller ones are under construction in the different parts of the country.

TRANSPORTATION

Specific conditions of the country predetermine the development of its transportation network, dominated by the auto-transportation regarding the inland territory and by railroad. Air-transportation is vital for the remote aimags. A small fleet of cargo boats operates on the lake of Khovsgol and Selenge river. Mongolia is also seeking to establish its own ocean fleet operating from the nearest port. Legislation regarding such matters as registration and domicile is being drafted and will be enacted.

The Trans-Mongolian Railroad connecting Russian and Chinese railroad network runs through Central Mongolia from north to south. The development of the rail system of Mongolia started in the 1930s with the construction of the 238 km long broad-gauge railway linking Choibalsan with the-ex Soviet Union in the east. A 400 km long railway, linking Ulaanbaatar with the Soviet Union was completed in 1949, and subsequently extended southward an additional 700 km to the

Chinese border. This 1,400 km stretch of railway today provides the major link for Mongolia with Russia and China and the rest of the world.

The main industrial and commercial centres such as Ulaanbaatar, Darkhan, Erdenet, Sainshand and Sukhbaatar are located along this railroad. The Mongolian rail system was established driven largely by an emphasis on expanding the mining industry. Since the completion of the Trans-Mongolian Railroad in 1956, spur routes have been constructed to support minerals development, including an 80 km line constructed to link with the Sharyn Gol coal mine, a 140 km line to link with Erdenet and a 96 km line to link with Bor-Ondor.

The spur railroads with length of about 45-150 km connecting the mining complexes to the Trans-Mongolian railroad have a vital role in the national economy. The city of Choibalsan, the centre of Dornod aimag, is directly connected with Russia. The total length of railroads of Mongolia is 1815 km.

The joint Mongolian-Russian concern "Ulaanbaatar railroad" operates Mongolian railroad.

The nearest Russian ports - Vladivostok, Vostochny and Nakhodka are located over 2004 km away. The route to the Chinese port of Tianjin enables much faster access to the sea and the distance is 1000 km from the Mongolian bor-der.

Mongolia and the People's Republic of China signed an agreement on transit which allows the transportation of Mongolian freight on the rail line from the Mongolia-China border through China to and from the port of Tianjin, providing Mongolia with direct access to the sea. Recently, new transhipment facilities have been put into operation in the Mongolian-Chinese border at Zamyn-Uud reducing significantly time of freight movement. (The Chinese railway gage is different from Mongolia's)

Auto-transportation is the most important mean of transport in the Mongolian conditions. Mongolia has 3076 km improved roads, out of which 1303 km are paved. There are 5 asphalt and concrete roads from Ulaanbaatar including the route to Russia through Darkhan, Sukhbaatar and to Arvaikheer, the centre of Ovorkhangai aimag.

An extensive domestic network of 42,000 km links the 21 major population centres and 160 smaller centres throughout the country. The vast majority of roads are simple dirt roads for which plans for improvements are being made.

All centres of aimags, somons and other towns have their filling stations.

Both state and private auto-transportation companies are operating in the domestic market. The introduction of the private sector has significantly improved the service. For Mongolia with its vast territory, the auto transport has a vital significance , and therefore it is important to create a reliable network of paved roads. Alongside with this, a need to build up improved railroads for international routes is emerging.

Taking into account the favourable geographical position of Mongolia located on the cross-roads linking the European continent and Pacific region it might be economically justified to develop air transport system.

The national air-transportation company (state enterprise) MIAT is the major domestic carrier. MIAT serves the regular links with Irkutsk, Moscow, Beijing and Alma-Ata. The company also operates charter flights to Seoul, Osaka, Singapore, Berlin and other cities.

Besides MIAT, three private air-transportation companies operate mainly in the domestic lines.

The main airport of Mongolia was reconstracted by ADB soft loan. According to the project, the main building of the airport is planned to be extended by 30 per cent and the runway - be reaped and lengthened. New hangars and warehouses will be added to the existing facilities.

Private Transportation Companies were established and playing the significant role in the transport industry of Mongolia.

TELECOMMUNICATIONS

The national integrated telecommunication network of the country consists of 4000 km analogue microwave and 30.000 km open wire lines connecting amigo centres and salmons. There are 325 switching systems with a capacity of 100.600 telephone lines in the network.

The establishment in 1990 of the ground station of the "Asiasat" and "Intelsat" system in Ulaanbaatar has enabled Mongolia to be connected automatically with a telex and fax network of over 190 countries. The international telecommunication services are handled through 74 channels of satellite systems including Intelsat, Intersputnik and Asiasat. In 1992-1993 a new Ulaanbaatar city digital technology telephone exchange with capacity of 40.000 lines was installed and is now in full use.

The postal service is rather inexpensive . In most cases, letters and parcels can be sent from post offices at a low cost. However, for reliable air freight service it is recommended that DHL be used.

Telegraph services are provided through teleprinters in post and telecommunications offices. The private sector has introduced telecommunications services such as E-mail and pager service.

Cellular net mobile telephone system is in place in Ulaanbaatar. Mongolia is committed to renew the whole communication system nation-wide.

Ref: http://www.magicnet.mn/datacom/"Datacom" Co., Ltd is the main service provider of world-wide Internet network communication. For average rate of international telecommunication tariffs please consult the home page of Mongolian Chamber of Comerce and Industry at http://www. Magicnet.mn/mccu.

LABOUR

High population growth rate during the 1960s and 1970s has provided an abundant labour force in the 1980s and 1990s. The developing national economy employed this labour pool. The centralised economy was providing new jobs for nearly 90.000 men and women yearly. A vast network of training and professional education was created. Graduates from secondary schools were sent to the former USSR and East European countries for higher education. Nearly 240.000 trainees completed the vocational schools between 1964-1990. New development projects had difficulties concerning shortage of labour force.

Today's labour market in Mongolia is characterised by increasing unemployment, and consequent decline in training process. The average registered unemployment is 657 per 10.000 persons. There is therefore a possibility to develop labour intensive industry.

FINANCIAL SYSTEM

The Mongolian Stock Exchange started its operations in February 1992. Now it has 29 broker firms each connected with the Stock Exchange with computer network. The national big privatisation programme is being realised through the Stock Exchange and it is planned to privatise altogether more than 400 companies with the registered capital worth 11 bln.togrog.

The main goal of the Mongolian Stock Exchange for the nearest future is to intensify capital investments into the production and service.

BANKING

The present banking system of Mongolia was formed in the beginning of 1990s when many newly founded commercial banks launched their operations along with state banking system. The transition to a two-tier banking system was completed in April 1993 when reserve management functions were moved to Mongolbank.

Until 1991, Mongolia had a monobank system, and all central and commercial banking activities were carried out by one institution. The state Bank of Mongolia functioned as a cashier, directing credit in line with the Planning Committee's instructions and handling foreign transactions in line with CMEA barter arrangements. It opened some 400 branches around the country which accepted savings deposits and disbursed credit to enterprises and government agencies.

In May 1991, a new Banking Law became effective, under which the State Bank was divided into a central bank, called the Bank of Mongolia, and a foreign trade bank called the State Bank of Mongolia /International/. The Bank of Mongolia's Chairman is responsible to the legislature /The State Great Khural/ thus making the central bank independent of the government. The Banking Law provides the framework for the development of a fully functioning central bank capable of managing money and credit using indirect instruments, leaving the allocation of resources to markets.

The Central Bank of Mongolia - Mongolbank - is responsible for the implementation of the laws and enactments concerning the banking. It also has functions to manage official foreign exchange reserves, issue bank notes, render banking service to the Government and to elaborate monetary policy. Also Mongolbank supervises the commercial banks.

The commercial activities of the former State Bank have been transferred to new commercial banks which were established in 1992. As of January 1, 1994, the commercial banks have to meetTg 400 mln paid-up capital requirement, up from the previous level of Tg 50 mln. Adoption of this rule led to the consolidation of several smaller banks and to the closure of others. Nowadays, there are operating 11 commercial banks including 1 privately owned bank. The year of 1994 had brought positive results in the monetary sector, which were early due to the strict monetary policy pursued by the Bank of Mongolia.

First year results under the new Enhanced Structural Adjustment Facility (ESAF) Program were reported in 1994. The ESAF program aims at developing the macro-economic management system which is necessary for a market economy. The successful implementation created conditions allowing the receipt of financial assistance from the International Monetary Fund (IMF) and other international financial institutions, as well as from donor countries. Thanks to IMF's assistance, the Bank of Mongolia developed a mechanism for clearing settlement at the Bank and made progress in solving the problems related to bad loans of commercial banks. Exchange Regime

There is free exchange of currency at the exchange rates determined by the floating togrog.

TAXATION

Mongolia's Parliament, the State Great Khural, has adopted ammendments to tax laws that scrap virtually all import duties, slash taxes on business , offer incentives to foreign investors and raise the income tax threshold. The radical reforms took effect from May 1, 1997.

The principal amendments to the tax laws are described below.

1. The main points of the ammendments to the Law on Individual Income Tax (1993) are given below:

The newly amended Law defines permanently residing, temporarily residing and non-residing persons as a taxpayer.

The newly amended Law points out in details the registration procedure of taxpayers. In tax calculations a camel, a cow and a horse is considered as 2 heads of animals, and a sheep and a goat is taken as 1 head of animal accordingly.

An individual with cattle in his ownership will be imposed 2-5% income tax. Income from 150-200 heads of animals is exempt from taxes.

Returns from use of copyright, programming, patents, models, trademarks, know-how, as well as cinema, video, audio and other records are subject to taxation.

Proceeds from art performance or sport awards, games of chance or lottery are levied income tax. · A permanently residing taxpayer engaged in production of crop, potatoes and vegetables is given 50% tax abatement as regards income from the above-mentioned activity.

2. The main points of the amendments to the Law on Business Entity and Organization Income Tax are given below:

Income from the sale of real estate is levied 2% tax.

The following income are exempt from taxes:
- Interest earned on Government debt;
- Membership fees and donation of non- governmental organizations;
- Monetary donation of taxpayers contributed to educational organizations; and registered with financial and taxation authorities;
- Income from donor blood, or other blood items;

A foreign oil company operating on the principle of production sharing contract with the Mongolian Government is exempt from tax on income based on its share or repatriation of profit abroad.

Producers of crop, potatoes and vegetables is given 50% tax abatement on their income from above-mentioned activities.

The list of taxpayers is enriched by non-state organizations, religious institutions, juridical persons of state and local ownership, as well as other juridical persons conducting economic activity.

Income tax is not imposed on assets directed to health insurance, routine repairs, temporary constructions, bonus item in the construction's budget, and to compensation of possible loss from exchange rate.

Bank loan loss provisions are tax deductible.

For the list of goods and rate of excise tax imposed as well as Foreign investment policy and regulations, please refer to the "Homepage of Mongolian Chamber of Commerce and Industry" http://www. Mongoliaonline.mn/mcci/

VISA REGULATIONS

The simplification of visa procedure comes next to the liberalization of the tax legislation, as the latest effort of the Government to open up the Mongolian market and create conditions near to free trade status.

The Government is now preparing two-level measures. Softening of visa regulations is expected to instigate the growth of the number of visitors to Mongolia, including businessmen and potential investors. Firstly, the draft of supplements and amendments to the Law on Legal Status of Foreign Citizens will be submitted to the Parliament in the nearest future. Secondly, new regulations enforced from May 1 comprise the changes as follows:

Visa for a foreign visitor is issued within 24 hours, if the duration of the stay in Mongolia is 30 days or less.

No invitation is needed for applicants to get Mongolian visa.

A citizen from a country where there is no Embassy of Mongolia or where there are certain difficulties in obtaining visa can get it at the international ports of the country as Buyant-Ukhaa, Zamyn Uud, Sukhbaatar and Altanbulag.

Honorary Consuls of Mongolia have the right to issue visas to travel to Mongolia on the approval from the Ministry of External Relations.

STOCK EXCHANGE

Mongolian Stock Exchange started its activities on February 7 , 1992 . Its activities include creation of necessary conditions for implementing privatization of the state - owned enterprises , establishing brokerage firms in local areas of Mongolia , and setting up computerized network throughout the country to conduct trading of the listed stocks. Law of Securities was approved by the Great Khural , in end of 1994 . Secondary securities market has started and first secondary trading was started on August 28, 1995 . At that stage foreigners will be allowed to buy stocks.

CAN MONETARY POLICY BE EFFECTIVE DURING TRANSITION?: LESSONS FROM MONGOLIA[1]

Mongolia has undergone dramatic changes during its transition to a market economy, with fundamental restructuring in both the real economy and the financial sector. How effective is monetary policy in such a changing environment?

A key element of each former centrally planned economy's transition to a market economy has been the establishment of financial markets and institutions that can support such an economy. But introducing and, in particular, creating confidence in, such markets and institutions has been a long process. Moreover, difficulties such as banking crises, high ratios of nonperforming loans to total loans, inexperienced management, political interference, currency appreciation, and high or moderate inflation rates have posed additional challenges for monetary policy.

The policy of Mongolia's monetary authorities has been to keep the growth rate of the money supply stable while dealing with these transition-specific challenges as they occur. In addition, because of Mongolia's climate, which is characterized by extremes of temperature, the Mongolian economy is highly seasonal, and the authorities have occasionally intervened in the foreign exchange market to avoid excessive exchange rate fluctuations stemming from large, weather-related swings in exports and imports. Such a pragmatic approach to monetary policy has been necessary in many transition economies. This article discusses whether Mongolia's approach has been facilitated by a stable money demand and a predictable relationship between inflation and monetary variables.

MONGOLIA'S EXPERIENCE

Mongolia's experience has been different from that of most other transition countries in four respects. First and most important, there has been a political consensus on the need for a bold and comprehensive approach to reforms. Despite significant shifts in the governing coalitions and periods of political gridlock, national governments have pursued essentially the same objectives. Second, Mongolia did not—unlike many other transition countries—experience a prolonged period of moderate inflation. Annual inflation fell below 10 percent in the first half of 1998 and has stayed low since then. Third, unlike the Central and Eastern European transition countries, Mongolia has not been a recipient of large capital inflows and has therefore not confronted the challenges that such inflows present for the monetary authorities. Fourth, the Mongolian economy has been significantly affected by both the Asian crisis of 1997 and, in particular, the Russian crisis of 1998. Consequently, its currency has appreciated considerably (in both nominal and real terms). This appreciation has been instrumental in lowering annual inflation rates from the moderate range to single digits, although this reduction was probably achieved at some cost to output.

The table on page 45 compares real GDP in 1989 and 1998 for Mongolia with that in the other transition economies and shows that Mongolia has done better than most. Out of 27 transition countries, only Poland, Slovakia, and Slovenia have been doing significantly better than Mongolia, while the Czech Republic and Hungary have performed equally well. This simple measure has limitations, however, and does not reveal much about the development of institutions or the role of policies in individual transition countries. To analyze the role of policies

[1] **Torsten Sløk** is an Economist in the World Economic Studies Division of the IMF's Research Department.

during the transition—in particular, thes role of monetary policy—one has to examine the relationship between monetary variables and inflation and real economic activity.

Development of real GDP in transition countries (1989 = 100)		
	1989	1998
Eastern Europe	100	93.4
CIS[1] countries	100	54.0
Baltic states	100	71.4
All of the above	100	64.5
Mongolia	100	93.1

Sources: United Nations, 1999, Economic Survey for Europe, No. 2, Appendix Table B.1. Data for Mongolia are IMF staff estimates.
[1] Commonwealth of Independent States.

MONETARY POLICY IN TRANSITION

A market-based monetary policy depends on the existence of a market for money and foreign exchange. Specifically, reserve requirements, refinance windows, government and central bank bills and bonds, and credit allocation through banks or credit auctions are needed. If the institutional framework for monetary policy and these specific monetary instruments are lacking or malfunctioning, the conduct and effectiveness of monetary policy will be impeded. Most transition economies have gradually established an institutional framework and introduced instruments and financial markets that function like those in developed countries, although they are smaller and less liquid.

Mongolia enhanced the role of monetary policy in the early stages of its transition. In May 1991, a two-tier banking system was introduced to replace the previous, central bank-based system.

Directed credits, which until 1991 had been determined by the credit plan, were limited to priority sectors and oil imports and were phased out in mid-1994. Bank-by-bank ceilings and interest rate controls on commercial bank deposit and lending rates that had been imposed in the initial transition phase were also eliminated. In addition, the central bank introduced reserve requirements on business and household demand deposits in 1991, central bank bills in 1993, and a regular refinancing auction at market-determined rates in 1995. The degree of independence given to the central bank, the Bank of Mongolia, is surprisingly similar to that observed in many developed countries.

The Banking Law of Mongolia, adopted in 1996, states that the two primary objectives of the Bank of Mongolia are to ensure a stable value for the Mongolian tugrik and to act as supervisor of the financial system. In summary, the institutions and financial markets required for an effective monetary policy in Mongolia have, to a large extent, been created.

Over the transition period, Mongolia's banking sector has faced major challenges, including a high volume of nonperforming loans. To strengthen the banking system, measures have been taken, under IMF-supported programs, to reduce operating costs, resolve the financial situations of insolvent banks, and increase loan recoveries. The ratio of foreign exchange deposits to broad money has for most years been less than 20 percent, the average for all transition countries since 1991. But the interest spread, defined as the difference at the end of the year between the rates on short-term bank loans in domestic currency and rates on deposits was, over the same period, one of the highest in the transition countries. The high interest rates have been maintained throughout the transition period to preserve and restore confidence in the banking system. While progress has been made in strengthening the system, problems remain, particularly in the balance-sheet positions of several private banks.

CAN MONETARY POLICY WORK IN TRANSITION?

A key challenge for monetary policy in transition is that inflation is not just a monetary phenomenon. Apart from the usual demand-pull and cost-push pressures, at least five additional influences pose challenges for the conduct of monetary policy. First, price liberalization at the beginning of transition results in an initial price level adjustment and substantial changes in relative prices and hence also in inflation. Second, this adjustment in relative prices brings about a significant reallocation of resources, and subsequent monetary financing of rising fiscal deficits resulting from a combination of declining fiscal revenues and rigid expenditure patterns also generates inflationary pressures. Third, downward rigidities in goods and labor markets, together with the indexation of prices, generate more permanent moderate inflation (15-40 percent a year) in many transition countries. Fourth, as income grows, so does the price level of the economy (in line with the so-called Balassa-Samuelson effect), and authorities have to determine to what extent inflation comes from this source.

Finally, privatization, institution building, and the creation of competitive markets take considerable time, and the speed with which competition and efficiency are introduced in the private sector significantly affects inflation rates during the transition. Given all these transition-specific influences on inflation, the existence of predictable relationships between key economic variables, necessary for monetary policy to be conducted effectively, cannot be taken for granted. To investigate the relationships among inflation, the exchange rate, reserve money, broad money, and net credit to the government in Mongolia, a causal analysis of relationships among economic variables has been carried out. Granger-causality tests give an indication of how these variables affect each other over time. All series measure 12-month changes, beginning in December 1995 and ending in June 1999. The chart on page 45 shows the causal relationships among the variables for different time periods.

One conclusion drawn from the results of the causality tests is that net credit to the government plays a key role. In the short run, this variable does not affect inflation directly but has an effect on it through the above-mentioned monetary variables. In the longer term (five to six months), net credit to the government becomes a function of the other monetary variables and affects inflation directly. A second conclusion is that the exchange rate has a significant effect on inflation during all time periods examined. In the very short term, it is the only variable explaining inflation directly. In other words, if the exchange rate changes, businesses immediately react by adjusting domestic prices. Third, in the longer term, the money supply explains inflation directly, and this indicates that it is the money-supply rule that has brought down inflation in Mongolia.

To explore this further, a money-demand relationship has been estimated using annual data covering 1993-98 for 22 Mongolian regions (see Sløk (2004) for details). The analysis provides two key insights. First, the money-demand estimation confirms that there is a significant and stable relationship between real money and real income over the sample period.

Second, the income elasticity is approximately one-half, which suggests that a 1 percent increase in income leads to a 0.5 percent increase in the demand for money. This elasticity is significantly below that for most member countries of the Organization for Economic Cooperation and Development, which is usually close to 1. The lower elasticity in Mongolia could indicate that considerably fewer and less complex transactions are carried out by its banks and firms than by their counterparts in highly developed economies. In other words, the lower income elasticity of the demand for money suggests that, in Mongolia, money is held primarily to carry out transactions.

In sum, a stable relationship exists between the money supply and economic activity in Mongolia, which has made it possible for the monetary authorities to use a money-supply-growth rule to guide monetary policy. Furthermore, their use of such a rule has been successful in bringing down inflation.

CONCLUSION

In a transition economy with institutions as rudimentary as Mongolia's, a stable demand for money and a predictable relationship between inflation and monetary variables can be found, and a market-based monetary policy can be implemented effectively. To strengthen the effectiveness of monetary policy, however, the authorities need to continue with reforms—in particular, banking sector and public administration reforms. Looking forward, other transition countries have managed to maintain annual inflation rates in the single digits by adopting inflation-targeting frameworks.

Such a framework has the advantages of being transparent and easily monitored by the public and of allowing monetary policy to keep inflation low while policymakers cope with domestic and international shocks. Inflation targeting, however, is not suitable for countries that have not completed structural adjustment, are starting with high inflation, or are susceptible to large shocks. In the event of such large shocks, inflation targeting could have sudden, marked effects on monetary instruments that could, in turn, have severe implications for the real economy. Moreover, as a consequence of its pronounced temperature fluctuations, Mongolia experiences seasonal movements in the exchange rate, which, if left unsmoothed, could have undesirable effects on inflation. In sum, it is not clear whether it would be useful for Mongolia to adopt an inflation-targeting framework at this stage of its transition.

Reference:
Torsten Sløk, 2004, "Monetary Policy in Transition: The Case of Mongolia," IMF Working Paper 00/21 (Washington: International Monetary Fund).

MINERAL POTENTIAL OF MONGOLIA

(Main minerals)

GOLD (AU)

Gold mineralization has taken place, with various intensity, during the early and late Precambrian-early Cambrian, Paleozoic, Mesozoic and Cenozoic time however the main gold mineralization is associated with magnetic activity during Permian and Triassic - Jurassic time. Placers were formed during the Cretaceous-late Neogene and Pliocene-Holocene time.

The known gold mineralizations in Mongolia are represented by three economic types: veins, mineralized zones, and placers. Although vein occurrences are the most widely developed of all gold occurrences the bulk of proven gold reserves associated with placers and mineralized zones.

On the base of geological data (tectonic structure, mineral occurrences, age of mineralization, gold content) ten main gold metallogenic provinces within Mongolia have been defined.

It should be emphasized that because of a very low level of geological knowledge, with respect to the western and southern portion of Mongolia and an emphasis on only placers and/ or quartz vein mineralization in the studied areas, the true gold potential of these large regions is largely conjectural. Nevertheless, the number of occurrences defined based on limited data clearly suggests a high gold potential overall for the region.

Additionally, although not identified, available geologic data would indicate that occurrences of (a) gold-bearing conglomerates of Cretaceous and Tertiary age should be expected in southern and western Mongolia, (b) gold mineralization associated with ancient volcano- sedimentary areas in Central Mongolia and (c) ancient epithermal gold occurrences (island arc associations) may be expected in the Kharkhira, Ulzeet, and Southern Mongolian gold provinces.

BASE METAL (CU, MO, PB, ZN)

Copper-molybdenum (Cu-Mo) mineralization in Mongolia is primarily of three deposit types, i.e., late Paleozoic-early Mesozoic Cu-Mo porphyries, Cu-Ni magmatic segregations associated with grabbo of unknown age and Paleozoic-Mesozoic stratabound coppers.

The Cu-Mo deposits previously described occur within four main base metal provinces in Mongolia, i.e., the Altai, North Mongolian and South Mongolian provinces.

In addition to the previously described Cu-Mo deposit types and provinces, Mongolia also has a large number of middle to late Mesozoic Pb-Zn deposits of various deposit types, largely in the eastern of the country. The main deposit types, skarn, mineralized explosive pipes, vein, mineralized zones. The known base metal deposits were mainly formed in the middle-late Mesozoic. They are located in eastern part of country.

The main Pb-Zn deposits located in Central Mongolian province, and several perspective occurrences in Altai province.

The Northern Central and Southern metallogenic provinces of Mongolia have a high potential for a discovery of new deposits of Cu, Mo, Pb, Zn. In the North and South Mongolian provinces, the potential is greater for Cu-Mo porphyries, in Central Mongolian and both Pb, Zn and Cu-MO porphyry deposits.

Most perspective for the discovery of large scale copper and/or polymetallic mineralization is the Altai province in South Mongolia where there is the intersecting of three regional geologic structures (Altai metallogenic province, Beitianshan tectonostratigraphic terrane and a complex zone of faults.

Regionally the Altai metallogenic province includes areas of Russia (Gornii Altai), China (Altai), and Mongolia (Mongolian Altai). In the Gornii Altai of Russia large deposits of lead and zinc have been discovered, whereas on the Russia-Mongolian border hydrothermal Pb-Zn deposits, and volcano-clastic Fe mineralization have been identified.

In the Altai zone of China, in mid-Paleozoic sandstone, shales and volcanoclastic deposits of synorogenic-synvolcanic massive Cu-Ni sulfides occurrences indicate that at least two major synorojenic massive sulphide deposits, in addition to Kuroko-type massive sulphide deposits will be discovered. Based on the same favorably criteria as used in the China Altai region it is estimated that similar deposits would occur in the adjacent Mongolian Altai. On the base of above-mentioned data is possible to predict the presence of economic deposits of Cu, Mo, Pb, Zn, and Ni in the Mongolian Altai. Recently, in the northern part of the Altai zone Cu occurrences of stratiform type have been discovered as well as synorogenic Cu-Ni mineralization associated with gabbro bodies.

In the southern Mongolia the Altai metallogenic province intersects the Bietianshan tectono-stratigraphic terrane and at this zone of intersection both areas are in turn intersected by a late-Devonian-Carboniferous fault zone extending NW from China through Mongolia. The fault zone is approximately 850-900 km in length and 30-50 km in width and which, based on recent epicenter studies, is tectonically active. This area of complex intersection of the three zones is known to contain Pb-Zn deposits however is considered highly prospective for the occurrence of several deposits and deposit types. In particular the complex rock types present include volcano-sedimentary, sandstone-carbonate formations, small to medium sized intrusions of tonalites, leucogranites, alkalic granites, syenites, gabbro and ultramafic rocks. Additinally, numerous crosscutting faults, of different orientation provide the host environment for diverse deposit types.

FLUORITE

Fluorite mineralization is widespread throughout Mongolia in rocks of Late Paleozoic to Late Mesozoic age. The major time of economically important mineralization took place during late Mesozoic / late Jurassic-early Cretaceous epochs). The fluorite mineralization represented by two economic types: epithermal vein and metasomatic ore bodies.

Late Mesozoic fluorite mineralization is associated with rare earth and lead-zinc mineralization but not in economical quantities. Three major fluorite provinces have been defined in Mongolia, i.e., the North Mongolia, Trans-Mongolian and South Mongolian with the Trans-Mongolian province having the largest reserves and being the most actively exploited.

The major characteristics of the main provinces are shown in the Table 7. The fluorite reserves/resources of Mongolia are estimated at 18/23-33, respectively.

RARE-EARTH ELEMENTS (REE)

Rare-Earth Metals (Ta, Nb, Zr, W, Sn)--REM

Genetically and spatially REE and REMs in Mongolia are primarily felsic and alkalic rocks of late-Mesozoic, early Mesozoic and late Paleozoic age. Known deposits of REE and REM are subdivided on the following basis:

REE, REM mineralization (metasomatic zones) with alkalic granitoids and volcano-plutonic complexes.

Tungsten (W) vein and stockwork mineralization in granitoids.

Tin (Sn) vein and skarn mineralization in granites and carbonate rocks.

Within Mongolia six REE and/or REM provinces have been identified; the Altai, North Mongolian Hentii, Hangai, Southeast Mongolian, South Mongolian and the geologic attributes of these provinces are given in Table 8.

REE and REM occurrences are widely distributed throughout Mongolia with the most promising areas, based on available data, being the Altai and South Mongolian provinces for Ta, Nb, Zr, Y, W and REE, respectively.

URANIUM

Uranium exploration in Mongolia has started in 1940's by Mongolian and former Soviet Union geological organisations. Prior to1966, numerous uranium occurrences were discovered in coal deposits. In the period from 1967 to 1988 the exploration work became more systematic. As result of these exploration works, four "uranium - bearing provinces" were defined Mongol - Priargun, Gobi - Tamtsag, Hentei - Daur and Northern Mongolian. Several deposits were discovered in that time Dornod, Gurvanbulag, Mardai in eastern and Kharaat in southern Mongolia. The proven uranium resources of Mongolia occur in these deposits, which represent 62004 tonnes of entire country are estimated to amount to 1 307 000 tonnes of uranium. Uranium mining in Mongolia started in 1989 with exploration of the Mardai open pit in eastern Mongolia. The ore is processed in the Russian Priargunsky ore dressing plant. The mine was operated by a Russian - Mongolian joint venture to 1993.

MAJOR MINERAL DEPOSITS OF MONGOLIA

COPPER DEPOSITS

Erdenetiin Ovoo

The Erdetiin-Ovoo (Erdenet) deposits is the site of Mongolia's largest mining activity and is operated as a Mongolian/ Russian joint venture. The deposit is located 365 km NNE of Ulaanbaatar and 165 km southwest of the trans-Mongolian railhead station at Darhan. Darhan provides railway between the mine and the trans-Mongolian railway and also linked to tte mine and its activities via both a highway and a 200 KV transmission line which provides the primary energy to the mine.

The Erdenet mine has been in operation since 1978 and has a present capacity of approximately 20 million tonnes of ore per year from which is produced approximately 354,000 T/yr of copper concentrate and 3,500 T/yr of Mo concentrate. In 1990, the Soviets purchased 90% of Mongolia's copper concentrate and 100% of its molybdenum concentrate. MONGOLEXPORT statistics cite copper concentrates as containing 27-35% Cu, plus selenium (50-60 gm/T), silver (50-70 gm/T), tellurium (8-9 gm/T) and gold (0.3-0.5 gm/T). Molybdenum concentrates are similarly cited to contain molybdenum (47-54%), rhenium (450 gm/T), selenium (90 gm/T) and tellurium (15 gm/T). Overall, approximately 124,000 T of Cu and 1,672 T of Mo are produced per year from Erdenet concentrate. A small but increasing amount of tungsten is also produced from the mine's ore.

The Erdenet Mine is located within a large porphyrite intrusive complex with associated volcanic rocks and as such recembles a typecal stockwork copper-molybdenum porphyry deposit. Within the larger intrusive/volcanic complex for spatially separated ore-bearing stockwork zones have been recognized with the Main (northwestern) stockwork, which occurs on the western flank of the system, usually considered the Erdenetiin-Ovoo (Erdenet) deposits. The main stockwork, like the other three zones, is a clearly defined vertical stockwork composed of discreet stringers 2-3 mm in thickness, and randomly oriented, occasionally ranging in thickness to 2-5 cm. The Main stockwork occurs in association with 2 small stocks, with numerous apophyses, cross-cut by numerous gently to steeply dipping dikes .

The Main stockwork is approximately 2.400 meters in length, 300-1,300 meters in width and in the central portion extends approximately 1,000 meters in depth whereas near the porphyry is approximately 600-700 meters in depth. Overall the Erdenet deposit, as represented by the Main Zone, is approximately 2 km^2 in total surface area. In plan the shape of the stockwork is roughly 2300 x 800 m as delimited by a cutoff grade of 0.25% Cu.

The principal minerals of economic importance in the oxidized/leached zone of the deposit are cuprite, delafessite, malachite, azurite, brochantite, pantellerite, turquoise and rarely native copper. The average grade of the oxidized/leached zone of 0.1% Cu. The zone of secondary enrichment, underlying the oxidized/leached zone, is characterized by chalcocite, bornite and covellite with a copper content rangeng from 0.65 to 1.35% and Mo ranging from 0.077 to 0.3% with the average values being 0.81% and 0.17% respectively. The primary ore of the Erdenet deposit is characterized by pyrite, chalcopyrite and molybdenite with lesser amounts of sheelite irregularly distributed through the ore body. The standard ores average 20-68 gm/T tungsten with local values ranging from 80-300 gm/T.

Estimated reserves of the Erdenet deposit (Main Zone) are 2.295% of ore grading 0.50% Cu, 0.014 Mo, 1.81 Ag and 0.05 gm/T Au. Indicative resrves at deeper stockwork horizons are estimated to contain approximately 1.4 MT of Cu metal and 37 KT of Mo metal.

TSAGAAN-SUVRAGA

The Surven-Sukhait (Tsagaan-Suvraga) deposit, located 164 km southwest of the Zuun-Bayan railroad station, is located in the semi-desert, unpopulated and water scarce region of Southeast Mongolia.

The Surven-Sukhait deposit is one of seven porphyry copper-molybdenum occurrences within the Tsagaan-Suvarguin district. Throughout the district, copper-molybdenum mineralization of various intensity can be discontinuously traced for approximately 10 km with a width of 0.8-3.0 km. Overall, the copper-molybdenum mineralization occurs within an extensive late Devonian-early Carboniferous intrusive massive of syenites. Although seven mineralized areas have been studied they are all considered to have less economic potential than the Surven-Sukhait locality.

Copper-molybdenum stockwork mineralization extends for approximately 1.980 meters with a width ranging from 180-500 meters and the maximum depth of drilled mineralization extending to a depth of 420 meters. The stockwork zone strikes NE and dips at an angle of 35-550 to the northwest.

All these rocks facially grade into each other. Stock-like bodies and dykes of the final stage of the massif formation are developed in the western part of the massif. They are represented by leucocratic aplite-like granites, granite-porphyries and granosyenite-porphyries undergone different degree of kalifeldspathization and molybdenum-copper mineralization.

The stockwork zone is strongly fractured, consists predominantly of quartz syenites and syenites which are intensely kaolinized, serecitized and silicified and is cross-cut throughout with quartz-chalcopyrite-molybdenite stringers.

In vertical section the stockwork zone consists of an upper mixed zone of oxidized and enriched ores, developed to a depth of 10-30 meters and reaching a maximum depth of 100meters along faults. Within the upper zone the zone of secondary enrichment is poorly developed, however, in areas of intensive fracturing it may persist to a depth of 150-180 meters.

The major primary ore minerals are chalcopyrite, bornite and molybdenite with lesser amounts of pyrite, chalcocite, sphalerite, galena and pyrrhotite. Principal gauge minerals are quartz, feldspar, muscovite and sericite.

Commercial ore reserves of the deposit have been estimated at 220 to 240 MT and marginal reserves at 77 MT. The commercial reserves contain 0.3-0.7% Cu, and 0.001-0.03% Mo with the average grades being 0.54% and 0.19% respectively. The average grades of the marginal reserves is estimated to be 0.25% Cu and 0.009% Mo. Associated elements of possible economic importance, in the economic reserves, are 2.64 gm/T Ag, 0.0084 gm/T Au, 0.39% gm/T Rh, 8.3 gm/T selenium, 12.8gm/T Te, 0.1-7.0gm/T Ga.

LEAD AND ZINC DEPOSITS

Tumurtiin-Ovoo

The Tumurtiin-Ovoo deposit is located in the east-northeast portion of Mongolia 180 km southwest of the Bayan-Tumen railroad station and the town of Choibalsan. Skarn deposits form the primary mineralization in the thick sequence of Devonian sedimentary-volcanogenic rocks which have been strongly hornfelsed or contact metamorphosed by the intrusion of a Late Paleozoic granitic complex. In the sequence the upper diabase unit has been converted to hornfels and hornfels blastides whereas the lower limestone and shale sequenceshave been converted to marble, with various skarns, and plagioclase-pyroxene hornfels, respectively. With the limestone (marble) sequence the skarns, consisting primarily of sphalerite form a distinct zone which coincides with garnet-magnetite skarns in the upper portion of the unit.

A main lenticular sphalerite orebody, with a number of associated lenses, define the orebody which extends for approximately 800 meters along strike, extends an average of 200-230 meters downward (the Central zone extends 480 meters downward) and averages 14 m in thickness. The upper 60m of the orebody are oxidized with the remainder consisting of primary sulphides-principally sphalerite. The deposit contains 7.7 M tonnes of ore with an average grade of 12.43% Zn and 0.024 Cd.

Ulaan

The Ulaan deposit is located in east-northeast Mongolia 110 km northwest of the town of Choibalsan and 6 km northeast of the Erdes (Mardai) uranium mine.

The Ulaan deposit represents an intricate fluidized-explosive structure consisting at the surface of four breccia pipes which at depths of 200-500 m in a single body. The main pipe, containing the bulk of the mineralization is a wedge-shaped structure (at the surface) 20-120m wide and filled with a large-to-small fragmented breccia consisting primarily of wallrock clasts. The clasts are centered by either (a) fine grained fluidized fragments or (b) by hydrothermally deposited material. Base metal mineralization has been traced to a depth of 800 m with no sign of attenuation. The ores are to a greater or lesser extent oxidized to a depth of 35-30 m and, occasionally, to a depth of 90 m. Within the deposit, therefore, oxidized and semi-oxidized ores are recognized. The deposit contains 68.1 M tonnes of ore, grading of 2.0% Zn, 1.2% Pb, 53 g/t Ag, and 0.21 g/t Au.

TUNGSTEN, TIN AND MOLYBDENUM DEPOSITS

Ondor-Tsagaan

The Ondor-Tsagaan deposit is situated in Central Mongolia 170 km east of the Baga-Nuur railroad station, 70 km northwest of the aimak administrative center of Undurhan. The deposits is localized in a synclinal fold where the folded axis sharply changes direction from NE to NW. Within the deposit the major structural features are folds and steep NW-trending faults. The rocks represented by lower Devonian quartz-sericite, quartz-biotite cherty and shales emplaced by gabbro-diabases bodies.

The deposit is elliptical in plan, and consists of a NW-trending (1500 x 500-700 m) stockwork form by variously oriented quartz-wolframite stringers ranging in thickness from fractions of mm to few cm. The maximum proved depth of mineralization (without signs of attenuation) is 550 m. The west portion of the area dominated by tungsten mineralization and un the east molybdenum mineralization which although more wide-spread becomes richer with depth. The mineralized host rock is strongly altered, giving a spotty appearance, is locally massive, drusy and brecciated, and crosscut by numerous stringers.

The primary ores contain over fifty minerals including wolframite, magnetite, hematite, pyrite, and chalcopyrite. The estimated reserves of the deposit are 186 M tonnes withan average grade of 0.17% W_2O_3, 0.018% Mo,0.07%Li, 0.13% Rb and 0.009 Cs.

Ygodzer

The Ygodzer deposit is located on the extreme SE of Mongolia, 280 km south of the Bayan-Tumen (Choibalsan) railroad station. The area is composed of an Ordovician sandy-siltstone sequence cut by Late Triassic-Early Jurassic intrusions of porphyritic granites.

The tungsten mineralization is represented by two morphological types--veins and a greisen body. The tungsten-bearing greisen body is localized in the apical portion of a porphyritic granite stock, is crescent-shaped in cross section and dips steeply and concordantly with the contact surface of the granites. The area of main mineralization is more than 2 sq km (1.700 x 100-120 m). Based on sampling using a cut-off grade of 0.5% WO_3, eleven tenses were outlined within the body. The largest of these, which contains 90% of the deposit's reserves, extends for 1.400 m along strike, has a width of 400 to 950 m and a thickness of 50 to 250 m and their thickness from 1 to 12 m. The greatest concentration of lenses occurs in the domal portion of the intrusion.

The principally economically-valuable minerals of greisen body include wolframite, molybdenite, and beryl. The average grade of the deposit is 0.197% tungstren, 0.056% molybdenum, higher-than-normal contents of beryllium oxide (0.08%) and bismuth (0.132%) are noted at individual sites. Total reserves are 21.6 MT with 42,500 of W_2O_3, at 12,000 t of MO.

GOLD DEPOSITS

Hailast

The Hailast placer occurs in the Zaamar gold district located 220 km northwest of Ulaanbaatar and is the best-studied and richest placer in the district. It lies in the valley of the Tuul tributary at the Tuul River and drains the northwestern slopes of the Zaamar-Nuruu range. The total length of the valley is 14 km, with an average width of 300-500 m. The fill of the valley is composed of alluvial and colluvial rubble-clay deposits 1-10 m thick; they are underlain by 3-5 to 20m thick Quarternary yellow and red-colored gravel with interbeds of sand, loam and clay with an aggregate thickness of 16-30 m.

Two paystreaks are defined in the vertical cross-section of the Hailast valley: the lower (main) pay-streak, with an average grade of 1-1.5 g/m^3 and approximately 10 t of reserves, occurs in the near-bedrock portion of the valley and is persistent in thickness, extent and width. The upper "suspended" paystreak occurs in grey-colored alluvium and has no economic value due to its discontinuity.

The placer gold is coarse to medium in size with tabular and sheet-like particle prevailing. The fineness is 899.

Boroo

The Boroo deposit is located 150 km south of Ulaanbatar and 24 km from the railroad station of Baruun-Haraa. The gold mineralization is associated with zones of intense hydrothermal alteration (chloritization, albitization and beresitization) occurring at the contacts of Late Permian-Early Triassic leucocratic and biotite granites and the sandy-flysch sequences of the Lower Paleozoic Kharin Group.

The mineralized zones have been traced 15-700 m along strike and for 150-300 m downdip at an angle of 10-20^0. Two ore horizons, a 7-8 m thick upper zone and a 3.5 m thick lower zone, separated by a 4 m thick zones of weakly mineralized granites, constitute the principle ore horizon. Ores are oxidized to a depth of 40m.

Gold content averages 3-4 g/t. Reserves of gold are approximately 30 t. Small amounts of silvet are present.

SILVER DEPOSITS

Asgat

The Asgat deposit, situated in the extreme northwest of the country near Russia/Mongolia frontier,170 km north of the town of Ulgii, the aimak administration center, was discovered in 1976 in an area of high mountains, with altitudes of 2,300-3,650 m.

Silver and accompanying base metals mineralization in the Asgat area is concentrated in 11 ore-bearing zones, with several radiating apophyses, which trend northeast to near north-south and which dip steeply to the southeast. The zones are from 1.5 to 12 km long, range in thickness from

5 to 80 m, and consist of a complex network of single branching quartz and siderite veins, quartz-siderite cemented breccias and siderite stringer. The viens have associated strong alteration consisting of argillization and silicification. Within the ore-bearing zones, individual orebodies, ranging in thickness from 0.8 to 3.3 m extend from 170-640 m along strike and to 500 m downdip.

The main ore minerals include tetrahedrite, chalcostibite, chalcopyrite, pyrite, arsenopyrite, bismuthitite, and native copper, silver, and bismuth. Subordinate minerals include sphalerite, galena, argentite, marcasite, melnikovite, and pyrrhotite. The main ore mineral is silver, and the principle by-products are copper, bismuth and antimony. Both silver and the by-products are distributed irregularly throughout the orebodies, however, the average contents of the major components change between individual orebodies within the following limits: silver from 100 to 450 g/t; bismuth from 0.03 to 0.09% antymony from 0.04 to 0.7%, copper from0.19 to 1.17%. Mercury is present in minor amounts. The estimated reserves of Ag are approximately 10,000 tonnes.

RARE EARTH ELEMENTS AND METALS

Halzan-Buregtei

The Halzan-Buregtei occurrence is situated on the left bank of the Hovdo River, 50 km northeast of the aimak center of Hovd (Kobdo). Complex tantalum-noibium-rare earth-zirconium mineralization is spatially and genetically associated with a Late Paleozoic (Carboniferous) multiple phase and multiple intrusion of alkaline granitoids.

The alkaline granitoids form the Halzan-Buregtei massif, which is small in size (800 to 2,000 m) and is elongated in the northwest direction. It is composed of nordmarkites, alkaline granites, rare-earth metal alkaline granites and has associated dykes of various composition. The principle ore mineralization is concentrated in alkaline mircrocline-albite granites of the third phase composing a stocklike body emplaced into nordmarkites.

Alkaline granites, containing rare-metal mineralization, are usually transformed into arfvedsonite-albite-quartz metasomatities. The total surface area of rare-earth metal metasomatites is 0.85 sq. km and is characterized by abundant fluorite (veins and impregnations). Rare metal mineralization is represented by evenly disseminated zircon, pyrochlore, columbite, rare-earth fluocarbonates (parasite, bastnaesite), pllylithionite, zirconium silicates (elpidite, tyttinsite), less frequently by xenotime, monazite, thorite and ferrithorite.

The average content of the ore is 0.20% Nb_2O_5; Ta_2O_5; 1.5% ZrO_2 and 0.35% Y_2O_3.

Estimated resources of rare earth metals, to a depth of 200 m, are estimated to be 600,000 t of niobium oxides, 35,000 t of tantalum oxides, 4,000,000 t of zirconium oxides, 1,000,000 t of rare earth oxides and more than 100,000 t of yttrium oxides.

It is highly probable that zircon-pyrochlore placers may have been formed near the rare- metal granites.

Lugeengol

The Lugeengol vein-carbonatite rare-earth deposit is in the South-Gobi aimak and occurs within the endo- and exocontact zones of the Early Jurassic (nepheline and pseudoleucite syenites Lugeengol massif. The massif occurs on the eastern flank of the South-Gobi belt of alkaline rocks.

The area is composed of hepheline-bearing syenites,pseudoleucite rocks accompanied by dykes of leucitephyries, nepheline syenites, rhyolites, and vien carbonatites intruded into a Permain shale-argillitic sequence, with interbeds of siltstones and limestones. These host rocks are converted into biotite-feldspathic hornfels, in locally fenitized contact aureole.

Seventeen carbonatite veins have been studied within the 0.2 sq km area of the mineralization occurring between the massif and the host rocks. Metasomatically altered syenites enriched in fluorite, feldsparsericite, muscovite, hematite, ironsulfides accompany carbonatite veins within the massif. The veins are arranged in an en-echelon pattern with individual veins ranging from a few meters to 430 m in length (the prevailing length being 200-259 m) and ranging in thickness from 0.2 to 1.0 m (0.5-0.4 m values being dominant). Two types of carbonatite viens are recognized: calcite and calcite-fluorite with their major component, synchysite, occurring as a fine dissemination. The REE oxide content ranges from 0.22-3.68%, the average being 3.23%. The content is somewhat higher on the surface due to leaching to calcite. The rare earths belong to the cerium subgroup with cerium comprising 50.77%, lanthanum 32.,96%, neodymium 9.14%, praseodymium 4.96%, samarium 0.97%; the remainder of the rare earths are present in fractions of tenths and hundredths of a present. The reserves are estimated about 200,000 t.

FLUORITE DEPOSITS

Bor-Undur Ore Field

The Bor-Undur ore field is the largest mineralized area in Mongolia. The Bor-Undur ore field is a tectonic block bounded by faults on all sides. In the core of the block there are Triassic granites cut by a system of crossing dykes and dyke-like bodies, composed of fluoritized breccias of trachyryolites. Permain acidic effusives occur to the north whereas Late Mesozoic andesitic basalts are developed to the east. More than 20 orebodies of economic importance represented by high-angled vein-like mineralization zones composed of breccias of host rocks with fluorite and quartz-fluorite cement have been discovered within the ore field. The ore bodies are grouped in four deposits (Bor-Undur, Adag, Bayan-Ulaan, Undur-Ovoo) spaced from 2-10 km apart.

Ore body thickness ranges from 0.5 to 32 m; extend for 100-3,400 m along strike and 20-350 m downdip. The average content of major components varies within the following limits (CaF_2 28-44%, SiO_2 40-55%, $CaCO_3$ 0.8-2.2%)

The Bor-Undur deposit is the largest in Mongolia. It is situated in the eastern part of the ore field where 14 high angle (65-85^0) orebodies extending for 150 to 2,280 m along strike, 60 to 400 downdip and averaging from 2 to 9 m thickness have been discovered and explored in detail. The orebodies occur both in Lower Permain acidic and Late Jurassic-Early Cretaceous basic effusives. NW- and NE-trending faults constitute the most important ore-controlling structures.

Initial identified reserves of the deposit, including orebodies of the nearly locality are as follows: 12.2 M t of ore with 5,200 t of contained fluorite at an average grade of 40-50% .

Urgen Ore Field

The Urgen ore field immediately adjoins the Transmongolia railroad 60 km southeast of the aimak center of Sainshand. The ore field is broken into a number of blocks by numerous variously oriented faults which control the fluorite mineralization. Within its area of 12 sq km 17 metasomatic ore zones and orebodies were discovered and to various extent studied. The ore zones are usually localized at the contacts of limestones and granites, limestones with schists and, less frequently, within granites. The orebodies extent for 50 to 520 m along strike and 30-

260 m downdip. They are from 1 to 70 m thick and dip at angles ranging from 30 to 60^0. Ore zone 9 (Urgen) is of the greatest economic importance.

The Urgen zone strikes approximately NS and is localized in the center of the ore field. The ore zone is composed of intercalated crystalline limestones, mica-feldspathic, quartz-intruded by Middle Paleozoic hyperbasites, Permian granites and accompanying dykes of microdiorites, diorite porphyrites and granite-porthyry.

The ore zone includes a major calcite-quartz fluorite ore mass of intricate structure and outline which on the surface extends for 520 m along strike and 30 to 260 m downdip. The width of the mass is 20-173 m on the surface and 17-113 m at depth. Individual orebodies are composed primarily of low carbonate calcite-quartz fluorite and high carbonate quartz- calcite-fluorite ores.

The Urgen field, which has been worked since 1981 and has total reserves 9.0 M t of ore containing 4.0 M t at average grade of 45% Ca_2F. Undiscovered resources at the deposit are estimated to be 1.1 M t.

COAL DEPOSITS

Tavan-Tolgoi

The Tavan-Tolgoi coal deposit is unique within the country both in terms of its size, covering over 90 sq km within the Ulannuur coal-bearing depression, and the high quality of the coal. The deposit is located 560 km south-southeast of Ulaanbaatar, 90 km east of Dalanzadgad, the administrative center of the Omnogov aimak. The deposit occurs in a large synclinal structure modified by faults and superimposed folding. The Late Permian coal-bearing sequence is as thick as 965 m in the central part of the syncline and occurs within units of intercalated sandstone, siltstone, and conglomerates. Overall, the coal-bearing sequence includes 16 coal seams ranging in thickness from 2 to 72 m. The aggregate thickness of coal beds, in the central part of the structure, reaches 163 m, with the maximum depth of the base of the lowermost seams occurring at 945m.

The central 9 sq. km of the deposit has been studied in detail to a depth of 340 m whereas the deeper horizons have undergone only reconnaissance exploration. Other areas of the Ulannuur basin, the Ukha-Khudag, Eastern and Bortolgoi localities, have been prospected to a depth of 340 m.

Chemical-analyses made by the Eastern Coal-Chemical Institute (Sverdlovsk, Russia) indicate that coals from the Tavan-Tolgoi deposits is comparable in quality to the principal types of coals exported by the U.S., Canada and Australia.

The overall coal resources the Ulannuur basin, including the Tavan-Tolgoi, Ukha-Khudag, Bortolgoi and Eastern areas (to the maximum coal seam depth of 940 m) are estimated to be 7.0 bln.t, which includes 4.0 bln t of coking coals of varying quality. The overall coal reserves of the Tavan-Tolgoi deposit proper are estimated to be 5.0 bln.t of which 2.8 bln.t are amenable to open pit mining to a depth of 340m.

Baga-Nuur

The Baga-Nuur deposit is located 110 km east of Ulaabaatar in the central part of the Tabunsubatuin depression and the deposit has been operation since 1978. The deposit is linked to the Transmongolian railroad through the railroad branch running from the Mant Station and with the towns of Ulaanbaatar and Underhaan via improved dirt road. The 480-500 m thick coal-bearing sequence, comprised of intercalated sandstones, claystones and siltstones, occur within a 5 km wide and 14 km long depression. Two coal-bearing horizons, containing 24 coal seams and interbeds are recognized within the coal-bearing sequence and contain approximately 600 mln. tonnes of coal amenable to open-pit.

CONCEPT OF INFORMATION AND COMMUNICATION TECHNOLOGY DEVELOPMENT OF MONGOLIA BY YEAR 2010

One. Mission

The mission of the ICT development vision in Mongolia is to develop a knowledge-based society and to improve the quality of people's lives.

Two. Principle

A principle to ensure accessible and flexible info structure, the main information service-provider.

Three. Goals

1. Within Government-Legislation framework: The government is the builder of the an informatized social structure, the open information and service-provider.
2. Within Business- Economy framework: To create a business environment capable to ensure efficient integration into the world's economy, to enhance intellectual capacities of domestic, national products and improve their competitiveness.
3. Within Human Development framework: Irregardless of where citizens live, to ensure opportunities for their equal and active participation in social life, for improving qualities of life and freely communication with each other and the world community.

FOUR. STRATEGY AND OPERATIONAL OBJECTIVES

I. OBJECTIVES OF GOVERNMENT-LEGISLATION FRAMEWORK

II. The following are strategic objectives to be implemented within government-legislation framework:

3. Creation and development of a favorable legal and development environment.
4. Creation of policy and regulatory regime.
5. Support and development government info structure through ICT

IMPLEMENTED THE FOLLOWING ACTIVITIES WITHIN FRAMEWORK OF FIRST STRATEGIC OBJECTIVES:

1. The following are directions to develop information and communications technology, creation of legal environment for coordination of information communication
1.1 Streamline the national information communications technology management, policy and regulatory regime.
1.2 Develop culture education and business environment for information society.
1.3 Establish conditions to promote citizens' equal participation, protection of intellectual property rights and copyright and development of fair competition.
1.4 Ensure the openness of government information to society and enable citizens' monitoring of government activities.

1.5 Develop electronic trade commerce and join international treaties and agreements.
2. Develop national standards and recommendations on information and communications technology in accordance with international standards and implement those standards.

IMPLEMENT THE FOLLOWING ACTIVITIES WITHIN FRAMEWORK OF SECOND STRATEGY OBJECTIVE:

3. Support and reward use and utilization of information communications technology and establish the financial structure
4. Establish a state find to develop information and communications technology
5. Initiate national movement from state to development information and communications technology.
6. Compile action plan to development information and communications technology, implement this action a plan through taking necessary coordinating measures to introduce economic and social development in the action plans of that year.
7. Provide state support to foreign and local investment into development of information and communications technology, implement projects and conduct monitoring activities.
8. Provide state support to create communication and information infrastructure based on national satellite.
9. Provide support and implement all kinds of services on ICT
10. Provide state support and implement fundamental and applied research on ICT
11. Provide support and implement national production of ICT products
12. Support the localization of hi-tech technology of information and communications technology
13. Ensure the state use of software application developed in Mongolia language.
14. Develop system to ensure information confidentiality, protection and reliable operation.

IMPLEMENT THE FOLLOWING ACTIVITIES WITHIN FRAMEWORK OF THIRD STRATEGIC OBJECTIVE.

15. Develop public administration information system.
15.1 Support public administration capacities through information technologies.
15.2 Develop efficient information relations between state organizations
16. Establish and develop step-by-step creation and implementation of office automation, information management system, support tools to assist administrative decision-making and management and monitoring automated system.
16.1 Improve level of office automation of civil servants,
16.2 Establish and develop the structure of government information network, database and search system
16.3 Introduce and promote use of electronic mailing, Internet and Intranet systems in activities of government.
17. Connect and further develop government information network in coordination with networks of non-governmental organization and business information networks.

Objectives within Business-Economy framework
The following are strategic goals to be implement within Business-Economy framework

4. Expansion of ICT business and make it highly efficient economic sector.
5. Establishment of economic - business profitable and operative info structure
6. Implement information and communications technology in national production and services.

IMPLEMENT THE FOLLOWING ACTIVITIES WITHIN FOURTH STRATEGIC OBJECTIVE.

18. Bring up an industry for exporting software, hardware and info ware
19. Develop market for software applications in Mongolian language

20. Establish in develop information service market.
20.1 Finalize necessary measures to acquire every economic entity with e-mail address in Ulaanbaatar by the year 2002 and for companies in the Aimags- by the year 2010
20.2 Transfer taxation, customs, insurance, banking, finance and other business services into electronic forms
21. Set up high-tech service centers to support small and medium size enterprises
22. Establish stock exchange for ICT products.

IMPLEMENT THE FOLLOWING ACTIVITIES WITHIN FIFTH STRATEGIC OBJECTIVE

23. Implement electronic commerce and introduce electronic payment tools such as smart card, electronic checks
24. Introduce Internet as main tool for business, finance and trade information sharing
25. Establish open information center for state and international tenders
26. Establish the open information environment for fair competition under market relations.
27. Set up public service virtual center to protect customers' rights and provide consultation.

IMPLEMENT THE FOLLOWING ACTIVITIES WITHIN SIXTH STRATEGIC OBJECTIVE

28. Implement electronic trade and commerce methods to improve the export of national products (such as cashmere, gold, copper, carpets, wool, tourism, fur and skins, raw materials, stamps and others)
29. Improve the production and productivity through introduction of bar codes, smart cards and other electronic methods
30. Widely implement electronic value-added services

III GOALS WITHIN HUMAN DEVELOPMENT FRAMEWORK

The following are strategic goals to be implemented within Human Development framework:

7. Provide opportunities for active and equal participation of citizens in social relations
8. Establish info-structure for open access to information by citizens.
9. Implement information and communications technology in social sector

IMPLEMENT THE FOLLOWING ACTIVITIES WITHIN SEVENTH STRATEGIC OBJECTIVE.

31. Ensure importance of information needs, intellectual wealth and capacities in human life.
32. Support and ensure equal participations of citizens in relations using ICT advantageous features, not depending from religions, political opinions, race, age and center.
33. Widely utilize information and communications technology for job search, employment, improve work performance quality and level.
34. Create structure to provide education on information and communications technology for all citizens.

IMPLEMENT THE FOLLOWING ACTIVITIES WITHIN EIGHTH STRATEGIC OBJECTIVE

35. Set up knowledge and education-based high-tech centers in Ulaanbaatar and the centers of the socio-economic development regions.
36. Create a set of possibilities to access information technologies at mobile sights running sustainable common services libraries and aimags and soum schools.
37. Provide opportunities for household to receive newspapers, press releases and other

information in timely manner from desirable sources of information.
38. Create info structure for the following branches of such as law, legislation, banking, insurance, agriculture, industry, infrastructure, trade and commerce, science, technology, health, education, environment, social protection, labor markets, history, culture, arts and others.
39. Resolve in detail human resource development issue of the national info structure (user, trainer, specialist)

IMPLEMENT THE FOLLOWING ACTIVITIES WITHIN NINTH STRATEGIC OBJECTIVES

40. Provide all kinds of information services to 30% or more households
41. Provide opportunities to make all types of electronic services accessible to every citizen:
41.1 Introduce electronic version of library system such as ordering, search and others
41.2 Provide opportunities for distance employment
41.3 Introduce electronic versions for all kinds of citizens' advisory services.
41.4 Develop open learning through distance learning and education
41.5 Implement tele - diagnosis, treatment expert system at soum and settlements level
41.6 Introduce electronic service for leisure and entertainment services (virtual libraries, museums, culture, centers, game centers, interest groups)
42. Widely use information and communications technology for questionnaires and social surveys.

INTERNATIONAL ASSISTANCE TO MONGOLIA

US ASSISTANCE

USAID's efforts to support Mongolia's ongoing economic and political transition address key U.S. national interests, including promoting economic prosperity and broad-based growth as well as democracy and the rule of law. USAID/Mongolia's two strategic objectives are mutually reinforcing and strongly support the U.S. Government's goal of helping Mongolia transform itself into a bastion of market-oriented and democratic stability in Northeast Asia. Mongolia now stands at a critical juncture in its transition to an open market and democratic society. Despite past reform successes, neither its political nor economic transformation is complete.

Public institutions are still run in a top down fashion, with decisions being made in the capital with little feedback from local areas. Economic hardships remain for many, particularly in rural Mongolia. Existing hardships have been exacerbated by the financial crisis in Asia that has adversely affected worldwide demand for two of Mongolia's principal exports – copper and cashmere. In Mongolia's vast rural areas, economic growth is not occurring at a rate sufficient to raise living standards, extend benefits to a larger population, reduce vulnerabilities to external shocks, and ensure the consolidation of the democratic transition.

Ultimately, the long-term success of Mongolia's democratic reform depends on all segments of Mongolian society feeling they have a stake in a new economic system and are able to benefit from market reform. USAID's assistance for Mongolia has been effective in assisting the Government to adopt policies and implement reforms, which greatly spurred economic development and growth in urban areas, particularly Ulaanbaatar, as well as facilitated democratic transition at the national level. In FY 1999, USAID began working under a new five-year strategy (FY1999-2003) which marks USAID's movement toward increased attention to rural area growth and development.

DEVELOPMENT CHALLENGE

The development challenge for Mongolia remains unchanged–it is to create a stable political and economic environment that enables it to attract the domestic and foreign investment necessary for broad-based, sustainable development. Key obstacles remain to the realization of Mongolia's development potential, specifically in rural areas: (1) undeveloped and insufficient energy supplies and transportation and communication systems impede the movement of goods, people and information throughout the country; (2) inefficient state-run institutions, including banking and capital markets, make it difficult to mobilize savings and investment and limit the productivity of resources; (3) inadequately developed judicial and enforcement services are unable to ensure the rule of law; and (4) in rural areas, inexperienced civil society organizations are unable to foster economic growth and provide feedback to government at the local and national levels on policies and programs.

Despite these obstacles, Mongolia has a number of strengths which can serve as a strong foundation for sustained development, namely (1) a broad commitment to the development of democracy and a market economy; (2) strong internal social cohesion; (3) a highly literate population; and (4) a government committed to reform and development.

USAID's strategy for Mongolia is to help it establish a market-oriented and democratic society by (1) consolidating Mongolia's democratic transition and (2) accelerating and broadening environmentally sound private sector growth, with a particular focus on bringing change to rural areas. To accomplish these results, USAID will establish the foundation for an effective rural society. Rural business associations, women's groups, local chambers of commerce, herders' associations, and progressive cooperatives will benefit from USAID assistance in selected regions and serve as vehicles to demonstrate a bottom-up approach to development heretofore untried in Mongolia. USAID also seeks to improve the effectiveness of Parliament and the judiciary so they become more accountable to the people they serve.

On the economic front, assistance will help accelerate and broaden private sector growth. USAID will facilitate the transfer to the private sector of productive assets in agriculture, industry, mining and infrastructure that are now under state control. A second key area of assistance will be to increase the efficiency of Mongolia's financial markets through privatizing banks, establishing independent and transparent capital market institutions, and putting the national pension system on a sound financial footing. Improving the environment for business is also a critical aspect of enhancing private sector growth. USAID will ensure that Mongolia's accelerated growth is environmentally sustainable by addressing issues critical to pasture and crop land degradation and better resource management.

OTHER DONORS

Among bilateral donors, the United States ranks third, behind Japan and Germany, in the amount of its grant assistance to the Government of Mongolia. The International Monetary Fund (IMF), the Asian Development Bank (ADB), the World Bank, and the Government of Japan also provide substantial development-related loans to Mongolia. Donor attention to, and funding for, Mongolia diminished somewhat over the past year, due to competing demands for significant donor assistance to address the Asia financial crisis as well as due to the impact of the crisis on Japan, Mongolia's major bilateral donor. The Government of Mongolia is taking steps to establish viable donor coordination mechanisms and reacted positively to USAID's offer to help in this effort. USAID has been coordinating with the IMF and the ADB in bank restructuring and privatization and has started discussions with the World Bank on issues related to the power sector.

PROGRAM

USAID's Rural Civil Society Program (RCSP) and the Farmer to Farmer (FtF) program are the primary vehicles for USAID's rural area focus. With technical assistance and training aimed at a wide range of selected civil society organizations (e.g., women's group, business associations, cooperatives), RCSP will develop and strengthen their institutional capabilities to become effective advocates and implementers of economic and democratic reform. RCSP will also foster cooperation between local governments and these civil society organizations to create a joint agenda for policy reform that will strengthen rural economies and civil society. FtF will use experienced U.S. volunteers to assist local organizations to develop private agriculture in Mongolia, with a focus on animal health, improved animal breeding and improved efficiency of the crop sector.

At the national level, USAID will continue to provide assistance to the government and parliament that helps ensure public awareness of parliamentary actions and key reform issues as well to help with the actual drafting of critical laws. Building on its success in developing judicial benchbooks (i.e., digests of laws and precedents), USAID will begin implementation of a more comprehensive program of judicial reform and enforcement that will include training to professionalize the judiciary.

On the economic front, USAID will continue to assist in the privatization of state-owned enterprises, increase the efficiency of financial markets, and improve the business environment. USAID intends to conclude its current programs of financial sector restructuring, pension reform, and energy sector sector restructuring in FY 2004. By supporting a joint effort with the U.S. Department of the Interior and the Philadelphia Academy of Sciences in the Lake Hovsgol region, USAID will demonstrate how development and natural resource management can be effectively joined.

SELECTED ASISTANCE PROJECTS

PROGRAM: MONGOLIA
TITLE AND NUMBER: Consolidate Mongolia's Democratic Transition, 438-SO01
STATUS: Continuing
PROPOSED OBLIGATION AND FUNDING SOURCE: FY 2004: $4,345,000 (ESF)
INITIAL OBLIGATION: FY 1993**ESTIMATED COMPLETION DATE:** FY 2003

Summary: USAID has supported Mongolia's democratic transition from the very beginning of its democratic movement. The first phase of USAID support was designed to open the doors to the west and to allow Mongolians to study other democratic systems. The second phase of USAID assistance sought to improve the capabilities of Mongolia's new democratic institutions and to foster the development of robust and sustainable citizen-initiated non governmental organizations in Mongolia.

A third phase was entered in FY 1999 with the introduction of the Mongolian Farmer to Farmer Program (FtF) and the Rural Civil Society Program (RCSP), which will assist in the development and strengthening of new and existing market-oriented civil society associations, local governments, and private sector business and support organizations able to address issues important to the economic growth of rural Mongolia. USAID, through the International Development Law Institute (IDLI), undertook to strengthen the judicial sector by developing and training in the use of "benchbooks" for judges that will serve as reference materials and self-training guides. Support to IDLI will last through FY 1999.

Key Results: Mongolia's overall accomplishments in embracing democracy have been profound: 1) a new constitution has been put into effect which guarantees basic democratic rights and protection; 2) a representative parliament has been created; 3) five free and fair national-level elections have been held; 4) a new, independent, judicial system has been established; 5) a vibrant community of citizen-initiated non governmental organizations has emerged and 6) the national parliament has passed legislation protecting and promoting the development of non governmental organizations. USAID assistance has played a role in all of these accomplishments and has been major contributor to the last two accomplishments listed above.

Performance and Prospects: Through support to the International Republican Institute (IRI), USAID is providing training and technical assistance to Members of Parliament and major political parties. Its efforts are focused on establishing democratic representative processes throughout Mongolia, particularly in the countryside. Funds are also being used to improve the organizational viability of political parties, especially at the provincial and local levels. USAID is actively engaged in efforts to improve the effectiveness of Government of Mongolia (GOM) ministries and the Great Hural (national parliament). Support to IRI will continue through FY 2001.

USAID is funding the rural institution development component of the Rural Civil Society Program and the Mongolian Farmer to Farmer Program. Rural institutions supportive of rural enterprise development will be fostered, such as business associations, women's groups, local chambers of commerce, herder's associations and cooperatives, that can provide training and support for the development of rural enterprises and agriculture, lobby local and national governments to support business growth, provide policy alternatives to rural business issues.

Possible Adjustments to Plans: USAID expects to continue assistance to the judicial and legal professions in FY 2004 to establish a competent judiciary and enforcement capacity able to ensure the rule of law in Mongolia. The program expects to include support for the development of a legal information system, the improved standards and ethical performance, and ensuring that individual protections and human rights are incorporated into the legal and judicial system. USAID's program will focus on reform of the existing system and will not have a significant training component, but will cooperate closely with other donors in the training arena to identify training needs. Outside the formal judicial system, support may be provided to establish a Mongolian bar association and an examination system for new lawyers to increase professionalism.

Other Donor Programs: The Asian Development Bank (ADB) is engaged in an effort to improve the quality of legal training, Gesellschaft Fur Technische Zusammenarbeit (GTZ) is supporting training of judges. The Soros Foundation may also be entering this field. No other donor is taking the systematic approach to rural development and civil society building that USAID is undertaking.

Principal Contractors, Grantees, or Agencies: USAID implements this activity through the following partners: The International Republican Institute, the International Development Law Institute, Mercy Corps International, and Agriculture Cooperation Development International/Volunteers in Overseas Cooperative Assistance (ACDI/VOCA).

Selected Performance Measures:

1. Civil society organizations providing services essential to rural growth.
2. Public policies changed consistent with rural civil society organizations advocacy.
3. Strategy for judicial development approved and implemented.
4. Public confidence in judiciary improved.

5. Parliament develops mechanism for incorporating public input into legislative process.

* Baseline and target indicators have not been developed for this program but will be within the next six months

PROGRAM: MONGOLIA
TITLE AND NUMBER: Accelerate and Broaden Environmentally Sound Private Sector Growth, 438-SO02
STATUS: Continuing
PROPOSED OBLIGATION AND FUNDING SOURCE: FY 2004: $7,655,000 ESF
INITIAL OBLIGATION: FY 1995 **ESTIMATED COMPLETION DATE:** FY 2003

Summary: The Economic Policy Support Project is the principle vehicle by which USAID is expanding its economic growth program under its new five year strategy (1999-2003). EPSP seeks to increase the standard of living of the people of Mongolia and to improve economic and social indices by assisting the Government of Mongolia's (GOM) transition from a centrally planned economy to a true private sector-led, market oriented economy. The project provides technical assistance, training and other inputs to establish sound, growth-oriented market-economy policies and practices, and to develop and strengthen select public and private-sector institutions that will help develop and sustain a market-oriented economy.

All Mongolians are benefiting from lower inflation and a more vibrant urban economy, for which USAID can fairly take partial credit. All Mongolians promise to benefit from the achievement of future activity goals including improved pensions, the development of a commercial power sector, and a better working financial sector. Activities in rural Mongolia promise to establish linkages between economic growth, improved environmental quality, and increased democratic participation.

In addition to the macroeconomic reform assistance referred to above, the following other activities are being supported:

USAID has begun providing assistance to the Mongolian State Property Committee for its privatization program. Over the next three years USAID will assist in the privatization of over 200 companies. Up to twelve of these will be suitable for foreign investors. --Sixteen Mongolians are benefiting from long-term economics and business training in the United States. In the future, USAID plans to broaden this training to cover our democracy as well as economic growth strategic objectives.
Through the U.S. Customs Service, USAID will provide assistance to the Mongolian Customs to bring it to international standards of effectiveness and efficiency.
USAID is funding the activities of a Global Technology Network in Mongolia (GTN-Mongolia). GTN-Mongolia assists Mongolian firms seeking to improve production efficiencies by adopting U.S. technology or to establish business relationships with U.S. companies. The resources of the International Executive Service Corps (IESC) complement the program.
Finally, USAID is funding two sustainable rural development activities. One is the Mongolia Farmer to Farmer (FtF) which is focusing on animal health, improving animal breeding stock, and improving the productivity of the crop sector. In the crop sector FtF will begin demonstration programs on proving the technical and economic feasibility of "no-till" agriculture, contract seed production, and cooperative development. The adoption of "no-till" methods of cultivation will have both economic and environmental benefits to Mongolia. The other program is an effort to develop the Lake Hovsgol region of Mongolia into an effective protected area that will lend itself to local economic development.

The hallmark of USAID assistance under EPSP has been its speed, flexibility and high quality. Senior Mongolian government officials have consistently identified EPSP as the single most important technical assistance activity in Mongolia. EPSP fully deserves credit for helping the GOM to go further, faster and achieve higher quality reform outcomes than would have been possible without the project

Key Results: With USAID provided advice and guidance, the Democratic Union Coalition has developed and is implementing a forward-thinking, macroeconomic reform agenda. Under this reform agenda, an improved energy pricing structure has been put in place which has enabled the Mongolians to recover costs of energy production and distribution; and bank restructuring, pension reform, capitol market development, and the privatization of state-owned enterprises have begun. The impact of this assistance has helped to bring down inflation and keeping it in check.

Performance and Prospects: USAID assistance under EPSP has played a key role in organizing the macroeconomic reform agenda of the Democratic Union Coalition. In the early days of the Coalition, EPSP organized a series of Economic Policy Workshops, which led to the development of a comprehensive economic reform agenda. EPSP later assisted the GOM to implement the agenda. Key achievements include: the setting of new and higher electricity, heat, coal and petroleum prices resulting in a more viable energy sector; the restructuring of two unviable banks and the development of a new banking strategy. Recently, an Energy Policy Workshop has helped the GOM in determining a course of action for energy privatization and commercialization. A similar workshop is planned for bank restructuring in FY 1999. EPSP has also played a key role in training a core cadre of economic analysts, capable of implementing the GOM's economic growth objectives. EPSP provided assistance in the legislative drafting for the GOM's new pension program and will provide the assistance needed for the Ministry of Health and Social Welfare to implement the new program. Similar assistance is anticipated for energy policy reform and financial sector bank reconstruction.

Possible Adjustment in Plans: Further assistance in the areas of macroeconomic reform, pensions, energy sector commercialization and financial sector restructuring may be undertaken, depending upon the activities of other donors and the level of need. In addition, efforts to help the Mongolian private sector link with U.S. technology and establish joint ventures with U.S. companies may continue depending on results achieved through FY 2004.

Other Donor Programs: The International Monetary Fund, the World Bank, the Asian Development Bank, the United Nations Development Program and the Japan International Cooperation Agency provide technical assistance in the fields of economic policy and public administration.

Selected Performance Measures:

1. Increased share of GDP attributable to private sector.
2. Independent and transparent banking, capital market and pension system resulting in increased savings and investment.
3. Effective energy regulatory authority established.
4. Increased value-added livestock production.
5. Increase in number of profitable, rural businesses and cooperatives.
6. Number of farmers adapting no-till agricultural practices.
7. Sustainable tourism established in Lake Hovsgol.

*Baseline and target indicators have not been developed for this program but will be within the next six months.

GOVERNANCE REFORM PROGRAM

U.S. consultants must also register with the ADB DACON (Data on Consulting Firms) system. DACON registration may now be completed on-line at . For loan projects, primary responsibility for hiring consultants rests with the executing agency in the borrowing country. A good way to facilitate contact with the executing agency is by working with the appropriate U.S. Commercial Service officer listed below.

Firms may also send a notification copy of their EOIs to U.S. Commercial Liaison Office for the ADB, Attention: Stewart Ballard, Senior Commercial Officer, PSC 500 Box 33, FPO AP 96515-1000, or to the same office at its international mailing address: 25th Floor Ayala Life-FGU Center, 6811 Ayala Avenue, Makati City, Metro Manila, Philippines 1226; Phone: (63-2) 887-1345; Fax: (63-2) 887-1164; E-mail: manila.adb.office.box @mail.doc.gov. This office works closely with the Office of the U.S. Executive Director to the ADB to increase American awareness of, and participation in, the ADB's activities.

The project listed in this report is now being actively processed by the ADB. For more information on this project, the name of the ADB project officer is indicated in the project brief. The U.S Commercial Liaison Office is ready to provide assistance to U.S. firms upon request. (Please see paragraph 4.)

The following loan project will be listed for the first time in the August 2003 issue of the Asian Development Bank's (ADB) Business Opportunities (ADBBO). (Note: The ADBBO is also available on the ADB's website .

NAME OF PROJECT: GOVERNANCE REFORM PROGRAM II
Project No.: MON35376-01
Executing Agency: Ministry of Finance and Economy
Contact: Mr. L. Enkhtaivan, Deputy Minister
Address: Negdsen Undestnii Street 5/1, Government Building No. 2, Mongolia
Fax: (976-11) 320247
Tel. No.: (976-11) 323442
Loan Amount: US$ 7 Million
Sector: Others

Objectives and Scope:
The goals of the Second Governance Reform Program (GRP-II) is to enhance accountability and efficiency of the public sector of Mongolia, to be measured by fiscal sustainability and tangible improvements in delivery of key public services. Its purpose, following the measures adopted under the GRP on a pilot basis, is to support the implementation of administrative and financial management reforms in a gradual manner within the public sector. GRP-II will adopt a three-pronged approach to: (i) enhance institutional capacity; (ii) improve fiscal sustainability; and (iii) initiate mainstreaming of governance reforms.

Procurement:
Goods: None
Services: None
Environmental Category: C
Project Processing Stage:
Second MRM completed: 3 Jul 2003

Project Officer: Ramesh Subramaniam; Tel.: (632) 632-6437
Governance, Finance, and Trade Division, ECRD
In-country Commercial Officer: c/o Michael Layne, Economic/Commercial Officer, American Embassy, Ulaanbaatar; E-mail: LayneMJ@state.gov

IMPLEMENTATION OF THE COUNTRY STRATEGY

A. PROGRESS UNDER THE PARTNERSHIP AGREEMENT ON POVERTY REDUCTION

10. Mongolia was the first developing member country to enter into a Poverty Partnership Agreement (PPA) with ADB. Since its signing in March 2004, the document, which adopted the MDGs as its strategic goals, has served as the general strategic framework guiding ADB operations in the country. The PPA is also regarded by the Government as one of its fundamental documents, on the basis of which the PRSP has been developed.

11. Annual review of the implementation of PPA noted the efforts made by the Government to refine and finalize the PRSP. It confirms the observations made in the Country Strategy and Program Update for 2003–2005 (the last CSPU) that Mongolia is on the right track to achieving many of the MDGs. With assistance from external funding agencies including ADB, good progress has been made in addressing non-income poverty, through maintaining and further improving the achievements in human development. Poverty reduction is hindered by slow economic growth that is unable to create sufficient jobs or ensure steady improvement of income, particularly for the poor. This situation, if continued, will limit the effectiveness and sustainability of the achievements attained in addressing non-income poverty.

B. PROGRESS IN THE COUNTRY STRATEGY AND PROGRAM FOCUS AREAS

12. The last CSPU noted that agriculture, finance, public sector reform, social services, urban development, and roads should continue to be the strategic focuses of ADB operations in Mongolia. It also highlighted the importance of involving Mongolia more actively in subregional cooperation. The planned CSP process will allow ADB to have a systematic review of its operations in Mongolia. It is envisaged that the planned CSP process will develop a more selective and focused operational strategy in view of the resource availability and comparative institutional advantages of ADB in the country. Prior to the new CSP, the current update is made selectively to present specific progress that has been made over the year in light of the last CSPU.

1. Financial Sector Reform

13. Since the mid-1990s, ADB has provided continued assistance, in cooperation with other external funding agencies including the World Bank, to promote the development of a sound financial sector to support private sector-led growth. These interventions have strategic importance in support of economic growth for poverty reduction. Mongolia has experienced rapid growth in financial intermediation over the past few years. During the period from 1999 to 2002, both bank deposits and bank loans increased very fast, at a compound annual rate of 86% and 38% respectively. Interest rates, although still high, have been declining, and the margins tightening, due to strengthened competition triggered by the entrance of new banks and, particularly, nonbank financial institutions (NBFIs).

14. Despite the progress made though, the financial sector in Mongolia remains undersized relative to the real economy. However, the rapid growth in bank lending and NBFI activity has increased systemic risk and fragility. Although the reported ratio of nonperforming loans remained

relatively low in 2002 at about 7.2%, there is a growing concern that lending quality and long-term sustainability will be jeopardized if risk management practices are not strengthened in a timely manner. To minimize the risk of adverse sector development and develop a sound financial sector through continued reforms, ADB and the Government have agreed that strengthening risk management (including supervision), and promoting long-term contractual savings and capital markets should be the priority of the next phase of financial sector reform. A project preparatory technical assistance (TA) is programmed for 2003. The ensuing loan is programmed for 2005 and is on stand by for 2004, subject to project preparedness and resource availability. The possibility of having equity investment by the Private Sector Operations Department of ADB in the newly privatized Trade and Development Bank is also being examined. Furthermore, a comprehensive private sector development assessment for Mongolia is under way, which includes a more detailed analysis of the critical role of the financial sector in promoting private sector-led growth.

2. Governance Reform

15. Mongolia's government sector is relatively large. On average, there is one public sector agency for every 350 people. The consolidated government expenditures account for about 39% of GDP, of which about 70% are required for current expenditures. Despite the moderate salary level of civil servants, the public sector wage bill, which stands at about 8.2% of GDP, is among the highest in the region in terms of its share in GDP. ADB has been involved in public sector reform since 1995. Supported by the Governance Reform Program (GRP)[2] and a series of TAs from ADB, the Government introduced public sector reforms, initially at six pilot agencies. Based on the lessons learned and experiences obtained from GRP, a general legal framework to guide comprehensive and systematic reforms across the public sector has been established through adoption of the Public Sector Management and Finance Law (PSMFL) in 2002.

16. ADB has been undertaking a country governance assessment for Mongolia. It has highlighted the importance of continued support for public sector reform and, particularly, the need for strengthening the Government's institutional capacity to implement the PSMFL in a gradual manner. Accordingly, ADB has helped the Government develop the second phase governance reform program. The purpose of the second phase is to support the implementation of administrative and financial management reforms to improve efficiency and accountability. As noted in the country governance assessment, these require enormous efforts for capacity building at both the central and local government levels, and administrative consolidation and institutional restructuring across the public sector. Given the complexity of the reforms involved, the second phase of the governance reform program will be implemented in a gradual manner, from 2003 to 2009 and will be supported through a cluster approach by two lending packages. The initial package comprising the first subprogram loan of $13.5 million and a TA loan of $2 million is in preparation and will be submitted for consideration by the Board of Directors within 2003. A TA for preparation of the follow-on lending package and the second subprogram loan are tentatively programmed for 2005 and 2006, respectively.

3. Provision of Essential Social Services

17. As a major thrust to reduce poverty, ADB has been active in improving provision of essential social services to the poor, including education, health, municipal services, and social security services. Apart from supporting rehabilitation and construction of social infrastructure, ADB has placed increased emphasis on policy and institutional issues to improve the efficiency and sustainability of service delivery systems and to ensure improved access of the poor, through integrated interventions for public sector reforms in general, and for specific social sectors in particular. Under the second phase governance reform program, ADB has attached great importance to supporting the implementation of reforms in the education, health, and social security sectors. The implementation of the ongoing Social Security Sector Development

Program[3] has made good progress in formulating a social security sector strategy to guide reforms in social insurance, pensions, and social assistance systems. Special attention has been given to assisting people with disabilities—the most vulnerable group among the poor. TA is provided in association with the Second Health Sector Development Project[4] to support health sector reform, particularly the health insurance system. Subject to good progress in implementation of this project and the associated TA and the findings and recommendations of the planned CSP process, a project preparatory TA for further intervention in the health sector is tentatively programmed for 2005–2006. As part of the planned CSP process, ADB will also undertake a country gender assessment in coordination with the World Bank (see para. 23).

18. The challenge resulting from internal migration calls for a review of the geographical focus of ADB support to ensure that social services be provided to meet the emerging needs in the expanded population centers on a timely basis. It should be recognized that this migration is driven by the forces of the market economy, and should lead to a generally more rational distribution of the population within the country in accordance with economic opportunities. A TA has been provided to help the Government develop its capacity for regional development planning. Assistance will also be provided under the second phase governance program to support the reforms in the service delivery systems through administrative consolidation. Subject to further review during the planned CSP process, a TA for integrated development for selected economic centers is tentatively programmed for 2004 to further study the options to address this emerging challenge.

19. In the education sector, following the approval of the loan for the Second Education Sector Development Project[5] in 2002, ADB has been working jointly with the Government and external funding agencies to explore the possibility of taking a more strategic and sector-wide approach to coordinate their activities. A TA for project preparation has been programmed for 2004 accordingly.

4. SUPPORT FOR AGRICULTURE SECTOR AND RURAL DEVELOPMENT

20. Agriculture is a vital sector for the economy, accounting for 21% of GDP and 45% of employment. Rural Mongolia is the home of 43% of the poor, many of whom may have to join the urban poor if they cannot find jobs or other economic opportunities. The agriculture sector has, therefore, a very important role to address poverty, both in rural and urban areas.

21. Successive harsh winters and severe droughts have kept agricultural output falling for the last few years, particularly due to losses in livestock. The agriculture sector has become a bottleneck constraining overall economic growth. To diversify the rural economic base and address rural poverty, the Government has attached high priority to promoting crop production and requested ADB support. The recently completed project preparatory TA for crop production project has revealed, however, the associated challenges and difficulties. These include the extreme climatic conditions, the relatively weak comparative advantage, and the lack of market-oriented physical and institutional support from both the public and private sectors. This has required more time to undertake an adequate and accurate assessment of the crop production sector, before an economically viable public sector intervention could be properly designed. As discussed and agreed with the Government, subject to availability of resources and project preparedness, the proposed crop production project has been rescheduled from the indicative lending program for 2003 to the indicative lending program for 2004. Furthermore, a TA for an agricultural sector study is being prepared as part of the process for the planned CSP next year.

5. Regional Cooperation

22. Given the geographical features of the country, support for Mongolia to participate in regional cooperation has two general dimensions, one in connection with the subregional cooperation initiatives in Northeast Asia and the other the subregional cooperation in Central Asia, both involving one of its two neighbors—the PRC. It has been agreed between the PRC and Mongolia that transport, environment, and trade and investment should be the three common priority areas for ADB-supported regional cooperation initiatives. Continued priority is attached to completing the north-south trunk road under the proposed regional road development project in 2004, and to link the road systems between the Russian Federation and the PRC through the major economic centers in Mongolia including Ulaanbaatar. Mongolia has also been actively involved in an ADB-supported regional cooperation initiative to establish a regional cooperation mechanism for prevention and control of the dust and sandstorms in Northeast Asia. A TA has been provided to help the Government undertake a review of its trade policy. In the general context of subregional cooperation in Central Asia, a new regional TA is in preparation in cooperation with the United Nations Economic and Social Commission for Asia and the Pacific to assess the viability of a newly proposed trunk road corridor between Xinjiang Uygur Autonomous Region, PRC and the Russian Federation through western Mongolia. This road is expected to help Mongolia break the isolation and remoteness of its less developed western region, and provide access to the markets in its two neighboring countries.

C. HIGHLIGHTS IN COORDINATION OF EXTERNAL FUNDING AND PARTNERSHIP ARRANGEMENTS

23. ADB has been the lead agency among the external funding agencies in many sectors, particularly in the social sectors. At the Consultative Group Meeting in July 2002, ADB and the World Bank agreed to strengthen coordination, at country strategy level, through formulation of their respective medium-term operational strategies, i.e., the CSP of ADB and the Country Assistance Strategy of the World Bank. Through follow-on coordination consultations, it was further agreed that the two institutions should jointly coordinate their sector and thematic analysis during strategy formulation, and further strengthen information sharing and policy and operational coordination, particularly in the areas of country performance assessment, governance reforms, sector interventions, and portfolio management. Collaboration with other external funding agencies has also been strengthened, particularly through the Mongolia Resident Mission (MNRM). For instance, in cooperation with the European Bank for Reconstruction and Development, TA has been provided to help the country develop a civil aviation policy with a view to promoting private sector involvement in the sector. An updated development coordination matrix is provided in Appendix 1, Table A1.5.

24. In conjunction with its lending program, ADB will continue to actively pursue cofinancing, particularly from grant and concessional cofinancing sources, to effectively address the important thematic priorities for ADB operations in Mongolia. In 2004, continued efforts will be made by ADB to help the Government mobilize cofinancing from concessional sources for the third road development project. To support the indicative lending program for 2005, specific efforts will be made to explore cooperation and cofinancing opportunities for the third education sector development project within the overall framework of the education sector master plan to be developed under the ongoing project preparatory TA. During the recent presidential visit of the PRC to Mongolia, a substantive bilateral aid package was announced. The assistance from the PRC, if provided on concessional terms in a transparent manner, might present an opportunity for cofinancing in conjunction with ADB lending. The implications of growing assistance from the PRC warrant assessment during the planned CSP process.

2. ADB. 1999. Report and Recommendation of the President to the Board of Directors on a Proposed Loan to Mongolia for the Governance Reform Program. Manila.
3. ADB. 2001. Report and Recommendation of the President to the Board of Directors on a Proposed Loan to Mongolia for the Social Security Sector Development Program. Manila.
4. ADB. 2003. Report and Recommendation of the President to the Board of Directors on a Proposed Loan to Mongolia for the Second Health Sector Development Project. Manila.
5. ADB. 2002. Report and Recommendation of the President to the Board of Directors on a Proposed Loan to Mongolia for the Second Education Sector Development Project. Manila.

ADB PROJECTS

Agriculture and Natural Resources

		PROJECT	TYPE	INITIAL	UPDATED	
▷	28201-01	Rural Finance	LOAN	1 Mar 1995	5 Nov 2001	
▷	31212-02	Agriculture Sector Development Project	LOAN	1 Apr 1997	1 Feb 2001	
▷	31212-01	Agriculture Sector Development Program	LOAN	1 Apr 1997	2 Jan 2001	
▷	30531-01	Cadastral Survey and Land Registration	LOAN	1 Apr 1998	14 Mar 2004	
▷	35097-01	Crop Production Project	PPTA	22 May 2001	14 Aug 2001	
▷	28201-01	Rural Finance	PPTA	1 Mar 1995	29 Feb 2004	
Energy						
		PROJECT	TYPE	INITIAL	UPDATED	
▷	31244-01	Energy Rehabilitation I	PPTA	1 Feb 1998	13 Jun 2002	
Transport and Communications						
		PROJECT	TYPE	INITIAL	UPDATED	
▷	29566-01	Second Roads Development	LOAN	1 Dec 1996	5 Nov 1999	
▷	35377-01	Road Development Project III	PPTA	16 Apr 2002	21 Nov 2002	
Social Infrastructure						
		PROJECT	TYPE	INITIAL	UPDATED	
▷	36245-01	ICT for Innovating Rural Education in Mongolia	GRNT	28 Jan 2003	14 May 2003	EOI
▷	36023-01	Improving the Living Environment of the Poor in Ger Areas of Mongolia's Cities	GRNT	12 Mar 2002	15 May 2002	
▷	31242-01	Second Health Sector Development	LOAN	5 Feb 2001	6 Jun 2003	
▷	31213-01	Second Education Development Project	LOAN	2 May 1998	22 Aug 2002	

▷	31243-01	Integrated Development of Basic Urban Services in Provincial Towns Project	LOAN	23 Mar 2004	7 Aug 2002	
▷	32017-01	Housing Finance Sector Loan	LOAN	17 Sep 1999	23 Oct 2001	
▷	31243-01	Integrated Development of Basic Urban Services in Secondary Towns	PPTA	23 Mar 2004	13 Jun 2002	
▷	31242-01	Second Health Sector Development	PPTA	5 Feb 2001	13 Jun 2002	
▷	32017-01	Housing Sector Finance	PPTA	17 Sep 1999	1 Jun 2004	
▷	31214-01	Second Education Development	PPTA	2 May 1998	22 Dec 1999	
Finance						
PROJECT			TYPE	INITIAL	UPDATED	
▷	30101-01	Second Financial Sector Program	LOAN	15 Nov 1999	24 Nov 2004	
▷	34135-01	Preparing the Third Financial Sector Program	PPTA	20 Dec 2002	30 Sep 2003	EOI
Multisector						
PROJECT			TYPE	INITIAL	UPDATED	
▷	35179-01	Expanding Employment Opportunities for Persons with Disabilities	GRNT	30 Oct 2001	7 May 2002	
▷	33335-02	Social Security Sector Development Program (Investment Loan)	LOAN	27 Mar 2001	14 Jun 2002	
▷	33335-01	Social Security Sector Development Program (Program Loan)	LOAN	1 Jan 1997	14 Jun 2002	
Others						
PROJECT			TYPE	INITIAL	UPDATED	
▷	35376-02	Capacity Building for Governance Reforms	LOAN	23 Jun 2003	12 Sep 2003	
▷	35376-01	Governance Reform Program II	LOAN	23 Jun 2003	12 Sep 2003	
▷	31597-01	Governance Reform Program	LOAN	23 Aug 1999	2 Dec 1999	

CUMULATIVE ADB LENDING

(as of 31 December 2002)

Sector	No. of Loans	$ Million	%[a]

Transport and Communications	5	134.5	24.9
Energy	4	93.8	17.4
Social Infrastructure	8	87.3	16.2
Agriculture and Natural Resources	6	73.6	13.6
Industry and Nonfuel Minerals	2	60.0	11.1
Finance	3	53.0	9.8
Others	1	25.0	4.6
Multisector	2	12.0	2.2
TOTAL	31	539.2	100.0

PRACTICAL INFORMATION FOR CONDUCTING BUSINESS[2]

DOING BUSINESS IN MONGOLIA

MARKET OVERVIEW

Prospects for 2014-2015: Mongolia's main economic and political challenges are all linked to ensuring steady growth through the boom and bust cycles likely to visit this resource-dependent economy. Double-digit economic growth over the past few years—2011's sizzling 17.3 % GDP growth, for instance—has been based on the investment in, and the production and export of, minerals. Mongolia is a major producer of several minerals including coal, copper, gold, zinc, and fluorspar. With extensive reserves, it has the potential to increase production considerably. For U.S. investors and firms, mining and mining-related services represent one of the most important and potentially most reliable sectors for long-term investment in Mongolia. Other promising sectors, based on Mongolia's economic development needs, include infrastructure, transportation, energy, construction, healthcare, and environmental products and services.

However, Mongolia has suffered ongoing setbacks to its economic advancement. Indeed, growth has steadily slowed from 2011's 17.3 % to 2013's 11.7 %. Both the International Monetary Fund (IMF) and World Bank estimate 2014 GDP to decline to 9.5%; and 2015, depending on Mongolian policy decisions, may range from a high of 12% to as low as 2%. The IMF cites loose fiscal and monetary policies as causes for negative growth. (For IMF: http://www.imf.org/external/pubs/ft/scr/2014/cr1464.pdf ; For WB: http://www.worldbank.org/en/news/feature/2014/07/03/mongolia-economic-update-july-2014 .)

Two factors have and will continue to affect Mongolia's economic condition. First, more than 90 percent of Mongolia's exports consistently go to China; and so, any slowing of China's growth affects Mongolia. Second, economic policies designed to protect Mongolia's sovereign interests and to respond to the expectations of the Mongolian public have discouraged FDI – despite statements from Mongolia's senior politicians that the government is committed to improving the business environment, reigniting foreign direct investment flows, and fostering Mongolian growth. Recent policy decisions have been influenced by the political realities of a coalition government representing multiple platforms, which has complicated reaching consensus on politically sensitive issues. There are a range of views represented within parliament on what constitutes an appropriate legal and regulatory framework for mining and other activities. Statutes and regulations are thus often crafted in a manner which incorporates multiple approaches and political imperatives. Investors have told us that this approach to legislation and regulation can give the impression that laws are hastily passed and that regulations are slowly created and partially implemented. Some investors are concerned that criticism

from some political quarters of current investment agreements and statutory obligations undertaken by past governments portends that commitments may not be fully respected.

Investors and companies may likely encounter bumpy short-run trends as Mongolia continues to come to terms with its mining endowments and how to bring them to the outside world, while satisfying domestic expectations that the mining sector should benefit the public. Investors may perceive, and have to accept that, the current political process creates an unclear policy

[2] This sections based in part on the materials of the US Department of Comemrce

environment that may increase investment risk, while Mongolian politicians see the process as yielding the necessary level of political comity. However, in the medium to long term, those willing to manage these issues and relationships with local partners with open eyes may find attractive opportunities in the aforementioned industries and sectors.

Political Situation: Mongolia has held twelve presidential and parliamentary elections in the past twenty years, during which power changed political hands peacefully, with the exception of some rioting in the aftermath of the disputed 2008 parliamentary elections. Concerns that this unprecedented political turbulence would continue to vex Mongolia were put to rest by the presidential election of 2009 and the elections of 2012 and 2013. In 2012, the Democratic Party (DP) peacefully unseated the long-ruling Mongolian People's Party (MPP), the much evolved successor of the Communist Party, and entered into a coalition to work on key economic and fiscal issues. The coalition, an unwieldy amalgamation of resource nationalists, free-marketers, and traditional socialists, struggles to develop consensus on key policies but shows no signs of breaking apart through the remainder of 2014. But these political changes have disrupted the local business environment and the administrative apparatus.

Mongolian-U.S. Relations: Mongolia calls the U.S. its "third neighbor" to balance relations with China and Russia. Good Mongolian-U.S. relations have developed rapidly to include humanitarian and technical assistance, military- to- military relations, business development, and a host of smaller programs. Mongolia has contributed peacekeeping forces to both Iraq and Afghanistan and to UN peace-keeping operations, including in Sierra Leone and Kosovo, Chad, and South Sudan. Aid programs reached a high point with the signing of the 2008 Millennium Challenge Compact for USD 285 million, which funded vocational education, health, land registration, infrastructure, and energy projects. The next phase of U.S. Mongolia relations will occur in commercial relations (business to business), as both nations seek to promote the bi-lateral trade relationship. In September 2013, the U.S. and Mongolia signed an agreement to promote transparency in matters of investment and commerce, although it has yet to be ratified by the Mongolian parliament and so is not yet in force. In 2005 Mongolia successfully hosted Speaker of the U.S. House of Representatives, the Secretary of Defense, Secretary of State, and President of the United States George W. Bush. In 2009, the John Boehner, Minority Leader in the U.S. House of Representatives, visited Mongolia, and Mongolian officials routinely meet with senior Cabinet officials when visiting Washington, D.C. Vice President of the United States Joseph Biden visited Mongolia in 2011; U.S. Secretary of State Hillary Clinton came to Mongolia in 2012; and Secretary of Defense Hagel visited in April of 2014, signing a joint vision statement with his counterpart. Over the past decade, we record no incidents of anti-American sentiment or politically motivated damage to American projects or installations.

Russo-Sino-Mongolian Relations: Relations with Russia and China are critical because Mongolia depends on both for power, petroleum, and transportation. Sour

relations among these neighbors invariably affects Mongolia's business environment. When the Dalai Lama visited in spring 2003, the Chinese temporarily halted all commercial rail shipments for "technical reasons." China seeks access to Mongolia's mineral and hydrocarbon resources, and remains the leading investor and customer in these fields. Aggressively re-asserting its claims to regional leadership, Russia has responded to Mongolia's growing ties with both China and "third neighbors" with robust attempts to limit the influence of the others.

MARKET CHALLENGES

* Weak rule of law

* Corruption in the bureaucracy

* Unfamiliarity with best commercial practices in the government and private sectors

* Lack of transparency in regulatory and legislative processes

* Some abuse of inspection, permitting, and licensing regimes to protect existing state and private interests

* Insufficient infrastructure in both urban and rural areas

MARKET OPPORTUNITIES

Mining: Over 6,000 deposits of approximately 80 minerals exist in Mongolia, among them coal, copper, uranium, rare earth oxides, iron ore, oil, tungsten, molybdenum and fluorspar. Of note are Mongolia's excellent metallurgic coal deposits. Mongolia's location next to China provides a ready market for Mongolia's mineral wealth. As with all resource sectors in Mongolia, the developing infrastructure, statutory, and regulatory environments remain works in progress.

Construction: The population of the Mongolian capital, Ulaanbaatar, has more than tripled in the last decade years from 450,000 to over 1.2 million. Quality commercial and residential stock remains in short supply and demand shows no signs of abating.

Meat Processing: Mongolia has vast herds of sheep, goats, and cattle, and hungry neighbors. Satisfying demand in Russia, China, Korea, and Japan offers an opportunity to American ranchers and meat processing and marketing technologies. However, quotas and restrictive health regulations inhibit the meat trade with Mongolia's her neighbors. Existing Mongolian processing facilities require upgrading to increase production capacity, quality, and sanitation.

Oil, Gas, and Unconventional Hydrocarbons: Mongolia seeks eventual energy independence and is encouraging development of its hydrocarbon resources. In addition to oil and natural gas, Mongolia has oil shale, shale gas, and shale oil deposits and the country hopes to attract companies that will bring coal-to-liquid, coal-to-gas, and coal-bed methane technologies.

MARKET ENTRY STRATEGY

* Personal Relations Key: Mongolians like to deal with *old friends.* Investors must establish and maintain close relationships with Mongolian counterparts and relevant government agencies. Family and school ties remain strong in Mongolia. Learn who is related to whom when establishing business connections.

* Use of Agents: Find a Mongolian advisor to guide through the ins and outs of local customs and business practices.

* Structure of ownership: The 2013 Investment Law of Mongolia does not require foreign investors to have Mongolian partners. Under the law, foreign investors are accorded national treatment and given the same protections as domestic investors with the exception of state-owned enterprises seeking to invest in mineral, banking and finance, and media and telecommunications.

* Product Pricing: Sensitive to price, Mongolian consumers will choose the less expensive product—unless they can be swayed by after-sales service or clear product superiority. They perceive American-branded goods as superior to others, and will more often than not pay a premium to avoid purchasing lower cost, lower quality items.

SELLING U.S. PRODUCTS AND SERVICES

USING AN AGENT OR DISTRIBUTOR

Distributors or agents who handle internal distribution and marketing represent many U.S. companies in Mongolia. The U.S. Embassy in Ulaanbaatar can help U.S. exporters find appropriate sales agents in Mongolia. An Embassy-assisted distributor search can help gauge interest in your product and begin the process of finding a suitable representative. Visiting a trade show or an International conference/forum in Mongolia is also a good occasion to review local businesses and to meet with potential partners.

ESTABLISHING AN OFFICE

The business registration process begins at the Invest Mongolia Agency of the Ministry of Economic Development (IMA: http://www.investmongolia.com). The 2013 Investment Law of Mongolia (IL) sets a minimum level for foreign investment into Mongolia of USD 100,000 and requires the State Registration Office of Mongolia (SRO: https://burtgel.gov.mn) to register all foreign-invested ventures.

For joint ventures, the foreign and Mongolian companies file an application and a joint venture agreement. A foreign-owned company submits information on its activities along with the application letter. The joint venture must register the company name written in Cyrillic letters with the SRO to insure no two companies have the same name and/or share confusing similarities.

The following fees apply for IMA services that are paid to the State Registration Office:

1. Opening of branch, representative's office and unit – 1 100 000Tg (USD 603)

2. Extension of branch, representative's office and unit – 750 000Tg (USD 411)

3. Establishing foreign invested entity – 750 000Tg (USD 411)

4. Extension of certificate – 75 000Tg (USD 42)

5. Registering change in contract and by-law of branch, representative's office and unit – 35 000Tg (USD 19)

6. New ID – 20 000Tg (USD 11)

7. Extension of ID – 10 000Tg (USD 6)

8. Lost ID – 50 000Tg (USD 28)

Registering with General Tax Authority of Mongolia (www.mta.mn)

To become a legal entity in Mongolia, the company must receive final approval from the General Tax Authority of Mongolia (GTA). The Tax Authority registers the business entity and makes the registration public. The GTA requires a US$10 filing fee and the following documents from investors:

* The agreement and charter signed by all parties involved in the venture.

* The certificate of approval from SRO.

* A notarized schedule showing the equity share held by each partner.

* The account numbers of Tugrik and hard currency accounts in a local

bank to be used by the venture.

* A copy of the foreign company representative's passport.

* A certificate showing the amount of capital held by the foreign

company in its home country.

* A certificate of approval from the local administration where the

venture will be based in Mongolia.

Applicants may need additional documents and (or) pay additional fees on a case-by-case basis.

District or *aimag* (province) tax offices will be informed about the registration of a foreign registered company. The foreign entity then should register with the district or *aimag* tax office within 14 days after the state registration certificate is issued. The entity needs to bring a copy of its state registration certificate along with the original certificate. If registering in a city district the representative office of the foreign invested company should be registered with the central tax office of that city, too.

Registering with General Authority for Social Insurance (www.ndaatgal.mn)

A newly established foreign invested entity must register with the Social Insurance office of their respective district or *aimag* (province) and get a social insurance certificate. The entity needs to bring a copy of its state registration certificate along with the original certificate.

FRANCHISING

2013 has seen several U.S. franchises penetrate the Mongolian market: Coffee Bean and Tea Leaf, Cinnabon, KFC, and Round Table Pizza. Several other food franchises

are in the process of opening in Mongolia. Of Mongolia's 2.9 million people, over 60% live in Mongolia's three major urban areas. Ulaanbaatar (UB) has over a million people— nearly 45% of the total. It is the key market and economic engine in Mongolia. With such a concentrated populace, investors need no far-flung network to tap the UB market.

American products enjoy a good reputation; and, generally find Mongolia an excellent fit. Mongolia is a very youthful country. Over 81% of Mongolia's 2.9 million people are under 40. Approximately 76% are under 35 years. Flexible, open to new products, services, and ideas, Mongolians particularly like American brands. Most city dwellers have radios, TVs or most likely both. Newspapers are cheap and billboards abound.

Mongolians appreciate quality and will pay for it. Personal appearance and lifestyle count for much in Mongolia. People are conscious of where they shop, how they communicate, what they wear, what they eat, and what they drive. Mongolians will pay to convey the *right* message and to own the *right* product. American products are often *the right product.*

Mongolians also have an increasing disposable income. Although the government estimates the minimum monthly wage at 144,000 Tugriks or about USD107, official figures do not capture actual economic capacity. 2013 estimates put annual per capita GDP of USD 5,885 on a purchasing power parity basis. In addition, to formal jobs, many Mongolians earn hundreds of dollars a month through gray market activities, and foreign remittances bring in hundreds if not thousands of dollars for some Mongolian families. A best guess puts the effective number willing and able to pay for American goods and services on a regular basis somewhere between -600-800 thousand people.

The ongoing success of the first franchise entrants into the Mongolian market shows that Mongols will buy American franchise products—even given the availability of cheaper competition, albeit of demonstratively lower quality. Where the price differentials are reasonable and the qualitative difference clear, franchisers and their franchisees seem to be succeeding.

The Foreign Investment Law of Mongolia identifies franchising as a potential foreign investment category; therefore, it is entitled to the same status as any other foreign investment under current Mongolian law.

DIRECT MARKETING

While individual firms may send employees out into the field to post bills and shove sales literature under doors or send text messages to cellular service customers advertising new products, there is no coherent system of direct marketing currently available in Mongolia. In-house experience at advertising firms is evolving and there is now some limited specialized expertise available for hire.

JOINT VENTURES/LICENSING

Investors should note that the 2013 Foreign Investment Law of Mongolia does not require foreign investors to have a Mongolian joint venture partner. Businesses may be 100% foreign-owned and operated.

SELLING TO THE GOVERNMENT

Donors have helped Mongolia bring its procurement practices in line with open and competitive bidding. Mongolia adopted a new public procurement law in 1999 making the process more transparent. Most tenders now follow World Bank procurement policies. The government's procurement code generally conforms to World Trade Organization standards. However, oversight of the process remains weak and inconsistent leading to irregularities in the process.

DISTRIBUTION AND SALES CHANNELS

Most products enter and exit Mongolia through three key ports of entry/exit:

* Zamyn-Uud, along a spur of the Trans-Siberian Railroad and a north-south road terminating at Mongolia's south-eastern border with China

* Sukhbaatar City, along a spur of the Trans-Siberian Railroad at Mongolia's north-central border with Russia

* Tsagaan Nuur, along Mongolia's north-western border with Russia

* Yarant, along the Mongolia's south-western border with China's Xinjiang Province

Zamiin-Uud is the most important of the four, and through it passes most of Mongolia's imports and exports, as well as many key Russian commodities—petroleum products, wood, copper, etc. bound for the Chinese market.

Products enter Zamiin-Uud or Sukhbaatar by rail, truck, or car. Products leaving Mongolia by rail are usually inspected at Mongolian Customs Authority (MCA) warehouses in Ulaanbaatar before being sent south or north. Products entering Mongol by rail are usually routed un-opened to the capital Ulaanbaatar (UB) for Customs inspections at the MCA warehouses. From UB, products are then distributed throughout the city and country. Increasingly, heavy equipment bound for Gobi mining sites clears customs in Zamyn-Uud for more direct shipment to the mine sites.

Products entering Mongolia by truck or auto are inspected at the border crossing points. In most cases, these are small traders bringing in limited quantities of food and dry goods for direct sale in rural Mongolia.

Products bound for sale in UB and in other Mongolian cities are trucked from Customs facilities to wholesale and retail outlets dispersed through the cities. Distribution of products to rural Mongolia is usually accomplished by small retailers who travel to urban centers in the Mongolian countryside by rented truck or auto. They purchase goods at local wholesale venues and bear the expense of transport back to their own retail outlets.

Currently, distribution of perishable livestock and organic products both in and out of Mongolia is hindered by the limited availability of refrigerated shipping facilities and infrastructure bottlenecks at ports of entry and along the shipping lines.

SELLING FACTORS/TECHNIQUES

* Personal relationships in business are critical. The Mongolians like to deal with *old friends.* Exporters, importers and investors must establish and maintain close relationships with their Mongolian counterparts and relevant government agencies. Equally important, American exporters should encourage strong personal relationships between their Mongolian agents or distributors and the buyers and end-users. A web of strong personal relationships can smooth development of business in Mongolia.

* Family and school ties are still very strong in Mongolia. It is important to learn who is related to whom when establishing business connections.

* Initial contacts with Mongolians can be in English, but it always helps to be accompanied by an interpreter at the start of any relationship. Mongolians look for cues

of serious intent by how much effort—time and material—a foreign investor puts in the early phases.

* It is a mistake to see Mongolians through the prism of their neighbors. That is, thinking that Mongolians are like the Chinese or the Russians or the Koreans, etc. While both historical and cultural ties exist between Mongolia and her neighbors, Mongolians are conscious and proud of their history and the progress of their country over the last decades. They become offended if confused with China and deeply resent being compared to other developing countries with similar commodity-dependent economies—especially those from Africa. They prefer to be compared to other former East-Bloc nations as Poland, Ukraine, the Czech Republic, etc.

* Promotional materials can be in English, but if possible, preparing a basic information sheet or packet in Mongolian is appreciated. Avoid Chinese language materials, as many Mongolians, fair or foul, associate China with poor quality products.

* Avoid letting cultural sensitivity to Mongolian norms get in the way of good judgment and commonsense. Some Mongolians tell investors that Mongolian customs preclude best commercial practices, insisting that an attractive deal *would* go through if only these practices are ignored. We advise investors to politely but firmly cleave to sound business principles. Investors who do so will earn the respect of the Mongolians and may protect their investment, too.

ELECTRONIC COMMERCE

While computers and the Internet have taken Mongolian by storm, E-Commerce has yet to blossom. Although UB consumer demand for E-services has grown along with size of the market, a not un-justified lack of faith in the security of Mongolian ISPs and public networks hobbles wide scale adoption outside of the banking sector applications. However, these assumptions remain perceptions rather than proven realities, because no formal market survey of the demand and ability of the consumers to pay for E-Services has been conducted.

TRADE PROMOTION AND ADVERTISING

Advertising is an effective way to create product awareness among potential consumers in Mongolia. Newspapers and magazines, radio, cell phones, television and billboard displays, and sports and entertainment sponsorships are mass advertising venues. Almost every household in Ulaanbaatar (over 50% of Mongolia's consumer market) has both TV and radio. In addition, most of Mongolians own or have access to cellular phones and service has become available in almost every part of the country, allowing advertisement by phone to reach all but the most remote corners of the nations. There are many advertising companies in Mongolia. The Mongolian Chamber of Commerce and Industry holds annual spring and autumn trade shows with participants from around Mongolia, Russia, China and Korea.

Two caveats about advertising:

1. In the US companies can deduct the cost of advertising as a legitimate business expense. In Mongolia deduction of advertising costs is limited to 5% of the gross profit—no matter how much a company spends on advertising.

2. The Law on Advertising of Mongolia restricts the sorts of information that may be presented. For example, advertisers must not *tarnish* the honor of Mongolia, promote alcohol or tobacco products, or directly compare products in their ads.

These issues aside, Mongolians have taken to advertising in a big way. Both buyers and sellers appreciate the value of advertising and are completely open to just about every method of providing information on products.

Major newspapers and business magazines:

Business Times - a monthly business paper, in Mongolian, published by the Mongolian Chamber of Commerce and Industry

http://www.mongolchamber.mn/en/index.php/publications/business-times-newspaper

Brand—a monthly business magazine

Mongol Messenger - weekly English language paper published by the Mongolian news agency www.mongolmessenger.mn

MONTSAME (the Mongolian national news agency) www.montsame.mn

Mongolyn Medee - (News of Mongolia) Genco

Odriin Sonin - (Daily News) daily newspaper www.dailynews.mn

UB Post - weekly English-language newspaper published by Mongol News Group ubpost.mongolnews.mn

Unoodor - (Today) independent daily newspaper published by Mongol News Group www.mongolnews.mn

Zuuny Medee - (Century News) daily newspaper www.zuuniimedee.mn
Ardyn Erkh - Mongol Mass Media group
Undesnii Shuudan - director B.Ganbold
Uls turiin toim
Ogloonii sonin-
Unen -
Ardchilal
Television stations include:
MNB - State-owned broadcaster
Channel 25
Mongol TV
RGB
UBS - (Ulaanbaatar Broadcasting System)
TV-5
TV-9
TM – private television station
TV8 - private television station
NTV
C1

Ekh oron
SBNEagle TV ETV
MNC

PRICING

Sensitive to price, Mongolian consumers will choose the less expensive product--unless they can be swayed by after-sales service or clear product superiority. However, Mongolians prefer to buy the best quality they can. They perceive American- branded goods as superior and will more often than not pay a premium to avoid purchasing lower quality items.

SALES SERVICE/CUSTOMER SUPPORT

Mongolian custom, law, and regulation are evolving in the area of sales service and customer support. Mongolian customers and businesses continue to explore the sets of services and practices that constitute an even basic support package for sales and customer support. In addition, Mongolians have not fully embraced—but no longer reject out of hand—the concept that after-sales service and support may justify upfront higher upfront costs they might incur by buying more expensive US products rather than cheaper Chinese or Russian-made ones.

Education about the value of after-sales service and experience with failed equipment has turned the corner for some American product lines in the heavy equipment sector. Currently, firms selling electronic equipment, autos, and mining equipment and tools pursue a variety of options. Generally, models based on best sales service and customer support practices used by well-known Western and Japanese firms have found favor among many Mongolians. Companies that follow such practices are perceived of as better and more reliable.

PROTECTING YOUR INTELLECTUAL PROPERTY

Mongolia supports intellectual property rights in general and has protected American rights. It has joined the World Intellectual Property Organization (WIPO); signed and ratified most treaties and conventions, including the WTO TRIPS agreement. The WIPO Internet treaties have been signed but remain un-ratified by the State Great Hural, Mongolia's Parliament. However, even if a convention is un-ratified, the Mongolian government and its intellectual property rights enforcer, the Intellectual Property Office of Mongolia (IPOM), make a good faith effort to honor these agreements. For more information on IPR services provided by the IPOM go to http://www.ipom.mn/ .

Protecting Your Intellectual Property in Mongolia

Several general principles are important for effective management of intellectual property ("IP") rights in Mongolia. First, it is important to have an overall strategy to protect your IP. Second, IP is protected differently in Mongolia than in the U.S. Third, rights must be registered and enforced in Mongolia under local laws. Your U.S. trademark and patent registrations will not protect you in Mongolia. There is no such thing as an "international copyright" that will automatically protect an author's writings throughout the entire world. Protection against unauthorized use in a particular country depends, basically, on the national laws of that country. However, most countries do offer copyright protection to foreign works under certain conditions, and these conditions have been greatly simplified by international copyright treaties and conventions.

Registration of patents and trademarks is on a first-in-time, first-in-right basis, so you should consider applying for trademark and patent protection even before selling your products or services in the Mongolia market. It is vital that companies understand that intellectual property is primarily a private right and that the US government generally cannot enforce rights for private individuals in Mongolia. It is the responsibility of the rights' holders to register, protect, and enforce their rights where relevant, retaining their own counsel and advisors. Companies may wish to seek advice from local attorneys or

IP consultants who are experts in Mongolia law. The U.S. Embassy in Ulaanbaatar can provide a list of local lawyers at http://mongolia.usembassy.gov/lawyer_list.html .

While the U.S. Government stands ready to assist, there is little we can do if the rights holders have not taken these fundamental steps necessary to securing and enforcing their IP in a timely fashion. Moreover, in many countries, rights holders who delay enforcing their rights on a mistaken belief that the USG can provide a political resolution to a legal problem may find that their rights have been eroded or abrogated due to legal doctrines such as statutes of limitations, laches, estoppel, or unreasonable delay in prosecuting a law suit. In no instance should U.S. Government advice be seen as a substitute for the obligation of a rights holder to promptly pursue its case.

It is always advisable to conduct due diligence on potential partners. Negotiate from the position of your partner and give your partner clear incentives to honor the contract. A good partner is an important ally in protecting IP rights. Consider carefully, however, whether to permit your partner to register your IP rights on your behalf. Doing so may create a risk that your partner will list itself as the IP owner and fail to transfer the rights should the partnership end. Keep an eye on your cost structure and reduce the margins (and the incentive) of would-be bad actors. Projects and sales in Mongolia require constant attention. Work with legal counsel familiar with Mongolia laws to create a solid contract that includes non-compete clauses, and confidentiality/non-disclosure provisions.

It is also recommended that small and medium-size companies understand the importance of working together with trade associations and organizations to support efforts to protect IP and stop counterfeiting. There are a number of these organizations, both Mongolia or U.S.-based. These include:

* The U.S. Chamber and local American Chambers of Commerce
* National Association of Manufacturers (NAM)
* International Intellectual Property Alliance (IIPA)
* International Trademark Association (INTA)
* The Coalition Against Counterfeiting and Piracy
* International Anti-Counterfeiting Coalition (IACC)
* Pharmaceutical Research and Manufacturers of America (PhRMA)
* Biotechnology Industry Organization (BIO)

IP Resources

A wealth of information on protecting IP is freely available to U.S. rights holders. Some excellent resources for companies regarding intellectual property include the following:

* For information about patent, trademark, or copyright issues -- including enforcement issues in the US and other countries -- call the STOP! Hotline: 1-866-999-HALT or register at www.StopFakes.gov .

* For more information about registering trademarks and patents (both in the U.S. as well as in foreign countries), contact the US Patent and Trademark Office (USPTO) at: 1-800-786-9199.

* For more information about registering for copyright protection in the US, contact the US Copyright Office at: 1-202-707-5959.

* For more information about how to evaluate, protect, and enforce intellectual property rights and how these rights may be important for businesses, a free online training program is available at www.stopfakes.gov .

* For US small and medium-size companies, the Department of Commerce offers a "SME IP Advisory Program" available through the American Bar Association that provides one hour of free IP legal advice for companies with concerns in Brazil, China, Egypt, India, Russia, and . For details and to register, visit: http://www.abanet.org/intlaw/intlproj/iprprogram_consultation.html

* For information on obtaining and enforcing intellectual property rights and market-specific IP Toolkits visit: www.StopFakes.gov This site is linked to the USPTO website for registering trademarks and patents (both in the U.S. as well as in foreign countries), the U.S. Customs & Border Protection website to record registered trademarks and copyrighted works (to assist customs in blocking imports of IP-infringing products) and allows you to register for Webinars on protecting IP.

* The U.S. Commerce Department has positioned IP attachés in key markets around the world. You can get contact information for the IP attaché who covers Mongolia at Ulaanbaatar-Econ-Comm@state.gov .

DUE DILIGENCE

The U.S. Embassy in Ulaanbaatar can assist by providing such verifiable non-confidential and proprietary information on both reputations and actions of firms and individuals active in Mongolia as circumstances allow.

LOCAL PROFESSIONAL SERVICES

Licensing technologies, opening representative offices, or establishing subsidiaries in Mongolia involve tax and other laws as well as questions on business practices that may best be addressed by attorneys and accountants familiar with Mongolian requirements.

Attorneys: Several US firms or US-Mongolian firms operate in Mongolia, in addition to competent Mongolian firms. You can find a complete list on the US Embassy website: http://mongolia.usembassy.gov , or contact Ulaanbaatar-Econ-Comm@state.gov .

WEB RESOURCES

Mongolian Resources
Invest Mongolia Agency: http://www.investmongolia.com/
General Tax Authority of Mongolia: www.mta.mn
State Registration Office of Mongolia: https://burtgel.gov.mn
General Authority for Social Insurance: www.ndaatgal.mn
Government of Mongolia: http://www.pmis.gov.mn
Intellectual Property Office: http://www.ipom.mn/
Mineral Resources and Petroleum Authority of Mongolia: http://www.mram.mn
Mongol Chamber of Commerce and Industry: http://www.mongolchamber.mn/en/
Mongolian Builders Association: http://www.buildersasso.mn
Embassy of Mongolia, Washington, DC: http://www.mongolianembassy.us
Parliament of Mongolia: www.parliament.mn
American Chamber of Commerce Mongolia: http://amcham.mn/
Business Council of Mongolia: www.bcmongolia.org/
U. S. Government Resources
Commercial Specialist: richmondmd@state.gov
U.S. Embassy, Ulaanbaatar: http://mongolia.usembassy.gov
U.S. Department of State: http://www.state.gov/
U.S. Department of Commerce: http://www.commerce.gov/
U.S. International Trade Administration: http://www.trade.gov/
U.S. Trade and Development Agency: http://www.ustda.gov
U.S. Export-Import Bank: http://www.exim.gov/
U.S. Overseas Private Investment Corporations: http://www.opic.gov

LEADING SECTORS FOR U.S. EXPORT AND INVESTMENT

MINING

	2010	2011	2012	2013
Total Exports	2 908.5	4 817.5	4 384.7	4 269.1
Total Import	3 200.1	6 598.4	6 738.4	6 357.8
Export to USA	11. 6	11.0	42.1	19.7
Import from USA	115.5	315.2	665.0	279.5
Total turnover USA	164.9	541.1	539.5	516.6

Millions USD/

Plentiful mineral endowments, proximity to strong markets in Asia, and general political stability make investing in and selling U.S. mining equipment and services to Mongolia's mining sector potentially promising activities. This promise is manifest in the strong growth: inward FDI in the geological prospecting, oil exploration, and mining sectors has increased from USD 336 million in 2007 to USD 2.2 billion in 2012—an increase of 85% in just 4 years. At 73% total inward FDI in 2012, the mining sector comprises the majority of investment in Mongolia, up from 67% in 2007 but down from a peak of 82% in 2011. In particular, two projects represent the promise of Mongolia's mining sector: The Oyu Tolgoi copper-gold project (OT) and the prospective Tavan Tolgoi coking coal project (TT). During the last three years, the mining sector's contribution to GDP has averaged 18.6%, to budget revenue 40%, and 90% to export income.

These marquee projects remain central to Mongolia's mineral sector. The OT mine alone contains over 35 million tons of copper and 1,275 tons of gold and will likely drive Mongolia's GDP growth well into the future. Production at OT started in 2013 and was scheduled to reach full capacity by 2017-18, although the progress has stalled repeatedly. At its full capacity, the OT mine is expected to supply 450,000 tons of copper a year, close to 3% of world output.1 Although in a more preliminary stage, TT

1 Asel Isakova, Alexander Plekhanov and Jeromin Zettelmeyer. "Managing Mongolia's resource boom." *EBRD*. Working Paper 138. January 2012.

holds estimated reserves of over 6 billion tons of high quality thermal and coking coals, approximately 100 years of production capacity. Together these mines will contribute substantially to Mongolia's projected GDP growth, which is anticipated to approach 9 - 10% in 2014, and continue at high levels, barring significant political changes.

In addition to these flagship projects, Mongolia continues to explore its significant potential in other areas, including but not limited to gold, copper, molybdenum, fluorspar, coal, zinc, tungsten, rare earths, iron, and uranium. Gold production grew by 5.1% in 2012, and new laws passed in 2014, providing a reduction in royalties for gold sold to the central bank of Mongolia, are expected to spur production. Iron ore production increased by over 30% in 2012. Mongolia ranks fifth among global fluorspar producers, producing both acid and metallurgical grades, with 4% of the world's total production. Mongolia's most common and potentially commercial rare earths are tantalum, niobium, yttrium, thorium, and zircon.

These opportunities have already positively impacted U.S. exporters of mining goods and services. Overall exports from the U.S. to Mongolia have expanded from USD 43 million in 2009 to USD 650 million in 2012, or 15 times, with at least a fifth of these exports directly linked to the OT mining project. Evening during recent periods of slower economic growth seen in 2013 and the first half of 2014, export volumes have remained relatively robust, hovering at around USD 300 million or approximately 7 times their 2009 levels. The hope is that as other mines are developed that ongoing successful performance of U.S. exports at OT and other high profile Mongolian mining projects will lead to expanded use of U.S. goods and services throughout the entire Mongolian mining sector. Exporters willing to consider ways to add value locally through employment and investment will find a welcoming environment.

RESOURCES

Mongolian Resources
Invest Mongolia Agency: http://www.investmongolia.com/
General Tax Authority of Mongolia: www.mta.mn
State Registration Office of Mongolia: https://burtgel.gov.mn
General Authority for Social Insurance: www.ndaatgal.mn
Government of Mongolia: http://www.pmis.gov.mn
Intellectual Property Office: http://www.ipom.mn/
Mineral Resources and Petroleum Authority of Mongolia: http://www.mram.mn
Mongol Chamber of Commerce and Industry: http://www.mongolchamber.mn/en/
Mongolian Builders Association: http://www.buildersasso.mn
Embassy of Mongolia, Washington, DC: http://www.mongolianembassy.us
Parliament of Mongolia: www.parliament.mn
American Chamber of Commerce Mongolia: http://amcham.mn/
Business Council of Mongolia: www.bcmongolia.org/
U. S. Government Resources
Commercial Specialist: richmondmd@state.gov
U.S. Embassy, Ulaanbaatar: http://mongolia.usembassy.gov
U.S. Department of State: http://www.state.gov/
U.S. Department of Commerce: http://www.commerce.gov/

U.S. International Trade Administration: http://www.trade.gov/
U.S. Trade and Development Agency: http://www.ustda.gov
U.S. Export-Import Bank: http://www.exim.gov/
U.S. Overseas Private Investment Corporations: http://www.opic.gov

CONSTRUCTION SECTOR

	2010	2011	2012	2013
Total Exports	2 908.5	4 817.5	4 384.7	4 269.1
Total Import	3 200.1	6 598.4	6 738.4	6 357.8
Export to USA	11. 6	11.0	42.1	19.7
Import from USA	115.5	315.2	665.0	279.5
Total turnover USA	164.9	541.1	539.5	516.6

Millions USD/

Although constrained by its harsh winters, Mongolia's construction sector continues to flourish, presenting opportunities for U.S. investors and exporters of U.S. construction goods and services–particularly those willing to employ and invest locally. The construction industry grew by 25.6% in 2012 led by public infrastructure investment. Paralleling this growth, inward FDI in the engineering and construction sector jumped significantly, from under USD 1 million in 2010 to 47 million in 2012.2 In 2013, the government and the central bank together provided MNT 3-4 trillion – equivalent to around 20 percent of GDP – to construction of infrastructure (mostly roads) and apartments, which led to 66.5 percent growth of the construction sector that year. While the construction stimulus measures and a low-cost mortgage program were politically popular and contributed to economic growth, the real estate market boom created by subsidized credit has raised concerns about possible overheating of the housing market.

Mongolia's rapid urbanization remains a strong driver of growing demand for social infrastructure and residential housing, as well as transportation and communications networks. While Mongolia's total population remains small at 2.9 million, 68% of the people reside in cities, with more than 42% living in the capital city.4 Cities have grown by 3% annually since 2000. From 1982-2009, the population of Ulaanbaatar more than doubled from 450,000 to over a million. With urbanization, a large housing market is rapidly growing; as a result, affordable residential stock is in short supply and demand shows no signs of slacking.

Short supply in the construction sector results from a myriad of factors. For one, there is a dearth of qualified construction companies. Mongolia's construction industry has only been fully privatized since 1998. Hence, the mix of private and public companies present in Mongolia—100 architectural and engineering design companies and over 800 construction companies—are learning how to work and prosper in the free market. Due to the nascent construction industry, companies are still learning to utilize technologies efficiently. Mongolia needs expertise and technology, specifically in the areas of concrete and cold weather construction, and heating, ventilation and air conditioning installation. Further, many companies have limited capacity; only 40 are large-scale operations with their own in-house design and engineering units or partnerships with companies that manufacture or import construction materials. As a result, there is an ongoing shortage of qualified companies to complete outstanding projects.

Growing industrial, service, and tourism industries also ensures a growing demand in for the construction sector. The number of visitors—both business and tourists—increased 70% from 2000 to 2010 (137,000 to 457,000 visitors); and revenues from tourism grew 85% over the same period to USD 258 million. These visitors will require more lodging and services.

The mining sector's development will also drive expansion. For example, with the government announced in January 2012 that 3,000 apartments, roads, a school and a kindergarten, as well as a hospital, hotel, and shopping centers, will be built near the OT mining site. These projects are valued at USD 73.26 million, and financed by Ivanhoe Mines, Rio Tinto and the state-run Tavan Tolgoi firm. This rapid expansion of the mining sector has fed into private demand, keeping construction humming at a clipper pace.

Of particular note is the growth in the luxury housing market. Prices for high-end residential units nearly doubled from the first quarter of 2010 to the first quarter of 2011, according to a local real estate firm.5 The prices for these units ranged from MNT 2 million (USD 1,465) per square meter to MNT 10 million (USD 7,326) per square meter, according to the National Statistical Office, as of May 2011. More generally, housing prices in Ulaanbaatar ranged from MNT 850,000 (USD 623) per square meter to MNT

1.48 million (USD 1,084) per square meter. In 2013 the total amount of housing stock by floor space built was 11,483.4 thous.m2 (excluded the traditional dwelling structure-the Mongolian felt *ger*), and residential quarters actually occupied was 1 237.3 thous.m2.

According to the Mongolian Builder's Association (MBA: http://www.buildersasso.mn), apartment prices per square meter fluctuate between US $750 to US $5,500 in Ulaanbaatar. Average price targeted to middle-income families is set at US $1,200/per square meter.

RESOURCES

Mongolian Resources
Invest Mongolia Agency: http://www.investmongolia.com/
General Tax Authority of Mongolia: www.mta.mn
State Registration Office of Mongolia: https://burtgel.gov.mn
General Authority for Social Insurance: www.ndaatgal.mn
Government of Mongolia: http://www.pmis.gov.mn
Intellectual Property Office: http://www.ipom.mn/
Mineral Resources and Petroleum Authority of Mongolia: http://www.mram.mn
Mongol Chamber of Commerce and Industry: http://www.mongolchamber.mn/en/
Mongolian Builders Association: http://www.buildersasso.mn
Embassy of Mongolia, Washington, DC: http://www.mongolianembassy.us
Parliament of Mongolia: www.parliament.mn
American Chamber of Commerce Mongolia: http://amcham.mn/
Business Council of Mongolia: www.bcmongolia.org/
U. S. Government Resources
Commercial Specialist: richmondmd@state.gov
U.S. Embassy, Ulaanbaatar: http://mongolia.usembassy.gov
U.S. Department of State: http://www.state.gov/
U.S. Department of Commerce: http://www.commerce.gov/
U.S. International Trade Administration: http://www.trade.gov/
U.S. Trade and Development Agency: http://www.ustda.gov
U.S. Export-Import Bank: http://www.exim.gov/
U.S. Overseas Private Investment Corporations: http://www.opic.gov

INFORMATION TECHNOLOGY

	2010	2011	2012	2013
Total Exports	2 908.5	4 817.5	4 384.7	4 269.1
Total Import	3 200.1	6 598.4	6 738.4	6 357.8

Export to USA	11. 6	11.0	42.1	19.7
Import from USA	115.5	315.2	665.0	279.5
Total turnover USA	164.9	541.1	539.5	516.6

Millions USD/

Over the last 10 years, Mongolian demand for computer goods and services has boomed. In absolute terms the numbers seem small: There are 210 400 telephone lines, 277 968 cable television subscribers, 186 television stations, 205 internet cafes, 762 200 permanent internet users and 505,596 computers for a population of 3 million people. However, the pace of growth is substantial. Revenue from telecommunication services in 2013 reached US $430 million or about 5% of the 2013 GDP. The penetration of Internet has reached 30% and the infrastructure for its use now covers much of Mongolia, albeit it only the populated parts. The growth in internet subscribers represents an increase of over 53% compared from 2009.6 Mongolians' use of mobile phones has also skyrocketed penetrating over 100% of the market (Note: Most Mongolian consumers subscribe to more than 1 IT and telecommunication service). Revenue from telecommunication services in 2013 reached US $430 million.

6 White Paper, GOM

Demand for both communications and internet technologies have been evolving rapidly. In the telecommunications sector, the use of fixed lines is minimal and declining, as Mongolia has largely bypassed this stage, proceeding directly to the use of mobile and wireless technologies. There are four major providers, Mobicom, Skytel, Unitel, and G-mobile—all offering pre-paid and post-paid plans for communication and computer services. By far, the use of pre-paid credit dominates the market. Halved prices for per minute charges have contributed to the expansion in users.

Introduction of new technologies has accompanied the boom in mobile phone use.

Since 2009, MobiCom, Skytel, and Unitel have launched 3G high-speed mobile broadband services in Mongolia. These services are accessible to all users, provided they have the supporting technology on their phones. 3G, as of 2010, is available in 31 soums and settlements, covering over 171,000 users.7 Several companies have also been successful marketing pre-paid long-distance direct calling card services.

7 White Paper, GOM

8 http://mongolia-briefing.com/news/2012/03/mongolias-it-sector-continues-to-see-rapid-growth.html

9 Data from the Information Communications Technology Post Authority of Mongolia

In the internet services sector, technology has also been improving steadily. Starting with the first VSAT technology that operated with 64kbps in 1996, Mongolia has now moved on. As of 2010, internet services available include xDSL (ADSL, HDSL, VDSL), Fiber optic, GPRS (including 3G, EVDO and EDGE), WiMax, WiFi technologies, dial-up and VSAT. The average speeds of bandwidth in Mongolia for downloading is 11.2Gbps and for uploading 11.2Gbps. According to Frontier Securities data, the wholesale price connection has dropped from USD 3,250 per 1 Mbps in 2004 to USD 80 in 2011.

The ICT sector presents substantial opportunity. Mongolia spends approximately USD 284 million on computer, communication, and other services imports, while exporting around USD 131 million in ICT services. The level of investment in the sector has been steadily increasing from USD 2.5 million in 2005 to USD 66 million in 2010. Of total ICT sector revenues—totaling USD 471 in 2010—about 73% were generated by mobile services, and the remaining from fixed telecommunications network, including VoIP, internet, cable TV, broadcasting, etc.

There is still considerable room for growth given that only about half of Mongolia's provincial towns have high-speed internet access. Of Mongolia's regular internet users, 18.7% rely on fiber-optic cables. Currently there are 17,900 kilometers of fiber-optic cables installed in Mongolia, covering about 70% of users. The ICTPA estimates that full coverage would require 40,000 kilometers of cables.8 Additionally, digital subscriber lines comprise about 12.6% of internet access, while wireless technologies, including Wi-Fi, WiMAX, and VSAT serve less than 1% of users.

Price sensitivity continues to affect consumers' choices regarding internet services as well as personal computing choices. By and large, although the number of computers per person jumped from 46 per 1000 in 2007 to 85 per 1000 in 20109, most Mongolia's are still reliant on internet cafes or other 3rd party devices for access. The number of internet subscriptions, therefore, is well below the number of computers—at approximately 351,758 subscriptions. However, the remainder of the market is likely to purchase personal computing equipment and/or internet services as soon as it becomes affordable, given Mongolians' familiarity with and frequent use of ICTs and social media resources.

As evidence of the popularity of computers and social media in Mongolia, the number of websites, blogs, etc. serving Mongolian users has grown rapidly. Intec, a local IT consulting firm, identified some 3,400 websites with Mongolia-related content. There are upwards of 1,823 Mongolia-themed blogs, with around one-third of them started in 2010. More than 160,000 Mongolians have a Facebook account, all predominantly youth, with 78% of subscribers aged between 18 and 34.

The use of social networking, websites, and email for advertising and business services is also on the rise. The most popular version of social networking in Mongolia is Biznetwork, with over 70,000 users that include corporations as well as individuals. Non-governmental organizations also use these types of platforms to organize events and convey messages to the public. Email advertising is becoming more commonplace as a conduit of information on products and services. A number of email marketing companies maintain databases of email addresses, which is the only way to reach individual consumers, aside from text messaging, given that the scarcity of postboxes in Mongolia.

Software development companies specialize in various areas, ranging from the creation of applications for use at stand-alone computers to enterprise software for networks and the development of websites and portal sites. More companies have shifted towards providing web-based applications. A break-down of companies shows that 20% work on development of websites while 16% specialize in software and application development.

Mongolia's IT infrastructure continues to evolve, striving to reach Western standards. Approximately 3 fixed broad band internet subscribers per 100 people, but growing rapidly from 0.1 in 2006. There are 54 secure internet servers in Mongolia. The fiber-optic network had reached 21 aimag (provincial) centers and over 300 soums (counties) by 2013. The development of the main infrastructure, fiber-optic cables, is predominantly owned and managed by the state-owned Information Communication Network Company and Railcom respectively. However, private operators, with Mobicom, Gemnet, Skytel, Unitel, have installed their own fiber optic and wireless networks.

RESOURCES

Mongolian Resources
Invest Mongolia Agency: http://www.investmongolia.com/
General Tax Authority of Mongolia: www.mta.mn
State Registration Office of Mongolia: https://burtgel.gov.mn
General Authority for Social Insurance: www.ndaatgal.mn
Government of Mongolia: http://www.pmis.gov.mn
Intellectual Property Office: http://www.ipom.mn/
Mineral Resources and Petroleum Authority of Mongolia: http://www.mram.mn
Mongol Chamber of Commerce and Industry: http://www.mongolchamber.mn/en/
Mongolian Builders Association: http://www.buildersasso.mn
Embassy of Mongolia, Washington, DC: http://www.mongolianembassy.us
Parliament of Mongolia: www.parliament.mn
American Chamber of Commerce Mongolia: http://amcham.mn/
Business Council of Mongolia: www.bcmongolia.org/
U. S. Government Resources
Commercial Specialist: richmondmd@state.gov
U.S. Embassy, Ulaanbaatar: http://mongolia.usembassy.gov
U.S. Department of State: http://www.state.gov/
U.S. Department of Commerce: http://www.commerce.gov/
U.S. International Trade Administration: http://www.trade.gov/
U.S. Trade and Development Agency: http://www.ustda.gov
U.S. Export-Import Bank: http://www.exim.gov/
U.S. Overseas Private Investment Corporations: http://www.opic.gov

AGRICULTURAL SECTORS

	2010	2011	2012	2013
Total Exports	2 908.5	4 817.5	4 384.7	4 269.1
Total Import	3 200.1	6 598.4	6 738.4	6 357.8
Export to USA	11. 6	11.0	42.1	19.7
Import from USA	115.5	315.2	665.0	279.5
Total turnover USA	164.9	541.1	539.5	516.6

Millions USD/

Agriculture remains a mainstay of Mongolia's economy both as a source of national revenue as well as employment. It contributes about 37 % of gross domestic product,10 constituting approximately a quarter of Mongolia's total economic growth in 2012.11 Agriculture and livestock is also source of direct and indirect employment for more than half of the population. Direct employment in the agricultural sector, as a percentage of total employment, has remained fairly steady at 40% from 2004-2009.

While central to Mongolia's economy, it is only recently that investors in the agriculture have moved to improve the efficiency and profitability of the sector. Initial privatizations of state farms and livestock cooperatives in the early 1990s, the deregulation of prices of major agricultural products, and the liberalization of agricultural trade hit the state-operated, state-owned sector hard. Early privatization was ill-timed, ill-conceived, and ill-executed. From 1991 to 1995, production of some commodities halted or declined to near subsistence levels. By 1996, the sector rebounded, and by 2002, most of the state farms were fully privatized under single (individual or company) ownership or limited partnerships of two or three owners.

The Government recognizes that sustainability in agriculture and rural areas depends largely on modernizing the livestock sector and improving land management. In 2002 the government passed legislation allowing long-term land leasing, strengthening sector institutions, privatizing service delivery wherever possible, and continuing with the privatization process. The government will not sell farm and grazing land. It will allow Mongolian citizens and foreigners to acquire the long-term use rights to these lands. Locals may be given preference. The need to brand the Mongolian food industry, expand domestic processing of agricultural products, as well as increasing technological capacity and standardizing production were all main topics at the Mongolia Economic Forum 2013. The government has signaled its intent to move forward on all of these fronts.

Food and Product Processing:

Although most of Mongolia's provinces have established private food plants and shops, there is a tendency to import food products from abroad, because domestic enterprises produce no food to international standards. Roughly, Mongolia spends around USD 772 million on food imports annually. This reliance on achieving higher quality through imports is driven, in part, by the low technological base in the food production industry. Likewise, Mongolia engages in very little domestic processing of foods and animal products. For example, by 2012 only 7% of domestic meat and 9% of domestic dairy products were processed in Mongolia.13 Failure to upgrade existing production technology continues to slow development of both food production, as well as export of higher value-added agricultural products, such as leather or cashmere.

Both the public and private sectors want to improve the operations at food processing plants, develop small and medium enterprises for processing and preserving vegetables and fruits, as well as produce sugar, vegetable oil, and grow some grains domestically to meet the demand. But lack of capacity is a serious constraint. For example, currently there are 44 meat factories producing 150 types of products in Mongolia, but they only operate at 10 percent capacity; and increasing capacity will require new technology and equipment, which will require funding of at least 200 billion MNT, as well as expansion of related infrastructure, which is also lagging. The value-added tax on the importation of equipment is one factor that slows the adoption of technology in the agricultural and food production sectors.14

Ranching and Meat Processing

The number of livestock reached 45.1 million head for the first time in Mongolia's recorded history: 2.6 million horses; 2.9 million cattle; 19.3 million goats; and 20.1 sheep. Mongolia has potentially excellent customers for these meat products in Russia, China, and other Asian markets. Much of Russian Siberia lacks good grazing land, so protein production remains a consistent problem. Although China has grazing land, much of that is given over to cereal production or, in the case of Inner Mongolia, cashmere. Mongolia has grasslands and livestock in abundance. Hungry markets to the North and South are a clear business opportunity for American ranchers and meat processing and marketing technologies.

Although these viable markets exist, several impediments remain. First, quotas and restrictive health regulations inhibit the meat trade between Mongolian and her neighbors. For example, Russia limits imports of beef from Mongolia to 35,000 metric tons a year, a quota Mongolia fills quickly. Sources at the various border posts suggest that at least that much (most likely much more) goes across as contraband. Much the same situation prevails at the Mongolian-Chinese border.

Both China and Russia's ascension to the World Trade Organization have increased the incentives for Asian countries to open borders and increase trade, giving Mongolia the leverage it needs to crack these tempting markets. The Mongolian Government has taken concrete steps to assist in increasing Mongolian meat exports, especially those beyond Siberia. In addition, USAID has supported programs to provide training in meat processing, project management, and product marketing.

Slow technological adoption also drags down Mongolia's production, especially for export markets. In 2012, there were 40.9 million livestock in Mongolia. Eight million were slaughtered for domestic meat consumption, producing approximately 220,000 tons of meat; only 3,000 tons were processed and exported. In part, both the low level of production, along with the meager revenues it produces (much of the export is raw commodities) stems from the inexperience in processing goods.

The Ministry of Industry and Agriculture, has highlighted the need for the upgrading and standardization of production practices. The government would like to adopt European standardization methods that will enable tracing of the origin of meat and dairy products but is finding lack of domestic capacity to hinder effective implementation.

The GOM's desire for improved technology and its vision that that the State, private sector, science, and research institutions work together to brand Mongolian meat provide opportunities for the involvement of U.S. companies specializing in these areas. In particular, existing meat processing plants require technological renovation to increase capacity and upgrade the quality and sanitation to expand their markets. There is also a need for food preservation technology, packaging and marketing techniques, as well as training in more modern butchering and processing techniques.

Wheat

Wheat is central to the diet and agricultural economy of Mongolia as the main crop in the country and a major food staple. Wheat flour comprises approximately 50% of the daily caloric intake of Mongolians. Until the mid-1990s, Mongolia was self sufficient in wheat

and an occasional exporter.15 Since, 1994, production levels have steadily declined, replaced by commercial imports. In addition to supplying these imports, there are additional opportunities for firms to assist in the upgrading the processing of consumer products for domestic consumption and export in wheat products manufacturing (noodles, bakery), small scale flour milling. In addition, a growing market exists for herbicides, fertilizers, and high quality wheat seed.

Vegetables

Contrary to popular belief, Mongolians do eat vegetables. Its young market is permeable to new foods. Lettuces, peppers, Washington apples, and California grapes appear in Ulaanbaatar's markets regularly. The total cereal crop was 387.0 thousand metric tons; potatoes 191.6 thousand tons; and vegetables of all types 101.8 thousand tons.

RESOURCES

Mongolian Resources

Invest Mongolia Agency: http://www.investmongolia.com/
General Tax Authority of Mongolia: www.mta.mn
State Registration Office of Mongolia: https://burtgel.gov
General Authority for Social Insurance: www.ndaatgal.mn
Government of Mongolia: http://www.pmis.gov.mn
Intellectual Property Office: http://www.ipom.mn/
Mineral Resources and Petroleum Authority of Mongolia: http://www.mram.mn
Mongol Chamber of Commerce and Industry: http://www.mongolchamber.mn/en/
Mongolian Builders Association: http://www.buildersasso.mn
Embassy of Mongolia, Washington, DC: http://www.mongolianembassy.us
Parliament of Mongolia: www.parliament.mn
American Chamber of Commerce Mongolia: http://amcham.mn/
Business Council of Mongolia: www.bcmongolia.org/
U. S. Government Resources
Commercial Specialist: richmondmd@state.gov
U.S. Embassy, Ulaanbaatar: http://mongolia.usembassy.gov
U.S. Department of State: http://www.state.gov/
U.S. Department of Commerce: http://www.commerce.gov/
U.S. International Trade Administration: http://www.trade.gov/
U.S. Trade and Development Agency: http://www.ustda.gov
U.S. Export-Import Bank: http://www.exim.gov/
U.S. Overseas Private Investment Corporations: http://www.opic.gov

TRADE REGULATIONS, CUSTOMS AND STANDARDS

IMPORT TARIFFS

Most imported goods are subject to 5% ad valorem Customs duty while some others are subject to seasonal duties. Certain goods for export are subject to specific Customs duties. Any person (physical or legal) engaged in foreign trade is liable to pay Customs duties as well as some other taxes and fees upon importation or exportation.

The following goods are subject to 15% customs duty between August 1 and April 1 every year. For the remaining period of the year, 5% customs duty applies.

* Potato

* Onion

* Cabbage

* Yellow carrot

* Yellow turnip

* Fluor (July 1 – April 1)

For more information on import and export tariffs and non-tariff regulations: http://ecustoms.mn/

TRADE BARRIERS

Mongolia generally offers exporters and investors a fairly free trade regime lacking quotas, onerous licensing requirements or local sourcing. However, the lack of transparency and consistency in how regulations are both crafted and applied remain obstacles to trading with and doing business in Mongolia.

IMPORT REQUIREMENTS AND DOCUMENTATION

Customs clearance for export and import consists of the following steps:

1. Declaring goods

2. Inspection of customs documents

3. Inspection of the goods and means of transport

4. Levying customs duties and other taxes and payments thereto

5. Granting permission and releasing goods to cross customs border.

For more information see: http://ecustoms.mn/

Export/Import of Strategic food:

According to the Interim Regulation on Issuing export/import license for strategic food, approved by Government resolution No 77 dated March 02, 2013, licensing of export and import of strategic food as defined in Article 3.1.6 of the Law on Food (a) liquid and powder milk, b) meat of cattle, horse, camel, goat and sheep processed other than heating, c) wheat flour, d) potable water shall be based on open tender for the given year. The National Council on Food Security shall define the type and amount of strategic food to be exported/imported based on proposals by the ministry in charge. The license is issued for each type of food and valid for 6 months.

U.S. EXPORT CONTROLS

For information on U.S. export controls applicable to Mongolia go to:

* http://www.state.gov/strategictrade/resources/c43182.htm

TEMPORARY ENTRY

Mongolia joined the Istanbul Convention on Temporary admission of goods in 2002. The Mongolian National Chamber of Commerce and Industry is assigned as an organization in charge of issuing ATA carnet and guarantee. Six annexes are being implemented (A, B1, B2, B3, B5 and C) and 11 customs organizations of Mongolia were approved for border crossing rights. These are:

1. Customs branch at Altanbulag, Selenge province

2. Customs office at Zamyn-Uud, Dornogobi province

3. Customs office of Ulaanbaatar city

4. Customs bureau of Darkhan-Uul province

5. Customs bureau of Orkhon province

6. Customs bureau at Khankh, Khuvsgul province

7. Customs branch at Tsagaannuur, Bayan-Ulgii province

8. Customs branch at Ereentsav, Dornod province

9. Customs branch at Bulgan, Khovd province

10. Customs branch at Borshoo, Uvs province

11. Customs office at Buyant-Ukhaa

More information available: http://ecustoms.mn/

Contact the Customs Control & Clearance Department of the General Customs Office at +976 11 353541.

LABELING AND MARKING REQUIREMENTS

By the amendments to the Law on Food of Mongolia (effective March 01, 2013), labels of imported food must be written in Mongolian, Russian or English languages. Only a properly registered legal entity of Mongolia is allowed to import food (not individuals). An Exporter needs to conclude an agreement with a Mongolian importer that introduces quality management and standards for agricultural, food and health.

Contact Export/Import Monitoring Department, General Agency of Specialized Inspection at: +976 51 264147.

PROHIBITED AND RESTRICTED IMPORTS

Prohibited items include drug/narcotics, devices and equipment for use and manufacturing of them and narcotic plants, all types of spirit, scrap metal, (ferrous and non-ferrous). Narcotics and narcotic plant for medical purposes are allowed only by the permission of the State central organization in charge of health.

Restricted items: highly toxic chemicals, organs and donor blood for the purpose of preventing and treatment under required medical control, guns, rifles, weapons, military equipment and devices and their spare parts, or explosives.

Mongolia restricts the import and export of certain items. Please consult Customs regulations in detail before importing or exporting these items. These include:

* Uranium and uranium concentrates;

* Poisonous chemicals

* Organs and blood products for the purpose of preventing and treatment under required medical control

* Firearms and ammunition, spare parts, outfit and explosives

* Artifacts and cultural property, including historical, cultural, fossils, archeological and similar items

* Breeding animals,

* Animal and animal originated raw materials, experimental samples and probes

* Animal embryos, microorganism culture

For more information http://ecustoms.mn/

CUSTOMS REGULATIONS AND CONTACT INFORMATION

Customs General Administration: http://www.ecustoms.mn/
Contact: Director International Cooperation Division
Tel: 976-51-266782
E-mail: info@ecustoms.mn

STANDARDS ORGANIZATIONS

The National standards body of Mongolia is the Mongolian Agency for Standardization and Metrology (MASM) http://masm.gov.mn/ . Its Chairman is appointed by the Government of Mongolia and reports to the Deputy Prime Minister's Office. The highest decision-making organ of MASM is its National Council, approved by the Cabinet with 19 members - representatives of the Ministries, agencies, nongovernmental organizations, scientific academia and industries. The aim of MASM in standardization is to contribute to the development of the Mongolian society, economy, industry and trade by establishing standards on the basis of mutual understanding and voluntary agreement between parties in governmental authorities, industry and business, with regard to consumers' rights, and in continuously developing standardization activities aligned to the market system. The preparation, application and promotion of national standards are set out in the Mongolian law on "Standardization and Conformity Assessment", adopted in 2003 but which is now being amended. MASM approves and publishes all Mongolian standards, represents Mongolia in international standardization within ISO, and is the Mongolian WTO/TBT Enquiry point.

The National Council of Standardization approves and adopts the standards used within the territory of the country after being reviewed and accepted by the standardization Technical Committee (TC). There are 49 TCs and sub-committees at the MASM. Department of Standardization and Technical Regulation is in charge of regulating TC activities and to define, resolve and develop national standards.

There are about 6210 national standards, 42% of which are in compliance with international or regional standards. Within the framework of the Agreement signed with the European Committee for Standardization (CEN), Mongolia aims to raise that to 90%. The list of national standards is available at:
http://www.estandard.gov.mn/index.php?module=menu&cmd=content&menu_id=132

Technical regulations:

Technical regulations shall be exercised in order to ensure the safety of products, which may harm the public interest, human health, the environment or security of nations, and to prevent from supply of deceptive products into the market. A regulation is approved by the Government Cabinet. The central body in charge of standards issues, MASM, shall review and draw conclusions on draft technical regulations. The Government Cabinet member in charge of trade issues, the Ministry of Economic Development, shall exercise the power to accept domestically the technical regulations, proposed by the member countries of the World Trade Organization (WTO) to apply in international trade (in

accordance to the Convention on Technical Barriers to Trade). The central body in charge of standard issues, MASM, shall inform other members of the WTO no less than three months in advance before the adoption of the technical regulations, proposed by the member countries of the WTO.

NIST Notify U.S. Service

Member countries of the World Trade Organization (WTO) are required under the Agreement on Technical Barriers to Trade (TBT Agreement) to report to the WTO all proposed technical regulations that could affect trade with other Member countries. Notify U.S. is a free, web-based e-mail subscription service that offers an opportunity to review and comment on proposed foreign technical regulations that can affect your access to international markets. Register online at Internet URL: http://www.nist.gov/notifyus/

CONFORMITY ASSESSMENT

The Department of Product and System Conformity conducts activities in following fields:

* Imported product conformity
* Exported product conformity
* Services conformity
* Domestic product conformity
* System conformity
* Approval of “MNS” mark for products and services
* Conformity for “Eco” mark

http://www.masm.gov.mn/index.php?module=divisions&cmd=conformity

PRODUCT CERTIFICATION

The national testing organization for *proficiency testing* is the Laboratory of Reference Materials at MASM. The laboratory is in charge of the laboratory requirements for proficiency of testing and calibration laboratories usually on food products, water and minerals. For more details call 976 7018 5279.

http://www.masm.gov.mn/index.php?module=divisions&cmd=conformity

ACCREDITATION

The Department of Accreditation of MASM has authority for accreditation of the following institutions:

* Accreditation for testing laboratory

* Accreditation for organizations of technical monitoring and confirmation

* Accreditation for human health and veterinary laboratory

* Accreditation for metrology laboratory

For more information contact the Department of Accreditation, call MASM at 976-51-263907.

http://www.masm.gov.mn/index.php?module=divisions&cmd=accreditation

PUBLICATION OF TECHNICAL REGULATIONS

Publication of technical regulations is a responsibility of MASM.

LABELING AND MARKING

TC on Labeling and Marking was established at the MASM. For more information contact Standardization & Technical Regulation Department at 976-11-455284.

CONTACTS

* Foreign Registration and Regulation Department: http://www.investmongolia.com/

* Ministry of Industry and Agriculture: http://mofa.gov.mn/

* Mongolian National Chamber of Commerce and Industry: http://www.mongolchamber.mn/en/

* National Statistical Office: http://www.nso.mn/contacts.php

* Mongolian National Center for Standardization and Metrology: http://masm.gov.mn/index.php

* General Agency for Specialized Inspection: http://inspection.gov.mn/

TRADE AGREEMENTS

* Mongolia has both signed and ratified most WTO treaties. For more information go to o http://www.wto.org/

* Mongolia has signed and ratified bilateral investment treaties with the following countries: UNCTD: http://www.unctad.org/sections/dite_pcbb/docs/bits_mongolia.pdf

Reporter	Partner	Date of Signature	Entry in to force
Mongolia	Austria	19-May-01	1-May-02
	Belarus	28-May-01	1-Dec-01
	Belgium/Luxembourg	3-Mar-92	15-Apr-04
	Bulgaria	6-Jun-00	------------
	China	25-Aug-91	1-Nov-93
	Croatia	8-Aug-06	------------
	Cuba	26-March-99	-----------
	Czech Republic	13-Feb-98	5-Jul-99
	Denmark	13-Mar-95	2-Apr-96
	Egypt	27-Apr-04	25-Jan-05
	Finland	15-May-07	------------
	France	8-Nov-91	22-Dec-93
	Germany	26-Jun-91	23-Jun-96
	Hungary	13-Sep-94	29-Aug-95
	India	3-Jan-01	29-Apr-02
	Indonesia	4-Mar-97	13-Apr-99
	Israel	25-Nov-03	2-Sep-04
	Italy	15-Jan-93	1-Sep-95
	Japan	15-Feb-01	24-Mar-02
	Kazakhstan	2-Dec-94	3-Mar-95
	DPR of Korea	10-Nov-03	-----------
	Republic of Korea	28-Mar-91	30-Apr-91
	Kuwait	15-Mar-98	1-May-00
	Kyrgyzstan	5-Dec-99	-----------
	Lao People's DR	3-Mar-94	29-Dec-94
	Lithuania	27-Jun-03	3-May-04
	Malaysia	27-Jul-95	14-Jan-96
	Netherlands	9-Mar-95	1-Jun-96
	Philippines	1-Sep-00	1-Nov-01
	Poland	8-Nov-95	26-Mar-96
	Qatar	29-Nov-07	------------
	Romania	6-Nov-95	15-Aug-96
	Russian Federation	29-Nov-95	------------
	Singapore	24-Jul-95	14-Jan-96
	Sweden	20-Oct-03	1-Jun-04
	Switzerland	29-Jan-97	9-Sep-99
	Tajikistan	20-Mar-09	16-Sep-09
	Turkey	16-Mar-98	22-May-00
	Ukraine	5-Nov-92	5-Nov-92
	UAE	21-Feb-01	-------------
	United Kingdom	4-Oct-91	4-Oct-91
	United States	6-Oct-94	4-Jan-97

Vietnam	17-Apr-00	13-Dec-01

The text of the U.S.-Mongolia Bilateral Investment Treaty can be found at http://www.state.gov/e/eb/ifd/43303.htm .

WEB RESOURCES

Mongolian Resources
Invest Mongolia Agency: http://www.investmongolia.com/
General Tax Authority of Mongolia: www.mta.mn
State Registration Office of Mongolia: https://burtgel.gov.mn
General Authority for Social Insurance: www.ndaatgal.mn
Government of Mongolia: http://www.pmis.gov.mn
Intellectual Property Office: http://www.ipom.mn/
Mineral Resources and Petroleum Authority of Mongolia: http://www.mram.mn
Mongol Chamber of Commerce and Industry: http://www.mongolchamber.mn/en/
Mongolian Builders Association: http://www.buildersasso.mn
Embassy of Mongolia, Washington, DC: http://www.mongolianembassy.us
Parliament of Mongolia: www.parliament.mn
American Chamber of Commerce Mongolia: http://amcham.mn/
Business Council of Mongolia: www.bcmongolia.org/
U. S. Government Resources
Commercial Specialist: richmondmd@state.gov
U.S. Embassy, Ulaanbaatar: http://mongolia.usembassy.gov
U.S. Department of State: http://www.state.gov/
U.S. Department of Commerce: http://www.commerce.gov/
U.S. International Trade Administration: http://www.trade.gov/
U.S. Trade and Development Agency: http://www.ustda.gov
U.S. Export-Import Bank: http://www.exim.gov/
U.S. Overseas Private Investment Corporations: http://www.opic.gov

INVESTMENT CLIMATE[3]

Mongolia's main economic and political challenges are all linked to ensuring steady growth through the boom and bust cycles likely to visit this resource-dependent economy. Double-digit economic growth over the past few years—2011's sizzling 17.3 % GDP growth, for instance—has been based on the investment in, and the production and export of, minerals. Mongolia is a major producer of several minerals including coal, copper, gold, zinc, and fluorspar. With extensive reserves, it has the potential to increase production considerably. For U.S. investors and firms, mining and mining-related services represent one of the most important and potentially most reliable sectors for long-term investment in Mongolia. Other promising sectors, based on Mongolia's economic development needs, include infrastructure, transportation, energy, construction, healthcare, and environmental products and services.

However, Mongolia has suffered ongoing setbacks to economic advancement. Indeed, growth has steadily slowed from 2011's 17.3 % to 2013's 11.7 %. Both the International Monetary Fund (IMF) and World Bank estimate 2014 GDP to decline to 9.5%; and 2015, depending on Mongolian policy decisions, may range from a high of 12% to as low as 2%. The IMF cites loose fiscal and monetary policies as likely causes for economic downturns. (For IMF: http://www.imf.org/external/pubs/ft/scr/2014/cr1464.pdf ; For WB: http://www.worldbank.org/en/news/feature/2014/07/03/mongolia-economic-update-july-2014 .)

[3] US Department of States materials

As with GDP, Foreign Direct Investment (FDI) has steadily declined, constraining development of the mining and infrastructure sectors. In 2012, FDI invested in Mongolia (mostly in the mining sector) reached USD $3.9 billion, which amounted to approximately 40% of that year's GDP. In 2013, FDI had contracted by nearly 45%. In the first five months of 2014, Mongolia's central bank reported that FDI through May was US $402.3 million compared to US $1.11 billion a year ago—a 64% year-on-year decline.

Two factors have and will continue to affect Mongolia's economic condition. First, more than 90 percent of Mongolia's exports consistently go to China; and so, any slowing of China's growth affects Mongolia. Second, economic policies designed to protect Mongolia's sovereign interests and to respond to the expectations of the Mongolian public have discouraged FDI – despite statements from Mongolia's senior politicians that the government is committed to improving the business environment, reigniting foreign

direct investment flows, and fostering Mongolian growth. Recent policy decisions have been influenced by the political realities of a coalition government representing multiple platforms, which has complicated reaching consensus on politically sensitive issues. There are a range of views represented within parliament on what constitutes an appropriate legal and regulatory framework for mining and other activities. Statutes and regulations are thus often crafted in a manner which incorporates multiple approaches and political imperatives. Investors have told us that this approach to legislation and regulation can give the impression that laws are hastily passed and that regulations are slowly created and partially implemented. Some investors are concerned that criticism from some political quarters of current investment agreements and statutory obligations undertaken by past governments portends that commitments may not be fully respected.

Investors and companies may likely encounter bumpy short-run trends as Mongolia continues to come to terms with its mining endowments and how to bring them to the outside world, while satisfying domestic expectations that the mining sector should benefit the public. Investors may perceive, and have to accept that, the current political process creates an unclear policy environment that may increase investment risk, while Mongolian politicians see the process as yielding the necessary level of political comity. However, in the medium to long term, those willing to manage these issues and relationships with local partners with open eyes may find attractive opportunities in the aforementioned industries and sectors.

1. OPENNESS TO, AND RESTRICTIONS UPON, FOREIGN INVESTMENT

1.1. Attitude Toward FDI

The Government of Mongolia (GOM) has consistently said that it supports foreign direct investment (FDI) in all sectors. Throughout 2013 and well into 2014, the President of Mongolia, Ts. Elbegdorj, and other senior officials have publicly stated in a variety of international and domestic venues that the GOM will keep key foreign investment commitments and pass investor-friendly legislation, because they recognize the value of FDI for Mongolia. On May 8, Parliament passed a resolution on "measures to spur economic activities" identifying steps to improve foreign currency flows, lower risk, and improve the business and investment environment; and on July 1, passed long-awaited amendments to the Minerals and Petroleum Laws respectively. However, some investors assert that Mongolia's support for FDI remains more aspiration than reality. Specifically, they report that, reform of a key investment law and resource laws notwithstanding, resolving disputes with Rio Tinto expeditiously according to the terms of the Investment and Share Holders Agreements and then moving to complete development of the Oyu Tolgoi (OT) project will explicitly demonstrate the GOM's commitment to the transparent rule of law, sanctity of contracts, and free market principles. Settling the outstanding issues with respect to OT will do much to convince hesitant investors that the GOM is able and willing to translate positive intentions into a welcoming and productive environment for investment.

1.2. Other Investment Policy Reviews

UNCTAD Mongolia IPR: http://unctad.org/en/pages/PublicationWebflyer.aspx?publicationid=758 .

WTO Mongolia IPR in the context of a Trade Policy Review: http://www.wto.org/english/tratop_e/tpr_e/tp245_e.htm .

OECD Mongolia IPRs: While OECD has not conducted a full-blown IPR of Mongolia, it has executed numerous economic studies related to investment and development in Mongolia available at http://www.oecd.org/countries/mongolia/ .

1.3. Laws/Regulations of FDI

Mongolia's legal system

Mongolia is a multiparty parliamentary democracy. Its legal code is based on Continental and Russian law, though ongoing justice sector reforms draw heavily from the American legal system. Most jurists have received their legal education at Mongolian State University and private universities.

The 1992 constitution empowered a General Judicial Council to select all judges and protect their rights. The Supreme Court is the highest judicial body. Supreme Court justices are nominated by the GCC and confirmed by the president; the State Great Hural (Parliament) must be made aware of the nominations but cannot block them. Specialized civil and criminal courts exist at all levels and are subject to Supreme Court supervision. Administrative courts exist at the province and city levels only and are also subject to Supreme Court supervision. The Supreme Court is constitutionally empowered to examine all lower court decisions upon appeal and provide official interpretations on all laws except the constitution. Local authorities--district and city governors--ensure that these courts abide by presidential decrees and State Great Hural decisions. At the apex of the judicial system is the Tsets or Constitutional Court, which consists of nine members, including a chairman, appointed for 6-year terms, whose jurisdiction extends solely over the interpretation of the constitution.

Trial Procedures

The law provides for the right to a fair public trial by a judge, although human rights groups and NGOs alleged that this right has been undermined by frequent bribery and large caseloads. Juries are not used. Defendants are innocent until proven guilty and can question witnesses, present evidence, and appeal decisions. Defendants have the right to be informed of the charges against them (with interpretation as necessary); to a fair, public trial without undue delay; to communicate with an attorney of their choice (or one provided at public expense); to adequate time to prepare a defense; to access government-held evidence; and to appeal. Defendants cannot be compelled to testify or confess guilt. These rights were generally observed in practice, although Amnesty International and other NGOs reported evidence that authorities, at times, used physical coercion to obtain confessions from suspects.

Civil Judicial Procedures and Remedies

Administrative and judicial remedies are available for alleged wrongs. Reports indicate that corruption, outside influence, and lack of enforcement of court orders remain problems in the civil judicial system. Private enterprises have reported cases where courts pressured businesses to pay bribes in civil cases involving property and tax disputes. Although by law victims of police abuse can sue for damages, in practice few are able to claim compensation.

The 2013 Investment Law of Mongolia

In October 2013, Parliament passed the Investment Law of Mongolia (IL). Entering into effect on November 1, the IL replaced the 1993 Foreign Investment Law of Mongolia (FILM), and the controversial 2012 Strategic Entities Foreign Investment Law (SEFIL), which most investors saw as being anti-foreign investment and one of the prime causes of the over 50% drop of FDI in the time between its passage and its revocation. Overall, the law sets down the legal rights and obligations of investors in Mongolia, stabilizes the tax environment, establishes the powers and responsibilities of the agency that will regulate investment, and provides incentives to encourage investment. Foreign investors are given the same protections as domestic investors.

Domestic vs. Foreign: It's Where You Are, Not Who You Are

Unlike FILM and SEFIL, what distinguishes a foreign from a domestic investor in the IL is not nationality but where the investor resides. A foreigner who resides permanently in Mongolia may be considered a domestic investor for purposes of the law while a Mongolian who lives abroad permanently may be considered a foreign investor. Investment may be made in any sector not prohibited or restricted by law. Accordingly, investments by private individuals or firms are no longer subject to special approval other than registration with the State Registration Office (SRO), which simplifies the procedures for doing business, unless sector-specific legislation mandates additional requirements. However investors claim the IL's level playing field has some regulatory bumps. In force for six months, the IL's implementation has already created concerns among foreign investors of unequal treatment. Specifically, the law increases the minimum capital requirements for foreign- invested companies in Mongolia, which have two or more foreign shareholders, by requiring that each foreign shareholder contribute US$ 100,000 if foreign investor(s) hold a 25% or more interest in the business entity, thus seeming to discriminate against foreign-invested firms.

Investment Sweeteners Include Tax and Non-Tax Incentives

A central feature of the law promoted by the GOM is the tax incentives in the form of tax stabilization certificates. New projects and some older projects that meet requirements may qualify for favorable tax treatment for periods up to 27 years. Affected taxes may include corporate income tax; customs duties; value-added tax; and mineral resource royalties. The most important criterion for tax stabilization is the amount of investment, determined by reference to specific sectors and the geographical area within which the investment is made.

The Invest Mongolia Agency

IL creates a new investment promotion agency, the Invest Mongolia Agency (IMA), under the Ministry of Economic Development to replace the Foreign Investment Regulation and Registration Department (FIRRD). Mandated to promote and regulate investment activities, the agency will issue tax stabilization certificates and monitor the activities of certificate holders but will have no role in registering companies or investors, a responsibility IL vests with the State Registration Office exclusively (SRO). To contact IMA go to www.investmongolia.com .

The Revised Securities Market Law of 2013

On May 24, 2013, the parliament of Mongolia amended the 2002 Securities Market Law with the Revised Securities Law of Mongolia (RSML), which entered into force on January 1, 2014. The RSML establishes a legal framework for a Mongolian capital market generally in line with international standards and practices; enhances regulation of market participants; increases market transparency; protects investors' rights and interests; and expands state authority to regulate and monitor market activity. Unlike the law it replaces, the RSML explicitly vests the Financial Regulatory Commission of Mongolia (FRC) with primary authority to regulate and monitor the operations of the securities market.

Of key interest to market participants, the RSML defines and creates an enabling environment for a series of standard market practices employed in most equity markets but long absent from Mongolia. These include the ability to dual-list on the Mongolian Stock Exchange and non-Mongolian exchanges; offer depository receipts and custodial services; and conduct IPO's. The RSML adopts a post-payment system for purchasing securities, while the old law required immediate settlement for all purchases. RSML requires MSE share transactions be made within three business days of the trade, the so-called T+3 settlement method practiced globally.

Of particular importance, the RSML introduces the concepts of beneficial and nominal ownership of securities. The old law only required that a nominal holder of securities be listed, who could be any one whom the beneficial owner designated. Under the old law, it was nearly impossible to discover the real owner. RSML replaces the concept of nominal ownership with that of a nominal holder: A regulated, FRC-approved entity registered as the depositor/custodian of a given security, and who is not the beneficial owner of such a security. RSML then statutorily defines beneficial owner as the real owner of the security and requires public disclosure of said ownership.

Public Private Partnership/Concession Law

In 2010, parliament authorized tendered concessions for certain government functions and for public-private partnerships (PPPs) in a variety of areas. As of May 2014, 880 separate projects—ranging from key power projects to major rail expansions to a horse-race track—are listed as available for private entities to engage with the GOM to support social and economic development by ostensibly providing commercial incentives for participation. However, some investors have criticized the law as offering too few incentives, particularly the short period during which an operator might realize a profit before the GOM assumes ownership of the project. Until the GOM amends the law to address these unattractive features, investors will likely pass on Mongolia's PPP opportunities.

Investor Concerns over Travel Bans

Investors and local legal experts have regularly reported that Mongolian public and private entities can use administratively imposed travel bans to pressure foreign investors to settle civil disputes. Immigration officials may impose a travel ban for a

variety of reasons, including an individual's involvement in civil disputes, pending criminal investigations, or for immigration violations. If banned for either a civil or criminal dispute, exit will not be allowed until either the dispute is resolved administratively or a court renders a decision. Neither current law nor regulation establishes a transparent process or clear time-table for settlement of such issues. Resolution of criminal and civil commercial cases has taken up to 2.5 years during which time the foreign citizen has remained in Mongolia. The GOM does not impose similar travel bans for Mongolian citizens with pending civil disputes. Mongolian nationals are only denied exit from Mongolia if an actual arrest warrant has been issued.

Two Mongolian laws, the Criminal Procedure Law of Mongolia (CPL) and the Law on the Legal Status of Foreign Citizens (FCL), regulate the administrative imposition of travel bans on foreign citizens seeking to leave Mongolia. Under the CPL, if the State decides that that the suspect will flee, then a measure of restraint, such as a travel ban, may be imposed, but even with a travel ban the State may allow temporary travel. The competent authorities, usually but not exclusively law enforcement authorities, inform Mongolian Immigration that an individual is a suspect and therefore banned from departing Mongolia.

The Law on the Legal Status of Foreign Citizens (FCL) applies to any foreign citizen in Mongolia, and bans foreign citizens from exiting Mongolia if anyone (Mongolian or foreign) files a claim or complaint against the foreign citizen for violation of rights, freedoms or lawful interests, and the State authority considers the claim or complaint to have merit. To our knowledge, the competent authority in these cases has been primarily individual investigating police officers and prosecutors to whom the complainant applies. These investigators then apply to Immigration to impose a travel ban on the foreigner. To our knowledge, there is no formal requirement for independent or higher level review of such detainments. Foreign travel is banned until the claim or complaint is resolved; and, in this case, the burden of proof seems to fall squarely on the foreigner. In many of these cases, the complainant and the investigating officer are known to each other. There does not appear to be a mechanism to regulate apparent conflicts of interest.

1.4. Investment Trends: Oyu Tolgoi Commences Operations but Challenges Persist

In October 2009, the GOM, Ivanhoe Mines of Canada, and Rio Tinto negotiated investment and share-holders agreements for the Oyu Tolgoi (OT) copper- gold deposit located in Mongolia's South Gobi desert. Rio Tinto eventually acquired control of Ivanhoe, renaming it Turquoise Hill Resources (TRQ). The OT agreements vest the government of Mongolia with 34% ownership of the project and TRQ with 66 %, and provide guarantees for local employment and procurement. With estimated development costs in excess of US $7 billion and a 40-year plus mine-life, OT is conservatively expected to double Mongolia's annual GDP by the time it reaches full production. In June 2013 production of copper concentrate and gold from the open pit portion of the mine commenced and has continued without interruption for almost a year.

Investors had hoped that commencement of operations and export of copper and gold would lead to approval of a project finance agreement for Phase II, which is to be an underground block-cave mine and which is expected to account for 80 % of OT's full value. However, throughout 2013 and likely through much of 2014, both Rio Tinto and

the GOM have failed to reach agreement on key issues related to project costs, management fees, taxation, and water usage, among other issues. This mutual inability to reach agreement has effectively halted Phase II financing. For their parts senior representatives from both sides have provided explicit representations that they want the project to go forward and that they are seeking to finalize agreement on project financing as expeditiously as possible. However, statements of senior Mongolian officials notwithstanding, GOM claims against OT, such as the June 2014 demand for $130 million USD in back taxes—which Rio Tinto disputes—raise the specter for investors that 2014 will see no progress at OT. Still, as of June 2014 both sides remain in talks to resolve the outstanding issues.

The domestic impact of failure to execute Phase II is that OT has trimmed over 2000 positions and the procurement that comes with moving to Phase II from its budget. For the GOM, this trimming represents a substantial reduction in revenue of between US $200 to US $300 million per year from the state budget for essential developments. For the people of Mongolia, these cuts mean that employees and contractors will not develop the skills needed to run OT and other mining developments, in addition the impact on vitally needed household income.

For foreign investors the delay to move to Phase II has equally dramatic significance. From its inception OT has embodied the investment prospects of Mongolia for investors. Positively, investors perceive that OT proves that Mongolia can say Yes to key projects undertaken with foreign involvement and investment; and demonstrates GOM willingness to amend laws and regulations to enhance and ensure the commercial viability of mining projects. This positive message for investors cannot be underestimated: OT is a barometer on foreign investment in Mongolia. The GOM's initial support for OT is largely considered responsible for spurring progress on other mining projects and for these projects' successful listing on foreign stock exchanges. Negatively, the dispute has raised doubts about the GOM's commitment to contract sanctity, has certainly become a factor in the downgrading of Mongolia's sovereign credit ratings, and has been blamed as a major factor in the severe drop in FDI since 2012.

1.5 Tables

TABLE 1: Mongolia's Ranking as a Place to Do Business

Measure	Year	Index or Rank	Website Address
TI Corruption Perceptions index	2013	83 of 177	http://cpi.transparency.org/cpi2013/results/
Heritage Foundation's Economic Freedom index	2013	97 of 177	http://www.heritage.org/index/ranking
World Bank's Doing Business Report "Ease of Doing Business"	2013	76 of 189	http://doingbusiness.org/rankings
Global Innovation Index	2013	72 of 142	http://www.globalinnovationindex.org/content.aspx?page=gii-full-report-2013#pdfopener
World Bank GNI per capita	2012	3,160 USD	http://data.worldbank.org/indicator/NY.GNP.PCAP.CD

TABLE 1B: Mongolia's MCC Scorecard

The Millennium Challenge Corporation, a U.S. Government entity charged with delivering development grants to countries that have demonstrated a commitment to reform, produced scorecards for countries with a 2012 per capita gross national income (GNI) of $4,085 or less. For a list of countries/economies, including Mongolia's, with MCC scorecards go to: http://www.mcc.gov/pages/selection/scorecards . For MCC indicators: http://www.mcc.gov/documents/reports/reference-2013001142401-fy14-guide-to-the-indicators.pdf . Find Mongolia's score at http://www.mcc.gov/documents/scorecards/score-fy14-english-mn-mongolia.pdf .

2. CONVERSION AND TRANSFER POLICIES

2.1. Foreign Exchange

The Mongolian government employs a liberal regime for controlling foreign exchange for investment remittances. Foreign and domestic businesses report no problems converting or transferring investment funds, profits and revenues, loan repayments, or lease payments into whatever currency they wish to wherever they wish. There remains no difficulty in obtaining foreign exchange in virtually any major world currency. However, in response to occasional shortages, most often of U.S. dollars, commercial banks can impose temporary, daily limits on the amounts they will exchange, transmit abroad, or allow to be withdrawn.

In regards to domestic transactions, current law requires all domestic transactions be conducted in Mongolia's national currency, the Tugrik (MNT), except entities granted limited waivers for non-Tugrik transactions by the Mongolia's central bank, the Bank of Mongolia (BOM).

Businesses report no delays in remitting investment returns or receiving in-bound funds. Most transfers occur within 1-2 business days or, at most, a single business week.

Ease of transfer aside, foreign investors criticize Mongolia's lack of sophisticated mechanisms for converting currencies and hedging forward exposure to MNT. Many Mongolian financial institutions lack experience with these arrangements. Moreover, Mongolian banking law currently provides incomplete statutory grounds and regulatory support for the activity to take place. Letters of credit remain difficult to obtain; and the government has recently taken to paying for goods and services rendered under domestic government contracts with promissory notes, which cannot be directly exchanged into other currencies. The immediate impact has been to limit access to

certain types of foreign capital, as international companies resist parking cash in Mongolian banks or in local debt instruments.

Mongolia has complied with the Financial Action Task Force (FATF's) requirements for passing anti-money laundering legislation. The next steps involve implementation of FATF-related laws pass in February 2014. For an analysis of Mongolia's status: http://www.state.gov/j/inl/rls/nrcrpt/2013/database/211182.htm#Mongolia .

3. EXPROPRIATION AND COMPENSATION

Mongolia has generally respected property rights for most asset types. However, investors have expressed concern over actions that they believe represent either "creeping expropriation" or more direct expropriation, especially but not exclusively those associated with the resource extraction sector.

Security of Ownership

The U.S.-Mongolia Bilateral Investment Treaty (BIT) entered in force in 1997. Under this BIT, Mongolia and the United States have agreed to international law standards for expropriation and compensation for expropriation. In addition, both Mongolian law and the national constitution recognize private property rights and the rights associated with its use, and specifically bar the government from expropriating such assets. To date, the GOM has been accused of a single act of expropriation against an American mining asset. (BIT: http://www.state.gov/documents/organization/43579.pdf)

Like most sovereigns, the Mongolian government may exercise eminent domain in the national interest. Under the current land law, Mongolian state entities at all levels can claim land or modify use rights for purposes of economic development; national security; historical preservation; and environmental and rangeland protection.

Investors have expressed little disagreement with such takings but worry that the lack of clear lines of authority among the various levels—central, provincial, and municipal—could lead to a loss of property rights. For example, the 2006 Minerals Law, still current as of June 2014, provides no clear limit on provincial control of permits and special use rights or guidance on how to apply these powers beyond codifying that the provincial and local authorities have some authority over activities occurring in their provinces, municipalities, and *soums* (counties). Faced with these unclear lines of authority, the central government often interprets the rules and regulations differently from the provincial and municipal authorities but declines to enforce its interpretation or even to assist in mediating among the disputing parties, all of which effectively suspends investors' access to property and licensed use rights for months and years. The central government acknowledges the problem but has taken no steps to resolve it.

National Security Concerns May Lead to Loss of Rights

In 2010, the President of Mongolia used his authority as head of the National Security Council of Mongolia (NSCM) to suspend the issuance and processing of both mining and exploration licenses. He argued that the flaws of the licensing regime constituted a threat to national security that justified the NSCM suspending issuances. Domestic and foreign investors and Mongolian government officials disputed this moratorium, claiming that neither the President nor the NCSM had constitutional or statutory authority to supersede the government's regulatory authority over mining. A constitutional crisis was only averted when Parliament imposed a moratorium on the issuance of the certain

types of mineral licenses. At the end of 2012, parliament extended the moratorium indefinitely until the 2006 Minerals Law is amended, which may happen in 2014. Consequently, since 2010, investors reportedly have faced limitations on claiming new land for exploration or converting exploration licenses into mining licenses, which effectively limits access to otherwise legally granted economic rights.

How the Amendment Process Affects Mineral Rights

Going into 2014, investors remain concerned over a legislative amendment process they claim halts or significantly delays the Mongolian regulatory process, and so, erodes rights granted under current law. For example, the ongoing amendment process to the 2006 Minerals Law has effectively stalled issuance of exploration and mining licensing. Since the President of Mongolia announced his concerns about the existing licensing regime in 2010, an amendment process for the entire law has been ongoing. This process, well into its fourth year, has produced numerous draft amendments between the government and Parliament. Although the 2006 Minerals Law remains in force, officials at all levels delay, or openly refuse to process, normal requests for extending or issuing exploration and mining licenses. They justify delay and refusal by stating that the amendment process renders the current law "effectively" invalid because any act may face post facto changes under a new statute. Overall, businesses suggest that the amendment process for mining and other laws has generated lengthy and costly bureaucratic delays for many commercial sectors, especially in mining.

The Use of Criminal Courts to Invalidate Use Rights

Recently, investors have vehemently criticized the revocation of economic rights by Mongolia's criminal courts. For example, in 2013 a criminal court judge revoked 106 mining licenses, because these had been granted during the tenure of an official subsequently found criminally guilty of corruption. At no time did the court offer specific evidence proving that these licenses, among the hundred granted during the official's term, were improperly granted. Local legal experts have noted that Mongolian law and regulation do not allow criminal courts to render administrative decisions, which is the formal statutory province of the Administrative Court of Mongolia. In effect, investors have had their economic rights expropriated by judiciary acting outside its jurisdiction without any opportunity to appeal these losses to a proper authority.

4. DISPUTE SETTLEMENT

Investors believe that both government and judiciary inconsistently support transparent, equitable dispute settlement; and argue these inconsistencies stem from both a lack of experience with standard commercial practices and the opportunistic targeting of foreign investors by some public and private Mongolian entities.

4.1. Legal System

As currently constituted, legal experts and investors argue that Mongolia's judicial system can support dispute settlement; however, problems with dispute resolution can and do arise. First, commercial law and broad understanding of it remain in flux. Even after nearly a quarter century of reform, the passage of new laws and regulations on contracts, investment, corporate structures, leasing, banking, etc., remains vitally

necessary. Generally, Mongolian civil law does not work from precedents but from application of the statute as written; and so, if a law is vague or does not cover a particular commercial activity, a judge's remit to adjudicate can be severely limited or non-existent. Further, because precedents are not legally binding on other judges and Mongolian courts, decisions reached in one case may have no legal force in others, even when the circumstances are similar or even before the same court and judges. In addition, many judges lack training in, or remain ignorant of, commercial principles, and some have appeared to willfully ignore what is considered sound practice elsewhere.

Based on what judges adjudicating contract disputes have said to investors or third party intermediaries it seems that the foreign identity of the plaintiff or defendant has incorrectly been taken into account in some cases. Arguments include: the foreign investor can afford the loss; the foreigner must be stealing from Mongolia in some way and so deserves to lose; or that Mongolian judges must support Mongolians or risk being accused of being unpatriotic.

4.2. Bankruptcy

Foreign investors and local banks argue that Mongolia's bankruptcy laws need comprehensive reform. While Mongolian law allows for mortgages and other debt instruments backed with securitized collateral, rudimentary systems for determining title and liens and for collecting on debts make lending on local security risky. Banks complain that onerous foreclosure rules are barely workable and unfair to creditors. Bankruptcy is an option on paper, but we can offer no example of a successful bankruptcy process. Indeed, local law firms state that the bankruptcy process is too vague, onerous, and time consuming to make it a practical step to end a business.

Although a system exists to register immovable property—structures and real estate—for the purpose of confirming ownership, the current system does not record existing liens against immovable property. Nor does a system currently exist to register ownership of, and liens on, movable property. Consequently, lenders face the added risk of lending on collateral that debtors may not actually own or which may have already been pledged as security for another debt. Overall, the legal system does recognize the concept of collateralized assets as security for loans, investment capital, and other debt-based financial mechanisms. The legal system also provides for foreclosure, but only through the judicial rather than administrative proceedings. Waits of up to 36 months for final liquidations and settlement of security are not uncommon.

4.3. International Arbitration

4.4.1. ICSID Convention and New York Convention

The Mongolian government generally supports and has submitted to both binding arbitration and international settlement procedures, but glitches remain in local execution. Mongolia ratified the Washington Convention and joined the International Centre for Settlement of Investment Disputes in 1991. It also signed and ratified the New York Convention in 1994. To our knowledge, the government of Mongolia has accepted international arbitration in several disputes. The government consistently declares it will honor resulting arbitral awards.

Mongolian businesses partnered with foreign investors often will accept international arbitration, as do government agencies that contract business with foreign investors, rather than avail themselves of the Mongolian Arbitration Bureau operated by the

Mongolian National Chamber of Commerce and Industry. Foreign investors tell us that they prefer international arbitration, because they perceive domestic arbitrators as too politicized, too unfamiliar with commercial practices, and too self-interested to render fair decisions.

Although arbitration is widely accepted among business people and elements of the government, support for binding international arbitration has not penetrated local Mongolian agencies responsible for executing judgments. Investors routinely report that the most common problem preventing resolution of debt-driven disputes is that the State Court Enforcement Office (SCO) often resists executing collection orders and court-ordered foreclosures.

The U.S.-Mongolia Bilateral Investment Treaty (BIT) entitles both U.S. and Mongolian investors to seek international arbitration in the case of investor-state disputes. (For the BIT: http://www.state.gov/documents/organization/43579.pdf .)

5. PERFORMANCE REQUIREMENTS AND INCENTIVES

5.1 WTO/TRIMS

There have been no reports that Mongolia employs measures inconsistent with World Trade Organization Trade Related Investment Measures (TRIMS) requirements, nor has anyone alleged Mongolia has violated TRIMS.

5.2 Investment Incentives

Under the current Tax Law of Mongolia, the GOM attempts to limit both exemptions and incentives and to make sure that tax preferences offered are available to both foreign and domestic investors. The GOM occasionally grants tax exemptions for imports of essential fuel and staple food products; or for imports in certain sectors targeted for growth, such as the agriculture sector. Such exemptions can apply to both import duties and Mongolia's value-added tax (VAT). In addition, the GOM will occasionally extend a 10% tax credit on a case by case basis to investments in such key sectors as mining, agriculture, and infrastructure. Under the 2013 Investment Law (IL) and related amendments, foreign-invested companies properly registered and paying taxes in Mongolia are treated as domestic-Mongolian entities; and therefore, can qualify for investment incentive packages that, among other incentives, include tax stabilization for a period of years. (For detail on IL see Chapter 1.)

5.3 Performance Requirements

Restrictions on hiring expatriate labor aside, foreign investors currently need not use local goods, services, or equity; or engage in substitution of imports. The government applies the same geographical restrictions to both foreign and domestic investors. Existing restrictions involve border security, environmental concerns, or local use rights. There are no onerous or discriminatory visas, residence, or work permits requirements imposed on American investors. Neither foreign nor domestic businesses need purchase from local sources or export a certain percentage of output; or require foreign exchange to cover their exports.

The GOM encourages value-added production and local sourcing of human and material inputs in Mongolia, especially for firms engaged in natural resource extraction. All Mongolian senior officials and politicians make in-country processing a consistent feature of their public and private policy statements regarding the development of mining. Although the GOM has not passed laws requiring local sourcing, government plans also call for increased investment in businesses and activities that keep the "value" of a resource in Mongolia. Consequently, companies should continue to expect the GOM to press aggressively for value-added production in Mongolia by companies registered in Mongolia.

Generally, foreign investors set their own export and production targets without concern for government imposed targets or requirements. There is no requirement to transfer technology. As a matter of law, the government generally imposes no offset requirements for major procurements. Certain tenders and projects on strategic mineral deposits may require agreeing to specific levels of local employment, procurement, or to fund certain facilities as a condition of the tender or project, but as matter of course such conditions are not the normal approach of the government in its tendering and procurement policies.

Investors, not the Mongolian government, make arrangements regarding technology, intellectual property, and similar resources and may generally finance as they see fit. Foreign investors currently need sell no shares to Mongolian nationals. Equity stakes are generally at the complete discretion of investors, Mongolian or foreign.

Although Mongolia has no statutory or regulatory requirement, the GOM sometimes negotiates restrictions on the sort of financing foreign investors may obtain and with whom investors might partner or to whom they might sell shares or equity stakes. These restrictive covenants will most likely be imposed in certain sectors where the investment is determined to have national impact or national security concerns—i.e., the mining sector.

Regarding employment, investors can locate and hire workers without using hiring agencies—as long as hiring practices follow Mongolian labor law. However, Mongolian law requires companies to employ Mongolian workers in certain labor categories whenever a Mongolian can perform the task as well as a foreigner. This law generally applies to unskilled labor categories and not areas where a high degree of technical expertise not existing in Mongolia is required.

6. RIGHT TO PRIVATE OWNERSHIP AND ESTABLISHMENT

Generally, unless otherwise forbidden by law, foreign and domestic businesses can establish and engage in any form of business activity. Under the U.S.-Mongolia Bi-lateral Investment Treaty (BIT: http://www.state.gov/documents/organization/43579.pdf), U.S. investors receive national treatment in Mongolia and can start up, buy, sell, merge; in short, do whatever they wish with their assets and firms, with exceptions in the banking and finance and real estate sectors, which are carved out for restrictive treatment under the BIT. In addition, the 2013 Investment Law of Mongolia (IL) guarantees that all foreign investors satisfying formal criteria are to be treated as Mongolian-registered entities and subject to the same rights and obligations related to ownership and establishment pertaining to any Mongolian entity. (For information on IL, go to Chapter 1.)

7. PROTECTION OF PROPERTY RIGHTS

7.1 Real Property

Mongolia recognizes the right to own private property, movable and immovable. Regardless of nationality (except for land located exclusively in municipalities and which only Mongolian citizens can own), owners can generally do as they wish with their property. Most of Mongolia's non-urban land, such as pasturage or mineral deposits, remains the property of the state, for which foreign and domestic investors may obtain use rights for terms varying from 3 to 90 years, depending on the purpose and relevant legislation. One can sell, transfer, or securitize structures, shares, use-rights, companies, and movable property, subject to relevant legislation and related regulation controlling such activities. Mongolian law does allow creditors to recover debts by seizing and disposing of property offered as collateral.

Mongolia's Current Regime to Protect Creditors

Investors tell us that Mongolian law does protect creditors but needs reform. Courts recognize property rights in concept, but have a checkered record of protecting them in practice. Part of the problem is ignorance of, and inexperience with, best international best practices regarding use-rights, land, leases, buildings, and mortgages. As noted in Chapter 1, some judges, whether out of ignorance or apparent partiality for Mongolian disputants over foreigners, fail to follow such practices. Investors tell us that newly trained judges make good faith efforts to uphold property rights but need more experience adjudicating such cases. The legal system also allows only judicial foreclosure for any contested foreclosure action. Because all contested foreclosure actions require court review and are subject to appeals up to the Supreme Court of Mongolia, final resolution can take up to 36 months. In addition, creditors report that it's often easier to get than to execute a court ruling. The problem remains inconsistent enforcement. The court orders the State Collection Office (SCO) to seize forfeited assets, which it then distributes to creditors. However, foreign and domestic investors routinely claim that SCO regularly fails to execute these responsibilities.

In addition, rudimentary systems for determining title and liens and for collecting on debts make lending on local collateral risky. Although a system exists to register immovable property—structures and real estate—for the purpose of confirming ownership, it does not record existing liens; nor does the system record ownership and liens on movable property. Consequently, creditors risk lending on collateral that debtors may not actually own or which may have already been offered as security for other debts.

7.2 Intellectual Property Rights

Mongolia supports intellectual property rights (IPR) in general. A member of the World Intellectual Property Organization (WIPO), Mongolia has signed and ratified most relevant treaties and conventions, including the World Trade Organization Agreement on Trade Related Aspects of Intellectual Property Rights (WTO TRIPS). However, Mongolia's parliament has yet to ratify the WIPO Internet treaties. (WIPO: http://www.wipo.int/directory/en/ .) Despite this, the Mongolian government and its intellectual property rights enforcer, the Intellectual Property Office of Mongolia (IPOM),

make a good faith effort to comply with these agreements. (See IPOM at http://www.ipom.mn/ .)

Under TRIPS and Mongolian law, the Mongolian Customs Authority (MCA) and the National Police (NP) also have an obligation to protect IPR. MCA can seize shipments at the border. The NP has the exclusive power to conduct criminal investigations and bring criminal charges against IPR pirates. The IPOM has the administrative authority to investigate and seize pirated goods administratively. Of these three, the IPOM makes the most consistent efforts to fulfill Mongolia's treaty commitments.

Problems stem from ignorance of the importance of intellectual property to Mongolia and of the obligations imposed by TRIPS on member states. Customs still hesitates to seize shipments, saying their statutory mandate bars them from seizing fake goods, but Mongolian statutory and constitutional laws clearly recognize that international treaty obligations in this area take precedence over local statutes and regulations. A clear legal basis exists for Customs to act, which has been recognized by elements of the Mongolian Judiciary, the Parliament, and the IPOM. Customs officers may occasionally seize fake products, but it seems that Mongolian customs law will have to be brought into formal compliance with TRIPS before Customs will routinely fulfill its obligations. The ECU has also hesitated to investigate and prosecute IPR cases, deferring to the IPOM.

The IPOM generally has an excellent record of protecting American trademarks, copyrights, and patents; however, tight resources limit the IPOM's ability to act. In most cases, when the U.S. Embassy in Ulaanbaatar conveys a complaint from a rights holder to the IPOM, it quickly investigates the complaint. If it judges that an abuse has occurred, it will (and has in every case, so far) seize the pirated products, under administrative powers granted in Mongolian law.

We note two areas where enforcement lags. Legitimate software products remain rare in Mongolia, with the IPOM estimating that 95% of the market uses pirated software. The IPOM enforces the law where it can but the scale of the problem dwarfs its capacity to deal with it. Pirated optical media are also readily available and subject to spotty anti-piracy enforcement. The growth of online downloads of pirated optical media by individuals and local Mongolian TV stations effectively eclipsed local production and imports of fake CD's, videos, or DVD's. The IPOM acknowledges that most of these local public and privately held TV stations, some 184 at latest count, regularly broadcast pirated materials; however, the IPOM hesitates to move on these broadcasters, most of which are connected to major government or political figures. The IPOM will act on specific complaints, but will rarely initiate action.

Resources for Rights Holders:

Contact at the U.S. Embassy in Ulaanbaatar: http://mongolia.usembassy.gov/

NAME: Economic and Commercial Section

TELEPHONE NUMBER: +976-7007-6001

EMAIL ADDRESS: Ulaanbaatar-Econ-Comm@state.gov

Mongolia Resources

For additional resources on protecting IPR in Mongolia, reach out to the American Chamber of Commerce in Mongolia at http://amcham.mn/ . The U.S. Embassy also provides a list of attorneys at http://mongolia.usembassy.gov/lawyer_list.html .

8. TRANSPARENCY OF REGULATORY SYSTEM

System Lacks Transparency

Generally, lack of laws and regulations is not Mongolia's problem; rather, legislators and government officials lack knowledge on what foreign and domestic investors need from the state to invest securely. Compounding this ignorance, these same officials frequently decline to consult meaningfully with those affected by legislative and regulatory acts. Corruption aside, the fact that laws and regulations change with little consultation creates chaos for all parties.

On paper the Mongolian legislative and regulatory process appears transparent, but investors and other observers report a gap between the theory of transparency inherent in Mongolian law and the actual practices of officials and legislators.

In 2011, Parliament passed the Law on Information Transparency and the Right to Information (LIT). LIT sets out which government, legislative, and non-governmental organizations must provide information to the public—both in terms of what information should be regularly disseminated and how these respective organizations should respond to requests for information by citizens and legal entities residing in Mongolia. LIT requires state policies, some legislative acts, and administrative decisions to be posted on the appropriate government websites in understandable language for no less than 30 days for comment and review. Comments may be incorporated in proposals if deemed appropriate. In addition, government entities must post public hiring processes, concessions, procurement, and budget and finance information. LIT specifically exempts the armed forces, the border protection and internal troops, and intelligence organizations from its provisions. Ongoing citizen complaints and petitions are not subject to LIT's provisions; nor does the law apply to intellectual property information, corporate or business information, or personal information.

In response to LIT, the Cabinet of Ministers requires ministries to post proposed regulatory changes on ministerial websites for comment and review at least thirty (30) days before approval. As with LML, the Cabinet decree does not specify a standard process for collecting and acting upon public comment and review.

In addition to LIT, the Law on Making Laws (LML) requires (or requests in the case of parliament) those who draft and submit laws to parliament—termed lawmakers in the LML—must subject their legislative acts to comment and review. Specifically, the President and the ministries must submit their legislative drafts for review and comment. Parliament, however, may solicit comment and review but is not required to do so. However, the LML does not specify who is to be consulted; how they are to be consulted; when or where; and what is to be done with comments and critiques of a given piece of legislation.

Such nods to transparency notwithstanding, investors find that the current process allows no statutory, systematic, and transparent review of legislation and regulations by stakeholders. Most ministerial initiatives still seem to go unpublished until the draft passes out of a given ministry to the full Cabinet. Typically, the full Cabinet discusses and passes bills on to Parliament, without public input or consultation. Parliament itself neither issues a formal calendar nor routinely announces or opens its standing committees or full chamber hearings to the public. While Parliament at the beginning of each session announces a list of bills to be considered during the session, this list is very general and often amended. New legislation is commonly introduced, discussed, and passed without public announcement or consideration. Members of the public requesting information on the voting record of their representative are often told that such information is not publicly available.

Informal Legislative and Regulatory Processes that Impede FDI

While foreign investors are most often invited by government agencies, NGOs, and industry associations to consult on an *ad hoc* basis on proposed laws and regulations affecting investments, they are strongly discouraged from taking any public role in such consultations. While this approach may avoid some of the controversies attending public comment by foreign investors, it also makes delivery of their advice less transparent and effectively unofficial, allowing the advice to be ignored by officials and Mongolian NGO's and industry associations.

United States and Mongolia Sign Bilateral Transparency Agreement in 2013

On September 24, 2013, the United States of America and Mongolia signed an Agreement on Transparency in Matters Related to International Trade and Investment (TA). The agreement, signed by United States Trade Representative Michael Froman and Mongolian Foreign Minister Luvsanvandan Bold, marks an important step in developing and broadening the economic relationship between Mongolia and the United States. The goal of the Transparency Agreement is to make it easier for American and Mongolian firms to do business. The agreement covers transparency in the formation of trade-related laws and regulations, the conduct of fair administrative proceedings, and measures to address bribery and corruption. In addition, it provides for commercial laws and regulations to be published in English, making it easier for international investors to operate in Mongolia.

Disappointingly, the TA remains unratified by the Mongolian parliament. U.S. and other foreign and domestic investors have explicitly stated that they see ratification of the TA as an unambiguous signal to businesses that Mongolia seeks to restore confidence in the statutory and regulatory processes affecting commerce and trade in Mongolia.

9. EFFICIENT CAPITAL MARKETS AND PORTFOLIO INVESTMENT

9.1 Money and Banking System

Mongolia is developing the experience and expertise needed to sustain portfolio investments and active capital markets. In 2013 parliament passed the Revised Securities Market Law (RSML), which most investors believe creates a sufficient regulatory apparatus for these activities. The government of Mongolia (GOM) imposes

few restrictions on the flow of capital in any of its markets. Multilateral institutions, particularly the International Monetary Fund (IMF), have typically found the regime too loose, especially in the crucial banking sector. (For more on the RSML see Chapter 1.)

Although the government has clear rules about capital reserve requirements, loan practices, and banking management practices, the Bank of Mongolia (BOM), Mongolia's central bank, has historically resisted restraining credit flows and interfering with operations at Mongolia's commercial banks, even when the need to intervene has been apparent. In 2013 and continuing through the first half of 2014, the BOM has embarked on a series of programs—a primarily a price stabilization program and a mortgage program—that have pumped trillions of Tugriks (MNT) into the economy leading to excessive liquidity, which the World Bank and the IMF say are among the leading, if not exclusive causes, for the 36% depreciation of MNT versus the U.S. dollar over the last two years, as well as gradual increasing in inflation from single digits through 2013 to currently 13%.

Banking Sector Concerns

Weakness in Mongolia's banking sector concerns all players, including the International Monetary Fund (IMF: http://www.imf.org). The system has been through massive changes since the socialist era, during which the banking system was divided into several different units. This early system failed through mismanagement and commercial naivety in the mid-90s, but over the last decade has become more sophisticated and somewhat better managed. As of February 2014, the combined assets of Mongolia's current 12 commercial banks add up to around US $11.5 billion. (For more details on Mongolia's banking sector, go to the Bank of Mongolia:

http://www.mongolbank.mn/eng/default.aspx .)

Mongolia has two large, generally well-regarded banks owned by both Mongolian and foreign interests. These two banks—Trade and Development Bank and Khan Bank—collectively hold approximately 50% ($6.0 billion) of all banking assets. They apparently follow international standards for prudent capital reserve requirements, have conservative lending policies, up-to-date banking technology, seem generally well-managed, and are open to foreigners opening bank accounts under the same terms as Mongolian nationals. If a storm descends again on Mongolia's banking sector, these banks appear able to weather it.

From 1999 through late 2008, BOM consistently refused to close any commercial bank for insolvency or malpractice. In late 2008, Mongol Bank took Mongolia's fourth largest bank into receivership. Most deposits were guaranteed and their depositors paid out at a cost of around US$150 million -- not an inconsequential sum in an economy then hovering at US$5 billion per annum GDP. In 2009, Mongolia's fifth largest bank went into receivership, and in 2010 two other mid-sized banks were merged; and in 2013, the BOM shut down Savings Bank for insolvency, merging it with the state-owned National Bank.

While the BOM and Mongolia's financial system have endured these chronic insolvencies, most observers note that each of these insolvent banks had shown clear signs of mismanagement, non-performing loans, and ill-liquidity for several years before the BOM moved to safeguard depositors and the financial sector. As with many issues in Mongolia, the problem is not lack of laws or procedures for dealing with troubled banks, which are sufficient to regulate the sector; but rather, the apparent lack of will and

capacity of the regulator, the BOM, to supervise and execute mandated functions, particularly in regard to prudential capital reserve requirements, bank management and corporate governance, and increasing portfolios of non-performing loans.

10. COMPETITION FROM STATE-OWNED ENTERPRISES IN THE MINING & ENERGY AND AUTOMOTIVE & GROUND TRANSPORTATION SECTORS

10.1 OECD Guidelines on Corporate Governance of SOEs

Mongolia has State-owned Enterprises (SOEs) in, among other areas, energy production, mining, and transport. Investors have been allowed to conduct activities in these sectors, although in some cases an opaque regulatory framework limits both competition and investor penetration. Indeed, both foreign and domestic private investors believe that the current regime favors Mongolian SOEs over private enterprises. However, in early 2014 President of Mongolia Ts. Elbegdorj articulated a policy to privatize SOE's as a shift toward *smarter government;* however, the practical steps remain to be developed. To our knowledge Mongolia does not encourage SOEs to adhere to OECD Corporate Governance Guidelines for SOEs: www.oecd.org/daf/ca/oecdguidelinesoncorporategovernanceofstate-ownedenterprises.htm)

Corporate Governance of Mongolian SOEs

Until recently, the formally independent State Property Committee (SPC) controlled almost all Mongolian SOEs (excluding Oyu Tolgoi, Tavan Tolgoi, and uranium properties and railroads). However, the 2012 government re-organization saw the SPC become a department of the Ministry of Industry and Agriculture. The implications of this change for state management of its portfolio remain unclear, because of inter-ministerial infighting. In any case, when investing with Mongolian SOEs, investors are strongly advised to contact all relevant government entities to learn what their respective interests are and what administrative and management authority they actually have.

All SOEs are technically required to submit to the same international best practices on disclosure, accounting, and reporting as imposed on private companies. When the SOEs seek international investment and financing, they tend to follow these rules. However, because international best practices are not institutionalized in, and are sometimes at odds with, Mongolian law, many SOEs tend to follow existing Mongolian rules by default. At the same time, foreign-invested firms follow the international rules, causing inconsistencies in corporate governance, management, disclosure, and accounting.

Competition from the State-Owned Sector

Mongolia passed and implemented a competition law applying to foreign, domestic, and state-owned entities active in Mongolia. As a practical matter, competition between state-owned and private businesses had been declining for the simple reason that many parastatals had been privatized. Exceptions include the state-owned power and telecom industries, a state-owned airline, the state-owned rail system (half-owned by Russia), several coal mines, and a large copper mining and concentration facility (also half-owned by Russia).

Currently, firms from Mongolia, China, Japan, Europe, Canada, and the U.S. are actively seeking opportunities for renewable and traditional power generation in Mongolia. However, few want to invest in the power generation field until the regulatory and statutory framework for private power generation firms up and tariffs are set at commercial rates.

Regarding its railway sector, Mongolia has no plans to privatize its existing railroad jointly held with the government of Russia, but current law does allow private firms to build, operate, and transfer new railroads to the state. Under this law several private mining companies have proposed rail links, and obtained licenses to construct these new lines from their respective coal mines to the Chinese border or to the currently operating spur of the Trans-Siberian Railroad.

Mongolia's rail policy and approach continue to be hotly debated in parliament. At the moment, the plan requires that railroads linking key coal deposits in the South Gobi desert region must first link those deposits to Russia's Pacific ports before linking with Chinese markets. Further, these projects may use international gauge used in China only after the links with Russia are completed, using Russian gauge. The GOM argues that this approach will keep Mongolia from being dependent on one market for its mining products, namely China. As construction on the Russian lines has stalled, there has been some progress on the China lines, with the road bed in the process of being laid.

Some observers question the rationale and sequencing of government plans. In their collective opinion, the Chinese market, the largest and most lucrative, should be developed first, followed by (or parallel with) diversification strategies. They see few commercial and economic benefits from the current GOM approach.

Government Re-enters the Mining Business

Although the trend had been for the GOM to extract itself from ownership of firms and other commercial assets, the 2006 Minerals Law of Mongolia and the newer 2009 Nuclear Energy Law keep the state in the mining business. Under both laws, the GOM grants itself the right to acquire equity stakes ranging from 34% up to 100% of certain deposits deemed strategic for the nation. Once acquired, these assets are vested with two state-owned holding companies respectively: Erdenes MGL, for non-uranium mining assets and MonAtom, for uranium resources. State mandates require these companies to use proceeds from their activities to benefit the Mongolian people.

The role of the state as an equity owner, in terms of management of revenues and operation of mines, remains unclear at this point. Many question the GOM's capacity to deal with conflicts of interest arising from its position as both regulator and owner-operator. Specifically, investors worry that the GOM's desire to maximize local procurement, employment, and revenues may comprise the long term commercial viability of mining projects.

Investors also question the GOM's capacity to execute its fiduciary responsibilities as both owner and operator of mines. For example, through the Erdenes MGL Tavan Tolgoi mining operation (EMTT), the GOM received a prepayment of US $250 million prepayment for coal from a Chinese state-owned entity. Rather than allowing EMTT to retain these funds to cover substantial startup costs, the GOM claimed the balance of

the payment, US$200 million, for its Human Development Fund, which has redistributed primarily mining revenues to the Mongolian public in the form of monthly cash payments. Throughout 2012, 2013, and it appears 2014, these and other GOM actions have left EMTT chronically insolvent, thereby crippling operational activities.

Consequently, investors worry that the GOM will divert future revenues gained from mining activities—for example capital raised through initial public offerings from strategic mines—for unrelated expenses. Going forward, the GOM will likely have to provide binding assurances that it can responsibly steward company interests rather than seeing state-owned companies as nothing more than transfer mechanisms for payments to the Mongolian public.

Observers are also concerned that the GOM may waive legal and regulatory requirements for state-owned mining companies that it imposes on all others. These concerns seem borne out by the GOM's treatment of state-owned EMTT. Generally, private mining firms take at least two years to submit and receive approval for relevant environmental and operating permits for coal mines in Mongolia. However, there is no indication that GOM required EMTT's two operating mining projects to follow the statutory or regulatory requirements imposed on other operations. A review of timelines suggests that the normally lengthy and costly approval processes cannot have been followed. This preferential treatment for this marquee SOE creates the appearance that the GOM has one standard for its SOEs and another for foreign-invested and private domestic invested companies; and also the appearance that SOEs receive substantial cost advantages via a more lenient interpretation or outright waiver of the legal requirements.

10.2 Sovereign Wealth Funds

Mongolia's Human Development Fund and Development Bank

In 2008, Parliament established the *Human Development Fund* (HDF), ostensibly Mongolia's first sovereign wealth fund; however, it does not currently function as a sovereign wealth fund. The stated purpose of the law was to fulfill campaign promises to provide every citizen with cash payments in excess of U.S. $1,000 so that the public could benefit from Mongolia's mineral wealth. The HDF is to be funded from the profits, taxes, and royalties generated by the mining industry as a whole, including large, medium and small scale projects. The HDF basically serves as an instrument to distribute mining revenues to the citizens of Mongolia in the form of social benefits: Payments for pension and health insurance premiums; mortgage support and other loan guarantees; and payments for health and education services. The GOM has no plans to use the HDF as a conduit for Mongolian investments abroad or for FDI into Mongolia. In that sense, we find no conflict between the HDF and private sector investment.

In 2011, Parliament created the *Development Bank of Mongolia* (DBM) for the explicit purpose of financing major infrastructure projects and support for export-oriented industries. Early plans were for the Development Bank to invest in cashmere processing, railways, power, and petroleum processing. At this point, the first tranche of sovereign debt, some U.S. $ 600 million, has been disbursed.

Mongolia passed its Fiscal Stability Law (FSL) in 2010 as part of its Stand-By Arrangement with the International Monetary Fund which ended on September 30, 2010. The FSL establishes a stabilization fund that sets aside certain mining revenues in excess of pre-set structural revenue estimates. Savings may then be used during a downturn to finance the budget. Under the FSL, a portion of the savings generated by the Fiscal Stability Fund can be used to finance domestic and foreign investments. For example, the government is allowed to use this money to purchase long term securities offered by the DBM to fund its activities. How the GOM and parliament will divide mining revenues between the HDF and the FSL remains to be determined.

11. CORPORATE SOCIAL RESPONSIBILITY

11.1 OECD Guidelines for Multinational Enterprises

It is early days for corporate social responsibility (CSR) in Mongolia. Most Western companies make good faith efforts to work with local communities. These efforts usually take the form of specific projects aimed at providing missing infrastructure—wells, power supplies, clinics or schools—or support for education such as books and scholarships. The larger Western firms tend to follow accepted international CSR practices and underwrite a full range of CSR activities across Mongolia; however, the smaller ones, lacking sufficient resources, often limit their CSR actions to the locales in which they work. Only the largest Mongolian firms regularly undertake CSR actions, with small- to medium –sized enterprises generally (but not always) hindered by limited resources from underwriting CSR actions. Generally, firms that pursue CSR are perceived favorably, at least within the communities in which they act. Nationally, responses range from praise from politicians to cynical condemnation by certain civil society groups of CSR actions as nothing more than an attempt to "buy" public approval. (For CSR in Mongolia refer to USAID sponsored Business Plus Initiative's web site: http://www.bpi.mn/ . For information on the U.S. government approach to CSR-related issues see U.*S. Government Approach on Business and*

Human Rights: http://www.humanrights.gov/2013/05/01/u-s-government-approach-on-business-and-human-rights/).

Mongolia has not statutory requirement for CSR actions. (Note: CSR is not statutorily required in the United States.) However, the GOM encourages CSR actions, normally using the bully-pulpit to exhort companies to adopt CSR practices, echoing admonitions of local NGOs and international institutions. However, these exhortation are not consistent with the CSR principles set forth in the OECD Guidelines for Multinational Enterprises or the United Nations Guiding Principles on Business and Human Rights (For OECD Guidelines: http://mneguidelines.oecd.org/ncps/ ; for UN Guiding Principles: http://www.ohchr.org/Documents/Publications/GuidingPrinciplesBusinessHR_EN.pdf .

In October 2011, Mongolia's parliament passed the Revised Company Law of Mongolia (RCL). The law concentrates almost exclusively on corporate governance issues and defines new types of corporate structures and does not require companies to adopt CSR practices as part of governance practices. The key features of the Revised Company Law are to broaden the personal liability of governing persons; introduce administrative sanctions for non-compliance and stricter corporate governance rules; and redefine

conflict of interest concepts and disclosure obligations. For more information of the RCL visit the Business Council of Mongolia: http://www.bcmongolia.org/en/laws-of-mongolia .

12. POLITICAL VIOLENCE

Mongolia is both peaceful and stable; political violence is rare. Mongolia has held eleven successful elections presidential and parliamentary elections in the past 17 years, though a brief but violent outbreak of civil unrest followed the disputed parliamentary elections on July 1, 2008. During that unrest, five people were killed and a political party's headquarters was burned. The violence was quickly contained and order restored, and no repeat of civil unrest has occurred since then. Indeed, Mongolia held peaceful presidential elections less than a year later in May 2009, in which the incumbent president was defeated and conceded at noon the next day; power was smoothly transitioned to the winner thereafter. Most recently, Mongolia held a politically robust, successful and peaceful series of elections (parliamentary in June 2012, local in November 2012, and presidential in June 2013), that were generally marked by good voter turnouts, and peacefully conducted campaigns. The Parliamentary elections resulted in a change of government, while the Presidential election resulted in a return of the incumbent to office.

Mongolia has an ethnically homogenous population: 97% of the population is Khalkh Mongol. The largest minority, numbering an estimated 130,000 people, is Kazakh (Muslim), concentrated in the far western part of the country.

A more resource nationalist tone in politics has become evident. Media and observer reports suggest a rising anti-foreigner sentiment among a few elements of the public, mostly based on the idea of wanting Mongolian resources developed in an environmentally sound way by Mongolians for the benefit of Mongolians. This nationalist sentiment has not led to any known incidents of anti-Americanism or politically motivated damage to American projects or installations in at least the last decade. However, there has been a gradual and perceptible level of rising hostility to Chinese and Korean nationals in Mongolia. This hostility has led to some instances of improper seizure of Chinese and Korean property, and in even more limited cases to acts of physical violence against the persons and property of Chinese—and to a lesser extent Korean—nationals resident in Mongolia. There have also been very isolated instances of physical violence directed at European foreigners in Mongolia, though these instances have been very rare and isolated ones.

CORRUPTION

13.1 UN Convention Against Corruption, OECD Convention on Combatting Bribery

Mongolia is a State Party to the United Nations Convention Against Corruption (UNCAC), but not the Convention on Combatting Bribery of Foreign Public Officials in International Business Transactions (the Anti-Bribery Convention). (UNCAC: www.unodc.org/unodc/en/treaties/CAC/signatories.html ; Anti-Bribery Convention:

www.oecd.org/daf/anti-bribery/countryreportsontheimplementationoftheoecdanti-briberyconvention.htm .)

Current Views on Mongolian Corruption

Since 2005, the USAID Mission to Mongolia, in collaboration with USAID/Washington and The Asia Foundation (TAF) has assessed corruption in Mongolia. (For USAID go to www.usaid.gov/mn .) These multiple reviews have found that opportunities for corruption have increased at both the "petty" or administrative and "grand" or elite levels. Both types of corruption should concern Mongolians and investors, but grand corruption should be considered a more serious threat because it solidifies linkages between economic and political power that could negatively affect or ultimately derail or delay democracy and development. Information from the USAID funded surveys are repeated in the U.S. Embassy's annual Mongolian Human Rights Reports (MHHR) and the Investment Climate Statements. For the MHHR go to http://www.state.gov/j/drl/rls/hrrpt/humanrightsreport/index.htm#wrapper .

Current Anti-Corruption Law

In 2006, Parliament passed the Anti-Corruption Law (ACL), a significant milestone in Mongolia's efforts against corruption. In addition the Criminal Code of Mongolia proscribes the acceptance of bribes by officials and provides for fines or imprisonment of up to five years. It also outlaws offering bribes to government officials. The ACL establishes the Independent Agency Against Corruption (IAAC) as the principal agency responsible for investigating corruption cases. The Criminal Police Department, the State Investigation Agency (both under the National Police Agency), and the Special Investigative Unit under the Prosecutor General's Office also investigate various types of corruption cases as well as assist the IAAC. (For a review of the IAAC's activities from its inception through the present see The Asia Foundation Mongolia: http://asiafoundation.org/publications .)

In 2013, the MHRR reported that implementation of the ACL remains inconsistent, allowing corruption to continue at all levels of government. Factors contributing to corruption include conflicts of interest, lack of transparency, lack of access to information, an inadequate civil service system, and weak government control of key institutions.

Of particular concern, members of parliament remain immune from prosecution during their tenure, which has prevented the prosecution of a number of allegations of corruption and, because all but two of 16 ministers are also members of parliament, seriously restricts the scope of corruption investigations more broadly. Corruption-related prosecutions, however, increased during 2013 year, including a number of high-level officials from across the political spectrum, although questions of political motivation remain.

Resources to report corruption:

Contact at Independent Agency Against Corruption (IAAC)

ADDRESS

District 5, Seoul Street 41 Ulaanbaatar, Mongolia 14250

TELEPHONE NUMBER

Telephone: +976-70110251; 976-11-311919 Fax: +976-7011-2458

EMAIL ADDRESS: contact@iaac.mn

Contact at Transparency International Mongolia

NAME: Tur-Od Lkhagvajav , Acting Executive Director

ADDRESS Bayanzurkh District, Mercy Corp Building 2nd Floor, Rooms #206, 207 Peace Avenue 24 Ulaanbaatar, Mongolia

TELEPHONE NUMBER

Telephone: +976 7015 4250 Fax: +976 7015 4250

EMAIL ADDRESS: naranzulb@yahoo.com

U.S. Foreign Corrupt Practices Act and Related Conventions

Corruption, including bribery, raises the costs and risks of doing business. Corruption has a corrosive impact on both market opportunities overseas for U.S. companies and the broader business climate. It also deters international investment, stifles economic growth and development, distorts prices, and undermines the rule of law.

It is important for U.S. companies, irrespective of their size, to assess the business climate in the relevant market in which they will be operating or investing, and to have an effective compliance program or measures to prevent and detect corruption, including foreign bribery. U.S. individuals and firms operating or investing in foreign markets should take the time to become familiar with the relevant anticorruption laws of both the foreign country and the United States in order to properly comply with them, and where appropriate, they should seek the advice of legal counsel.

The U.S. Government seeks to level the global playing field for U.S. businesses by encouraging other countries to take steps to criminalize their own companies' acts of corruption, including bribery of foreign public officials, by requiring them to uphold their obligations under relevant international conventions. A U. S. firm that believes a competitor is seeking to use bribery of a foreign public official to secure a contract should bring this to the attention of appropriate U.S. agencies, as noted below.

U.S. Foreign Corrupt Practices Act: In 1977, the United States enacted the Foreign Corrupt Practices Act (FCPA), which makes it unlawful for a U.S. person, and certain foreign issuers of securities, to make a corrupt payment to foreign public officials for the purpose of obtaining or retaining business for or with, or directing business to, any person. The FCPA also applies to foreign firms and persons who take any act in furtherance of such a corrupt payment while in the United States. For more detailed information on the FCPA, see the FCPA Lay-Person's Guide at: http://www.justice.gov/criminal/fraud/

Other Instruments: It is U.S. Government policy to promote good governance, including host country implementation and enforcement of anti-corruption laws and policies pursuant to their obligations under international agreements. Since enactment of the FCPA, the United States has been instrumental to the expansion of the international framework to fight corruption. Several significant components of this framework are the OECD Convention on Combating Bribery of Foreign Public Officials in International Business Transactions (OECD Antibribery Convention), the United Nations Convention against Corruption (UN Convention), the Inter-American Convention against Corruption (OAS Convention), the Council of Europe Criminal and Civil Law Conventions, and a growing list of U.S. free trade agreements. This country is party to [add instrument to which this country is party], but generally all countries prohibit the bribery and solicitation of their public officials.

OECD Antibribery Convention: The OECD Antibribery Convention entered into force in February 1999. As of March 2009, there are 38 parties to the Convention including the United States (see http://www.oecd.org/dataoecd/59/13/40272933.pdf). Major exporters China, India, and Russia are not parties, although the U.S. Government strongly endorses their eventual accession to the Convention. The Convention obligates the Parties to criminalize bribery of foreign public officials in the conduct of international business. The United States meets its international obligations under the OECD Antibribery Convention through the U.S. FCPA. [Insert information as to whether your country is a party to the OECD Convention.]

UN Convention: The UN Anticorruption Convention entered into force on December 14, 2005, and there are 158 parties to it as of November 2011 (see http://www.unodc.org/unodc/en/treaties/CAC/signatories.html). The UN Convention is the first global comprehensive international anticorruption agreement. The UN Convention requires countries to establish criminal and other offences to cover a wide range of acts of corruption. The UN Convention goes beyond previous anticorruption instruments, covering a broad range of issues ranging from basic forms of corruption such as bribery and solicitation, embezzlement, trading in influence to the concealment and laundering of the proceeds of corruption. The Convention contains transnational business bribery provisions that are functionally similar to those in the OECD Antibribery Convention and contains provisions on private sector auditing and books and records requirements. Other provisions address matters such as prevention, international cooperation, and asset recovery. [Insert information as to whether your country is a party to the UN Convention.]

OAS Convention: In 1996, the Member States of the Organization of American States (OAS) adopted the first international anticorruption legal instrument, the Inter-American Convention against Corruption (OAS Convention), which entered into force in March

1997. The OAS Convention, among other things, establishes a set of preventive measures against corruption, provides for the criminalization of certain acts of corruption, including transnational bribery and illicit enrichment, and contains a series of provisions to strengthen the cooperation between its States Parties in areas such as mutual legal assistance and technical cooperation. As of December 2009, the OAS Convention has 34 parties (see http://www.oas.org/juridico/english/Sigs/b-58.html) [Insert information as to whether your country is a party to the OAS Convention.]

Council of Europe Criminal Law and Civil Law Conventions: Many European countries are parties to either the Council of Europe (CoE) Criminal Law Convention on Corruption, the Civil Law Convention, or both. The Criminal Law Convention requires criminalization of a wide range of national and transnational conduct, including bribery, money-laundering, and account offenses. It also incorporates provisions on liability of legal persons and witness protection. The Civil Law Convention includes provisions on compensation for damage relating to corrupt acts, whistleblower protection, and validity of contracts, inter alia. The Group of States against Corruption (GRECO) was established in 1999 by the CoE to monitor compliance with these and related anti-corruption standards. Currently, GRECO comprises 49 member States (48 European countries and the United States). As of December 2011, the Criminal Law Convention has 43 parties and the Civil Law Convention has 34 (see www.coe.int/greco.) [Insert information as to whether your country is a party to the Council of Europe Conventions.]

Free Trade Agreements: While it is U.S. Government policy to include anticorruption provisions in free trade agreements (FTAs) that it negotiates with its trading partners, the anticorruption provisions have evolved over time. The most recent FTAs negotiated now require trading partners to criminalize "active bribery" of public officials (offering bribes to any public official must be made a criminal offense, both domestically and trans-nationally) as well as domestic "passive bribery" (solicitation of a bribe by a domestic official). All U.S. FTAs may be found at the U.S. Trade Representative Website: http://www.ustr.gov/trade-agreements/free-trade-agreements . [Insert information as to whether your country has an FTA with the United States: Country [X] has a free trade agreement (FTA) in place with the United States, the [name of FTA], which came into force. Consult USTR Website for date: http://www.ustr.gov/trade-agreements/free-trade-agreements.]

Local Laws: U.S. firms should familiarize themselves with local anticorruption laws, and, where appropriate, seek legal counsel. While the U.S. Department of Commerce cannot provide legal advice on local laws, the Department's U.S. and Foreign Commercial Service can provide assistance with navigating the host country's legal system and obtaining a list of local legal counsel.

Assistance for U.S. Businesses: The U.S. Department of Commerce offers several services to aid U.S. businesses seeking to address business-related corruption issues. For example, the U.S. and Foreign Commercial Service can provide services that may assist U.S. companies in conducting their due diligence as part of the company's overarching compliance program when choosing business partners or agents overseas. The U.S. Foreign and Commercial Service can be reached directly through its offices in every major U.S. and foreign city, or through its Website at www.trade.gov/cs .

The Departments of Commerce and State provide worldwide support for qualified U.S. companies bidding on foreign government contracts through the Commerce

Department's Advocacy Center and State's Office of Commercial and Business Affairs. Problems, including alleged corruption by foreign governments or competitors, encountered by U.S. companies in seeking such foreign business opportunities can be brought to the attention of appropriate U.S. government officials, including local embassy personnel and through the Department of Commerce Trade Compliance Center "Report A Trade Barrier" Website at tcc.export.gov/Report_a_Barrier/index.asp .

Guidance on the U.S. FCPA: The Department of Justice's (DOJ) FCPA Opinion Procedure enables U.S. firms and individuals to request a statement of the Justice Department's present enforcement intentions under the anti-bribery provisions of the FCPA regarding any proposed business conduct. The details of the opinion procedure are available on DOJ's Fraud Section

Website at www.justice.gov/criminal/fraud/fcpa . Although the Department of Commerce has no enforcement role with respect to the FCPA, it supplies general guidance to U.S. exporters who have questions about the FCPA and about international developments concerning the FCPA. For further information, see the Office of the Chief Counsel for International Counsel, U.S. Department of Commerce, Website, at http://www.ogc.doc.gov/trans_anti_bribery.html . More general information on the FCPA is available at the Websites listed below.

Exporters and investors should be aware that generally all countries prohibit the bribery of their public officials, and prohibit their officials from soliciting bribes under domestic laws. Most countries are required to criminalize such bribery and other acts of corruption by virtue of being parties to various international conventions discussed above.

POST INPUT: Public sector corruption, including bribery of public officials, [remains a major/minor challenge for U.S. firms operating in xxx xxx. Insert country specific corruption climate, enforcement, commitment and information about relevant anticorruption legislation.

Anti-Corruption Resources

Some useful resources for individuals and companies regarding combating corruption in global markets include the following:

* Information about the U.S. Foreign Corrupt Practices Act (FCPA), including a "Lay-Person's Guide to the FCPA" is available at the U.S. Department of Justice's Website at: http://www.justice.gov/criminal/fraud/fcpa .

* Information about the OECD Antibribery Convention including links to national implementing legislation and country monitoring reports is available at: http://www.oecd.org/department/0,3355,en_2649_34859_1_1_1_1_1,00.html . See also new Antibribery Recommendation and Good Practice Guidance Annex for companies: http://www.oecd.org/dataoecd/11/40/44176910.pdf .

* General information about anticorruption initiatives, such as the OECD Convention and the FCPA, including translations of the statute into several languages, is available at the Department of Commerce Office of the Chief Counsel for International Commerce Website: http://www.ogc.doc.gov/trans_anti_bribery.html .

* Transparency International (TI) publishes an annual Corruption Perceptions Index (CPI). The CPI measures the perceived level of public-sector corruption in 180 countries and territories around the world. The CPI is available at: http://www.transparency.org/policy_research/surveys_indices/cpi/2009 . TI also publishes an annual *Global Corruption Report* which provides a systematic evaluation of the state of corruption around the world. It includes an in-depth analysis of a focal theme, a series of country reports that document major corruption related events and developments from all continents and an overview of the latest research findings on anti-corruption diagnostics and tools. See http://www.transparency.org/publications/gcr .

* The World Bank Institute publishes Worldwide Governance Indicators (WGI). These indicators assess six dimensions of governance in 213 countries, including Voice and Accountability, Political Stability and Absence of Violence, Government Effectiveness, Regulatory Quality, Rule of Law and Control of Corruption. See http:// info.worldbank.org/governance/wgi/index.asp . The World Bank Business Environment

and Enterprise Performance Surveys may also be of interest and are available at: http://data.worldbank.org/data-catalog/BEEPS .

* The World Economic Forum publishes the *Global Enabling Trade Report*, which presents the rankings of the Enabling Trade Index, and includes an assessment of the transparency of border administration (focused on bribe payments and corruption) and a separate segment on corruption and the regulatory environment. See http://www.weforum.org/s?s=global+enabling+trade+report .

* Additional country information related to corruption can be found in the U.S. State Department's annual *Human Rights Report* available at http://www.state.gov/g/drl/rls/hrrpt/ .

* Global Integrity, a nonprofit organization, publishes its annual *Global Integrity Report*, which provides indicators for 106 countries with respect to governance and anti-corruption. The report highlights the strengths and weaknesses of national level anti-corruption systems. The report is available at: http://report.globalintegrity.org/ .

BILATERAL INVESTMENT AGREEMENTS

14.1 Bilateral Taxation Treaties

(UNCTD: http://www.unctad.org/sections/dite_pcbb/docs/bits_mongolia.pdf)

Reporter	Partner	Date of Signature	Entry in to force
Mongolia	Austria	19-May-01	1-May-02
	Belarus	28-May-01	1-Dec-01
	Belgium/Luxembourg	3-Mar-92	15-Apr-04
	Bulgaria	6-Jun-00	------------
	China	25-Aug-91	1-Nov-93
	Croatia	8-Aug-06	------------
	Cuba	26-March-99	-----------
	Czech Republic	13-Feb-98	5-Jul-99
	Denmark	13-Mar-95	2-Apr-96
	Egypt	27-Apr-04	25-Jan-05
	Finland	15-May-07	------------
	France	8-Nov-91	22-Dec-93
	Germany	26-Jun-91	23-Jun-96
	Hungary	13-Sep-94	29-Aug-95
	India	3-Jan-01	29-Apr-02
	Indonesia	4-Mar-97	13-Apr-99
	Israel	25-Nov-03	2-Sep-04
	Italy	15-Jan-93	1-Sep-95
	Japan	15-Feb-01	24-Mar-02
	Kazakhstan	2-Dec-94	3-Mar-95
	DPR of Korea	10-Nov-03	-----------
	Republic of Korea	28-Mar-91	30-Apr-91
	Kuwait	15-Mar-98	1-May-00

Kyrgyzstan	5-Dec-99	-----------
Lao People's DR	3-Mar-94	29-Dec-94
Lithuania	27-Jun-03	3-May-04
Malaysia	27-Jul-95	14-Jan-96
Netherlands	9-Mar-95	1-Jun-96
Philippines	1-Sep-00	1-Nov-01
Poland	8-Nov-95	26-Mar-96
Qatar	29-Nov-07	------------
Romania	6-Nov-95	15-Aug-96
Russian Federation	29-Nov-95	------------
Singapore	24-Jul-95	14-Jan-96
Sweden	20-Oct-03	1-Jun-04
Switzerland	29-Jan-97	9-Sep-99
Tajikistan	20-Mar-09	16-Sep-09
Turkey	16-Mar-98	22-May-00
Ukraine	5-Nov-92	5-Nov-92
UAE	21-Feb-01	-------------
United Kingdom	4-Oct-91	4-Oct-91
United States	6-Oct-94	4-Jan-97
Vietnam	17-Apr-00	13-Dec-01

Although Mongolia and the United States have no bi-lateral tax or free-trade agreements, the two have signed and ratified a Bi-Lateral Investment Treaty. For a copy of the treaty go to http://2001-2009.state.gov/documents/organization/43579.pdf .

15. OPIC AND OTHER INVESTMENT INSURANCE PROGRAMS

The U.S. government's Overseas Private Investment Corporation (OPIC: (www.opic.gov) offers loans and political risk insurance to American investors involved in most sectors of the Mongolian economy.

In addition, there is an Investment Incentive Agreement in force between the United States and Mongolia that requires the GOM to extend national treatment to OPIC financed projects in Mongolia. For example, under this agreement mining licenses of

firms receiving an OPIC loan may be pledged as collateral to OPIC, a right not normally bestowed on foreign financial entities.

The U.S. Export-Import Bank (EXIM: www.exim.gov) offers programs in Mongolia for short-, medium-, and long-term transactions in the public sector and for short- and medium-term transactions in the private sector.

Mongolia is a member of the Multilateral Investment Guarantee Agency (MIGA: www.miga.org).

16. LABOR

The Mongolian labor pool is generally educated, young, and adaptable, but shortages exist in most professional categories requiring advanced degrees or vocational training. These shortages include all types of engineers and professional trades in the construction field. (For more on labor needs see: http://www.mca.mn/document/LMSReportMNG.pdf.) Unskilled labor is sufficiently available. Foreign-invested companies deal with these shortages by providing in-country training to their staffs, raising salaries to retain employees, or hiring expatriate workers to provide skills and expertise unavailable in Mongolia.

Mongolian labor laws are not particularly restrictive. Investors can locate and hire workers without using hiring agencies—as long as hiring practices are consistent with the Mongolian Labor Law. However, Mongolian law requires companies to employ Mongolian workers in all labor categories whenever a Mongolian can perform the task as well as a foreigner. This law generally applies to unskilled labor categories and not areas where a high degree of technical expertise is required but does not exist in Mongolia. The law does provide an escape hatch for employers. Should an employer seek to hire a non-Mongolian laborer and cannot obtain a waiver from the Ministry of Labor for that employee, the employer can pay a monthly waiver fee. Depending on a project's importance, the Ministry of Labor can exempt employers from 50% of the waiver fees per worker. However, employers report difficulty in obtaining waivers, in part because of public concerns that foreign and domestic companies refuse to hire Mongolians at an *appropriate level*.

The labor law, including related regulations and statutory instruments, entitles workers to form or join independent unions and professional organizations of their choosing without previous authorization or excessive requirements and protects the rights to strike and to collective bargaining. Nevertheless, some legal provisions restrict these rights for groups such as foreign workers, public servants, and workers without formal employment contracts. The law bars certain public servants from striking, although all groups have the right to organize. The law protects the right of workers to participate in trade union activities without discrimination, and the government has protected this right in general. The law provides for reinstatement of workers fired for union activity.

The law on collective bargaining regulates relations among employers, employees, trade unions, and the government. Wages and other conditions of employment are set between public or private employers and employees, with trade union input sometimes. Laws protecting the right to collective bargaining and freedom of association generally were enforced. The tripartite Labor Dispute Settlement Committee resolved the majority of disputes between workers and management. Cases that could not be resolved at the Labor Dispute Settlement Committee were referred to the courts. (For Mongolian labor laws' relation to union activity refer to Mongolia Country Reports on Human Rights Practices
http://www.state.gov/j/drl/rls/hrrpt/humanrightsreport/index.htm#wrapper .

ILO conventions (http://www.ilo.org):

Convention	Ratification date	Status
C29 Forced Labor Convention, 1930	15:03:2005	ratified
C59 Minimum Age (Industry) Convention (Revised), 1937	03:06:1969	denounced on 16:12:2002
C87 Freedom of Association and Protection of the Right to Organize Convention, 1948	03:06:1969	ratified
C98 Right to Organize and Collective Bargaining Convention, 1949	03:06:1969	ratified
C100 Equal Remuneration Convention, 1951	03:06:1969	ratified
C103 Maternity Protection Convention (Revised), 1952	03:06:1969	ratified
C105 Abolition of Forced Labor Convention, 1957	15:03:2005	ratified

C111 Discrimination (Employment and Occupation) Convention, 1958	03:06:1969	ratified
C122 Employment Policy Convention, 1964	24:11:1976	ratified
C123 Minimum Age (Underground Work) Convention, 1965	03:12:1981	ratified
C135 Workers' Representatives Convention, 1971	08:10:1996	ratified
C138 Minimum Age Convention, 1973	16:12:2002	ratified
C144 Tripartite Consultation (International Labor Standards) Convention, 1976	10:08:1998	ratified
C155 Occupational Safety and Health Convention, 1981	03:02:1998	ratified
C159 Vocational Rehabilitation and Employment	03:02:1998	ratified

(Disabled Persons) Convention, 1983

C182 Worst Forms of Child Labor Convention, 1999 26:02:2001 Ratified

17. FOREIGN-TRADE ZONES/FREE PORTS

The Mongolian government launched its free trade zone (FTZ) program in 2004. Two FTZ areas are located along the Mongolia spur of the trans-Siberian highway: one in the north at the Russia-Mongolia border town of Altanbulag; the other in the south at the Chinese-Mongolia border at the town of Zamyn-Uud. Both FTZs are relatively inactive, with development pending at either site. A third FTZ is located at the port of entry of Tsagaan Nuur in the far western province of Bayan Olgii.

In April 2004, the USAID sponsored Economic Policy Reform and Competitiveness Project expressed the following concerns about Mongolia's FTZ Program, which remains valid in 2014. First, benchmarking of Mongolia's FTZ Program against current successful international practices shows deficiencies in the legal and regulatory framework as well as in the process being followed to establish FTZs in the country.

Second, FTZ's lack of implementing regulations required to implement key international best practices. Third, a process of due diligence, including a cost-benefit analysis, has never been completed for the FTZs. Fourth, sufficient funding has never been mobilized for on-site infrastructure requirements for the three FTZ sites. Finally, deviations from international best practices in the process of implementing FTZs repeats mistakes made in other countries and may lead to "hidden costs" or the provision of subsidies that the government of Mongolia did not foresee or which will have been granted at the expense of higher priorities.

18. FOREIGN DIRECT INVESTMENT STATISTICS

The Invest Mongolia Agency (IMA), the successor to the Foreign Investment Registration and Review Department of the Ministry of Economic Development (IMA), collects and disseminates data for tracking foreign direct investment (FDI) in Mongolia, but the IMA's data has limitations. (Invest Mongolia Agency: www.investmongolia.com)

The most recent data has been collected under the recently passed Investment Law of Mongolia (IL). The law requires all foreign investors to turn in their certificates in calendar year 2014 for new certificates and may lead to different ways to account for FDI in Mongolia, according to the IMA. For example, the IMA has not clarified if the new statistics will reflect the cumulative investment from past years, or will allow the investors to reflect only the minimum amount of $100,000 USD required under the IL for foreign direct investors.

In addition many foreign firms provide IMA with incomplete data on their annual investment amounts. IMA's pre-2014 data registration regime requires companies to document business plans and total FDI for the coming year. IMA uses these reports to determine FDI for the year. However, concerns in the business community that IMA cannot secure proprietary and confidential business information means that many firms withhold data on their activities.

Mongolia suffers from promised investment that does not materialize or which comes in at a lower level than originally stated. IMA does not update reports to account for these or other changes to investments during the year.

Some investors claim certain jurisdictions as tax homes to minimize taxes, a fact not conveyed by IMA's data. Consequently, this data suggests that much of Mongolia's investment originates from such places as the British Virgin Islands, the Netherlands, or Singapore, when, in fact, the investment comes from Canada, the United States, Australia or other jurisdictions.

Data not Available on Mongolian Investment Abroad

To our knowledge neither the IMA nor any other Mongolian agency tracks Mongolia's direct investment abroad.

TABLE(S) 1: Mongolian Investment Statistics (All statistics in Tables 1a to 1h are from the

Invest Mongolia Agency: www.investmongolia.com)

A. TRADE TURNOVER (USD MLN.)

Year	Total Turnover	Percent comp.	Exports	Percent comp.	Imports	Percentage comp.	Balance
2000	1,150	119%	536	118%	615	120%	-79
2001	1,159	101.%	513	97%	638	104%	-116
2002	1,215	105%	524	101%	691	108%	-166
2003	1,417	117%	616	116%	801	116%	-185
2004	1,891	133%	870	141%	1,021	128%	-152
2005	2,249	119%	1,065	122%	1,184	116%	-120
2006	3,018	134%	1,529	144%	1,489	126%	39
2007	4,119	136%	1949	126%	2,170	146%	-221
2008	6,155	149%	2,539	130%	3,616	167%	-1077
2009	4,023	65%	1,885	74%	2,138	59%	-253
2010	6,109	152%	2,908	154%	3,200	150%	-292
2011	11,416	187%	4,817	166%	6,598	206%	-1781
2012	11,123	97%	4,385	91%	6,738	102%	-2353
2013	10,627	96%	4,273	97%	6,355	94%	-2,082

B. TOP 10 INVESTOR COUNTRIES (THOUSAND USD)

№	Country	%	Total	1990-2004	2005	2006	2007	2008	2009	2010
1	Netherlands	29.96	4,225,310,12	5,265,58	221,70	475,86	58,50	4,069,20	51,028,60	232,962,1
2	China	26.65	3,757,607,62	441,786,38	227,922,28	172,014,03	339,614,67	497,800,88	613,058,80	176,038,3

3	Luxemburg	8.17	1,151,702,03	2,911,70	1,809,30	10,00	3,118,917	195,80	1,012,65	25
4	UK Virgin Islands	7,87	1,109,543.62	48,394,23	5,033,92	6,111,67	35,449,00	6,157,89	19,305,18	10
5	Singapore	5,14	724,855,27	8,513,28	4,645,78	728,60	700,00	32,339,86	9,359,44	31
6	Canada	3,53	498,056,74	174,206,58	1,542,25	72,180,37	497,15	2,739,57	1,028,00	14
7	South Korea	2,69	379,267,82	85,180,14	19,004,49	16,434,78	22,991,38	41,765,41	31,673,98	38
8	USA	2,19	308,230,57	45,25,48	5,564,06	37,165,78	4,285,67	6,466,89	2,571,52	13
9	Russia	2,11	297,674,26	37,163,16	7,450,14	11,654,52	39,774,38	3,795,42	6,139,20	2,2
10	Australia	1,84	260,026,89	3,730,19	12,066,75	384,40	289,20	3,361,90	516,50	2,2

C. TOP 25 INVESTOR ENTITIES (FDI – 2010)

No	Entity	Equity	Foreign	Domestic	Sectors	Countries
1.	Oyutolgoi	*65,005,920*	*65,005,913*	-	Geological prospecting and exploration	Netherlands-Mongolia
2.	MD Securities	*43,603,000*	*43,500,000*	-	Trade and catering service	Virgin Islands (UK)
3.	MCS mining	*25,100,000*	*25,000,000*	-	Geological prospecting and exploration	Singapore
4.	HSBC	*10,000,000*	*9,990,000*	-	Others	South Korea
5.	Wagner Asia Leasing	*9,890,224*	*9,890,224*	-	Trade and catering service	USA
6.	Seoul Senior Tower	*7,840,000*	*7,140,000*	-	Health and beauty services	South Korea
7.	Khan Bank	*20,599,356*	*7,073,699*	*3,393,576*	Bank and financial services	USA-China /Hong Kong/-Japan-Mongolia
8.	Gyantbaylag	*7,000,000*	*7,000,000*	-	Geological prospecting and exploration	Virgin Islands (UK)
9.	Globalcom	*4,500,000*	*4,500,000*	-	Trade and catering service	Virgin Islands (UK)
10.	Louis Vuitton Mongolia	*6,000,000*	*4,000,000*	-	Trade and catering service	France
	LLC					
11.	Credit Bank	*9,585,108*	*3,900,686*	-	Bank and financial services	Cyprus
12.	MCS Asia Pacific	*15,000,000*	*3,850,000*	*3,150,000*	Production of foods and beverages	Singapore-Mongolia
13.	Shangri-La Ulaanbaatar Hotel	*10,000,000*	*3,820,000*	-	Trade and catering service	Virgin Islands (UK)

14.	EAM Bayan-Ulgii	*3,548,107*	*3,538,107*	-	Geological prospecting and exploration	Canada
15.	Handy Soft Rich	*3,000,000*	*2,900,000*	-	Trade and catering service	South Korea
16.	Tethys Mining	*26,992,495*	*2,793,974*	-	Geological prospecting and exploration	Switzerland
17.	Big Mogul Coal and Energy	*4,627,722*	*2,776,633*	*1,851,089*	Geological prospecting and exploration	Luxemburg-Mongolia
18.	Hong Kong Sunkfa group Mongol	*1,600,000*	*1,600,000*	-	Transportation	China-China /Hong Kong/
19.	EAM Exploration	*1,511,710*	*1,501,710*	-	Geological prospecting and exploration	Canada
20.	Santanmores	*5,300,000*	*1,500,000*	-	Geological prospecting and exploration	South Korea

D. FDI by COUNTRY (THOUSAND USD)

№	Country	%	Total	2009	2010	2011	2012*	2013.10.31*
1	Netherlands	29.96	4,225,310,12	51,028,60	232,962,18	1,816,714,10	1,253,215,65	861,298.74
2	China	26.65	3,757,607,62	613,058,80	176,038,36	1,015,265,04	243,194,70	30,912.48
3	Luxemburg	8.17	1,151,702,03	1,012,65	25,589,47	476,652,07	634,384,11	6,018.01
4	UK Virgin Islands	7,87	1,109,543.62	19,305,18	101,986,27	610,933,11	274,331,09	1,841.28
5	Singapore	5,14	724,855,27	9,359,44	31,075,00	402,738,17	227,281,96	7,473.19
6	Canada	3,53	498,056,74	1,028,00	147,11,12	72,288,16	18,629,50	7,134.04
7	South Korea	2,69	379,267,82	31,673,98	38,763,43	54,972,59	54,025,32	14,456.29
8	USA	2,19	308,230,57	2,571,52	13,911,20	127,238,95	62,592,42	2,708.62
9	Russia	2,11	297,674,26	6,139,20	2,273,18	58,11,87	129,589,99	1,822.40
10	Australia	1,84	260,026,89	516,50	2,273,80	82,453,32	96,479,16	58,471.68
11	China /Hong Kong /	1,62	228,549,21	11,032,44	80,148,35	54,366,84	37,741,42	9,089.96
12	Japan	1,47	207,138,50	5,594,78	7,125,37	21,460,68	34,243,99	12,863.46

13	Bermuda	30,30	6,46		114,455,56	4,387,49	3,560,70	
14	Great Britain	2,429,00	6,057,76	972,15	693,07	17,910,90	46,773,38	700.00
15	Switzerland	366,52	90,00	22,190,40	3,850,22	37,161,16	17,239,55	7,231.27
16	Barbados					30,098,89	12,759,89	41,870.85
17	Cayman Islands		35,069,33	321,45	10,363,06	25,404,54	329,94	
18	Germany	817,49	580,01	13,281,00	932,64	26,631,80	5,683,70	1,463.16
19	France	12,550,00	170,08	2,376,34	4,499,79	15,050,66	13,375,83	682.82

20	Bulgaria	15,00	7,50		50,00	150,00	82,00	
21	Italy	37,50	856,97	340,00	448,00	4,482,74	6,861,29	246.10
22	Vietnam	674,73	1,270,11	442,00	780,00	519,70	431,00	845.29
23	China /Taiwan/	590,80	6,443,49	997,50	161,30	99,74	185,00	
24	Islands of Saint Kitts & Nevis	10,00		173,70	19,529,56	90,00	100,00	
25	Malaysia	60,75	5,340,69	445,12	331,50	2,882,37	1,909,25	426.86
26	Kazakhstan	11,522,22	214,57	1,515,00	418,00	1,195,19	1,986,12	529.00
27	The Bahamas				90,00	10,50	3,65	
28	Portugal							
29	Cyprus	7,091,52	71,00	190,00	4,001,05	100,00	89,87	1,548.72
30	Mauritius					9,950,91	216,77	
31	Ukraine	66,90	45,00	725,63	190,04	502,50	1,319,97	168.00
32	Czech Republic	80,61	2,015,04	80,00	436,00	457,47	1,587,67	313.60
33	Israel	23,70	15,00		193,07	754,66		
34	Turkey	114,30	338,60	514,50	379,00	2,259,35	1,861,46	558.66
35	India	4,925,00	690,00	1,155,00	285,69	75,00	67,50	140.00
36	New Zealand	225,95	1,706,28	580,00	100,00	759,58	249,00	74.00
37	Belgium	134,46	75,00	27,62	100,00	807,43	704,78	

38	Thailand			3,00	108,10	100,00	2,500,00		2,000.00
39	China /Macao/								
40	Spain	20,00	10,00				1,702,82	1,828,78	100.00
41	Lichtenstein								
42	British Man Island					200,00	839,97	1,969,98	
43	Austria	101,87	6,40	191,52		40,50		421,94	184.00
44	Poland	16,00	20,00	10,00	150,00	50,00	319,89	270,00	164.50
45	Lebanon	7,92					333,74	2,113,35	
46	Hungary	54,20	18,00		240,00	408,29	203,40	335,92	
47	Uzbekistan			100,00	756,10	845,00	269,28		100.00
48	Sweden		466,00	30,00	40,10	100,00		1,270.12	100.00
49	Philippines		4,90				90,00	1,868,39	
50	DPRK	22,75	50,00			100,00	159,42	100,00	193.33
51	Samoa							200,00	1,333.49
52	Panama				100,00	130,50	163,50		
53	Syria	15,00		105,00			1,021,03		
54	Slovakia	273,00	50,00					180,00	
55	British Guernsey Island						417,65	849,96	
56	Pakistan	6,00	21,10	80,00		110,00			100.00
57	Belize	175,88			85,00	102,00	199,99	349,97	100.00
58	Kyrgyzstan				120,00	60,00	80,00	190,00	60.00
59	United Arab Emirates						375,49	577,98	
60	Denmark						141,97	540,00	100.00
61	Belarus			56,00		186,06	314,90	250,00	0.90
62	Seychelles Islands		10,00	17,00		43,00	100,00	643,00	

63	Antigua & Barbuda								

64	Malta						252,09	441,00	
65	Bangladesh		10,00		105,00	100,00	200,00	100,00	175.00
66	Iran		2,00			233,00	100,00	200,00	95.00
67	Azerbaijan		20,00			190,00	140,00	100,00	100.00
68	Ireland		9,00		76,54	179,35	213,10		
69	Slovenia						230,99	300,11	
70	Mauritania			30,00	480,00				
71	Anguilla					200,00	200,00		
72	Norway	5,00	6,00	90,00		15,00	89,55	104,98	
73	Indonesia	20,00			84,00		215,95	19,00	
74	Gibraltar					100,00			
75	Yugoslavia								
76	Armenia	6,60		8,55					
77	Romania					100,00			100.00
78	Saudi Arabia								
79	Kuwait						179,96		
80	Estonia							102,00	50.00
81	Cambodia	15,00							
82	Croatia								
83	Finland	7,00		6,50			15,97	83,89	
84	Qatar			10,00	30,00			100,00	
85	Turkmenistan					30,00		100,00	
86	South Africa						126,00		
87	Iraq					100,00			
88	Nepal				30,00				60.00
89	Jordan	3,33							50.00
90	Georgia		5,00		50,00				

91	Argentina		55,00				
92	Greece						
93	Moldavia						
94	Egypt					33,33	
95	Turks and Caicos Islands			27,90			
96	Tajikistan						
97	Sri Lanka	28,00					
98	British Indian Ocean territory						
99	Liberia						
100	Morocco	20,00					

101	Honduras						
102	Serbia Montenegro						
103	Cameroon						
104	Latvia						
105	Marshall Islands						
106	Myanmar						
107	Outlying Islands						
108	Saint Helena						
109	Dominion of Melchizedek						
110	Nigeria						
111	Ethiopia						
112	US Virgin Islands						
	TOTAL	708,922,55	801,158,33	1,025,995,88	4,986,034,12	3,198,731,30	1,076,054.71

*Note: 0.1.2012** - FDI figure as of Q4 of 2012 does not include Balance of payment by Central Bank of Mongolia. (The Bank defines the Balance of payment based on data

from commercial banks). *0.2.* Data on imported goods purchased by foreign investment is not added to above statistics. (Customs General Administration) *0.3.* Investment of the ongoing investment projects is not added to the statistics.

E. FOREIGN INVESTED COMPANIES BY COUNTRY

№	Country	%	Total	1990-2004	2005	2006	2007	2008	2009	2010	2011	2012	2013.10.31
1	China	48,77	6,225	1,534	532	827	876	859	299	376	434	346	142
2	Korea	17.64	2,251	632	203	274	332	302	113	117	122	101	55
3	Russia	6.56	837	433	54	105	72	51	37	17	34	21	13
4	Japan	4,22	539	190	29	56	60	58	35	23	35	39	14
5	USA	2,35	300	98	19	28	27	44	11	14	36	15	8
6	UK Virgin Islands	2.02	258	27	9	12	26	17	23	37	67	38	2
7	Germany	1,59	203	102	10	18	13	13	8	7	9	16	7
8	Singapore	1,49	203	52	9	5	10	21	4	22	31	34	15
9	China /Hong Kong/	1,44	184	54	9	5	10	14	10	27	20	18	17
10	Vietnam	1,28	163	25	14	34	46	21	3	8	3	2	7
11	Great Britain	1,16	148	61	14	12	10	15	4	5	12	7	8
12	Canada	1,00	128	38	8	13	10	17	9	13	8	9	3
13	Australia	0.92	117	18	5	8	12	4	4	21	21	20	4
14	Czech Republic	0.63	80	40	3	7	8	4	1	4	2	6	5

15	Malaysia	0,55	70	17	8	9	3	11	5	7	3	5	2
16	Switzerland	0,53	68	25	2	3	4	3	3	1	4	20	3
17	Turkey	0.49	62	18	4	3	4	8	5	4	6	4	6
18	Ukraine	0,47	60	21	1	12	7	3	3	1	7	3	2
19	Kazakhstan	0,49	62	16	3	4	11	5	1	5	9	5	3
20	Netherlands	0.45	58	14	3	2	6	7	6	4	6	9	1
21	France	0,45	58	14	2	12	4	9	3	4	4	2	4
22	China /Taiwan/	0,42	54	33	1	3	6	7	2		1	1	
23	Italy	0,39	50	15	3	2	4	13	3	4	4		2
24	Pakistan	0,35	45	31	1	2	4	4		2			1
25	Poland	0,27	35	16	1	2	2	1	2	1	3	4	3
26	India	0,26	33	5	1	5	11	4	1	3	1	1	1
27	New Zealand	0.24	30	11	1	3	2	3	1	1	4	3	1
28	Luxemburg	0,24	30	2		1		2	1	5	8	9	2
29	Hungary	0,20	25	7	1	5	3		3	4		2	
30	Bulgaria	0,16	21	12		2	2	1		1	2	1	
31	Austria	0,17	22	7	1	2	2	6				1	3
32	Belgium	0,13	17	7		4	2	1		1		2	
32	DRPK	0,14		9	1	2	1			1	2	1	1

			18										
34	Israel	0,12	15	7	1	3	2	2					
35	Bermuda	0,10	13	8		3	2						
36	Spain	0,10	13	6		1					2	3	1
37	Uzbekistan	0,09	12		1			1	2	6	2		
38	Syria	0,09	12	10				2					
39	The Bahamas	0,09	11	8		2				1			
40	Antigua & Barbuda	0,09	11	11									
41	Belarus	0,08	10	2				1		3	1	3	
42	Cyprus	0,09	11				5	3	1		1		1
43	Iran	0,07	9		2					3	1	2	1
44	Kyrgyzstan	0,07	9	4					1	1	1	1	
45	Bangladesh	0.07	9				1		1	1	2	2	2
46	Sweden	0,06	8	2	1		1	2		1			1
47	Seychelles Islands	0.05	7				1	2			1	3	
48	Cayman Islands	0,06	7	2		3		1	1				
49	Slovakia	0,05	7	3		2	2						
50	Lebanon	0,05	6	3		1					1	1	
51	Norway	0,05	6	2	1	1	1					1	
52	Barbados	0.05	6	2	1						3		
53	Arab United Emirates	0.04	5								3	2	
54	Thailand	0,04	5	2					1	1	1		
55	Panama	0,04	5	3					1		1		
56	Denmark	0.03	4		1						2		1
57	Jordan	0,03	4	3									1

58	Estonia	0.04	5	1		1						2	1
59	Anguilla	0.03	4							2	2		
60	Ireland	0.03	4				1			1	2		
61	Gibraltar	0,03	4	1	2					1			
62	Liberia	0,03	4	1		3							
63	Yugoslavia	0,03	4	4									
64	Saudi Arabia	0,03	4	4									
65	Mauritius	0.03	4		1						2	1	
66	Azerbaijan	0.04	5				1			1	1	1	1
67	Saint Kits and Nevis	0.02	3	1						1		1	
68	Qatar	0,02	3					1	1			1	
69	Philippines	0,02	3				1				1	1	
70	Indonesia	0.02	3	1					1		1		
71	Belize	0,03	4		2					1			1
72	Mauritania	0,02	3					3					
73	Moldavia	0,02	3	2			1						
74	Turkmenistan	0,02	2							1		1	
75	South Africa	0,02	2								2		
76	Isle of Man	0,02	2							2			
77	Iraq	0,02	2	1						1			
78	Georgia	0,02	2		1				1				
79	Sri Lanka	0,02	2					2					
80	Armenia	0,02	2		1			1					
81	Tajikistan	0,02	2	1		1							
82	Ethiopia	0,02	2	1		1							
83	China /Macao/	0,02	2	2									
84	Samoa	0.01	1									1	
85	Egypt	0.01	1									1	
86	British Guernsey Island	0.01	1								1		
87	Kuwait	0.01	1								1		
88	Romania	0,02	1							1			1
89	Nepal	0,02	1						1				1
90	Argentina	0,01	1						1				
91	Finland	0,01	1					1					
92	Morocco	0,01	1					1					
93	Marshall Islands	0,01	1			1							
94	Myanmar	0,01	1		1								
95	Turks and Caicos Islands	0,01	1		1								
96	Cambodia	0,01	1		1								
97	Honduras	0,01	1		1								
98	Portugal	0,01	1	1									
99	Lichtenstein	0,01	1	1									
100	Croatia	0,01	1	1									
101	Greece	0,01	1	1									

102	Serbia Montenegro	0,01	1	1									
103	Cameroon	0,01	1	1									
104	Latvia	0,01	1	1									
105	Dominion of Melchizedek	0,01	1	1									
106	Nigeria	0,01	1	1									
	TOTAL	100	12,764	3,691	971	1,505	1,609	1,551	613	769	933	774	348

F. FDI by SECTORS (THOUSAND USD)

No	Sectors	%	Total	2010	2011	2012*	2013.10.31*
1	Mining, exploration, Petroleum	73.3	10,331,467.88	819,762.15	4,083,218.51	2,217,906.92	871,626.04
2	Trade, Catering services	17.0	2,397,779.62	162,567.18	620,567.90	694,336.18	169,173.49
3	Others	3.4	484,205.62	14,012.70	207,216.65	38,728.09	6,475.19
4	Banking & financial services	1.4	201,162.15	12,979.58	24,893.87	17,753.36	17,753.36
5	Transport	1.3	176,695.37	2,892.00	7,374.49	135,062.51	6,219.07
6	Engineering services & construction material manufacturing	0.9	73,337.16	980.10	5,177.47	47, 615.15	2,477.41
7	Light industry	0.8	108,372.57	153.76	99.24	365.17	
8	Processing: animal raw materials	0.4	57,20243	236.89	656.60	49.97	1,084.85
9	Tourism	0.4	53,656.36	371.40	22,458.16	12,458.16	175.35
10	Information & Communications Technology	0.3	45,966.40	125.00	8,971.86	502.37	383.60
11	Food manufacturing	0.3	47,999.76	3,850.00	4,586.98	21,428.30	
12	Culture, education & science products, printing	0.1	16,286.09	60.48	415.65	833.64	353.00
13	Agriculture, crop production, animal husbandry	0.1	15,908.75	403.36	554.00	431.12	109.86
14	Health & beauty products	0.1	14,607.29	7,492.00	905.55	1,074.84	135.50
15	Wooden Furniture manufacturing	0.0	5,994.23	33.60	12.48	45.00	50.00
16	Energy	0.0	5,515.80				

17	Public utilities services	0.0	2,841.29	83.07			38.00
18	Jewelry, souvenirs	0.0	2,648.18				
19	Electric appliance manufacturing	0.0	1,809.20				
20	Household items manufacturing	0.0	1,432.50				
	Total FDI	100	14,101,138.77	1,025,995.12	4,986,034.12	3,198,731.30	1,076,054.71

Note: 0.1.2012 , 2013.10.31** - FDI figures do not include Balance of payment by the Central Bank of Mongolia.

G. FOREIGN INVESTED COMPANIES by SECTORS

No	Sectors	%	Total	1990-2004	2005	2006	2007	2008	2009	2010	2011	2012	2013.10.31
1	Trade, Catering services	68.9	8,796	969	522	1,112	1,505	1,515	572	731	872	689	309
2	Others	12.2	1,562	860	297	262	21	3	15	14	15	50	25
3	Mining, Geological exploration, Petroleum	3.3	415	272	27	22	23	4	12	14	22	19	
4	Engineering services and construction material manufacturing	3.1	396	327	15	14	20	4	6		1	4	5
5	Tourism	2.5	314	176	57	35	23	12	1	2	6		2
6	Light industry	1.5	190	167	7	14	1	1					
7	Food manufacturing	1.4	181	172	5	2							
8	Processing: animal raw materials	1.2	158	149	4	4							
9	Transport	1.0	132	101	7	3	1	1	2	3	9	3	2
10	Information & Communications Technology	0.8	108	72	7	11	7	6	2	1		2	
11	Agriculture, crop production, animal husbandry	0.8	108	86	8	5	1		1	1	4	1	1
12	Wooden Furniture manufacturing	0.6	78	71	2	4							1

13	Culture, education & science products, printing	0.5	67	60	1	3							
14	Banking & financial services	0.5	64	36	2	5	7	4	2	1	2	2	3
15	Health & beauty services	0.4	53	47	1	2		1		1	1		
16	Energy	0.3	44	39	4	1							
17	Public utilities services	0.3	40	36	2	2							
18	Electric appliance manufacturing	0.2	29	23	3	3							
19	Household items manufacturing	0.2	21	21									
20	Jewelry, souvenirs	0.1	8	7		1							
	Total number of foreign invested companies	100	12,764	3,691	971	1,505	1,609	1,551	613	769	933	774	348

H. REGISTERED FOREIGN DIRECT INVESTMENT IN MONGOLIA BY COUNTRIES – 2014

No	Country	%	Total number of companies	Investment
1	Australia	1.52	1	$100,000
2	Azerbaijan	1.52	1	$100,000
3	Belgium	1.52	1	$100,000
4	Canada	1.52	1	$100,000
5	Chile	1.52	1	$100,000
6	China	43.94	29	$3,734,923
7	Hong Kong (China)	9.09	6	$5,515,425
8	Japan	4.55	3	$396,078
9	Macao	1.52	1	$100,000
10	Russia	1.52	1	$200,000
11	Seychelles	1.52	1	$100.00
12	Singapore	1.52	1	$2,368,186
13	South Korea	19.70	13	$2,376,941
14	Turkey	4.55	3	$704,146
15	USA	1.52	1	$100,000
16	British Virgin Islands	3.03	2	$200,000
	Total FDI	100	66	$16,300,699

TABLE 3: Sources and Destination of for FDI to Mongolia 2012 (Source: http://cdis.imf.org)

Direct Investment from/in Counterpart Economy Data					
From Top Five Sources/To Top Five Destinations (US Dollars, Millions)					
Inward Direct Investment	Outward Direct Investment				
Total Inward	13,458	100%	Total Outward	NA	NA
Netherlands	7,637	57%	NA	NA	Na
Singapore	1,424	11%			
United Kingdom	906	7%			
China, P.R.: Mainland	657	5%			
China, P.R.: Hong Kong	544	4%			
"0" reflects amounts rounded to +/- USD 500,000.					

TABLE 4: Sources of Portfolio Investment for Mongolia, 2012(Source: http://cpis.imf.org/)

Portfolio Investment Assets
Top Five Partners (Millions, US Dollars)
Total
Equity Securities
Total Debt Securities

World	469	100%	World	468	100%	World	1	100%
China, P.R.: Hong Kong	404	86%	China, P.R.: Hong Kong	403	86%	Korea, Republic of	0.26	52%
Australia	28	6%	Australia	28	6%	Russian Federation	0.16	33%
United States	10	2%	United States	10	2%	China, P.R.: Hong Kong	0.06	12%
Canada	9	2%	Canada	9	2%	Japan	0.01	2%
Singapore	7	2%	Singapore	7	2%	Australia	0.01	1%

19. CONTACT AT THE U.S. EMBASSY IN ULAANBAATAR TO LEARN MORE

NAME: The Economic and Commercial Section
ADDRESS OF MISSION:
U.S. Embassy in Mongolia
P.O. Box 341
Ulaanbaatar 14192 Mongolia
TELEPHONE NUMBER: +976-7007-6001
EMAIL ADDRESS: Ulaanbaatar-Econ-Comm@state.gov

Web Resources

Mongolian Resources
Invest Mongolia Agency: http://www.investmongolia.com/
General Tax Authority of Mongolia: www.mta.mn
State Registration Office of Mongolia: https://burtgel.gov
General Authority for Social Insurance: www.ndaatgal.mn
Government of Mongolia: http://www.pmis.gov.mn
Intellectual Property Office: http://www.ipom.mn/
Mineral Resources and Petroleum Authority of Mongolia: http://www.mram.mn
Mongol Chamber of Commerce and Industry: http://www.mongolchamber.mn/en/
Mongolian Builders Association: http://www.buildersasso.mn

Embassy of Mongolia, Washington, DC: http://www.mongolianembassy.us
Parliament of Mongolia: www.parliament.mn
American Chamber of Commerce Mongolia: http://amcham.mn/
Business Council of Mongolia: www.bcmongolia.org/
U. S. Government Resources
Commercial Specialist: richmondmd@state.gov
U.S. Embassy, Ulaanbaatar: http://mongolia.usembassy.gov
U.S. Department of State: http://www.state.gov/
U.S. Department of Commerce: http://www.commerce.gov/
U.S. International Trade Administration: http://www.trade.gov/
U.S. Trade and Development Agency: http://www.ustda.gov
U.S. Export-Import Bank: http://www.exim.gov/
U.S. Overseas Private Investment Corporations: http://www.opic.gov

TRADE AND PROJECT FINANCING

METHODS OF PAYMENT

Payment in cash is the most common method of payment, although electronic payments are becoming more common. Although the Tugrik is the official currency for all domestic transactions, dollars may be used for some exchanges. These payments can be in hard currency or through wire transfers into and from Mongolian-bank accounts. Letters of credit remain hard to obtain due to weaknesses in banking supervision and difficulties in collecting on defaults.

Pay-as-one- goes should be the mantra for American investors active in Mongolia. We do not recommend paying cash in advance or extending credit until a clear record of trust and successful transactions exists. Tight control of finance and procurement is recommended.

There are no private collection or credit rating agencies currently active in Mongolia.

BANKING SYSTEM

The banking system has become more efficient and reliable, although supervision lags and some banks do not measure up to international standards. Prior to 1991, no western-style commercial or central banking system existed in Mongolia. The State Bank was the only bank in Mongolia. In October 1990, the Mongolian Government, in line with free market economic reforms, dissolved the State Bank.

In 1991, Mongolia enacted a new banking law to create a western-style banking system. The law re-organized the banking system into a two-tier structure. The Bank of Mongolia or Mongol Bank acts as the central bank, implementing monetary policy. Other private and public banks provide commercial services.

The Trade and Development Bank (TDB), Golomt Bank, and Khan Bank are the three largest commercial.

A foreign company or organization (such as a joint venture or wholly owned firm) may open an account by presenting the following information to their bank:

1. Registration by the Foreign Investment Registration and Regulation Department (FIRRD) \

2. Authorization from the Ministry of Finance.

3. A letter requesting the account.

A private foreign individual may open an account upon written request. Banks usually have forms that serve as written requests. A passport is required.

Exchange Services

MONGOLIAN BANKS PROVIDE EXCHANGE SERVICES FOR ALL AMOUNTS; HOWEVER, LARGER AMOUNTS MAY BE SUBJECT TO REGULATORY DELAYS OR DELAYS DUE TO CURRENCY AVAILABILITY.

Transfers and Withdrawals

Most of Mongolia's banks make international money transfers. The three largest banks maintain correspondent relations with several foreign banks and maintain accounts in major world currencies with several of them. Clients may transfer money into and out of their domestic accounts, subject to domestic reporting requirements. There are no set limits on the amount that may be withdrawn from an account. The bank charges a small commission on cash withdrawals in hard currency. There is no commission on cash withdrawals in Tugriks at the day's buying rate. The bank charges a commission on all transfers of hard currency within Mongolia and to other banks abroad.

Most banks will cash personal checks but that process can take up to one month while the bank waits for the check to clear. The check casher will not have access to the funds until the check clears.

Travelers' Checks, Credit Cards, and ATMs

The Trade and Development Bank is one of the main banks that cashes and sells American Express, Thomas Cook, Visa, and MasterCard U.S. dollar-denominated travelers' checks. The bank sells travelers' checks for U.S. dollars without commission. There is a commission on drawing travelers' checks from an account. The checks may be cashed for Tugriks with no commission charge. If cashed for hard currencies or deposited into an account, the client pays a small commission.

Major hotels accept American Express, Visa, Master Card, and JCB credit cards. More major stores, restaurants, and travel agencies also accept credit cards. Most banks offer cash advances on major credit and charge cards. Most banks maintain ATMs that allow cash withdrawals through international networks. Merchants can add a 3 %- 4% surcharge on both credit and charge card purchases.

FOREIGN-EXCHANGE CONTROLS

The tugrik (MNT) is the national currency of Mongolia and the only legal currency. Since July 1996 and renewed in 2009 legislation, all cash payments and transactions are made in Tugriks (with exceptions for certain bank and government transactions). Mongolia maintains a floating exchange rate policy. Over the past several years, the exchange rate has been relatively stable. In June 2013, the rate was approximately US

$1 = 1,430 MNT. Individuals may exchange money at authorized currency exchange points, as well as at banks and hotels. English language newspapers and radio and TV programs regularly report exchange rates.

There are no foreign exchange controls affecting either investment or trade in Mongolia. Infrequently, the commercial banking system has shortages of dollars that slightly delay remittances. The local currency, the Tugrik, floats freely. Several banks and exchange kiosks are licensed by the BOM to engage in foreign currency exchange. Large transactions are subject to government reporting requirements.

U.S. BANKS AND LOCAL CORRESPONDENT BANKS

INTERNATIONAL SERVICE BANKS IN MONGOLIA

Khan Bank of Mongolia: https://www.khanbank.com/en.html

Tel: 976-11-332-333 Fax: 976-7011-7023 Hotline: 1917

Seoul Street-25 PO.BOX-192, Ulaanbaatar-44 Mongolia Golomt Bank: http://www.golomtbank.com/en/home/site-map/

Tel: 976-7011-7676 Fax : 976-11-312-307; 311-958 Hotline: 1646 Telex: 79247 GLMT MN Sukhbaatar Square Ulaanbaatar 210620 Mongolia

Trade and Development Bank: http://www.tdbm.mn

PROJECT FINANCING

In Mongolia's market economy, there are many ways to finance imports. The most common is the letter of credit. The Trade and Development Bank and Golomt Bank are familiar with letters of credit, as are major importers/distributors in Mongolia. However, credit tends to be quite tight in Mongolia. Many domestic and foreign investors seek financing outside Mongolia.

Sources of financing available for US exporters and investors are:

THE WORLD BANK (www.worldbank.org or www.worldbank.org/mn):

The World Bank, based in Washington, D.C., publishes bidding opportunities in the United Nations publication "Development Business." This is available by subscription from United Nations, PO Box 5850, Grand Central Station, New York, New York 10163-5850.

The World Bank conducts procurement by the rules of international competitive bidding through Mongolian government agencies; nonetheless, successful bidding requires close coordination with the Mongolian government entity responsible for development of a project at the consulting stage, when specifications are being established. The World Bank Mongolia Office can be contacted at (976-11) 312-647 or by email at eastasiapacific@worldbank.org .

THE INTERNATIONAL FINANCE CORPORATION (www.ifc.org or www.ifc.org/ifcext/eastasia.nsf/Content/mongolia):

IFC maintains an office in Ulaanbaatar and plans more activities in Mongolia. IFC's core business is financing projects with cash flows that can cover debt-service repayment to lenders and payment of dividends to shareholders. Such financing is without government guarantees. IFC can be contacted through its Washington, D.C. headquarters at (202) 473-1000 or at its Ulaanbaatar office (976-11) 312-694 or by email at Ntuyen@ifc.org .

ASIAN DEVELOPMENT BANK (www.adb.org or http://www.adb.org/Mongolia):

The ADB largely provides loans for infrastructure and agricultural projects. Once the ADB and the Mongolian government initially approve a project, it is included in a monthly publication called "ADB Business Opportunities." Available by subscription from the Publications Unit, Information Office, ADB, PO Box 789, Manila, Philippines, fax (632) 632-5122 or 632-5841.

The U.S. Commerce Department has established a multilateral development bank operations office (fax: 202/273-0927) that publishes information to assist companies in winning such contracts.

EUROPEAN BANK FOR RECONSTRUCTION AND DEVELOPMENT (http://www.ebrd.com/pages/country/mongolia.shtml):

EBRD maintains an active portfolio in Mongolia in all sectors of the Mongolian economy. Contact the EBRD at Tel: (976 11) 317 974/298; Fax: + 976 11 315 844.

US TRADE AND DEVELOPMENT AGENCY (TDA: http://www.tda.gov):

The Trade and Development Agency occasionally participates in Mongolian projects. Once active sectors and potential projects are identified for possible feasibility study financing or technical assistance, TDA will hire its own technical consultant to review the project. TDA's basic criteria for project funding are:

* The project is a developmental priority of the host country

* There is a likelihood of project financing

* The US export potential is significant

* There is foreign competition for the project

Contact the US Trade and Development Agency at 1000 Wilson Boulevard, Suite 1600 Arlington, Virginia 22209, Tel: 703/875-4357, fax: 703/875-4009.

EXPORT-IMPORT BANK (EXIM: http://www.exim.gov), INTERNATIONAL FUNDING INFORMATION SERVICE (IFIS), AND THE OVERSEAS PRIVATE INSURANCE CORPORATION (OPIC: http://www.opic.gov)

Currently, EXIM and OPIC are open for Mongolian projects.

WEB RESOURCES

Mongolian Resources
Invest Mongolia Agency: http://www.investmongolia.com/
General Tax Authority of Mongolia: www.mta.mn
State Registration Office of Mongolia: https://burtgel.gov
General Authority for Social Insurance: www.ndaatgal.mn
Government of Mongolia: http://www.pmis.gov.mn
Intellectual Property Office: http://www.ipom.mn/
Mineral Resources and Petroleum Authority of Mongolia: http://www.mram.mn
Mongol Chamber of Commerce and Industry: http://www.mongolchamber.mn/en/
Mongolian Builders Association: http://www.buildersasso.mn
Embassy of Mongolia, Washington, DC: http://www.mongolianembassy.us
Parliament of Mongolia: www.parliament.mn
American Chamber of Commerce Mongolia: http://amcham.mn/
Business Council of Mongolia: www.bcmongolia.org/
U. S. Government Resources
Commercial Specialist: richmondmd@state.gov
U.S. Embassy, Ulaanbaatar: http://mongolia.usembassy.gov
U.S. Department of State: http://www.state.gov/
U.S. Department of Commerce: http://www.commerce.gov/
U.S. International Trade Administration: http://www.trade.gov/
U.S. Trade and Development Agency: http://www.ustda.gov
U.S. Export-Import Bank: http://www.exim.gov/
U.S. Overseas Private Investment Corporations: http://www.opic.gov

IMPORTANT CONTCTS

A. MONGOLIAN GOVERNMENT

Office of the Prime Minister
Tel: (976-11) 320-123
Fax: (976-11) 327-825
Website: http://www.pmis.gov.mn/pmis_eng/index.php
* Open government: http://www.open-government.mn/
* Central Intelligence Agency: http://www.gia.gov.mn/
* Information Technology and Post Agency: http://itpta.gov.mn/
* Communications Regulatory Committee: http://www.crc.gov.mn

Office of the Deputy Prime Minister
Tel: (976-11) 260535, 976-11) 321956
Fax: (976-11) 321956
Website: www.pmis.gov.mn
* Intellectual Property Office: http://www.ipom.mn/
* Center of Standardization and Metrology: http://www.masm.gov.mn/
* Agency for Fair Competition and Consumer Protection: http://www.afccp.gov.mn/?lang=en
* State Professional Inspection Agency: http://www.inspection.gov.mn
* Procurement Policy Department: http://www.mof.gov.mn/page/?lan=en&c=3514
* National Emergency Management Agency: http://www.nema.gov.mn/

Cabinet Secretariat of Government of Mongolia
Tel: (976-11) 262408
Fax: (976-11) 310011
Website: http://cabinet.gov.mn/

Ministry of Culture, Sports, and Tourism

Tel: (976-11) 310-986
Fax: (976-11) 310-985
Web: www.mcst.gov.mn

Ministry of Construction and Urban Development
Website: http://www.mcud.gov.mn
* Administration of Land Affairs, Construction, Geodesy and Cartography: http://www.gazar.gov.mn

Ministry of Defense
Tel: (976-51) 261-718
Fax: (976-11) 322-904
Website: http://www.mod.gov.mn/index.php
* General Staff of the Mongolian Armed Forces: http://gsmaf.gov.mn/

Ministry of Economic Development
Tel: (976-51) 264-878
Fax: 976-51) 263-333
Web: http://www.med.gov.mn/mn/
Foreign Investment and Foreign Regulation Department: www.investmongolia.com

Ministry of Education and Science
Fax: (976-11) 323-158
Website: www.mecs.gov.mn/
E-mail: Info@mecs.gov.mn

Ministry of Energy
Tel: (976-11) 320-126
Fax: (976-11) 319-335
Website: http://www.energy.gov.mn/weblink

Ministry of Environment and Green Development
Tel: (976-51) 261-966
Fax: (976-511) 266-171
Website: http://www.mne.mn/
* Agency of Metrology and Environment Monitoring : http://www.namhem.pmis.gov.mn/

Ministry of Finance
Tel: (976-11) 260-247, 262-712
Fax: (976-11) 320247
Website: http://www.mof.gov.mn/welcome?lan=en
* Mongolian Tax Administration: http://en.mta.mn/pages/18
* General Customs Office: http://www.ecustoms.mn/

Ministry of Foreign Affairs
Tel: (976-51) 262-788
Fax: (976-11) 322-127
Website: http://www.mfa.gov.mn

Ministry of Health
Tel. (976-51) 263-913
Fax: (976-11) 320-916
Website: www.moh.mn

Ministry of Industry and Agriculture
Tel: (967-11) 262204
Fax: (976-11) 450258
Website: http://www.mofa.gov.mn
* State Property Committee: http://www.spc.gov.mn/eng/
* Agency for Veterinary and Animal Breeding: vetsermongolia@magicnet.mn

Ministry of Justice & Internal Affairs
Tel: +976-51-267-533
Fax: +976-51-267-533
Website: www.moj.gov.mn
* General Police Department: http://www.police.gov.mn/
* General Authority for Border Protection: http://bpo.gov.mn/
* General Authority for State Registration: http://www.citizenmongolia.com/
* General Authority for Implementing Court decisions: http://www.court-decision.gov.mn/
* National Archives: http://www.archives.gov.mn/
* Immigration Agency: www.immigration.gov.mn/

Ministry of Labor
Tel: (976-51) 261-418
Fax: (976-51) 261-516
Website: http://www.mol.gov.mn/

Ministry of Mining
Tel: (976-51) 263-506, 265-814
Fax: (976-11) 318-169
Website: http://www.mm.gov.mn/mn/
* Mineral Resources Authority: http://www.mram.gov.mn/index.php?lang=en
* Petroleum Authority - http://www.pam.gov.mn/

Ministry of Population Development and Social Welfare
Tel: (976-51) 264-791
Fax: (976-11) 328-634
Website: www.mpdsp.gov.mn

* General Authority for Social Insurance: http://www.ndaatgal.mn/
* General Office for Social Welfare Service: www.hun.gov.mn
* National Authority for Children: http://www.nac.gov.mn/

Ministry of Roads and Transportation
Tel: (976-11) 322-406; (976) 7011-2333 Fax: (976-11)312-315 Website: www.mrt.gov.mn

* Civil Aviation Authority: http://www.mcaa.gov.mn/index.php/page-en/10
* Railway Authority: http://www.mtz.mn/

B. PARLIAMENT OF MONGOLIA

http://www.parliament.mn/

* National Audit Office: http://www.mnao.mn/mn
* National Statistical Office www.nso.mn
* Bank of Mongolia http://www.mongolbank.mn/
* Government Service Council http://csc.gov.mn/
* Financial Regulatory Commission http://www.frc.mn/

* National Human Right Commission http://www.mn-nhrc.org/
* General Election Commission http://www.gec.gov.mn/
* Constitutional Court http://www.conscourt.gov.mn/
* Independent Authority Against Corruption http://www.iaac.mn/

C. OFFICE OF THE PRESIDENT OF MONGOLIA

www.president.mn/eng/
* National Security Council of Mongolia: http://www.nsc.gov.mn/

D. CHAMBERS OF COMMERCE/TRADE ASSOCIATIONS

Mongolian National Chamber of Commerce and Industry
Website: www.mongolchamber.mn

Mongolian Employers Federation
Website: www.monef.mn

Mongolian Stock Exchange
Website: www.mse.mn

D. MARKET RESEARCH FIRMS

U.S.-Mongolia Advisory Group, Inc.
Dr. Alicia Campi
6002 Ticonderoga Court
Burke, VA 22015
Phone/Fax in Virginia: 703-451-6456
Phone in New York City: 212-861-9460
E-mail: usmagcampi@aol.com

Business Council of Mongolia (BCM)
Mr. Jim Dwyer, Executive Director
Mr. I. Ser-Od, Vice Director
Tel/Fax: (976-11) 332345
Email: serod@bcmongolia.org Website: www.bcmongolia.org

North America Mongolia Business Council, American Office (NAMBC)
Mr. Steve Saunders, President
Phone: (703) 549-8444
Fax: (703) 549-6526
Address: 1015 Duke Street, Alexandria, Virginia 22314, USA
Email: steve@nambc.org
Website: www.nambc.org

Sant Maral
Mr. I Sumati
Tel: (976) 9911-6367
Email: Isumati@magicnet.mn

E. BANKS

Mongol Bank (Central Bank)
Website: www.mongolbank.mn

Trade and Development Bank

Website: www.tdbm.mn

Khan Bank
Website: www.khanbank.com

Golomt Bank
Website: http://www.golomtbank.com

Khas Bank
Website: http://www.xacbank.mn

F. US EMBASSY CONTACTS

The United States Embassy
Mr. Michael Richmond, Ph.D., Senior Commercial Specialist
E-mail: richmondmd@state.gov
Web Site: www.mongolia.usembassy.gov/

Mongolia Mailing Address:
U.S. Embassy in Mongolia P.O. Box 341 Ulaanbaatar-14192 MONGOLIA
U.S. Mailing Address:
American Embassy Ulaanbaatar
Department of State
Washington, DC 20521-4410
Attention Senior Commercial Specialist Michael Richmond

G. WASHINGTON-BASED USG MONGOLIA CONTACTS

Washington-Based USG Mongolia Contacts
US Department of Commerce
International Trade Administration
Mongolia Desk Officer Zhen Gong Cross
14th And Constitution Avenue
Washington, DC 20230
Tel: (202) 482-3583
Fax: (202) 482-1576

U.S. Trade Development Agency
1000 Wilson Boulevard
Suite 1600
Arlington, Virginia 22209
Tel: 703/875-4357
Fax: 703/875-4009
Web site: www.tda.gov.

TPCC Trade Information Center
Tel: 800-USA-Trade

US Department Of State
Office of China and Mongolia
Bureau of East Asia & Pacific Affairs
Room 4318, 2201 C Street, NW
Washington, DC 20520
Tel: (202) 647-6796
Fax: (202) 647-6820

US Department of Agriculture
International Trade Policy
Asia American Division
Foreign Agricultural Service Stop 1023
11th And Independence Ave., SW
Washington, DC 20250-1023
Tel: (202) 720-1289
Fax: (202) 690-1093

Office of US Trade Representative
600 17th Street, NW
Washington, DC 20506

Embassy of Mongolia 2833 M Street,
N.W. Washington, D.C. 20007 USA
Tel: (202) 333-7117
Fax: (202) 298-9227
Email: monemb@aol.com
Web Site: http://www.mongolianembassy.us

AMENDMENT TO THE FOREIGN INVESTMENT LAW OF MONGOLIA

Article 1. Incorporate the following articles, sections and provisions to the Foreign Investment Law of Mongolia.

1/ Article 19:

"Article 19. Stability Agreement

1. In the event of a request by the investor intending to undertake an investment project of not less than US$ 2 million or equivalent amount in Mongolian national tugrigs in Mongolia, the Cabinet Member responsible for taxation policy issues as permitted by the Government of Mongolia may sign an agreement with that investor on a stability as a legal guarantee for a stable environment to conduct business activities.

2. A sample of a stability agreement will be approved by the Government of Mongolia. This agreement sample shall contain provisions to ensure stable tax conditions during certain period and state objectives and amount of the investment, its implementation period and rationale to revoke the agreement.

3. If a start-up investment amount of the project to be implemented by a foreign investor is US$ 2.0-10.0 million or equivalent amount of Mongolian national tugrigs a stability agreement can be signed for l0 years and if the amount is over US$ 10.0 million or its equivalent in Mongolian national tugrigs for 15 years.

4. In the event of a termination of activities by sole initiative of an investor before the period stated in the stability agreement when a business entity with foreign investment and/or a branch of a foreign legal entity was not bankrupted in accordance with the laws of Mongolia or their activities were not stopped by the respective authorities or the parties did not terminate the contract upon

their mutual agreement the amount of tax discounts and/or exemptions awarded to that investor shall be compensated by the investor."

2/ Article 20:

"Article 20. Conclusion of a Stability Agreement

1. An investor willing to conclude a Stability Agreement shall submit its application and draft Stability Agreement to the State central administrative body in charge of taxation policy issues.

2. The Government member in charge of taxation policy issues shall examine the application and the draft agreement within 14 business days following the receipt and shall conclude the Stability Agreement with the applicant, if no clarifications are required. If additional clarifications are required, the applicant shall be notified of it within 7 business days.

3. Relevant organizations shall be notified of such Stability Agreement."

3/ Article 3, section 4, 5:

"4/ "Investment agreement" is an agreement and/or a contract on concession, product sharing, marketing, management, financial leasing and franchise investment concluded by foreign investors for implementation of concrete project without having to establish a legal entity.

5/ "One stop service" is a complex service including to receive applications and other relevant materials on establishing a business entity with foreign investment or a branch of foreign legal entity, issuing certificate, license and special permission in order to start a business activity, making a conclusion, appraisal at one place and to organize activities to solve of these issues by relevant authorities, and to provide investors with necessary information as well as consultancy service."

4/ Article 17, section 2:

"2. An investment agreement shall be removed from the registration and a certificate of approval shall be revoked when duration of the investment agreement expires and/or the investor annuals the agreement or violates laws of Mongolia."

5/ Article 18, section 2:

"2. Tax incentives and/or exemptions to a business entity with foreign investment, branch of a foreign legal entity and an implementing entity of an investment agreement will be subject to Income tax law of Business entities and organizations1, Customs tariff law2, Value added tax law3, Excise tax law4 and Land law5 of Mongolia."

6/ Article 6, section 5, 6:

"5) Conclude a contract for marketing and management,

6) Make an investment through financial leasing and franchise."

Article 2. Add the phrase of "concession and product sharing" after "resolution" in the provision 4 of section 1 of article 6; "branch of a foreign legal entity" after "business entity with foreign investment" in the section 1 and 2 of article 16; section 1, 2, 3, 4 and 5 of article 17; section 1 of article 18; section 1, 3, 5 and 6 of article 21; section 1, 2 and 3 of article 22; article 23; section 1, 2 and 3 of article 24; article 25.

Article 3. Rephrase the following articles, sections and provisions of the Foreign Investment Law as below:

1/ Article 14:

"Article 14. Plenary rights of the state administrative body in charge of foreign investment

1. The State Central administrative body in charge of foreign investment shall have the following plenary rights with respect to foreign investment:

(1) to formulate foreign investment policy in accordance with the Government general action plan on development country's economy and society, and monitor its implementation;
(2) to ensure and supervise the implementation of legislation regard to foreign investment;
(3) to work out a proposal on leading sectors and directions of foreign investment.

2. The State administrative body in charge of foreign investment shall have the following plenary rights:

(1) to implement policies and legislation with respect to foreign investment;
(2) to research possibilities to increase foreign investment, to organize investment promotional activities, to provide investors with relevant information, and to involve foreign investors to project tender;
(3) to render foreign investors with complex "One-stop service";
(4) to prepare information on foreign investment statistics;
(5) to approve and/or disapprove establishment of a business entity with foreign investment or a branch of a foreign legal entity;
(6) to terminate, temporarily or completely, the activities of a business entity with foreign investment or a branch of a foreign legal entity;
(7) other rights specified in legislation.

3. The State administrative body in charge of foreign investment issue shall render some of the services specified in the provision 3 of section 2 of this Article on charge base."

2/ Article 15:

"Article 15. Registration of Business entity with foreign investment, branch of a foreign legal entity and Investment agreement

1. A business entity with foreign investment and a branch of a foreign legal entity that received a certificate from the State administrative body in charge of foreign investment shall be registered by the National General Taxation Office with state registration.

2. Any amendment to the Agreement or Statute of a business entity with foreign investment and a branch of a foreign legal entity shall be registered with the National General Taxation Office as approved by the State administrative body in charge of foreign investment.

3. The State administrative body in charge of foreign investment will register an Investment agreement based on an application to register an investment agreement and a notarized copy of the investment agreement, and will issue a certificate within 10 business days after the receipt of the application."

3/ Article 11, section 1:

"1. Business entity with foreign investment is a entity, established in accordance with the legislation of Mongolia, of which not less than 25 percent of the equity is constituted with an investment of a foreign investor."

4/ Article 13, section 1:

"1. Investors of a business entity with foreign investment shall negotiate on evaluation of the property and intellectually valuable items invested from them to form the equity of the entity following the same principle sued for convertible currency and tugrug (local currency). If investor considers it as necessary, the evaluation can be done by either Mongolian or foreign specialized company licensed to conduct asset evaluation."

5/ Article 6, provision 3:

"3/ a foreign investor makes a direct investment by buying stocks, shares and other securities of the Mongolian business entities under the legislation of Mongolia;"

6/ Article 10, provision 4 of section 1:

"4. Remit the following income, profit and payments to abroad without any barriers:

(a) allotted stockholders income and share dividends;
(b) allotted income after property and securities' sale, transfer of property right to other party, completion of an investment agreement and liquidation of an entity;
(c) principal and interest of debt or other identical payments;
(d) compensation payment for confiscated property;
(e) other income gained under the legislation of Mongolia."

7/ Article 10, provision 2 of section 2:

2/ Follow commitments stated in the Agreement and Statute of the business entity with foreign investment, branch of a foreign legal entity and in Investment agreement;"

8/ Article 24, provision 3 of section 1:

"Issues on importing labour forces and experts shall be regulated by the relevant legislation of Mongolia."

Article 4. Add the phrase of "the State Central administrative body in charge of foreign investment " before "National General Taxation Office" in section 1 of article 17."

Article 5. Rephrase the following words and phrases in the relevant provisions, sections and articles of the Foreign Investment Law of Mongolia as below:

The title of the section 3 as "activities of a foreign invested entity and branch of a foreign legal entity"; the title of article 16 as "terminating a foreign invested entity and branch a foreign legal entity"; the title of article

17 as "liquidating a foreign invested entity and branch of a foreign legal entity"; the title of article 21 as "land utilization by a foreign invested entity and branch of a foreign legal entity"; the provision "related to activities of a foreign invested entity" as "related to foreign investment" in the article 1; "of a business entity" in the section 3 of article 22, article 25, section 1 and 2 of article 16 as "business entity"; "to a business entity" in section 1 of article 18, section 1, 3 and 5 of article 21, section 2 of article 24 as "a business entity"; "State General Taxation Office" in section 4 of article 17 as "National General Taxation Office"; "in registered capital" in provision 1 of section 1 of article 10, section 4 of article 21 as "in equity"; "status" in the title of article 24 and section 2 of same article as "security"

Article 6. Remove the following words and phrases from the relevant provisions, sections and articles of the Foreign Investment Law of Mongolia as below:

"nationalize" in the section 2 of article 8, "registered capital" in the section 2 of article 15; "about business entity" from the section 1 of article 16.

SELECTED INVESTMENT AND BUSINESS OPPORTUNITIES

AGRICULTURE SECTOR STRATEGY STUDY PROJECT

The ADB selects a consultant for a TA grant based on its prior Expression of Interest (EOI). An EOI can be transmitted on-line through the ADB's website (www.adb.org); afterward it will be acknowledged automatically. Firms may opt to send a hardcopy follow-up EOI addressed to Mr. S. Thuraisingham, Director, Consulting Services Division, with a copy to the ADB Project Officer. The EOI should relate a firm's experience and expertise to the ADB project. It is important for a U.S. firm to emphasize its similar project experience in the country or in a similar geographic area rather than presenting a general profile of its consulting activities. A separate EOI should be submitted for each project. The project name indicated in the EOI should exactly match that listed in the ADB Business Opportunities publication to avoid confusion.

To be considered for employment, consultants must register on the ADB's DACON (Data on Consulting Firms) and DICON (Data on Individual Consultants) Systems, otherwise, their EOIs will not be accepted. DACON and DICON registration can now be done on-line at www.adb.org/consulting.

Firms may also send a notification copy of their EOIs to the U.S. mailing address for the U.S. Commercial Liaison Office for the ADB, Attention: Stewart Ballard, Senior Commercial Officer, PSC 500 Box 33, FPO AP 96515-1000, or to the same office at its international mailing address: 25th Floor Ayala Life-FGU Center, 6811 Ayala Avenue, Makati City, Metro Manila, Philippines 1226;
Phone: (63-2) 887-1345; Fax: (63-2) 887-1164; E-mail: manila.adb.office.box @mail.doc.gov. This office works closely with the Office of the U.S. Executive Director to the ADB to increase American awareness of, and participation in, the ADB's activities.

The project listed in this report is now being actively processed by the ADB. For more information on this project, the name of the ADB project officer is indicated in the project brief. The U.S Commercial Liaison Office is ready to provide assistance to U.S. firms upon request. (Please see paragraph 4.)

The following TA project will be listed for the first time in the August 2003 issue of the Asian

Development Bank's (ADB) Business Opportunities (ADBBO). (Note: The ADBBO is also available on the ADB's website .

NAME OF PROJECT: AGRICULTURE SECTOR STRATEGY STUDY
Project No.: MON36477-01
Executing Agency: Ministry of Food and Agriculture
Contact: Dr. Gochoo DAAVADORJ, Director
Address: Ministry of Agriculture, Government Bldg. #9,
- Enkhtaivan Avenue 16a, Ulaanbaatar -210 349 Mongolia
Fax: (976-11) 454-742
Tel. No.: (976-11) 454-742
TA Amount: US$ 400.0 Thousand
Sector/Subsector: Agriculture and Natural Resources/Agricultural Support Services

Objectives and Scope:
The goal of the TA is to help the Government and ADB to develop a common strategy and roadmap for Mongolia's agriculture and rural development. The objective is to help the Government and ADB to identify the specific and concrete measures that could be rapid incorporated in ADB operations, to maximize the utility and effectiveness of ADB resources that are available to help Mongolia meeting its goal of economic development in the rural communities, specially in the poorer provinces. The proposed TA will make use of the available sector study results, and focus on identifying concrete measures that can be readily operationalized, through discussions with concerned key Government officials and other stakeholders.

Consulting Services: Consulting services yet to be determined.
Recruitment of Consultants: Recruitment of consulting services to be completed during fact-finding mission.

Project Processing Stage:
Beginning of Fact-finding Mission: Aug 2003.

Project Officer: Joji Tokeshi; (63-2) 632-6722
Agriculture, Environment, & Natural Resources Division, ECRD
In-country Commercial Officer: c/o Michael Layne, Economic/Commercial Officer, American Embassy, Ulaanbaatar; E-mail: LayneMJ@state.gov

OIL & GAS SECTOR OPPORTUNITIES

Ministry of Fuel and Energy
Ulaanbaatar 46, Baga Toiruu 6
Mongolia
Tel: +976 1 291 16

Mongol Petroleum Company
Uildverchnii, Gusamj MGT, Ulaanbaatar 37
Mongolia
Tel: +976 1 331 176
Fax: +976 1 331 176

Petroleum Authority of Mongolia
Uildverchinii str-37/81, Ulaanbaatar
Mongolia

Tel: +976 1 331 208 , 976-1-3312
Fax: +976 1 331 239
E-mail: petromon@magicnet.mn
URL: www.pam.mn/

INVESTMENT CLIMATE

- Mongolia is risk free politically and offers an open commercial environment.

- Favorable legal condition; The Petroleum Law of Mongolia is one of the top 10 petroleum laws (AAPG, Explorer, Aug. 1995, van Meurs rates)

- Open 16 blocks (each acreage approximately 10,000 sq. km) and more acreage available

- Stable politically and regulatory condition

- One of the most favorable Tax condition in the world

  Exemption from:

  - Corporate Income Tax
  - Customs Tax
  - Excise Tax
  - Value Added Tax

- Mutually beneficial fiscal terms (Production Sharing Contract)

- Stability agreement for Stabilized tax environment for 10-15 years
(The Amendments to Foreign Investment Law of Mongolia, Jan 2002)

- High possibility of recourse
Recoverable petroleum resource estimated to be 4-6 billion barrels by American experts. (CNPC attributed original oil-in-place in Tamsag Basin to be approximately 1.5 billion barrels. Chinese recovery factors in analogous basins range around 30%. (Oil and Gas Journal, Oct. 29, 2001, Vol. 99-44, p. 37)

- Near oil market in North Chinese refineries.

The vast Chinese energy market is about to move to the center stage of world oil industry activity and senior oil company executives are likely to be spending the coming months signing contracts running into billions of dollars. The long-predicted boom in the region is about to burst into reality (OGJ, Oct 29, 2001, p. 38).

BIDDING INFORMATION

On 22 August 2003 the Tender Comission had its meeting and decided to award the Bidding to the Chinese company Shi Ji Yang Guang one of the four companies that applied for oil exploration operations in the Nyalga XVI Exploration area of the Central Mongolian Basin.

The Tender Comission was appointed by the Order from 20 August 2003 of Chairman of the Petroleum Authority of Mongolia (PAM), Government Implementing Agency.

A final negotiations between PAM and winner Shi Ji Yang Guang company will start shortly.

PIPELINE PROJECT

The Petroleum Authority of Mongolia has cooperation with the companies, participating parties of a pipeline project. Kovyktinskoye gas is planned to be used to supply both the Irkutsk region market, neighboring areas, and the large and growing markets of China and South Korea through a long distance pipeline. There is also possibility of supply to markets in Mongolia and Japan.

Discussion between Russia, China, South Korea, Japan and Mongolia regarding gas supplies from KOVYKTINSKOYE have been held on a number of occasions on a "five nations" multilateral basis.

Kovykta is expected to be proven to be one of the largest natural gas accumulations in the world. Estimated reserves are more than one trillion cubic meters of natural and more than 40 million tons of gas liquids that are as condensate.

The long-distance pipeline will be transporting 30 billion cubic meters per year of gas for regional use and for export, for a more than 25 years.

SELECTED INFORMATION

COMPLETION OF INITIAL VIETNAM DRILLING PROGRAMME

SOCO International plc ("SOCO" or "the Company")

SOCO is an international oil and gas exploration and production company, headquartered in London. The Company has interests in Vietnam, Mongolia, Yemen, Libya, Tunisia, Thailand and North Korea with production operations in Yemen, Tunisia and Mongolia.

SOCO Vietnam Limited ("SOCO Vietnam"), SOCO's 80% owned subsidiary, and partners have completed the final well in the initial four well exploration drilling programme offshore Vietnam in the Cuu Long Basin. The Ca Ong Doi-1X ("COD-1X") vertical exploration well was drilled to a total depth of 4,618 metres terminating in granite wash.

The well encountered more than 1,050 metres of oil shows from inter-bedded Oligocene sands and shale source rocks. A drill stem test ("DST") was conducted over an open hole section from 3,565 metres to 4,618 metres. However, the interval was not heavily fractured and reservoir quality was therefore inadequate to yield commercial quantities of hydrocarbons.

From seismic re-interpretation, the COD-1X well appeared to be approximately five kilometres from the top of the Basement structure in a location chosen to test both Oligocene and Basement potential. On the basis of information gained from this well, the Company expects a subsequent exploration well will be drilled on the newly interpreted crest of the Basement structure.

The COD-1X was the fourth and final well drilled under terms of a 2002 farm-out agreement wherein SOCO Vietnam was carried up to a maximum amount of US$50 million by PTT Exploration and Production Public Company Limited of Thailand. Following its release from this well, the drilling rig will be moved immediately to a location on Block 16-1 to spud another exploration well on prospect "A" as a follow-up to the Voi Trang discovery last year which tested 3,500 barrels of oil per day ("BOPD"). This will be the first of an expected four to five exploration/appraisal well programme for 2003.

SOCO Vietnam holds a 25% working interest in Block 9-2 and a 28.5% interest in Block 16-1, pending finalisation of a transaction to acquire one half of the interest in the Block currently held by a subsidiary of Amerada Hess. Both Blocks are contiguous to the Bach Ho field, which is producing approximately 250,000 BOPD and 150 million cubic feet of gas per day, and the Rang Dong field, which is producing approximately 65,000 BOPD and 85 million cubic feet of gas per day.

Ed Story, President and Chief Executive of SOCO, commented:

"We've enjoyed the rare success of having drilled four exploration wells in the Basin and encountering oil in all the wells. Two of these were significant discoveries. Although the COD-1X well location lacked adequate reservoir in the Oligocene, the well penetrated over 1,000 metres of oil bearing source rock on the flank of this large Basement structure. This geological setting arguably ranks this structure as one of the best sourced oil regimes in the world. We remain very enthusiastic about the potential of prospect "C" on Block 9-2 and expect to demonstrate this potential with another well once all of the data can be integrated into a new interpretation. In the meantime, we will continue an active four to five well exploration and appraisal programme in 2003 on the prospects in Blocks 16-1 and 9-2."

SUCCESSFUL DRILLING RESULTS ON FIRST TWO WELLS IN MONGOLIAN SOCO INTERNATIONAL PLC ("SOCO" OR "THE COMPANY")

Successful Drilling Results on First Two Wells in Mongolian 2004 Drilling Campaign and Re-commencement of Crude Oil Sales to China

SOCO is an international oil and gas exploration and production company headquartered in London. In addition to its interests in Mongolia, the Company has operations in Yemen, European Russia, Vietnam, Tunisia, Thailand and North Korea.

SOCO's total crude oil production net to its working interest during the first six months of 2004 has averaged approximately 8,525 BOPD (7,205 BOPD in 1999). Average prices received for total crude oil sold by the Company during the period has been approximately US$25 per barrel ($16.70 per barrel in 1999).

SOCO announces that it has successfully completed the 19-9 and 19-10 wells, the first two wells drilled this year on Contract Area 19 in the Tamtsag Basin of Mongolia. Initial log, core and production results indicate that both wells appear to equal or exceed results from the 19-3 well drilled in 1997. The 19-3, which open-hole tested from a net 36 metre interval at a stabilised rate of approximately 690 barrels of oil per day was produced on pump during 1999 at a stabilised rate of 250 barrels of oil per day (BOPD). The new wells were not drill stem tested during drilling operations in order to avoid potential formation damage which is believed to have hampered the production rates of the 19-3 well. Each of the new wells is producing at approximately 250 BOPD at pump capacities which may not reflect ultimate flow potential. Full assessment of the stabilised production capabilities of the new discoveries is pending completion of pumping and production facilities.

The results are particularly encouraging in that these wells are the first to be drilled based upon the 3D seismic acquired in 1999 and under the reduced cost drilling contract. The 19-9 well was drilled as an appraisal well to the 19-3 discovery well and the 19-10 tested a new structure approximately 2.5 kilometres north of the 19-3 well. Upon completion, both wells flowed oil to surface. Log analysis on the 19-10 exploratory well indicate a net productive reservoir of approximately 77 meters in a gross interval from 2,324 meters to 2,449 meters that could yield in excess of thirty million barrels of recoverable oil.

A third well, the 19-11 was spud on 2 July as an exploratory test of a structure approximately 1.5 kilometres east of the 19-3 location. It is anticipated that a further two wells could be drilled this year, one of which will test the extent of the 19-10 discovery. Under the terms of the reduced cost drilling programme (from approximately $2.2 million per well to approximately $0.5 million per well), Huabei Oilfield Services, a Chinese company providing the drilling services, would earn the right to elect to participate in Contract Area 19 after completion of the full eight well programme. Huabei's participation of up to 20% would be on a working interest basis and fully funded by Huabei going forward. Petrovietnam, the Vietnamese national oil company has a 5% interest, carried through the exploration phase, in each of SOCO's Mongolia production sharing contracts, including Contract Area 19.

Sales of crude oil to China, which had been suspended earlier in the year, have been reinitiated as of this week under a sales contract signed 29 June 2004 with China National United Oil Corporation. As with the previous contract, crude oil will be trucked to a pipeline in the Aershan Oilfield for further delivery to the Horhot Refinery in the Inner Mongolia Autonomous Region of China. Although the volumes sold are not significant from a turnover standpoint, the sales program will free storage capacity to gather production data on the new discoveries, while allowing some recovery of costs.

Ed Story, Chief Executive Officer of SOCO, stated, " We are particularly pleased that we have advanced our exploration programme while continuing to build the Company's cash balances, which currently exceed £32 million. The 3D seismic program has provided a tool to significantly improve the predictability of drilling results in the Tamtsag Basin. Of equal importance, is that we are drilling these wells through our contract with Huabei Drilling at a fraction of the cost of the earlier wells. Moreover, the new field discovery potentially places the Company at the threshold of having sufficient reserves to justify planning a comprehensive development program."

SOCO'S MONGOLIAN EXPLORATION PROGRAM SEEN AS ENCOURAGING

SOCO International PLC, London, has conducted its four-well 2001 drilling program in the Tamtsag basin in Mongolia, OGJ Online reported.
Ed Story, CEO and President of SOCO, said, "The 2001 drilling campaign in Mongolia confirmed the value of 3D seismic and repeated the 75% wildcat success rate of the previous year. With the drilling success of a Chinese company just across the border from our project in the Tamtsag basin coupled with our success, we expect interest in the project to grow significantly."
The 19-13 and 19-14 wells were completed and fracture-stimulated in the Tsagaantsav zone (OGJ, Dec, 7 1992, p93). "Although only portions of the indicated productive intervals were perforated in each well and tests were restricted by pump capacity, the wells still tested at initial rates of approximately 350 b/d of oil", said SOCO.

ONE OF THE TOP 10 LAWS IN WORLDWIDE

Pedro van Meurs of takes a strictly fiscal approach to comparing international prospects.
His consulting company, van Meurs&Associates Ltd. recently conducted an analysis of 226 fiscal systems in worldwide petroleum exploration.
He evaluates the government's share, or "take" in exploration terms for each country, then ranks

the attractiveness (or lack of appeal) for prospects overall
Based on those results, van Meurs rates the following countries as his own **TOP 10** for exploration investment :

1. Lebanon
2. Ireland
3. Urugway
4. Spain
5. The Bahamas
6. The United Kingdom
7. Paraguay
8. Portugal
9. Israel
10. **Mongolia**

"My way of doing thing is somewhat different from what an oil company would actually do", van Meurs said. "I am comparing countries solely for the purpose of comparing fiscal systems "He makes no judgment on geology, cost difference, price difference or the handful of other factors an exploration company would evaluate.
AAPG EXPLORER, august 1995

TELECOM AND IT SECTOR IN MOGOLIA: STRATEGIC INFORMATION AND OPPORTUNITIES

BASIC INFORMATION

COMMUNICATION AND INFORMATION TECHNOLOGY

In 1234, the Mongol Empire of Chinggis Khaan set up the world's first long-distance postal transmission system, known as "Morin urtuu" (Horse relay station). Then it could take a letter from Kharkhorum to the Caspian Sea in one week. The horse relay service remained so until 1930s. The modern communication development began in the 1930s with the first international telephone exchange. Those days are gone, but now Mongolia is enjoying another information boom.

The Government of Mongolia recognizes that Information and Communication Technologies (ICT) have an important role to play in the development of the country. They offer a platform for building and applying knowledge; facilitate participation in trade for isolated communities, and small and medium enterprises as well as corporations; are critically important for national competitiveness; and allow for improved delivery of public services.
Before 1990, the country applied only analogue networks. New information technology has been effectively introduced into Mongolia with high speed since 1992.

Mongolia Telecom Company (MTC) is the national telecommunications company of Mongolia . MTC is a joint venture between the Mongolian government, which holds 60 per cent of the company, and the Korean Telecommunications Company, owning all remaining shares.

The company is planning to expand its services into the areas of cellular phones and internet-services in the near future. Deregulation of the telecommunications market is expected to enhance competition and provide new opportunities for growth. The government intends to privatize a portion of the state-owned shares of the Mongolia Telecom to strategic investor through a competitive tender.

Mongolia takes a high place in the international arena with a number of computers and mobile phones per person. The telecommunications network of the country was renovated and installed according to international standards by Alcatel of France, EWSD of Germany and KDD of Japan, with future projects coming from Germany and Korea . The country is connected with more than 150 countries via American Intelsat, Asiasat-1 and Intersputnik satellite links. Moreover, mobile telephone services, paging and data networks, cable TV networks, radio and TV broadcasting, and intranet networks are presently operating in Mongolia.

The Government Action Plan for 2000-2004 aims to provide technical facilities to connect Aimag centers with domestic and international communications and information networks. It is planned to upgrade the automatisation rate to 85 percent and to increase the number of telephone users by 20 per cent by the end of 2004. VSAT satellite communication stations were installed in a number of aimags under the Communications II and III project. As a result of the measures to upgrade and improve communication services all Aimags have now been provided with access to automatic dial, and Internet and e-mail services through dial up tone services.

The first- ever cellular telephone service company "Mobicom" was established in 1995 with Japan 's investment. Since then, digital technology has been introduced to the communication sector of the country in the short term. Any foreigner visiting Mongolia can enjoy using mobile phones within GSM and CDMA systems. Today number of mobile users has reached 256.8 thousand.

Nowadays, all aimags, except three, have access to cellular phone service provider in the country, is planning a $5.3 million investment to expand its CDMA system network that will transfer all customers in rural areas currently using the AMPS system.

The government of Mongolia supports the introduction of new state of the art information technology to this sector by granting taxation relief.

By unofficial estimates, every day there are approximately over 1000 calls from Mongolia to foreign countries and 14.000 calls to Mongolia from Korea, Russia, USA and China, where many Mongolians work and live.

New international telephone prepaid cards such as the "Smart" card was recently put into service. Sky C & C Company launched the smart card on May 2, 2002 . The card may be used from any telephone, to over 260 countries. Because of lower costs, higher quality of connections and easier use, the card is called "Smart".

The internet was first brought to Mongolia by DataCom in January 1996. Since then, various internet-based services such as e-mail, internet connections, internet taxing, internet-telephone, e-accounts, e-shopping, and internet café are available to users in Mongolia . The information technology is being introduced in Mongolia rapidly, and the total speed of the outgoing line is reaching 1472 Kbit/s, whereas the incoming is 2592 Kbit/s. There are four main Internet service providers in Mongolia such as Datacom, Micom and Bodicomputer Co., Ltd. The number of internet cafes has reached 80.

The Government of Mongolia approved the Medium Term Strategy for the Development of the ICT sector and an Action Plan for its implementation in January 2003. Furthermore, in 2001, Ikh Khural approved the Communications Law and the Communications Regulatory Commission to regulate the telecom sector has been established.

Mongolia has made considerable progress in developing its information and telecommunications infrastructure in recent years, particularly in the area of availability of modern basic service and cellular services. The number of main lines grew from 3.5 per 100 inhabitants in 1996 to 5.4 in 2002. The number of cellular subscribes grew from 1800 in 1996 to 235.000 in 2002 with the licensing of two operators. The internet service market fully liberalized and there are approximately 50000 internet users. A number of licensed VSAT service providers also provide various value added services such as managed network services, which allow businesses to utilize ICTs. Approximately 90 per cent of the current fixed network infrastructure is digitized. Further, Mongolia Railways also owns fiber optic infrastructure. This provides the opportunity to provide affordable bandwidth while increasing returns on state owned assets and investments.

Mongolia will ensure that the policy and regulatory environment allows for fair and competitive provision of infrastructure and services. The challenge Mongolia faces is to increase rural access to ICT infrastructure and services.

As the broadcast media has an important role to play in the development of Mongolia by providing information to its citizens, the equipment of radio and TV studios will be improved and transmission systems and stations for TV broadcasting will be upgraded. Within this framework, Mongolia will start broadcasting the 4 domestic digital TV (including the National TV) and 4 FM radio channels throughout the whole Mongolia , at the end of 2003.

In 2002, communication revenue was 38.7 billion tugrugs of which revenue from the population was 14 billion tugrugs. As compared with 2001, the total revenue from communication increased by 4 billion tugrugs, whereas, the revenue from the population increased by 2.2 billion tugrugs.

Postal service. Postal service is the most basic means of communications, which has served the public for a long time. Despite other alternative means of communications, the postal service is here to stay.

There are 9 business entities that conduct postal activities in Mongolia . To date, the Mongol Post Company is the only 100 per cent state-owned company of the existing 9 postal entities, the other 8 companies being private businesses. Mongolia joined the World Post Organization in 1963.

The Postal Law approved by the Parliament of Mongolia in May 2003. According to the law, the first time there will be free and fair competition between the companies

Mongolia has come a long way since Genghis Khan introduced a point-to-point horseback postal system in the 13th century. The country now has 3 telecommunications companies, 6 ISPs, 2 mobile phone operators, and over 50 software development companies. There are an estimated 50,000 people working in the ICT sector. The sector contributed 6.3 percent to the country's GDP in 2003; this contribution has been rising steadily from 2002 - 2003.

A number of progressive changes occurred in the ICT sector in Mongolia during 2003 - 2004. A new Department of Information and Communications Technology (ICT Department) has been set up at the Ministry of Infrastructure; previously, there was only one person looking after the ICT sector at the ministry. This department drafted a law on ICT in consultation with various stakeholder groups. These groups include representatives of government organisations and agencies, NGOs, donor and international organisations, as well as representatives of the media. The draft law has been presented to the government. It will be submitted for another round of discussion and lobbying within the government and among members of parliament after the June 2004 national elections led to the formation of a new coalition government and the election of new members of parliament. The new government, recognising the importance of ICT for development, has established the Information and Communications Technology Agency (ICT Agency).

The acquisition of a major portion of shares in Magicnet, the first ISP in Mongolia, by Bodicomputer, the second ISP in the country, has laid the groundwork for more mergers and acquisitions within the ICT sector. The number of ISPs has now been reduced to six. However, the total bandwidth to Mongolia has grown owing to connections established by RailCom, in collaboration with TransTelecom and China Unicom, and the resulting access it obtained to fibre optic links with neighbouring China.

The telecommunications sector is headed for change with the announcement that a third mobile operator will be licensed and the Mongolian Telecommunications Company (MTC) will be privatised. These two plans were unveiled by the previous government but left to the new government to implement.

The merger of the two NGOs dealing with ICT issues in Mongolia -- the Mongolian Information Development Association (MIDAS) and the Mongolian Information Technology Association (MONITA) -- has helped to raise the visibility of Mongolian ICT stakeholders in the global ICT community. Mongolian NGOs have now joined the World Information Technology and Service Alliance and the Asian-Oceanian Computing Industry Organization, thereby increasing the opportunity for Mongolian ICT stakeholders to participate in international initiatives.

ONLINE SERVICES

The total number of active Internet subscribers has grown by 8 percent since 2002, when there were about 40,000 registered subscribers and over 140,000 Internet users. The number of names registered under the ".mn" domain has been growing steadily, and 1,300 names were registered as of mid-2004. An increasing number of local organisations are registering ".mn" domain names.

TELEMEDICINE

A telemedicine project was started linking six locations in the country to the Third Hospital. Chest X-rays taken in these six locations are transmitted to the Third Hospital where they are reviewed by the country's leading cardiologists, who then send their diagnosis and advice back to the doctors at the six locations.

DISTANCE EDUCATION AND E-LEARNING

The public administration reform programme of the Asian Development Bank has supported the installation of videoconferencing facilities connecting 12 *aimag*

INFORMATION AND COMMUNICATION TECHNOLOGY SECTOR

ICT SECTOR HIGHLIGHTS

The ICT sector contributes to 8% of GDP growth.
There are currently 140 companies in this industry
The sector employs 11,500 people.

The Mongolian government is committed to the long term development of this sector as a means of promoting Mongolia's future economic growth. There are tax waiver schemes for foreign investors. The government is also promoting the privatization of private telecom assets.
The availability of low cost and qualified labor contributes to the attractiveness of this industry for foreign investors.

KEY PRODUCT SEGMENTS

Segment	Total Revenue 2002	Key Market Players	Current Trends
Voice (fixed phone)	20 US$ mil	1 Mongolia Telecom 2 Mongolian Railway Authorities 3 Mongolian Civil Aviation Authorities	1 The industry has limited infrastructure – There are over 30,000 people waitlisted for a phone line 2 It is being challenged by the cellular phone market segment
Cellular phone	20 US$ mil	1 Mobicom Co Ltd 2 Skytel Co Ltd	1 Current market exceeds that of fixed phones 2 Market growing since 1990s – poor infrastructure for fixed phones have contributed to growth 3 Subscribers are primarily in urban areas – 85% of all subscribers are in Ulaanbaatar
Internet/	2 US$ mil	1 Magicnet	1 There was a big increase in demand

Datacom		2 Micom 3 MCS Electronics 4 Bodicom	for Internet hosts and ISPs from 1999 to 2002 as more consumers utilized the internet 2 Market penetration continues to remain strong in the urban centers. Although, the rural sector is catching up with 50% of provincial centers having high speed internet access
Software	3 US$ mil	1 Grape City Mongolia 2 Engineersoft 3 Interactive	1 Highly fragmented industry with many small market players 2 The industry is young and unsophisticated 3 Local players are making strides in reaching global standards 4 Most domestically developed software applications are web related

FUTURE OF FOREIGN DIRECT INVESTMENT IN THE ICT SECTOR

Since 1990 20.9 million USD have been invested into Mongolia. International companies will continue to outsource their ICT needs to Mongolia to benefit from the country's competitive advantages, namely cheap labor markets and continued government support for the industry.

More partnerships will develop between domestic and foreign corporations. Currently, most key market players are partially foreign owned.

Company	Ownership Structure
Mobicom	12% Japanese ownership
Skytel	60% foreign ownership
Mongolian Railway Authority	JV Mongolian and Russian governments
Mongolia Telecom	JV Mongolian government and Korean Telecom

Business	Comment
Cellular Services	This market is experiencing continued growth. Care should be taken as there could be a tendency for over saturation as the market matures
Software Outsourcing	With the availability of cheap and well qualified labor resources, there are plenty of opportunities in this market to assist foreign firms in cutting their costs
Telecom Infrastructure	Currently, Mongolia lacks the necessary infrastructure to continue to maintain its long term goals for growth. Foreign investment in this segment would be strongly encouraged by the Mongolian government

NATIONAL IT STRENGTHS & WEAKNESSES

Mongolia has committed to continuing efforts to promote and improve its IT sector. A lot has been accomplished, but there is still room for improvement. To illustrate, below are the most important strengths and weaknesses characteristic of Mongolia's IT sector at the present time.

NATIONAL IT STRENGTHS

1. Infrastructure including ICT is among the high priority issue in the government development agenda. Mongolian Parliament approved a nationwide construction project "Millennium Road" to establish a main transversal auto road (Jan., 2001) and "ICT Vision - 2010" (Feb., 2000). Physical road infrastructure is the base for development, to create better livelihood environment and market condition, while ICT is to intensify development improving human capabilities and opening new opportunities for improvement of quality of life of the Mongolian people.[21]

2. Creation of a model of public accessible Infostructure along the Millennium Road:

- Create Development E-contents & Library: E-books, e-documents on planning, policy, project activities, business, and environment, other information related to Millennium road project.
- Create Millennium Road Database: mapping of road and its buffer area, road construction materials, technology, feasibility study reports, master plans, geo-engineering, environment, ecology, standards, norms, legal, policy documents, etc.
- Establish IT Platform with terminals at selected rural area along the Millennium Road: Virtual networking and partnership, Open Forums on development issues.

Development of Integrated Infostructure along the Millennium Road at the possible early stage would enable accumulation and sharing of information, knowledge and best practices, improve human capabilities, double the productivity, efficiency of road construction and lead to intensify development process. Such a benefit is vital for country socio-economic growth.

NATIONAL IT WEAKNESSES

1. Mongolian ICT development is not recognized by world ICT market and lack of experience with international competition.

There is:

A lack of skilled human resource / IT project managers, experts/ and ICT business support mechanism.
A weak standards on electronic data exchange.
A weak communication facilities, especially in the rural area.
A low rate of investment, as high Investment leads to high value of ICT products
A slow growth of need for ICT use.

2. Mongolia is a nation with an age-old history and culture. But as for development and progress it has been lagging behind many nations of world for many years. Low developed infrastructure limits access to market and social services for sparsely located population. Literacy rate,

education level of population is considered high, but application of information technology to intensify socio-economic development of country is insignificant.

GROWING POTENTIAL

Mongolia has one of the smallest income differentials in the world. This serves as a tremendous stabilizing factor in Mongolian political life. It is an advantage for the Mongolian economy, and must be maintained. The labor force is well-educated and well-disciplined, and are massive assets in establishing new enterprises and absorbing standard production technologies readily available in many areas of the world.

The country is bordered by China and Russia, two of the largest markets in the world. If Mongolia can produce good-quality products, these countries will become excellent markets for its exports. Moreover, Mongolia's most-favored-nation status in the United States is very useful in attracting direct investment from countries that would like to export to the US.

SIZE OF DOMESTIC IT MARKET

Mongolia has taken significant and consistent steps towards market economy. In 1997, Mongolia has joined the World Trade Organization (WTO). Despite some attempts at diversification of exports, the Mongolian economy remains highly vulnerable with external factors. Mongolia has narrow productive base that is built on animal originated raw materials such as hides, skins, dehaired cashmere etc. and mineral resources namely copper, gold and flour spar.

NATIONAL GDP

National Statistical Office data for a year of 2001 shows that in the structure of GDP agriculture share remains predominant, which is represented as 48.9 percent of total labor force and produces nearly 30 percent of GDP. This constitutes 30% of exports having a strong comparative advantage. Mining and processing industry share is 8.5 per cent and 5.6 per cent respectively. Rest of GDP is produced by wholesale and retail trading and service sectors.

During the economic transition period from the centrally planed economy to the market based economy, the former trading system was completely destroyed. Liberalization of foreign trade activity in one hand and giving freedom in domestic trade in the other hand had completely changed structure of trade sector of the country.

Mongolia's domestic trade sector is represented by over 100 wholesale trading private companies. One of the obstacles existing trade structure is an inadequate service condition for rural population, including people live in the provincial centers (aimag and sum centers). Nearly 95 per cent of consumer goods are imported or produced in city of Ulaanbaatar and accordingly distributed to the provinces through the retail channel. This inappropriate trade structure that can be so called one door outflow system raises vast problems with supply of provincial population by consumer goods in terms of article of goods, quality and price.

Mongolia's import consists mainly from processed goods such as petroleum products, equipment, machinery and consumer goods. The import exceeds the export that contributes bad trade balance.

Economic Indicator:

Exchange rate: $1 = Tg 1099 (Sep 25, 2001)
GDP: Tg 1,044,580.6 million
GDP per capita: Tg 436,971.6
Inflation: 219.6 per cent (1995=100), 8.1 annual inflation rate
State budget expenditure: Tg 412.9 billion
State budget revenue: Tg 350.2 billion
Foreign aid (1991-97): U.S. 478 million
Official external debt: Tg 522 billion (Oct 97)
Industrial output: Tg 582.3 billion
Exports: $466.1 million
Imports: $614.5 million
Workforce: employed: 809,000, unemployed 38,570

Source: State Statistical Office

COMPUTING & INTERNET DIFFUSION

Its Internet infrastructure is far from perfect, but nevertheless Mongolia has improved its communications capability dramatically in just two years. So much so that it has attracted the attention of other developing countries facing similar problems.

Mongolia is a sparsely populated country located in Central Asia and occupies a vast territory. The country has an under-developed infrastructure. Mongolia is ranking in the 116th place in terms of the human development index by the UN human development report. Population literacy rate is 96.8%. All the key factors show the importance of penetration and use of ICT in all sectors of Mongolia.

INTERNET SERVICE PROVIDERS

Based on the reports from the ICT institutions there are 7 ISPs, 1 Internet Exchange Point, 50000 group users of the Internet, 10000 dedicated Internet subscribers and over 40 Internet service points(public centers and café). Total bandwidth of satellite link is 10 mbps download.

At present the ICT sector is most growing sector with more than 70 private companies (over 7000 employees), working in Internet service, software and hardware development, online information services and consultancy.

Mongolia has 3100 ICT professionals and about 2000 students are studying ICT related higher education institutions.

There are total of 11 Internet Service Providers (ISPs) in Mongolia. The top five ISPs are:[3]

1. Datacom Co., Ltd. (since 1995) - Datacom Co., Ltd, a data communications systems company, was the first to introduce Internet and its services to Mongolia in 1995. Datacom provides data communications services such as domestic PC-mail service, VSAT X.25, international PC-fax services, DirectPC service, WWW, and Internet E-mail service. Datacom Co., Ltd. has VSAT Internet connection to the United States with a bandwidth of 512 Kbps. They are the major ISP in Mongolia and they have more than 2,000 subscribers, which does not include the users at the corporate level. Most universities and research institutes, government organizations, agencies, banks, companies, international organizations in Ulaanbaatar and other main cities are using a

LAN connected to the Internet. Datacom provide VSAT Internet connection to USA with a bandwidth of 512 kbps. Dial-up users can have an access at 33.6 kbps speed. Corporate users have 64 to 115 kbps access.

2. CSMS (since 1998) - The Computer science and management school of the Technical University of Mongolia has connected ten universities with 400 PC's. They have about 100 dial-up users and are connecting 33 schools via dial-up and three schools via radio modem. The CSMS leases 115 kbps radio line and 400 kbps DirecPC satellite line from Datacom.

3. Bodicomputer (since January 1999) - They have about 200 users and their bandwidth is 374 kbps. The Bodicomputer provides high speed Galactic satellite Internet (GSI). They lease telecommunication lines of the MTC (Telecom).

4. Micom (since March 1999) - The Micom is a subsidiary of the MTC (Telecom) and have about 300 users at present with bandwidth of 374 Kpbs. An advantage of them is that dial-up users pay local tariff for the Internet connectivity in provinces.

5. Mobinet - An Internet provider formed by the Mobicom Corporation.

IT Development Indicator for Mongolia (per 1000 people)

Country	Daily Newspaper	Radios	Televsion Sets	Cable Subscribers	Personal Computers	Internet Users	ISP Charge	Telephone Usage	Secure Servers
Mongolia	30	50	72	16.5	14.6	40	52	0.17	1

Sources: World Bank - Information Age 5.1

INTERNET DIFFUSION

D. Ganbold, General Director of Interactive, local software company, states "The Mongolian private sector has achieved good progress in building ICT infrastructure." Today 7 Internet service providers and 2 mobile service providers operate in Mongolia. One in ten Mongolians use a mobile phone, and there are now over 50, 000 Internet users in Mongolia. The mobile service providers, with Korean and Japanese investment, have delivered fiber optic cable loops within Ulaanbaatar City, as well as many rural areas and smaller cities within the country. Around 60 software development companies produce applications for e-commerce and banking, as well as producing content and applications software in both Mongolian and other languages.

Mongolia has strength in human resources, basic infrastructure, and supportive government policies. With a positive business environment, the next phase for ICT development is involvement in the global economy, and creating further opportunities for Mongolian companies. "That is the mission of the second stage of ICT development in the country," D. Enkhbat says.

John Savageau, American CEO of MagicNet, the first Mongolian Internet Service Provider, believes Mongolians can do any job needed to compete in the global economy. As long as Mongolian software developers and network providers can produce a world class product, it makes no difference whether the product is produced by an American, Indian, European, or Mongolian. The important discriminator is quality the, and a desire to do the best.

At the same time some local experts criticize Mongolia's situation. D. Enkhbat explains the "The Mongolian market is not aggressive towards using knowledge and information. Business habits of the local people are different. Today in Mongolia there are more people with cars than with computers." He says, "It is important for Mongolian people to understand that ICT is tool that delivers knowledge and enables new efficiencies when employed. This means additional knowledge needs to be added into all business processes to be more competitive, and introducing more value added products and services."

J. Savageau says "Thought leadership is missing in leading Mongolian business people." "In many cases business leaders have no experience or knowledge of how to use the tools and resources to manage their business processes better." Savageau sees tremendous potential and opportunity for local enterprises to improve the efficiency of their business, and to extend current markets using communications technology as an enabling tool.

ELECTRONIC COMMERCE & E-BUSINESS

E-commerce are transactions conducted over networks across organizational boundaries. The traditional types of e-commerce are those that involve transactions between business and consumers (B2C) and between business partners (B2B).[4]

Information and Communications Technology (ICT) has changed the rules of the global economy. The idea that many of today's business successes in world are small companies with flexible and high speed responses to the demands of markets and their clients is in stark contrast to the traditional factors related to a company's size and capital.

In the new global economy ICT is considered an essential tool in linking Mongolia, particularly business community with the global economy. This makes Mongolia more competitive in both local and international markets. ICT is turning the country's disadvantages; landlocked, remote areas with small population into advantages. Advantages are possible as we continue to develop an economy based on knowledge and information technology.

The Government of Mongolia pays serious attention to ICT sector by considering it as an economic key sector in the 21st century. ICT Committee represented by members from the Government, science organizations, and business community chaired by Prime Minister have been formed and been working on the long term program on development of ICT sector in Mongolia.

E-COMMERCE IN MONGOLIA

In 1997, government program on Establishment of Wholesale Network has been developed to be a B2B e-commerce system that supplies consumer goods to the people in the rural areas and raw materials to the industry.

Success of the Government program for establishing the wholesale network will depend on the development of its B2B e-commerce. E-commerce development will bring its input in implementation of national priorities that could foster and emulate the human development outcomes and will render assistance in improving living standards of Mongolian citizens and also in reducing economic vulnerabilities. This in affect will increase the living standards of Mongolian population in rural area.

The project objective is to ensure that there will be a formed operational wholesale information network connecting provinces, cities, and rural areas that provide real time trade. The trade is related to data exchange between suppliers and buyers and e-commerce environment with its appropriate components with gateway to international network.

The project is to establish inter-media oriented market placing B2B e-commerce service centre that would support e-commerce trading actions. Participating companies in wholesale trading actions would have accesses to B2B service centre database through the Internet. B2B Service Centre will be a business organization financed with membership fees of registered companies at the centre and transaction commissions. It is estimated that $120,000 (USD) is necessary for establishment of B2B Service Centre as an initial investment for a year term. The Centre will have an international Internet access.

Some of the business entities have set up e-commerce system of B2C for their commercial actions. For instance, approximately 10 companies created their online shopping for their retail sales.

Since August 2002, banks of Golomt and Capitron have commenced providing Internet banking services to the customers in Mongolia.

Over the last couple of years, the growth of the Mongolian domestic IT industry has led more and more firms to use ICT in their business activities, enabling them to move into e-commerce and e-banking.

SOFTWARE AND HARDWARE

There are many companies in the country offering hardware and software products. Import taxes for these kinds of goods are low due to the ICT policies of the government. Hence, purchasing IT products in the country is easy and prices are relatively low. The majority of small businesses have at least one computer which is used for word processing and spreadsheet purposes and in retail related businesses as cheap point of sales terminals. On the other hand mid-size to large-size businesses tend to have a computer for each employee and servers running e-mail systems as well as departmental databases. The majority of PCs owned by small and mid-sized businesses are "generic", i.e., assembled from purchased parts. At the same time, larger businesses tend to buy brand name computers. Computer networks are very common in mid-sized to large size businesses, while they are almost non-existent in small businesses. There are very few mainframes in operation in the country which are owned by government institutions and state universities.

USE OF LEASED LINES

Lines for interconnecting businesses to different sites can only be leased from the state owned telecom company RACSA. The prices of these lines are relatively high. Hence, only larger businesses can afford them.

INTERNET

The majority of small businesses do not have permanent connections to Internet; they only have one, or in some cases, a couple of dial-up accounts. Broadband services are available through dedicated connections through Telecom Mongolia or – in some very limited areas of the capital city Ulaan Baatar – through cable modems. However, businesses tend not to use cable modems. The reason is twofold: one, cable modem services are not available everywhere, and two, the level of security is inadequate. Finally, where high speed Internet is not available, such as some rural areas as well as remote areas of the country, satellite Internet (VSAT) is available.[5]

CURRENT STATUS AND PROSPECTS OF E-COMMERCE

ICT Committee represented by members from the Government, science organizations and business community and chaired by Prime Minister have been formed and been working on the medium term program on development of ICT sector in the country. Government program on Establishment of Wholesale Network is a supply chain or B2B e-commerce system that supplies consumer goods to the rural people and raw materials to the industry.

Success of the Government program for establishing the wholesale network will depend on development of its information component or in other word its B2B e-commerce. E-commerce development will bring its input in implementation of national priorities that could foster and emulate the excellent human development outcomes and will render assistance in improving living standards of Mongolian citizens and in reducing economic vulnerabilities.

Some of the business entities have set up e-commerce system of B2C for their commercial actions. For instance around 10 companies created their online shopping for their retail sales. Since August 2002, banks of Golomt and Capitron have commenced providing Internet banking services to the customers.

SOFTWARE DEVELOPMENT, HARDWARE MANUFACTURING, R&D

Today's global economy is rapidly shifting from business strongly focused on natural resources, software development, hardware manufacturing, and to service-based industries, particularly those using information and communication technology. These rapid changes open up new development opportunities for Mongolia, and the digital highway could bring many blessings to the landlocked country. However, to benefit from it, action has to be taken soon.

Generally speaking, Mongolia is actively seeking to engage in software development in the recent yearsr, but there are no hardware manufacturing and research and development (R&D) activities as of this year.

FUTURE OF SOFTWARE DEVELOPMENT, HARDWARE DEVELOPMENT, AND R&D:

The essence of the science and technology information policy is to create information supply infrastructure and ensure its operational procedures and mechanism to enable effective use of science and technology information resources for national economic development. For this purpose the results of the research and development works accumulated at the research institutions need to be transferred to an electronic form and works should be organized for expanding the user's group and benefits to the users.

The measures are being taken to promote domestic companies that will supply their products to both domestic and international market through establishing technopark and incubators of information technology.

It is necessary to establish a centralized science and technology information network and a database to expand the future of information communications technology and improve their utilization.

IT WORKFORCE

Mongolia's national ICT policy is formulated in ICT Vision 2010 in the Education Sector of Mongolia. This vision seeks to meet its mission by establishing a flexible system to implement and manage international-standard ICT training for all educational levels. The vision covers four areas - training, hardware, teaching staff and information ware.

Labor Market Statistics[9]

Labor force: 1.4 million
Labor force by occupation: Primarily herding / agricultural
Unemployment rate: 20%
Industrial production growth rate: 2.4%
Adult literacy rate: 62.3%
Primary school net enrollment: 84%
Secondary school net enrollment: 54%
Physicians: 27 per 10,000

BACKGROUND IN EDUCATION

Unlike some newly developing countries, Mongolia is not burdened with a low literacy rate which could hamper its economic growth. In fact, at 87%, Mongolia can claim one of the highest literacy rates in the world. However, with the transition from a Russian soviet-dependent economy to a market-driven one, Mongolia's education systems are changing, and not always for the better.

Mongolian students go to school for eleven years, from age 7 to 17. The education system consists of preschool, primary school (grades 1-6), secondary school (compulsory to grade 8, complete at grade 10), vocational and technical training, and universities. Schooling is considered to be very important; in the rural areas where there may be no schools, children of nomads are often sent to the aimag (province) centers to attend boarding schools, only returning home on breaks and summer vacation.[10]

Currently, there are 29 state universities and 40 private universities in Mongolia, and in the last 10 years many kinds of schools have surfaced that are teaching everything from computer technology to traditional medicine, reflecting the changing needs of students. Most of these schools are located in the capital city of Ulaanbataar, so those students who live in the rural areas must find a way to get to the city. With 43% of the total Mongolian population under the age of 14, students' education is the key to Mongolia's continued success.

Mongolia, with the assistance of many nation-donors and international NGOs, has begun to revamp its educational system. Laws urging and monitoring change were passed in 1991 and 1995 but it has become apparent that many of the revisions are slow in being implementing. Students in remote provincial areas can see that their education system is lagging behind.

An increasing number of students (16.5%) are dropping out, mostly young men who are choosing to stay in rural areas to help their herder families, and the number of children attending the rural boarding schools has also decreased by 35%. At the same time, the Mongolian National Statistical Office survey reports that the number of female students far exceeds the males by a large margin. In fact, women now make up more than 63% of university students and 65% of those earning master's degrees. Even among the employed rural population, women are consistently more educated than their male counterparts. And the 1997 Human Development Report stated that 80% of medical doctors, 70% of lawyers and 73% of teachers in Mongolia are women. The problem now is to continue encouraging young women while addressing the obstacles young rural men face. Distance education is a possibility for some of these rural students and it's one of the best alternatives that Mongolia is seeking at the moment.

ICT ACTION PLAN OF EDUCATION SECTOR OF MONGOLIA

Within basic education, the Government will conduct training towards improving knowledge and skills of the most popular and commonly used software such as word processing, spreadsheet, information exchange and communication.

Starting from the academic year 2002 to 2003, the curriculum of the basic education will be revised to include a specification that by completion of 8th grade, students will have been taught at least 70 hours of "Informatics".[11]

Furthermore, free access will be provided for students of secondary schools who do not have access to modern and well equipped ICT training labs through a voucher system. Mobile labs will be set up for short term training and information services for school lacking modern ICT facilities.

For upper secondary, vocational and technical education, opportunities will be provided to gain knowledge and skills on the use of the most popular and latest application software, such as desktop publishing, Internet applications and e-mail, access to ICT applications, and to search and use necessary and available information.

Model textbooks will be developed in 'Information Sciences" for all levels of education.

Pre and in-service teacher education initiatives will be established for staff in secondary schools, in revision of contents and curriculum, expansion of professional teachers' training activities considering the increase of professional teaching staff in information sciences up to 50 percent by 2003 and up to 90 percent by 2007.[11]

Training will also be organized for teachers who wanted to use ICT in teaching their subjects and favorable conditions will be nurtured to run ICT supported training programs.

LABOR FORCE

By the end of 2000 Mongolia had 809.0 thousand employed persons and the economically active population constituted 68.5 per cent of the whole workforce. The number of unemployed people has been increasing despite the growth of the population leading to a rapid increase in the number of the economically active population, particularly among young people. High population growth rate during the 1960s and 1970s has provided an abundant labor force in the 1980s and 1990s.

The developing national economy employed this labor pool. The centralized economy was providing new jobs for nearly 90.000 men and women yearly. A vast network of training and professional education was created. Graduates from secondary schools were sent to the former USSR and East European countries for higher education. Nearly 240.000 trainees completed the vocational schools between 1964-1990. New development projects had difficulties concerning shortage of labor force.

Today's labor market in Mongolia is characterized by increasing unemployment, and consequent decline in training process.

Informal Sector Employment, 2000

Indicators	Employment in the capital city (thous.persons)	Employment in Aimags (thous.persons)	Total (thous.persons)
Population of working age	-	-	1 374.4
Economically active population	221.7	625.9	847.6
Employed	215.5	593.5	809.0
Unemployed	61.5	324.2	385.7
Labor force participation rate, %	-	-	62.9
Employment rate, %	-	-	60.0
Unemployment rate, %	2.8	1.8	4.6
With higher education	85.6	125.1	210.7
With special secondary education	72.7	413.7	486.4
Graduated training centers	173.6	765.4	939.0
Untrained	28.2	193.8	222.1

Employees, by divisions

Divisions	Total (thous.persons)
Agriculture, hunting	393.5
Mining	18.6
Manufacturing	54.6
Electricity, gas and water supply	17.8
Construction	23.4
Wholesale and retail trade, repair of motor vehicle, motorcycle. And personal and household goods	83.9
Hotels and restaurants	13.3
Transport, storage and communication	34.1
Financial intermediation	6.8
Real estate, renting and business activities	7.2
Public administration and defense	34.7
Education	54.4
Health and social security	33.5
Community, social and personal services	29.0
Others	4.2

Social Data:

Life expectancy: 62.5 years

Infant mortality rate: 32.8 per 1000
Under five mortality rate: 56.4 per 1000
Maternal mortality: 81
One-year-old immunization rate: tuberculosis 97 per cent, measles 86 per cent
Access to safe drinking water: rural 89.9 per cent, urban 46.1 per cent (1995)
Access to sanitation: 74 per cent
Adult literacy rate: 62.3 per cent
Primary school net enrollment: 84 per cent
Secondary school net enrollment: 54 per cent
Physicians: 27 per 10,000
Hospital beds: 7.5 per 1000
Daily calorie intake: 2462.3
Television sets: 7 per 100
Newspapers: 7.5 per capita, pcs
Number of telephones: 112,200
Marriage: 9.0 per 1000 over 18
Divorce: 0.6 per 1000 over 18
Number of pensioners: 287,200
Crimes reported: 23463 . As percentage of same period in 1999: 100.5 per cent.

Sources: State Statistical Office, Human Development Report Mongolia 1997

IT GEOGRAPHICS

Mongolia is vast and landlocked country that situated in the central Asia with an area of over 1.5 million sq km and population of only 2.5 million (as of 2000). Mongolia has one of the lowest population densities of the world. The capital, Ulaanbaatar, has a population of over 600,000. The country is divided into 21 aimags (provinces), plus autonomous capital region. Landlocked geographical location, abominable climate and lower population density exerts negative impacts to the economic development growth of the country and vast distances in the country raises difficulties on infrastructure development in terms of transportation and communication.

IT GEOGRAPHICS IN MONGOLIA

The main geographic concentrations of Information Technology (IT) exist in Ulaanbaatar, which is the capital of Mongolia. In particular, the National Information Technology Park (NITP) has been established as information and communication technology has become an increasingly crucial accelerator in the development of Mongolia in the twenty-first century.

The NITP was established in 2002 under the Government Act 107. The Charter of the NITP was approved by the joint order 210/216 of 19 July 2002, by the Minister of Science, Technology, Education and Culture and the Minister of Infrastructure. The NITP is a non-profit governmental organization.

The NITP officially commenced its activities on 6 August 2002. In the years 2002 and 2003 the park has successfully implemented the "Information Technology Park" project with the grant aid of U.S. $1 million from the Republic of Korea, and created the environment for incubator services.

The main objectives of the NITP are to support the development of information technology in Mongolia, and serve as the incubator for turning new and unique ideas of venture businesses into competitive products and services. The NITP also aims to establish a scientific and technological database with comprehensive services to increase the contribution of information technology to the economic growth of Mongolia and to become a hub of IT in the country.

The NITP represents Mongolia in the Asia Pacific Information Network (APIN) and the International Center for Scientific and Technical Information (ICSTI).

- **National Information Technology Park (NITP) of Mongolia**
  - Internet address:
    - http://www.itpark.mn/
  - Language of data presentation:
    - Mainly in Mongolian
    - English
  - The following are the key NITP activities:
    - Establishment of the modern high-speed broadband Internet and provision of services associated with it
    - Creation of a favorable incubator environment for newly established information technology companies and support for their growth
    - Identification of the works and projects for governmental and international organizations and facilitation of these works to be executed by start-up IT companies
    - Establishment of contacts with IT, banking, business and R&D institutions abroad and implementation of joint projects
    - Support to the development of policies of the government of Mongolia on information technology
    - Establishment of an integrated scientific and technological library and network and provision of related information
  - The NITP has the library with scientific and technological materials and is able to provide the following services:
    - Database of R&D reports
    - Dissertations database
    - "Erdemten" (Scientist) database
    - Polytechnic databases
    - Development of business and business services
  - Database contains following information databases:
    - Information library of Natural Sciences
    - Information library of Technical and Applied Sciences
    - Information library of Medical Sciences
    - Information library Agricultural Sciences
    - Information library Human and Social Sciences

The NITP officially commenced its activities on 6 August 2002. In the years 2002 and 2003 the park has successfully implemented the "Information Technology Park" project with the grant aid of U.S. $1 million from the Republic of Korea, and created the environment for incubator services offered by the following companies located in Ulaanbaatar.

NATIONAL INFORMATION TECHNOLOGY PARK (NITP)

1. STARSOFT

a. Established in 2002, the company focuses its activity are focused on computer software development, professional and non-professional trainings.
b. Website: **http://www.starsoft.mn**
c. E-mail Address: support@starsoft.mn

2. **INTERACTIVE**
   a. Established in 1996, the company activity is focused on automation of interior accounting, establishment of database, web-based on-line software, portal site development, business integration, software development, and domain name selling.
   b. Website: http://www.interactive.mn
   c. E-mail Address: interactive@mongolnet.mn

3. **ECM**
   a. Established in 2001, the company focuses its activities on e-commerce, financial and organizational activity software, Internet programming, and web-based software development.
   b. Website: http://www.ecm.mn
   c. E-mail Address: ecm@mongolnet.mn

4. **CISCO**
   a. Established in 2003, the company activities include introduction and development of new information technology initiatives in Mongolia, development of new database and adapting; elaboration and implementation of information network and e-commerce draft, consulting services regarding the activities mentioned above, and training programs.
   b. Website: http://www.cisco.mn
   c. E-mail Address: altanoch@magicnet.mn

5. **SPEAKER GROUP**
   a. Established in 2001, the company activities include software development, Website design, e-production, publishing and information services.
   b. Website: http://www.stormpages.am/speaker
   c. E-mail Address: speaker@mol.mn

6. **MONEXE**
   a. Established in 2003, the company activity include software and Web-based program development.
   b. Website: http://www.monexe.mn
   c. E-mail Address: saikhnaa@mongoleducation

7. **E-MONGOLIA**
   a. Established in 2001, the company activities include Website design, Website service/domain name registration, Website installation, Internet marketing creating, introduction, practice, consulting and transfer.
   b. Website: http://www.mongolmedia.com
   c. E-mail Address: emongol@mongol.net

8. **SKY POWER MEDIA**

a. Established in 2003, it is the Mongolian-Korean joint company with activity such as production of digital goods, and computer graphics services.
b. Website: http://www.skypowermedia.mn
c. E-mail Address: eamarsaikhan@mogicnet.mn

9. **SOFTNET**
   a. Established in 2002, the company activities include E-commerce and e-service Website, software development, Website installation, and domain name selling.
   b. Website: http://www.softnet.mn
   c. E-mail Address: softnet@magicnet. mn

10. **CITICOM**
    a. Established in 1998, the company's main activities include development of financial and far-distance training program and Web-based software, software and technical repair services.
    b. Website: http://www.citicom.mn
    c. E-mail Address: siticom@mobinet.mn

11. **IMT**
    a. Established in 2001, the company focuses its activity on on-line trainings, multimedia, network planning and protection.
    b. Website: http://www.imt.mn
    c. E-mail Address: shinee@imt.mn

12. **Geo-Information Center**
    a. Established in 2001, the company focuses its activity on information technology, environmental research and analysis, establishment of geo-information service network and database, trainings, books, publishing services, and consulting services.
    b. Website: http://www.geoinfo.mn
    c. E-mail Address: jemr@majicnet.mn

IT FINANCING

Although Mongolian government realizes the importance in the development of IT by financing and has been gradually engaging in this process recently via near by Asian countries like, South Korea, China, Russia, Phillipines, and Singapore, the government is actively pursueing to receive sufficient funds on natural disaster frequently occuring in Mongolia

INFORMATION ON FINANCING FOR NATURAL DISASTER OCCURRING IN MONGOLIA

Mongolia is situated in high regions of Central Asia with severe climatic conditions, and therefore difference in daily temperatures during warm and cold seasons, is enormous. If earlier, draughts and zuds occurred only once in three years, now, due to the overall world climatic changes, frequency of those natural disasters got even closer, and the last three years it happened consequently.

This kind of change in climate has very negative impacts on agricultural development of the country, where non-irrigated crop production and pasture livestock production systems are dominated.

During the last three years Mongolia had lost 10.8 million heads of livestock, 8.8 million out of which died due to zud, which could be converted to 269.5 million tugriks in total. These figures will increase dramatically if the following issues are included such as: decrease in numbers of offsprings produced from every hundred of breeding animals, deterioration of animal quality and productivity, increase of abortions and number of barren animals, state direct and indirect expenses for draught and zud damage alleviation, amount of international and donor loan and assistance, decrease in overall domestic production of processing enterprises, as well as reduction of export incomes against import increase and all other economic losses caused by those natural disasters.

In 2000, the total amount of humanitarian aid and financial assistance reached to 30.0 million US dollars which were offered by many foreign countries, international organizations, donors and private persons in order to help us to overcome damage and losses that were facing Mongolia. People of Mongolia are sincerely grateful for that financial as well as moral support during those hard years.

Due to the increasing frequency and extent of draught and zud, "National programme for protecting livestock from draught and zud" was approved by the Government of Mongolia in 2001. Within the framework of the programme implementation, state reserve points were additionally established in all Aimags, and certain measures are taken regarding establishment of Aimag and Soum level reserves, that are based on former state reserve facilities.

With a view to restore Aimag and Soum emergency reserves, the Government of Mongolia also distributed Tug 1.050 billion in 2001 from the state budget to Aimags for the preparation of hay and fodder reserves in Aimags and Soums.

The state budget is spending Tug 5.1 billion for measures to improve livestock health, Tug 850.0 million for combating pasture pests, rodents and insects and over Tug 440.0 million for the improvement of water supply in pasture land and repair of wells.

In connection with these conditions the Government of Mongolia is taking additional measures such as:

1. The Government approved to spend Tug 1.0 billion totally in order to increase hay and fodder amounts at the regional state reserves up to 50%;

2. To extend repayment of Tug 1050.0 million, which was issued last year as loan for establishment of fodder funds at Aimags and Soums within project "Hay & Fodder - 2001"; the funds would be used temporarily for preparing livestock for wintering and repaid in 2003.

3. A decision was made to allot 116.5 million tugriks to repair engineered wells and drill new ones in rich pasture (otor) regions. The work had been done.

4. In connection with current excessive dry climate, a resolution was passed to repair and reestablish low-pressure irrigation systems and support citizens in having irrigated hay fields and grow vegetables. In the first place, twenty million tugriks, with repayment condition, were allotted to repair Hurhree irrigation system in Chandman soum of Gobi-Altai province.

5. In order to help herders to prepare hay themselves and improve their abilities rakes, silk thread dews and horse driven (morin) machines were given for half-price with repayment condition.

E-GOVERNMENT

ccording to the World Bank, E-government refers to “the use of information and communications technologies to improve the efficiency, effectiveness, transparency and accountability of government”. E-government can be divided into Government-to-Government (G2G) and Government to Citizens (G2C).

E-GOVERNMENT IN MONGOLIA

The delivery of information through the use of information and telecommunication technology is strategically important for developing countries like Mongolia.

E-Government is the new topic in the area of Information Technology (IT) of Mongolia. Recognizing the importance of IT, Mongolian Government adopted a policy paper entitled "Vision for the development of information and communication technology until 2010". The paper details the basic scope of the promotion of information technology and the priorities of IT application in Mongolia. [6]

In order to establish a development of government IT system among the government-legislation, business-economic, and people-society, there are three main frameworks as follows:

1. Framework is within the government-legislation: The Government is the Founder of a social system with Information and Communication Technologies, an open source for information and data and it should offer the main service

2. Within business-economic framework: Set up a business environment that can be integrated efficiently with the world economy

3. Framework is the people-society: Create a favorable environment for Mongolian citizens to communicate freely among themselves and with the world community regardless of location, and to provide equal and active involvement and participation in the social relationships

The major objectives of the vision mentioned above are:

Harmonize Information and Communication Technology standards Internationally
Set up an Information and Communication Technology structure
Set up a system to make government information accessible
Promote the favorable legal and development environment of e-commerce
Meet the requirements of the international agreements

"Information and Communications Technology for Sustainable Human Development" (ICT for SHD) project of Cabinet Secretariat of Government of Mongolia and United Nations Development Programme has started its activities from June 1997. The main purpose of the project was to establish the Government Information Network (GIN), assist the Ministries and Government agencies on the setting up LAN's and provide the possibility of exchanging information in electronic format between government organizations.

Since the project implementation, 27 government organizations, agencies and the governor's offices of provinces were connected to the GIN. More than 800 government employees have been trained on various Windows Operating Systems, Microsoft Office packages and web publishing application.

The Mongolian Government recognizes the potential role that emergent Internet-based distance education technologies can play in its educational system, to spread and make available the teaching resources from the capital, Ulaanbataar, to the country's vast rural provinces.

According to Mr R Bat-Erdene, the State Secretary of the Ministry of Science, Technology and Culture (MOSTEC), the Government aims to deliver distance education to 75% of the population by the year 2010. There is great optimism that this mission will succeed due to Mongolia's high literacy rate - at 82.9%, it is one of the highest in the world. Through this project, the government is assisting the educational authorities in Mongolia to strategize a plan for technology-based distance education within its national education policy framework.

It is highly optimistic that the Mongolian distance education model will become a prototype from which it can transfer and share the lessons learnt to other Asian countries which are looking to the new educational technologies to help solve the problems of access to education for their rural populations.

INFORMATION TECHNOLOGY DEVELOPMENT

The Government of Mongolia is sensitively feeling the great implication of information technology's advanced achievement on social and economic development and gives high priority to it. The modern way of information dissemination (inter-network) is not new for Mongolians, even in the period Chinggis Khaan the success of his great victories was based on it. The digital infrastructure is in place and growing and there has already been experience with the implementation of ICT in a variety of fields. There are currently 7 Internet service providers and 2 mobile operators run their business in the country. One of every ten Mongolians uses mobile phone and there are over 50 000 Internet users.

Around 60 ICT companies deal with development of software application and local contents including e-commerce and e banking. With regard to deepening liberalization and competitiveness in this sector, the Communication law was renewed in 2001, which aims to create more favorable and clearly defined legal environment in communication sector. According to the newly revised law, General service fund is to be set up distributing communication services to the population of remote local areas. In February 2000, Parliament of Mongolia has adopted the "Concept on Information and Communication Technology Development of Mongolia up to 2010". The Government of Mongolia set up the National Committee for Information and Communication Technology headed by the Prime Minister.

NATIONAL ICT POLICIES

ICT policies are extremely important for developing countries like Mongolia. "ICT can be a powerful enabler of development goals because its unique characteristics dramatically improve communication and the exchange of information to strengthen and create new economic and social networks. ICT can contribute to income generation and poverty reduction. It enables people and enterprises to capture economic opportunities by increasing process efficiency, promoting participation in expanded economic networks, and creating opportunities for employment."

ICT POLICIES IN MONGOLIA

As evidence that Mongolia is fully aware of the importance of Information Communications Technology (ICT), the mission of the ICT Development concept of Mongolia has been adopted by the Government in 1996. The key strategic goal with respect to the Information Technology (IT) development has been defined as "introduction of world wide and nation wide IT into production, services and public life, organization of new software and IT industry, and establishment of scientific and technological information network".[2]

The Ministry of Enlightenment which is the policy making and coordinating government authority in the field of education, science, technology and culture, and responsible for library and information service's development policy has been set up following the political election of 1996.

In December of 1997, the Government of Mongolia has established a Working group (GWG) on coordination of the development of the national information technology. GWG consists of 18 representatives of the telecom and network operators, experts of the research institutes, relevant ministries and government agencies. GWG focuses on development of the efficient and fair competition or regulatory environment to be adopted by the government.

In January of 1999, the Ministry of Enlightenment has formed an Advisory committee on improvement of Education information network. The committee consists of 14 representatives from Technical University, higher education institutes, and Center for Scientific and Technological Information (CSTI).

As a result of the Mongolian ICT Summit in June of 1999, "Mongolian ICT Vision 2010" has been approved by the Summit and endorsed by the government. The vision consists of Mongolia's mission, principles and objectives.

1. The mission of the ICT development vision in Mongolia is to develop a society based on knowledge and intellectual potentials and to develop the quality of people's lives

2. A principle to ensure accessible and flexible informatics policies promoting dynamic and sustainable development in an open and fair society shall be pursued to achieve the mission

3. The main objectives are divided into three groups (government-legislation, business-economy, and people-society):

   - The government is the builder of an informative social structure and the open information source, and the main information service-provider
   - To create a business environment capable of ensuring efficient integration into the world's economy, enhance intellectual capacities of domestic and national products, and improve the competitiveness
   - To ensure opportunities for Mongolian citizens' equal and active participation in social life, for improving qualities of life and freely communicating with each other and the world community
   - The Government Action Program 2000 includes "establishment of nation wide information network of 240 institutions including universities, higher educational institutes, and libraries with an Internet gateway"

The Government of Mongolia is sensitively feeling the great implication of information technology's advanced achievement on social and economic development and gives high priority to it. The new generation of Mongolia has a potential to produce computer software programs if we restructure the education system adjusting to the present trend of information technology. The modern way of information dissemination (inter-network) is not new thing for Mongolians, even in the period Chinggis khaan of the success of his great victories was based on it. Mongolian people are generally well educated, and have many talents in technical fields. The digital infrastructure is in place and growing and there has already been experience with the implementation of ICT in a variety of fields. Mongolia has a large, young, eager and well-qualified workforce. Mongolia has a democratic and stable government, and information is open and accessible to everyone.

POLICIES AND LEGISLATION

In May 1996 Parliament of Mongolia has adopted the Concept of Development of Mongolia in which the key strategy of national development in the nearest 15-25 years. Communications and Information technology development related laws are as Law on status of Mongolian Academy of Science, Law on Patent, Law on Copyright, Law on technology Transfer and Law on Telecommunications.

In February 2000, Parliament of Mongolia has adopted the "Concept on Information and Communications Technology Development of Mongolia up to 2010 years". A principle to ensure accessible and flexible infostructure promoting dynamic and sustainable development in an open and fair society shall be pursued to achieve the mission. The government, the private sector and the public, indeed all sectors of society and of the economy, needs to harness the potential of the information and knowledge revolution to improve the health, wealth and well being of everyone.

The National Seminar on "Development of Mongolia-information and Communication Technology," held on Feb. 7, 2001, is an evidence of that Mongolian Government has been furthering its strategic policies to support ICT development initiatives and implement corresponding. As result of this event, the National Committee for ICT, headed by Prime Minister, is established and approved by Government.

All of these factors give Mongolia the potential to attract ICT-related business from overseas.

ICT DEVELOPMENT

ICT National Summit was held in 1999 and created an ICT work group headed by the prime minister.
In 2000 Parliament adopted the “National Vision for ICT development of Mongolia up to 2010” and established the ICT Expert Council (MIDAS).
The National seminar in February 2001 established the National Committee of ICT, headed by the prime minister of Mongolia. ICT recognized it as one of the priority sectors.
Currently, the Law of Mongolia on Telecommunications is adopted and the draft law on legal rights of regulating public administration information, law on Information, and information security and the law on postal communication are being prepared.

In 2002, the Foreign Investment forum in Mongolia organized the ICT sector meeting in Ulaanbaatar.

In May of 2002, the National ICT Park was established according to the government decision. Starting from 2003, the Authority for ICT policy and regulation has been established and functioning under the Ministry of Infrastructure.

According to the Law on Mongolian Government, the Ministry of Infrastructure is in charge of ICT policy and regulations, and MOSTEC is responsible in managing ICT policy and regulations for Education, Culture and Science organizations.

CONCEPT OF INFORMATION AND COMMUNICATION TECHNOLOGY DEVELOPMENT OF MONGOLIA BY YEAR 2010

One. Mission The mission of the ICT development

vision in Mongolia is to develop a knowledge-based society and to improve the quality of people’s lives.

Two. Principle

A principle to ensure accessible and flexible info structure, the main information service-provider.

Three. Goals

1. Within Government-Legislation framework:
The government is the builder of the an informatized social structure, the open information and service-provider.
2. Within Business- Economy framework:
To create a business environment capable to ensure efficient integration into the world's economy, to enhance intellectual capacities of domestic, national products and improve their competitiveness.
3. Within Human Development framework:
Irregardless of where citizens live, to ensure opportunities for their equal and active participation in social life, for improving qualities of life and freely communication with each other and the world community.

Four. Strategy and operational objectives

I. Objectives of Government-Legislation framework
II. The following are strategic objectives to be implemented within government-legislation framework:
III. Creation and development of a favorable legal and development environment.
IV. Creation of policy and regulatory regime.
V. Support and development government info structure through ICT

Implemented the following activities within framework of first strategic objectives:
1. The following are directions to develop information and communications technology, creation of legal environment for coordination of information communication

1.1 Streamline the national information communications technology management, policy and regulatory regime.
1.2 Develop culture education and business environment for information society.
1.3 Establish conditions to promote citizens' equal participation, protection of intellectualproperty rights and copyright and development of fair competition.
1.4 Ensure the openness of government information to society and enable citizens' monitoring of government activities.
1.5 Develop electronic trade commerce and join international treaties and agreements.

2. Develop national standards and recommendations on information and communications technology in accordance with international standards and implement those standards.

Implement the following activities within framework of second strategy objective:

3. Support and reward use and utilization of information communications technology and establish the financial structure
4. Establish a state find to develop information and communications technology
5. Initiate national movement from state to development information and communications technology.
6. Compile action plan to development information and communications technology, implement this action a plan through taking necessary coordinating measures to introduce economic and

social development in the action plans of that year.
7. Provide state support to foreign and local investment into development of information and communications technology, implement projects and conduct monitoring activities.
8. Provide state support to create communication and information infrastructure based on national satellite.
9. Provide support and implement all kinds of services on ICT
10. Provide state support and implement fundamental and applied research on ICT
11. Provide support and implement national production of ICT products
12. Support the localization of hi-tech technology of information and communications technology
13. Ensure the state use of software application developed in Mongolia language.
14. Develop system to ensure information confidentiality, protection and reliable operation.

Implement the following activities within framework of third strategic objective.

15. Develop public administration information system.

15.1 Support public administration capacities through information technologies.
15.2 Develop efficient information relations between state organizations

16. Establish and develop step-by-step creation and implementation of office automation, information management system, support tools to assist administrative decision-making and management and monitoring automated system.

16.1 Improve level of office automation of civil servants,
16.2 Establish and develop the structure of government information network, database and search system
16.3 Introduce and promote use of electronic mailing, Internet and Intranet systems in activities of government.

17. Connect and further develop government information network in coordination with networks of non-governmental organization and business information networks.

II.Objectives within Business-Economy framework

The following are strategic goals to be implement within Business-Economy framework

4. Expansion of ICT business and make it highly efficient economic sector.

5. Establishment of economic - business profitable and operative info structure

6. Implement information and communications technology in national production and services.

Implement the following activities within fourth strategic objective.

18. Bring up an industry for exporting software, hardware and info ware
19. Develop market for software applications in Mongolian language
20. Establish in develop information service market.

20.1 Finalize necessary measures to acquire every economic entity with e-mail address in Ulaanbaatar by the year 2002 and for companies in the Aimags- by the year 2010

20.2 Transfer taxation, customs, insurance, banking, finance and other business services into electronic forms

21. Set up high-tech service centers to support small and medium size enterprises
22. Establish stock exchange for ICT products.

Implement the following activities within fifth strategic objective

23. Implement electronic commerce and introduce electronic payment tools such as smart card, electronic checks
24. Introduce Internet as main tool for business, finance and trade information sharing
25. Establish open information center for state and international tenders
26. Establish the open information environment for fair competition under market relations.
27. Set up public service virtual center to protect customers' rights and provide consultation.

Implement the following activities within sixth strategic objective

28. Implement electronic trade and commerce methods to improve the export of national products (such as cashmere, gold, copper, carpets, wool, tourism, fur and skins, raw materials, stamps and others)
29. Improve the production and productivity through introduction of bar codes, smart cards and other electronic methods
30. Widely implement electronic value-added services

III Goals within Human Development framework

The following are strategic goals to be implemented within Human Development framework:

7. Provide opportunities for active and equal participation of citizens in social relations

8. Establish info-structure for open access to information by citizens.

9. Implement information and communications technology in social sector

Implement the following activities within seventh strategic objective.

31. Ensure importance of information needs, intellectual wealth and capacities in human life.
32. Support and ensure equal participations of citizens in relations using ICT advantageous features, not depending from religions, political opinions, race, age and center.
33. Widely utilize information and communications technology for job search, employment, improve work performance quality and level.
34. Create structure to provide education on information and communications technology for all citizens.

Implement the following activities within eighth strategic objective

35. Set up knowledge and education-based high-tech centers in Ulaanbaatar and the centers of the socio-economic development regions.
36. Create a set of possibilities to access information technologies at mobile sights running sustainable common services libraries and aimags and soum schools.
37. Provide opportunities for household to receive newspapers, press releases and other

information in timely manner from desirable sources of information.
38. Create info structure for the following branches of such as law, legislation, banking, insurance, agriculture, industry, infrastructure, trade and commerce, science, technology, health, education, environment, social protection, labor markets, history, culture, arts and others.
39. Resolve in detail human resource development issue of the national info structure (user, trainer, specialist)

Implement the following activities within ninth strategic objectives

40. Provide all kinds of information services to 30% or more households
41. Provide opportunities to make all types of electronic services accessible to every citizen:

41.1 Introduce electronic version of library system such as ordering, search and others
41.2 Provide opportunities for distance employment
41.3 Introduce electronic versions for all kinds of citizens' advisory services.
41.4 Develop open learning through distance learning and education
41.5 Implement tele - diagnosis, treatment expert system at soum and settlements level
41.6 Introduce electronic service for leisure and entertainment services (virtual libraries, museums, culture, centers, game centers, interest groups)

42. Widely use information and communications technology for questionnaires and social surveys.

IT LEGAL ENVIRONMENT

As well as guaranteeing physical property, the Mongolian Government ensures protection for intellectual property. Mongolia became a member of the World Intellectual Property Organization in 1979. Mongolia also has joined eleven International Conventions including the Paris Convention on the Protection of Industrial Property and Madrid Agreement on International Registration of Trademarks.

Capital: Ulaan Baatar
Population: 2,422,000
IP Internet website: http://www.ipom.mn, http://www.mongol.net/ipom

INTELLECTUAL PROPERTY

The Mongolian Government guarantees physical property and ensures protection for intellectual property. Mongolia became a member of the World Intellectual Property Organization (WIPO) in 1979. Mongolia also has joined eleven International Conventions including the Paris Convention on the Protection of Industrial Property and Madrid Agreement on International Registration of Trademarks.

Administration:

- Supervisory Ministry
- Ministry of Justice and Home Affairs
- Intellectual Property Office of Mongolia

Membership of WIPO Treaties:

- WIPO Convention, since February 1979.
- Paris Convention (Industrial Property), since April 1985.
- Berne Convention (Literary and Artistic Works), since March 1998.
- PCT (Patents), since May 1992.
- Madrid Agreement (International Registration of Marks), since April 1985.
- Madrid Protocol (International Registration of Marks), since June 2001.
- Hague Agreement (International Deposit of Industrial Designs), since April 1997.
- Nice Agreement (International Classification of Goods and Services), since June 2001.
- Locarno Agreement (International Classification for Industrial Designs), since June 2001.
- Strasbourg Agreement (International Patent Classification), from March 2002.
- Nairobi Treaty (Protection of the Olympic Symbol), since August 2002
- WCT (WIPO Copyright Treaty), since October 2002
- WPPT (WIPO Performances and Phonograms Treaty), since October 2002

Membership of WTO:

- Member and Signatory to TRIPS Agreement, since January 1997.

On October 25 2002, Mongolia became party to the WIPO Copyright Treaty and the WIPO Performances and Phonograms Treaty.

INTELLECTUAL PROPERTY OFFICE OF MONGOLIA:

Patents: Patent Law of Mongolia (as of June 1993) covers inventions, industrial designs, innovation certificates, and utility models, and has been last amended in April 1995 and again in February 1997.

Trademarks: Law on Tradenames and Trademarks (as of February 1997) and prior to that, the Statute on Trademarks, 1967, and has been last amended in September 1987.

Copyright: Copyright Law (as of September 1993) and has been last amended in 1999.

- Supervisory Ministry
- Copyright Office
- Mongolian Society of Rights of Authors and Composers (MOSRAC)

APPLICATIONS FILED AND/OR REGISTERED IN MONGOLIA:

		Patents	**Trademarks**	**Industrial Designs**
Applications by:	**Residents**	106	726	90
	Non-residents	76	1,863	310
Grants to:	**Residents**	86	376	75
	Non-residents	90	1,836	310

Educational Institutions in Intellectual Property:

There are three educational institutions that have specialized classes in teaching Intellectual Property.

- State University of Mongolia Law School
- Mongolian University of Science and Technology
- Otgontenger University

Mongolian Authorities Enforcing Intellectual Property:

Intellectual Property Tribunal
Any Mongolian courts can deal with infringement cases.

Trade-related Intellectual Property in Mongolia:

Mongolia's laws in the field of intellectual property rights are in conformity with the provisions of the Agreement on the Trade Related Aspects of Intellectual Property Rights (TRIPS), and Mongolia fully applies the provisions of the Agreement on TRIPS on the date of its accession to the WTO.

MINERAL AND MINING SECTOR IN MONGOLIA

STRATEGIC INFORMATION

Until the late 1960s, mining in Mongolia consisted primarily of coal extraction. In the 1970s, however, joint exploitation of mineral resources by the Soviet Union and other Comecon nations commenced on a large scale. Comecon and joint Mongolian-Soviet geological teams surveyed the country's natural resources and discovered valuable mineral deposits, such as copper, molybdenum, wolfram, fluorite, gold, and tin. Several joint stock companies, such as Mongolsovtsvetmet, Mongolchekhoslovakmetall, and Mongolbolgarmetall, were formed to develop and to exploit these deposits. By the late 1980s, mining was an important sector of the economy, and accounted for 42.6 percent of exports in 1985. Little information was available on mining output.

In 1985 Mongolia mined 6.5 million tons of relatively lowgrade varieties of coal, of which only 225,200 tons, or 3 percent, was exported. Exploited lignite deposits were located at Aduun Chuluu, near Choybalsan; Baga Nuur; Nalayh, near Ulaanbaatar; and Sharin Gol, near Darhan. The Aduun Chuluu coal mine's annual output was 300,000 tons. The Baga Nuur strip mine, developed in the 1980s, produced 2 million tons annually by 1985. The Nalayh coal mine, the country's oldest, produced 800,000 tons annually in the 1980s. The Sharin Gol strip mine, developed in the 1960s, had an annual output of 1.1 million tons in the 1980s. The large Tavan Tolgoy deposit of coking coal remained unexploited because of its remoteness from transportation and industrial centers. The Eighth Plan called for raising coal production to 9 million tons, labor productivity 22 to 24 percent, and the capacity of the Baga Nuur mine.

The copper and molybdenum deposit at Erdenetiyn-ovoo was discovered by Mongolian and Czechoslovak geologists in the mid1960s and was developed with massive Soviet assistance in the 1970s. Erdenet's development required the construction of a branch railroad line from Salhit, near Darhan to Erdenet; a highway from Darhan to Erdenet; a water pipeline from the Selenge Moron; an electric line from the Soviet Union; and factories, housing, and other facilities. A Mongolian-Soviet construction force numbering 14,000 built the Joint Mongolian-Soviet Erdenet Mining and Concentrating Combine, which included a mine, a concentrating plant, a material and technical supply base, a mechanical repair plant, and a high-capacity thermal and electric power plant. The first stage of the Erdenet combine went into operation in 1978, with a planned output of 50,000 tons for 1979. With the completion of the fourth stage in 1981, planned annual production capacity was 16 million tons of concentrate. From 1979 to 1982, Erdenet's output of concentrates amounted to 250,000 tons of copper and 3,400 tons of molybdenum, with concentrates containing 33 percent copper and 50 percent molybdenum. In 1983 the Erdenet combine was completed. During the Eighth Plan, annual capacity was to reach 20 million tons. No information was available on actual output or exports.

Other nonferrous metals exploited by Mongolsovtsvetmet and other joint ventures were fluorite, wolfram, tin, and gold. The Berh, Bor Ondor, Burentsogt, and Har-ayrag fluorite deposits had an annual output of 786,700 tons; fluorite was exported to the Soviet Union, but no figures were available. The Eighth Plan called for expanding fluorite production capacity by an unspecified amount. No figures were available on output or on exports of wolfram, tin, and gold. In the late 1980s, plans to open the Urandosh phosphate strip mine near Hatgal were delayed by concerns for environmental pollution in Hovsgol Nuur. Exploitation of the Burenhaan phosphate deposit still was planned. Further development of Mongolia's other mineral resources was also planned, and the Eighth Plan called for continued cooperation with Comecon countries in geological prospecting and mining.

Mongolia can be considered one of the "last frontiers" for mineral exploration. The country is surrounded by some of the world's largest mineral deposits but exploration efforts within Mongolia are still in the early stages. QGX recognized this potential several years ago and the recent discovery of a world class deposit, Oyu Tolgoi, has confirmed the country's mineral potential. As a result, an increasing number of mining and exploration companies (both juniors and majors) are active in Mongolia.

Some of the reasons for this increasing attention are:

The local geology is highly prospective for large size mineral deposits
The country is under-explored
The Government has firmly demonstrated its commitment to developing the mineral sector by attracting foreign capital
Appropriate laws have been adopted to encourage foreign investment
Proximity to major metal markets in China and Japan

At present, gold production in Mongolia originates primarily from alluvial deposits although there are small hard rock operations in the north part of the country.
Mongolia is a major exporter of copper and molybdenum as well as a leading world producer of fluorspar. A significant proportion of the country's exports come from the Erdenet copper deposit, which is one of the largest copper reserves in the world.

Mongolia possesses one of the most progressive mineral regimes in Asia. Introduced in 1995 and modified in 1997, the Minerals Law of Mongolia provides a transparent licensing system that has served to encourage investment in the sector. The Law clearly establishes the state as having primary control of its mineral resources, a central premise of modern minerals legislation throughout the world.

The law allows any Mongolian citizen, foreign citizen or legal person to hold any number of mineral exploration licenses of up to 400,000 hectares each. An exploration license holder is afforded the exclusive right to conduct exploration for minerals within the boundaries for seven years (three years initially plus two extensions of two years each), the exclusive right to obtain a mining license for any part of the exploration license, and the right to transfer or pledge any part of the exploration license. Exploration license fees are US$.05 per hectar for the first year, US$.10 per hectar for the second and third years, US$1.00 per hectar for years four and five and US$1.50 per hectar for the sixth and seventh years.

Mining license holders have the right to engage in mining of minerals within the license area for sixty years (with the right to extend for an additional 40 years), the right to sell mineral products internationally, the right to transfer or pledge all or part of the license, and the exclusive right to conduct exploration for minerals within the license area. A mining license holder must pay royalties to the government equal to 2.5% of the sale value of products sold (with the exception of alluvial gold on which the royalty is 7.5%). Mining license fees are US $5.00 per hectar for years one to three, US$7.50 per hectar for years four to five, and US$10.00 per hectar thereafter.

CURRENT STATUS OF THE MINERAL INDUSTRY

Today the mining sector is Mongolia's single largest industry, accounting for 55% of industrial output and more than 40% of export earnings (Fig. 1).

In recent years, gold mining has emerged as on of the most dynamic sectors of the Mongolia's economy. Gold production has grown ten-fold from 1993 to 2000, with 11.5 metric tons of gold having been produced in 2000 (Fig. 2 and 3). Gold production is expected to continue to increase annually for the foreseeable future as a result of new exploration and investment.

Mongolia also has substantial proven reserves of coal, and annual coal production is presently about 5 million metric tons, almost all of which is used for steam and electricity generation (Fig. 4). The country is estimated to have potential coal reserves of some 100 billion metric tons. Most of these reserves are proven but have not been developed due to a lack of infrastructure. For example, the Tavan Tolgoi deposit in the south Gobi contains over 5 billion metric tons of coking and hard coal, however it is located 400 km from the nearest rail-line (see section 4.8). Mongolia also has potential to become a significant oil exporter. There is currently one operating oil field in the Gobi region and initial results from oil exploration in eastern and western Mongolia are very promising. The country has recently been exporting limited amounts of crude oil to China.

The Mongolian Geological Survey, in conjunction with geological survey teams from numerous other countries, has been actively conducting mineral exploration in Mongolia since the 1960's. These geological field expeditions have produced a vast body of information on the geology of Mongolia, including 5,300 geological reports. Most of these reports are written in either Mongolian or Russian languages and are available at the Geological Information Center in Ulaanbaatar (see section 7.5). The geology of over 93% of the country has been mapped at a scale of 1:200,000, while 18% of the country has been geologically mapped at a scale of 1:50,000. Various airborne geophysical survey techniques (e.g. gravimetric and magnetic surveys) have been used to map 67% of Mongolia's national territory at a scale of 1:200,000, and 32% of national territory at a scale of 1:50,000.

More than 6,000 significant deposits of 80 different minerals have been discovered, and more than 160 of the 400 deposits surveyed in detail have been, or are now are being developed for production. Another 170 deposits of construction grade materials, such as granite and marble, have also been studied, of which 35 are presently in production while a further 90 are being developed for production.

Prior to 1970, Mongolia was not able to develop its vast mineral resources due to a lack of infrastructure and lack of financing for mineral resource development. However, beginning in 1970, numerous deposits of copper, gold, fluorspar, uranium, and coal were developed by joint ventures formed in partnership with the former Soviet Union and its allies. Today the Government of Mongolia has adopted a number of long term programs to explore for and develop promising mineral deposits, especially of gold, silver, copper, coal, and oil. Foreign investment and direct participation in a wide range of mining related industries are actively encouraged, particularly in connection with the exploration, extraction, and processing of mineral resources. Mongolia's national policies concerning its mineral sector are continuously under review to insure that Mongolia remains favorable for foreign mineral investment and globally competitive with other nations.

EXPENDITURES FOR GEOLOGICAL EXPLORATION BY EXPLORATION LICENSE HOLDERS IN 1997-2000

(By June 19, 2000)

Million Tugriks (Rate: USD1» 1090Tug)

Year	Item	Total Organizations	Of which: Mongolian Organizations	Foreign Organizations

		No. of Reports	Cost	No. of Reports	Cost	No. of Reports	Cost
1997	Total cost for geological exploration	75	8,963	50	1,743	21	5,600
1998	Total cost for geological exploration	136	7,816	67	2,606	30	2,404
1999	Cost for geological exploration	89	3,982	55	828	19	1,863
2000	Cost for geological exploration	100	6,043	44	568	33	3,785

Joint Ventures		Entities		Private Persons	
No. of Reports	Cost	No. of Reports	Cost	No. of Reports	Cost
3	572	1	86	0	0
24	369	2	10	13	28
4	1,011	1	7	10	109
14	1,573	1	30	8	86

Source: Office of Geology (Mongolian Geological Survey), Mineral Resources Authority of Mongolia

MINERAL RESOURCES AND MINING INDUSTRY[4]

Mongolia is rich in many types of mineral resources which will be of interest to international investors.

Over 6,000 deposits of 80 different minerals have been discovered. Over 160 deposits out of 400 surveys deposits are being exploited. A further 170 deposits of construction materials, such as granite and marble also exist, of which 35 are now being worked and 90 are in the process of development.

In the past Mongolia was not able to develop or exploit discovered mineral resources because of a lack of infrastructure and capital investment. Since 1973, Mongolia, with financial and technical assistance from Eastern European countries, has set up and operated joint ventures to explore and develop major deposits of gold, copper, molybdenum, uranium, coal and fluorspar.

Mongolia is now becoming one of the largest producers of several of these metals and minerals. Mongolia produces nearly 15% of the world's fluorspar and is a major producer and exporter of copper, molybdenum and uranium.

Gold, silver, tungsten, tin and precious stones mines are typically small-scale operations, but some of these are planned for expansion. Nearly half of the gross industrial output and 60% of the country's export earning come from the mining sector.

The Mongolian Government has adopted a package of long-term programs to explore and develop large promising mineral deposits such as gold, silver, oil, coal, copper and other metals and minerals.

[4] ***By Dambyn Galsandorj***

Mining operations are mostly state owned but foreign investment in a wide range of industries is openly invited, especially in exploration, extraction and processing of Mongolia's mineral resources. The World Bank has funded a mining and minerals sector's study. It is also reviewing present and potential mineral operations.

The Mongolian National Geological Organization, the Mongolian Joint expedition with the socialist countries, and the International Geological Expedition "IGE" have worked on the territory of Mongolia since 1963. These agencies have produced a wealth of geological data and more than 4,000 reports.

The entire has been mapped geologically at a scale of 1:1,500,00, much of the country to 1:1,000,000 and 1:50,000, and selected areas to larger scales. Gravity, aeromagnetic and geochemical data are also available.

GOLD

Mongolia is blessed with a number of important gold deposits which will be developed in joint ventures with new international partners. Substantial proven reserves of both primary and placer gold exist. Most primary deposits are goldsulfide quartz veins, while secondary gold is found associated with copper molybdenum, copper-pyrite, polymetallic, silver and rare metallic ores.

The Mongolian Government adopted a Gold Industry Development Program aimed at increasing existing gold production by more than ten times over the present level and creating a gold refining capability. Current major mines in development will dominate in the future.

The Boroo deposit measures up to 700m long at the surface and extends 150-300m down dip. The ore bearing zone is 20-40m thick averaging 3-4 gm/t gold. Initial measurements indicate a resource of 40 tons of gold with some silver. Other gold deposits situated near Boroo include those at Narantolgoi, Sujigtei and Tsagaanchuluut.

Another gold district soon to be developed is at Zaamar, in the Zaamar hills about 160 km northwest of Ulaanbaatar. Total gold reserves in the Zaamar area are estimated at over 100 tons. Of 150 gold-quartz veins so far explored, twenty are considered commercially exploitable, averaging 20 gms gold. Veins in the hills will be developed as underground mines while the gold in the valleys will be worked as placer operations.

The Bumbat hard rock gold ore area is situated 220 km west of Ulaanbaatar in the Tuul river valley. About 150 veins have been discovered in this area of 45 sq. km, and seven of these investigated in detail. Gold deposits discovered range from 100m to 800m in length, and are 100-200m deep with vein thickness of 0.8-3.2m, averaging 7-30 g/t gold. Reserves discovered at Bumbat are about 17 tons of gold.

Several other gold deposits have been discovered or evaluated in two main districts: at Hentii (free, a Altat, and Zuunmod) in the north and Bayanhongor (Zedin) in the west.

Some gold deposits are operated by the Mongolian-Russian joint venture "Mongolrostsvetmet" and produce 1.5 tons of gold per year.

The Mongolian-Bulgarian joint venture "Mongol-Bulgarmetal" has been successfully mining and processing the Mukhar Ereg alluvial deposits in Bayankhongor Province since 1981.

SILVER

Two important silver deposits have been discovered in Mongolia: silver-sulfosalts at Asgat, and silver polymetallic deposits at Mongon Ondoriin.

The Asgat silver deposit is located in the northern part of the Mongol Altai mountains at an altitude of 2,700-3,100m, and is about 170 km from Olgii, the nearest town. The length of the silver ore zone is 1.5-12km, with a thickness of 580m, to a depth of 400-500m. The orebody is 0. 8-3.3m thick and averages: 100-450 g/t Ag, 0. 03-0. 09% Bi, 0. 04-0.7% Sb and 0. 19-1.17% Cu.

The ore is easily concentrated and can produce: 82% Ag, 75% Bi, 81% Sb and 84% Cu in concentrates. Preliminary exploration at the deposit has assessed ore reserves as 24. 8 million tons and several similar ore zones have been discovered nearby.

The Mongon Ondoriin deposit is 310 km Northwest of Ulaanbaatar and 200 km from the Baganuur coal mine and railway station near the Ondortsagaan molybdenum-tungsten deposit and 90 km from Berkh fluorspar mine.

The main metals of this deposit average 70 g/t Ag, 0. 09% Sn, 1. 09% Pb and 0. 85% Zn. Estimated metal reserves are about 280,000 tons Pb, 230,000 tons Zn and 24,000 tons Sn.

COPPER

Mongolia's primary copper reserves are located at Erdenetiin Ovoo and Tsagaansuvarga. Chalcopyrite skarns, copper-nickel and sandstone copper deposits also exist, but have not yet been studied in detail. Erdenetiin Ovoo deposit is situated 165 km southwest of Darkhan and both railway and high-voltage lines connect to this deposit. Selective collective-flotation methods are used to concentrate this ore and oxidation and concentration facilities are technically advanced.

The Mongolian and Russian Erdenet joint-venture has been operating since 1981 with a capacity of 20 million tons of copper ore which has expanded 24 million tons. Reserves of this deposit include 7,556,000 tons of 0.8% copper and 400,000 tons of0.018% molybdenum.

The newest copper-molybdenum project under consideration for development is at Tsagaan Suvarga where the deposit has reserves of 128 million tons of 0.53% copper and 43,600 tons of 0.018% molybdenum concentrate using collective-selective flotation methods have been positive.

MOLYBDENUM

Most molybdenum reserves are situated at the Erdenetiin Ovoo and Tsagaanchuluut deposits. Smaller reserves have also been discovered at Aryn Nuur (Mo-Cu), Ondortsagaan, and Yegzer (W-Mo), and Tsagaanchuluut, and Ih Uul in central and northern Mongolia. Molybdenum deposits at Tomortiin Ovoo, Tsav and Ulaan have been studied and are for exploitation.

The deposit at Aryn Nuur, 145 km from Choibalsan city and the Bayantumen railway station and 50 km from the Tomortiin Ovoo zinc deposit is also interesting. Aryn Nuur has four belts, the central being 1,000m x 400-600m. Oxidized and secondary enriched belts of not more than 30m and primary ore are continuous to 250m depth. Average grades are: 0.03-0. 57% averaging 0. 08% Mo with 0.02-0. 153% Cu. Aryn Nuur is suitable for open-cast mining and total molybdenum reserves are 25,000 tons. Flotation methods could produce 89.5% metal, including 54% molybdenum concentrate.

At present, Mongolia does not produce oil or gas, and lacks a petroleum infrastructure such as refinery and pipelines. The country has imported and is still importing all petroleum products - about 800,000 tons per year (or about 15,000 to 20,000 barrels per day) - by rail from Russia, China, Singapore and the UK.

Using Mongolian data from 1939 to 1989, Exploration Associates International of Texas Inc. (EAIT) made an oil gas resource appraisal of Mongolia, which indicated that recoverable oil resources are probably more than 5.0 billion barrels of oil equivalent, based on the current geological and geophysical data. Possible oil resources may be significantly greater than this. The current data also indicates that the size of the largest oil fields within the major basins (Tsagaan Els and Zuunbayan oil fields) may be in the 100 to 700 million barrel range.

Mongol Gazryn Tos (MGT), the State Petroleum Company formed in 1990 is planning to open up the country to western oil companies. 370,000 square kilometers, almost a quarter of the country is now under offer in nine contract areas in the west and the south. MGT is also organizing another bid, including a further 11 contract areas in the eastern part of the country, covering 156,000 square kilometers, for which a seismic survey is available. In the longer term Mongolia is intending to export oil. With the nearest port over 1,000 km distant, pipeline transportation through Russia and China will be necessary.

FLUORSPAR

More than 60 fluorspar deposits and about 300 prospects have been discovered, mainly in the central and eastern provinces. Estimated reserves are about 18 million tons of fluorspar. Most of the resources are at the Berkh, Kharairag and Bor-Ondor ore districts. Three large joint-ventures with Russia have operated successfully since end of 1970, and about 860,000 tons of fluorspar is mined at Bor-Ondor. Concentrate production is over 120,000 tons. The modem expansion of existing mines is required. Some 15 deposits and more than 60 occurrences are found in the Bor-Ondor ore district with estimated resources of 17 million tons.

At the Berkh district 24 deposits and more than 60 sites contain about 2 million tons of fluorspar resources. There are fifteen deposits and more than 30 occurrences with about 7 million tons at the Kharairag district. The biggest deposit of this kind is the Orgon deposit. More than 30 occurrences have been located at the Choibalsan fluorspar district, but none have been mined and estimated.

PHOSPHORITE

Mongolia is rich in phosphorite resources. A huge of phosphorite occurs in the north, 300 km long and 70 - 120 km wide. About 20 deposits were discovered during the geological survey with an estimated resource of 2.4 billion tons.

The Burenkhaan deposit is 370 km northwest of Erdenet, 20-40 km north of Moron city, and 100 km south of Khovsgol Lake. The main component here is carbonate-phosphor anhydrite and it's content averages 20%. The total resource of this deposit is 300 million tons of which 192 million tons could be open pit mined. There are also several smaller deposits and occurrences near Burenkhaan deposits.

There is also a very large phosphorite deposit at Lake Khovsgol, a freshwater lake 100 km from the Burenkhaan deposit. Development of this deposit will be subject to an environmental assessment.

LEAD AND ZINC

Polymetallic deposits in central Mongolia are situated mainly in the Mesozoic volcano-plutogene zones and in the throats of volcano eruptions skarns and vein formations. About 30 lead and zinc prospects have been discovered at Tomortiin Ovoo (Sarn-polymetallic) and at Ulaan and Tsav (silver-polymetallic). Total reserves are estimated at 3.0 million tons. Estimated reserves at the Tsav deposit,

based upon recent exploration, are at 9 million tons.

Several other deposits and prospects have been found nearby. The Ulaan deposit is situated 120 km to the north of Choibalsan and near to the railway running north to Russia. Open-cast operations could produce up to 757,000 tons of 1.92% zinc, and 430,000 tons of 1.1% lead. The average silver content is 30-58 gram/ton. At the surface level, 300,000 tons of lead and 600,000 tons of zinc can be produced.

A smaller polymetallic mine, Mukhar Ereg is situated 1 km from Ulaan. Mukhar Ereg's reserves are estimated at 430,000 tons of zinc and 90,000 tons of lead. Tsav is a rich vein-like deposit, with estimated reserves of 330,000 tons of lead and 280,000 tons of zinc contents average 10-1 1% with 80-240 gms/ton silver.

Some small tin mines and placer deposits are operating, and many other deposits require further evaluation, as variety have been discovered. The Elst placer tin deposit and placer deposits in Narsan Hondlon, Oortsog and Janchivlin deposits all offer large reserves. The Oortsog cassiterite-skarn deposit is situated 90 km from the Kharairag railway station to the southwest in the Middle Gobi Aimag. The tin content in the ore is 0. 02-2.0% with zinc, lead and silver in the ore as accessories. Concentrating tests have been done under laboratory conditions. Tin reserves averaging 0.60% content are estimated as 40,000 tons. Most deposits should be mined as open-pit.

TUNGSTEN

Tungsten deposits and prospects are widespread throughout Mongolia with most in the eastern and central part of the Mongolia Altai in the west. About 350 tons of tungsten a year has been mined and concentrated since 1943.

The Ondortsagaan deposit is located 70 km northwest of Ondorkhaan and 170 km from Baga-Nuur railway station to the east. This deposit is 1,500 by 500-700 meters and 550m depth. The ore contains 0.124% WO3, 0.019% Mo, 0.08% Bi and 0.011% BaO. Total reserves are 175,000 tons and 26,000 tons of W03 and can be mined by open pit down to 300m depth. Ondortsagaan may also be developed together with the Mongon Ondor silver-polymetallic and Tsagaanchuluut molybdenum deposits in an integrated operation. One of the more interesting tungsten deposits is at Yegzer, in the south east of the country, 230 km from railway station at Bayantumen. The average content is 0.197% W03, 0.56% Mo, 0.08% BaO, 0.132% BO. Total tungsten oxide reserves are 42,500 tolls with 12,000 tons Mo.

RARE METALS

Tantalum, niobium, lutetium, rare elements and other rare metals resources are available in the south and west of the country. Rare elements belts have been discovered at Mushgai Hudag, Lugiin Gel, Shartolgoi and Ulaantolgoi. Exploration at Lugiin Gol revealed more than 400,000 tons of reserves. Rare metals have been located in the north of the country as well.

MINERAL POTENTIAL OF MONGOLIA (MAIN MINERALS)

GOLD (AU)

Gold mineralization has taken place, with various intensity, during the early and late Precambrian-early Cambrian, Paleozoic, Mesozoic and Cenozoic time however the main gold mineralization is associated with magnetic activity during Permian and Triassic - Jurassic time. Placers were formed during the Cretaceous-late Neogene and Pliocene-Holocene time.

The known gold mineralizations in Mongolia are represented by three economic types: veins, mineralized zones, and placers. Although vein occurrences are the most widely developed of all gold occurrences the bulk of proven gold reserves associated with placers and mineralized zones.

On the base of geological data (tectonic structure, mineral occurrences, age of mineralization, gold content) ten main gold metallogenic provinces within Mongolia have been defined.

It should be emphasized that because of a very low level of geological knowledge, with respect to the western and southern portion of Mongolia and an emphasis on only placers and/ or quartz vein mineralization in the studied areas, the true gold potential of these large regions is largely conjectural. Nevertheless, the number of occurrences defined based on limited data clearly suggests a high gold potential overall for the region.

Additionally, although not identified, available geologic data would indicate that occurrences of (a) gold-bearing conglomerates of Cretaceous and Tertiary age should be expected in southern and western Mongolia, (b) gold mineralization associated with ancient volcano- sedimentary areas in Central Mongolia and (c) ancient epithermal gold occurrences (island arc associations) may be expected in the Kharkhira, Ulzeet, and Southern Mongolian gold provinces.

BASE METAL (CU, MO, PB, ZN)

Copper-molybdenum (Cu-Mo) mineralization in Mongolia is primarily of three deposit types, i.e., late Paleozoic-early Mesozoic Cu-Mo porphyries, Cu-Ni magmatic segregations associated with grabbo of unknown age and Paleozoic-Mesozoic stratabound coppers.

The Cu-Mo deposits previously described occur within four main base metal provinces in Mongolia, i.e., the Altai, North Mongolian and South Mongolian provinces.

In addition to the previously described Cu-Mo deposit types and provinces, Mongolia also has a large number of middle to late Mesozoic Pb-Zn deposits of various deposit types, largely in the eastern of the country. The main deposit types, skarn, mineralized explosive pipes, vein, mineralized zones. The known base metal deposits were mainly formed in the middle-late Mesozoic. They are located in eastern part of country.

The main Pb-Zn deposits located in Central Mongolian province, and several perspective occurrences in Altai province.

The Northern Central and Southern metallogenic provinces of Mongolia have a high potential for a discovery of new deposits of Cu, Mo, Pb, Zn. In the North and South Mongolian provinces, the potential is greater for Cu-Mo porphyries, in Central Mongolian and both Pb, Zn and Cu-MO porphyry deposits.

Most perspective for the discovery of large scale copper and/or polymetallic mineralization is the Altai province in South Mongolia where there is the intersecting of three regional geologic structures (Altai metallogenic province, Beitianshan tectonostratigraphic terrane and a complex zone of faults.

Regionally the Altai metallogenic province includes areas of Russia (Gornii Altai), China (Altai), and Mongolia (Mongolian Altai). In the Gornii Altai of Russia large deposits of lead and zinc have been discovered, whereas on the Russia-Mongolian border hydrothermal Pb-Zn deposits, and volcano-clastic Fe mineralization have been identified.

In the Altai zone of China, in mid-Paleozoic sandstone, shales and volcanoclastic deposits of synorogenic-synvolcanic massive Cu-Ni sulfides occurrences indicate that at least two major synorojenic massive sulphide deposits, in addition to Kuroko-type massive sulphide deposits will be discovered. Based on the same favorably criteria as used in the China Altai region it is estimated that similar deposits would occur in the adjacent Mongolian Altai. On the base of above-mentioned data is possible to predict the presence of economic deposits of Cu, Mo, Pb, Zn, and Ni in the Mongolian Altai. Recently, in the northern part of the Altai zone Cu occurrences of stratiform type have been discovered as well as synorogenic Cu-Ni mineralization associated with gabbro bodies.

In the southern Mongolia the Altai metallogenic province intersects the Bietianshan tectono-stratigraphic terrane and at this zone of intersection both areas are in turn intersected by a late-Devonian-Carboniferous fault zone extending NW from China through Mongolia. The fault zone is approximately 850-900 km in length and 30-50 km in width and which, based on recent epicenter studies, is tectonically active. This area of complex intersection of the three zones is known to contain Pb-Zn deposits however is considered highly prospective for the occurrence of several deposits and deposit types. In particular the complex rock types present include volcano-sedimentary, sandstone-carbonate formations, small to medium sized intrusions of tonalites, leucogranites, alkalic granites, syenites, gabbro and ultramafic rocks. Additinally, numerous crosscutting faults, of different orientation provide the host environment for diverse deposit types.

FLUORITE

Fluorite mineralization is widespread throughout Mongolia in rocks of Late Paleozoic to Late Mesozoic age. The major time of economically important mineralization took place during late

Mesozoic / late Jurassic-early Cretaceous epochs). The fluorite mineralization represented by two economic types: epithermal vein and metasomatic ore bodies.

Late Mesozoic fluorite mineralization is associated with rare earth and lead-zinc mineralization but not in economical quantities. Three major fluorite provinces have been defined in Mongolia, i.e., the North Mongolia, Trans-Mongolian and South Mongolian with the Trans-Mongolian province having the largest reserves and being the most actively exploited.

The major characteristics of the main provinces are shown in the Table 7. The fluorite reserves/resources of Mongolia are estimated at 18/23-33, respectively.

RARE-EARTH ELEMENTS (REE)

Rare-Earth Metals (Ta, Nb, Zr, W, Sn)--REM

Genetically and spatially REE and REMs in Mongolia are primarily felsic and alkalic rocks of late-Mesozoic, early Mesozoic and late Paleozoic age. Known deposits of REE and REM are subdivided on the following basis:

REE, REM mineralization (metasomatic zones) with alkalic granitoids and volcano-plutonic complexes.

Tungsten (W) vein and stockwork mineralization in granitoids.

Tin (Sn) vein and skarn mineralization in granites and carbonate rocks.

Within Mongolia six REE and/or REM provinces have been identified; the Altai, North Mongolian Hentii, Hangai, Southeast Mongolian, South Mongolian and the geologic attributes of these provinces are given in Table 8.

REE and REM occurrences are widely distributed throughout Mongolia with the most promising areas, based on available data, being the Altai and South Mongolian provinces for Ta, Nb, Zr, Y, W and REE, respectively.

URANIUM

Uranium exploration in Mongolia has started in 1940's by Mongolian and former Soviet Union geological organisations. Prior to1966, numerous uranium occurrences were discovered in coal deposits. In the period from 1967 to 1988 the exploration work became more systematic. As result of these exploration works, four "uranium - bearing provinces" were defined Mongol - Priargun, Gobi - Tamtsag, Hentei - Daur and Northern Mongolian. Several deposits were discovered in that time Dornod, Gurvanbulag, Mardai in eastern and Kharaat in southern Mongolia. The proven uranium resources of Mongolia occur in these deposits, which represent 62000 tonnes of entire country are estimated to amount to 1 307 000 tonnes of uranium. Uranium mining in Mongolia started in 1989 with exploration of the Mardai open pit in eastern Mongolia. The ore is processed in the Russian Priargunsky ore dressing plant. The mine was operated by a Russian - Mongolian joint venture to 1993.

MAJOR MINERAL DEPOSITS OF MONGOLIA

COPPER DEPOSITS

Erdenetiin Ovoo

The Erdetiin-Ovoo (Erdenet) deposits is the site of Mongolia's largest mining activity and is operated as a Mongolian/ Russian joint venture. The deposit is located 365 km NNE of Ulaanbaatar and 165 km southwest of the trans-Mongolian railhead station at Darhan. Darhan provides railway between the mine and the trans-Mongolian railway and also linked to tte mine and its activities via both a highway and a 200 KV transmission line which provides the primary energy to the mine.

The Erdenet mine has been in operation since 1978 and has a present capacity of approximately 20 million tonnes of ore per year from which is produced approximately 354,000 T/yr of copper concentrate and 3,500 T/yr of Mo concentrate. In 1990, the Soviets purchased 90% of Mongolia's copper concentrate and 100% of its molybdenum concentrate. MONGOLEXPORT statistics cite copper concentrates as containing 27-35% Cu, plus selenium (50-60 gm/T), silver (50-70 gm/T), tellurium (8-9 gm/T) and gold (0.3-0.5 gm/T). Molybdenum concentrates are similarly cited to contain molybdenum (47-54%), rhenium (450 gm/T), selenium (90 gm/T) and tellurium (15 gm/T). Overall, approximately 124,000 T of Cu and 1,672 T of Mo are produced per year from Erdenet concentrate. A small but increasing amount of tungsten is also produced from the mine's ore.

The Erdenet Mine is located within a large porphyrite intrusive complex with associated volcanic rocks and as such recembles a typecal stockwork copper-molybdenum porphyry deposit. Within the larger intrusive/volcanic complex for spatially separated ore-bearing stockwork zones have been recognized with the Main (northwestern) stockwork, which occurs on the western flank of the system, usually considered the Erdenetiin-Ovoo (Erdenet) deposits. The main stockwork, like the other three zones, is a clearly defined vertical stockwork composed of discreet stringers 2-3 mm in thickness, and randomly oriented, occasionally ranging in thickness to 2-5 cm. The Main stockwork occurs in association with 2 small stocks, with numerous apophyses, cross-cut by numerous gently to steeply dipping dikes .

The Main stockwork is approximately 2.400 meters in length, 300-1,300 meters in width and in the central portion extends approximately 1,000 meters in depth whereas near the porphyry is approximately 600-700 meters in depth. Overall the Erdenet deposit, as represented by the Main Zone, is approximately 2 km^2 in total surface area. In plan the shape of the stockwork is roughly 2300 x 800 m as delimited by a cutoff grade of 0.25% Cu.

The principal minerals of economic importance in the oxidized/leached zone of the deposit are cuprite, delafessite, malachite, azurite, brochantite, pantellerite, turquoise and rarely native copper. The average grade of the oxidized/leached zone of 0.1% Cu. The zone of secondary enrichment, underlying the oxidized/leached zone, is characterized by chalcocite, bornite and covellite with a copper content rangeng from 0.65 to 1.35% and Mo ranging from 0.077 to 0.3% with the average values being 0.81% and 0.17% respectively. The primary ore of the Erdenet deposit is characterized by pyrite, chalcopyrite and molybdenite with lesser amounts of sheelite irregularly distributed through the ore body. The standard ores average 20-68 gm/T tungsten with local values ranging from 80-300 gm/T.

Estimated reserves of the Erdenet deposit (Main Zone) are 2.295% of ore grading 0.50% Cu, 0.014 Mo, 1.81 Ag and 0.05 gm/T Au. Indicative resrves at deeper stockwork horizons are estimated to contain approximately 1.4 MT of Cu metal and 37 KT of Mo metal.

TSAGAAN-SUVRAGA

The Surven-Sukhait (Tsagaan-Suvraga) deposit, located 164 km southwest of the Zuun-Bayan railroad station, is located in the semi-desert, unpopulated and water scarce region of Southeast Mongolia.

The Surven-Sukhait deposit is one of seven porphyry copper-molybdenum occurrences within the Tsagaan-Suvarguin district. Throughout the district, copper-molybdenum mineralization of various intensity can be discontinuously traced for approximately 10 km with a width of 0.8-3.0 km. Overall, the copper-molybdenum mineralization occurs within an extensive late Devonian-early Carboniferous intrusive massive of syenites. Although seven mineralized areas have been studied they are all considered to have less economic potential than the Surven-Sukhait locality.

Copper-molybdenum stockwork mineralization extends for approximately 1.980 meters with a width ranging from 180-500 meters and the maximum depth of drilled mineralization extending to a depth of 420 meters. The stockwork zone strikes NE and dips at an angle of 35-550 to the northwest.

All these rocks facially grade into each other. Stock-like bodies and dykes of the final stage of the massif formation are developed in the western part of the massif. They are represented by leucocratic aplite-like granites, granite-porphyries and granosyenite-porphyries undergone different degree of kalifeldspathization and molybdenum-copper mineralization.

The stockwork zone is strongly fractured, consists predominantly of quartz syenites and syenites which are intensely kaolinized, serecitized and silicified and is cross-cut throughout with quartz-chalcopyrite-molybdenite stringers.

In vertical section the stockwork zone consists of an upper mixed zone of oxidized and enriched ores, developed to a depth of 10-30 meters and reaching a maximum depth of 100meters along faults. Within the upper zone the zone of secondary enrichment is poorly developed, however, in areas of intensive fracturing it may persist to a depth of 150-180 meters.

The major primary ore minerals are chalcopyrite, bornite and molybdenite with lesser amounts of pyrite, chalcocite, sphalerite, galena and pyrrhotite. Principal gauge minerals are quartz, feldspar, muscovite and sericite.

Commercial ore reserves of the deposit have been estimated at 220 to 240 MT and marginal reserves at 77 MT. The commercial reserves contain 0.3-0.7% Cu, and 0.001-0.03% Mo with the average grades being 0.54% and 0.19% respectively. The average grades of the marginal reserves is estimated to be 0.25% Cu and 0.009% Mo. Associated elements of possible economic importance, in the economic reserves, are 2.64 gm/T Ag, 0.0084 gm/T Au, 0.39% gm/T Rh, 8.3 gm/T selenium, 12.8gm/T Te, 0.1-7.0gm/T Ga.

LEAD AND ZINC DEPOSITS

Tumurtiin-Ovoo

The Tumurtiin-Ovoo deposit is located in the east-northeast portion of Mongolia 180 km southwest of the Bayan-Tumen railroad station and the town of Choibalsan. Skarn deposits form the primary mineralization in the thick sequence of Devonian sedimentary-volcanogenic rocks which have been strongly hornfelsed or contact metamorphosed by the intrusion of a Late Paleozoic granitic complex. In the sequence the upper diabase unit has been converted to hornfels and hornfels blastides whereas the lower limestone and shale sequenceshave been converted to marble, with various skarns, and plagioclase-pyroxene hornfels, respectively. With the limestone (marble) sequence the skarns, consisting primarily of sphalerite form a distinct zone which coincides with garnet-magnetite skarns in the upper portion of the unit.

A main lenticular sphalerite orebody, with a number of associated lenses, define the orebody which extends for approximately 800 meters along strike, extends an average of 200-230 meters downward (the Central zone extends 480 meters downward) and averages 14 m in thickness. The upper 60m of the orebody are oxidized with the remainder consisting of primary sulphides-principally sphalerite. The deposit contains 7.7 M tonnes of ore with an average grade of 12.43% Zn and 0.024 Cd.

Ulaan

The Ulaan deposit is located in east-northeast Mongolia 110 km northwest of the town of Choibalsan and 6 km northeast of the Erdes (Mardai) uranium mine.

The Ulaan deposit represents an intricate fluidized-explosive structure consisting at the surface of four breccia pipes which at depths of 200-500 m in a single body. The main pipe, containing the bulk of the mineralization is a wedge-shaped structure (at the surface) 20-120m wide and filled with a large-to-small fragmented breccia consisting primarily of wallrock clasts. The clasts are centered by either (a) fine grained fluidized fragments or (b) by hydrothermally deposited material. Base metal mineralization has been traced to a depth of 800 m with no sign of attenuation. The ores are to a greater or lesser extent oxidized to a depth of 35-30 m and, occasionally, to a depth of 90 m. Within the deposit, therefore, oxidized and semi-oxidized ores are recognized. The deposit contains 68.1 M tonnes of ore, grading of 2.0% Zn, 1.2% Pb, 53 g/t Ag, and 0.21 g/t Au.

TUNGSTEN, TIN AND MOLYBDENUM DEPOSITS

Ondor-Tsagaan

The Ondor-Tsagaan deposit is situated in Central Mongolia 170 km east of the Baga-Nuur railroad station, 70 km northwest of the aimak administrative center of Undurhan. The deposits is localized in a synclinal fold where the folded axis sharply changes direction from NE to NW. Within the deposit the major structural features are folds and steep NW-trending faults. The rocks represented by lower Devonian quartz-sericite, quartz-biotite cherty and shales emplaced by gabbro-diabases bodies.

The deposit is elliptical in plan, and consists of a NW-trending (1500 x 500-700 m) stockwork form by variously oriented quartz-wolframite stringers ranging in thickness from fractions of mm to few cm. The maximum proved depth of mineralization (without signs of attenuation) is 550 m. The west portion of the area dominated by tungsten mineralization and un the east molybdenum mineralization which although more wide-spread becomes richer with depth. The mineralized host rock is strongly altered, giving a spotty appearance, is locally massive, drusy and brecciated, and crosscut by numerous stringers.

The primary ores contain over fifty minerals including wolframite, magnetite, hematite, pyrite, and chalcopyrite. The estimated reserves of the deposit are 186 M tonnes withan average grade of 0.17% W_2O_3, 0.018% Mo,0.07%Li, 0.13% Rb and 0.009 Cs.

Ygodzer

The Ygodzer deposit is located on the extreme SE of Mongolia, 280 km south of the Bayan-Tumen (Choibalsan) railroad station. The area is composed of an Ordovician sandy-siltstone sequence cut by Late Triassic-Early Jurassic intrusions of porphyritic granites.

The tungsten mineralization is represented by two morphological types--veins and a greisen body. The tungsten-bearing greisen body is localized in the apical portion of a porphyritic granite stock, is crescent-shaped in cross section and dips steeply and concordantly with the contact surface of the granites. The area of main mineralization is more than 2 sq km (1.700 x 100-120 m). Based on sampling using a cut-off grade of 0.5% WO_3, eleven tenses were outlined within the body. The largest of these, which contains 90% of the deposit's reserves, extends for 1.400 m along strike, has a width of 400 to 950 m and a thickness of 50 to 250 m and their thickness from 1 to 12 m. The greatest concentration of lenses occurs in the domal portion of the intrusion.

The principally economically-valuable minerals of greisen body include wolframite, molybdenite, and beryl. The average grade of the deposit is 0.197% tungstren, 0.056% molybdenum, higher-than-normal contents of beryllium oxide (0.08%) and bismuth (0.132%) are noted at individual sites. Total reserves are 21.6 MT with 42,500 of W_2O_3, at 12,000 t of MO.

GOLD DEPOSITS

Hailast

The Hailast placer occurs in the Zaamar gold district located 220 km northwest of Ulaanbaatar and is the best-studied and richest placer in the district. It lies in the valley of the Tuul tributary at the Tuul River and drains the northwestern slopes of the Zaamar-Nuruu range. The total length of the valley is 14 km, with an average width of 300-500 m. The fill of the valley is composed of alluvial and colluvial rubble-clay deposits 1-10 m thick; they are underlain by 3-5 to 20m thick Quarternary yellow and red-colored gravel with interbeds of sand, loam and clay with an aggregate thickness of 16-30 m.

Two paystreaks are defined in the vertical cross-section of the Hailast valley: the lower (main) pay-streak, with an average grade of 1-1.5 g/m^3 and approximately 10 t of reserves, occurs in the near-bedrock portion of the valley and is persistent in thickness, extent and width. The upper "suspended" paystreak occurs in grey-colored alluvium and has no economic value due to its discontinuity.

The placer gold is coarse to medium in size with tabular and sheet-like particle prevailing. The fineness is 899.

Boroo

The Boroo deposit is located 150 km south of Ulaanbatar and 24 km from the railroad station of Baruun-Haraa. The gold mineralization is associated with zones of intense hydrothermal alteration (chloritization, albitization and beresitization) occurring at the contacts of Late Permian-Early Triassic leucocratic and biotite granites and the sandy-flysch sequences of the Lower Paleozoic Kharin Group.

The mineralized zones have been traced 15-700 m along strike and for 150-300 m downdip at an angle of 10-20^0. Two ore horizons, a 7-8 m thick upper zone and a 3.5 m thick lower zone, separated by a 4 m thick zones of weakly mineralized granites, constitute the principle ore horizon. Ores are oxidized to a depth of 40m.

Gold content averages 3-4 g/t. Reserves of gold are approximately 30 t. Small amounts of silvet are present.

SILVER DEPOSITS

Asgat

The Asgat deposit, situated in the extreme northwest of the country near Russia/Mongolia frontier,170 km north of the town of Ulgii, the aimak administration center, was discovered in 1976 in an area of high mountains, with altitudes of 2,300-3,650 m.

Silver and accompanying base metals mineralization in the Asgat area is concentrated in 11 ore-bearing zones, with several radiating apophyses, which trend northeast to near north-south and which dip steeply to the southeast. The zones are from 1.5 to 12 km long, range in thickness from 5 to 80 m, and consist of a complex network of single branching quartz and siderite veins, quartz-siderite cemented breccias and siderite stringer. The viens have associated strong alteration consisting of argillization and silicification. Within the ore-bearing zones, individual orebodies, ranging in thickness from 0.8 to 3.3 m extend from 170-640 m along strike and to 500 m downdip.

The main ore minerals include tetrahedrite, chalcostibite, chalcopyrite, pyrite, arsenopyrite, bismuthitite, and native copper, silver, and bismuth. Subordinate minerals include sphalerite, galena, argentite, marcasite, melnikovite, and pyrrhotite. The main ore mineral is silver, and the principle by-products are copper, bismuth and antimony. Both silver and the by-products are distributed irregularly throughout the orebodies, however, the average contents of the major components change between individual orebodies within the following limits: silver from 100 to 450 g/t; bismuth from 0.03 to 0.09% antymony from 0.04 to 0.7%, copper from0.19 to 1.17%. Mercury is present in minor amounts. The estimated reserves of Ag are approximately 10,000 tonnes.

RARE EARTH ELEMENTS AND METALS

Halzan-Buregtei

The Halzan-Buregtei occurrence is situated on the left bank of the Hovdo River, 50 km northeast of the aimak center of Hovd (Kobdo). Complex tantalum-noibium-rare earth-zirconium mineralization is spatially and genetically associated with a Late Paleozoic (Carboniferous) multiple phase and multiple intrusion of alkaline granitoids.

The alkaline granitoids form the Halzan-Buregtei massif, which is small in size (800 to 2,000 m) and is elongated in the northwest direction. It is composed of nordmarkites, alkaline granites, rare-earth metal alkaline granites and has associated dykes of various composition. The principle ore mineralization is concentrated in alkaline mircrocline-albite granites of the third phase composing a stocklike body emplaced into nordmarkites.

Alkaline granites, containing rare-metal mineralization, are usually transformed into arfvedsonite-albite-quartz metasomatities. The total surface area of rare-earth metal metasomatites is 0.85 sq. km and is characterized by abundant fluorite (veins and impregnations). Rare metal mineralization is represented by evenly disseminated zircon, pyrochlore, columbite, rare-earth fluocarbonates (parasite, bastnaesite), pllylithionite, zirconium silicates (elpidite, tyttinsite), less frequently by xenotime, monazite, thorite and ferrithorite.

The average content of the ore is 0.20% Nb_2O_5; Ta_2O_5; 1.5% ZrO_2 and 0.35% Y_2O_3.

Estimated resources of rare earth metals, to a depth of 200 m, are estimated to be 600,000 t of niobium oxides, 35,000 t of tantalum oxides, 4,000,000 t of zirconium oxides, 1,000,000 t of rare earth oxides and more than 100,000 t of yttrium oxides.

It is highly probable that zircon-pyrochlore placers may have been formed near the rare- metal granites.

Lugeengol

The Lugeengol vein-carbonatite rare-earth deposit is in the South-Gobi aimak and occurs within the endo- and exocontact zones of the Early Jurassic (nepheline and pseudoleucite syenites Lugeengol massif. The massif occurs on the eastern flank of the South-Gobi belt of alkaline rocks.

The area is composed of hepheline-bearing syenites,pseudoleucite rocks accompanied by dykes of leucitephyries, nepheline syenites, rhyolites, and vien carbonatites intruded into a Permain shale-argillitic sequence, with interbeds of siltstones and limestones. These host rocks are converted into biotite-feldspathic hornfels, in locally fenitized contact aureole.

Seventeen carbonatite veins have been studied within the 0.2 sq km area of the mineralization occurring between the massif and the host rocks. Metasomatically altered syenites enriched in fluorite, feldsparsericite, muscovite, hematite, ironsulfides accompany carbonatite veins within the massif. The veins are arranged in an en-echelon pattern with individual veins ranging from a few meters to 430 m in length (the prevailing length being 200-259 m) and ranging in thickness from 0.2 to 1.0 m (0.5-0.4 m values being dominant). Two types of carbonatite viens are recognized: calcite and calcite-fluorite with their major component, synchysite, occurring as a fine dissemination. The REE oxide content ranges from 0.22-3.68%, the average being 3.23%. The content is somewhat higher on the surface due to leaching to calcite. The rare earths belong to the cerium subgroup with cerium comprising 50.77%, lanthanum 32.,96%, neodymium 9.14%, praseodymium 4.96%, samarium 0.97%; the remainder of the rare earths are present in fractions of tenths and hundredths of a present. The reserves are estimated about 200,000 t.

FLUORITE DEPOSITS

Bor-Undur Ore Field

The Bor-Undur ore field is the largest mineralized area in Mongolia. The Bor-Undur ore field is a tectonic block bounded by faults on all sides. In the core of the block there are Triassic granites cut by a system of crossing dykes and dyke-like bodies, composed of fluoritized breccias of trachyryolites. Permain acidic effusives occur to the north whereas Late Mesozoic andesitic basalts are developed to the east. More than 20 orebodies of economic importance represented by high-angled vein-like mineralization zones composed of breccias of host rocks with fluorite and quartz-fluorite cement have been discovered within the ore field. The ore bodies are grouped in four deposits (Bor-Undur, Adag, Bayan-Ulaan, Undur-Ovoo) spaced from 2-10 km apart.

Ore body thickness ranges from 0.5 to 32 m; extend for 100-3,400 m along strike and 20-350 m downdip. The average content of major components varies within the following limits (CaF_2 28-44%, SiO_2 40-55%, $CaCO_3$ 0.8-2.2%)

The Bor-Undur deposit is the largest in Mongolia. It is situated in the eastern part of the ore field where 14 high angle (65-85^0) orebodies extending for 150 to 2,280 m along strike, 60 to 400 downdip and averaging from 2 to 9 m thickness have been discovered and explored in detail. The orebodies occur both in Lower Permain acidic and Late Jurassic-Early Cretaceous basic effusives. NW- and NE-trending faults constitute the most important ore-controlling structures.

Initial identified reserves of the deposit, including orebodies of the nearly locality are as follows: 12.2 M t of ore with 5,200 t of contained fluorite at an average grade of 40-50% .

Urgen Ore Field

The Urgen ore field immediately adjoins the Transmongolia railroad 60 km southeast of the aimak center of Sainshand. The ore field is broken into a number of blocks by numerous variously oriented faults which control the fluorite mineralization. Within its area of 12 sq km 17 metasomatic ore zones and orebodies were discovered and to various extent studied. The ore zones are usually localized at the contacts of limestones and granites, limestones with schists and, less frequently, within granites. The orebodies extent for 50 to 520 m along strike and 30-260 m downdip. They are from 1 to 70 m thick and dip at angles ranging from 30 to 60^0. Ore zone 9 (Urgen) is of the greatest economic importance.

The Urgen zone strikes approximately NS and is localized in the center of the ore field. The ore zone is composed of intercalated crystalline limestones, mica-feldspathic, quartz-intruded by Middle Paleozoic hyperbasites, Permian granites and accompanying dykes of microdiorites, diorite porphyrites and granite-porthyry.

The ore zone includes a major calcite-quartz fluorite ore mass of intricate structure and outline which on the surface extends for 520 m along strike and 30 to 260 m downdip. The width of the mass is 20-173 m on the surface and 17-113 m at depth. Individual orebodies are composed primarily of low carbonate calcite-quartz fluorite and high carbonate quartz- calcite-fluorite ores.

The Urgen field, which has been worked since 1981 and has total reserves 9.0 M t of ore containing 4.0 M t at average grade of 45% Ca_2F. Undiscovered resources at the deposit are estimated to be 1.1 M t.

COAL DEPOSITS

Tavan-Tolgoi

The Tavan-Tolgoi coal deposit is unique within the country both in terms of its size, covering over 90 sq km within the Ulannuur coal-bearing depression, and the high quality of the coal. The deposit is located 560 km south-southeast of Ulaanbaatar, 90 km east of Dalanzadgad, the administrative center of the Omnogov aimak. The deposit occurs in a large synclinal structure modified by faults and superimposed folding. The Late Permian coal-bearing sequence is as thick as 965 m in the central part of the syncline and occurs within units of intercalated sandstone, siltstone, and conglomerates. Overall, the coal-bearing sequence includes 16 coal seams ranging in thickness from 2 to 72 m. The aggregate thickness of coal beds, in the central part of the structure, reaches 163 m, with the maximum depth of the base of the lowermost seams occurring at 945m.

The central 9 sq. km of the deposit has been studied in detail to a depth of 340 m whereas the deeper horizons have undergone only reconnaissance exploration. Other areas of the Ulannuur basin, the Ukha-Khudag, Eastern and Bortolgoi localities, have been prospected to a depth of 340 m.

Chemical-analyses made by the Eastern Coal-Chemical Institute (Sverdlovsk, Russia) indicate that coals from the Tavan-Tolgoi deposits is comparable in quality to the principal types of coals exported by the U.S., Canada and Australia.

The overall coal resources the Ulannuur basin, including the Tavan-Tolgoi, Ukha-Khudag, Bortolgoi and Eastern areas (to the maximum coal seam depth of 940 m) are estimated to be 7.0 bln.t, which includes 4.0 bln t of coking coals of varying quality. The overall coal reserves of the Tavan-Tolgoi deposit proper are estimated to be 5.0 bln.t of which 2.8 bln.t are amenable to open pit mining to a depth of 340m.

Baga-Nuur

The Baga-Nuur deposit is located 110 km east of Ulaabaatar in the central part of the Tabunsubatuin depression and the deposit has been operation since 1978. The deposit is linked to the Transmongolian railroad through the railroad branch running from the Mant Station and with the towns of Ulaanbaatar and Underhaan via improved dirt road. The 480-500 m thick coal-bearing sequence, comprised of intercalated sandstones, claystones and siltstones, occur within a 5 km wide and 14 km long depression. Two coal-bearing horizons, containing 24 coal seams and interbeds are recognized within the coal-bearing sequence and contain approximately 600 mln. tonnes of coal amenable to open-pit.

MONGOLIA'S FUTURE LIES IN MINING[5]

During its 70-year history, the People's Republic of Mongolia has been dominated by its neighbor to the north, the Soviet Union. Today, preoccupied with domestic crises, the Soviet Union is disengaging politically and military from this landlocked nation. It is reducing substantially its financial and technical assistance to Mongolia.

In the past, Soviet aid has been directed primarily to Mongolia's mining industry, which accounts for nearly one-fifth of the Mongolian gross national product and about half of its export earnings. With decreased Soviet aid and a new drive in Mongolia towards economic openness, new opportunities exist for Western countries in the areas of lending and joint mineral ventures.

Trade with the Soviet Union has accounted for 90% of Mongolia's foreign trade revenues. Annual trade between the two countries had been near $2.4 billion, with minerals comprising the major share.

But foreign trade fell 7.3% in 1990, to $1.40 billion. Along with the sharp reduction Soviet financial aid and trade, Mongolia's economy has slowed considerably. Industrial production has dropped, while prices and unemployment have risen.

Faced with mounting economic woes, Mongolia authorities are viewing their nations' huge and largely untapped minerals endowment as a possible long-term source of revenue to rebuild the economy. In this direction, Mongolian officials are revising investment and taxation codes to attract overseas investors in the mining sector.

[5] James P. Dorian, Ph.D., is a research fellow in the program on resources, energy and minerals of the East-West Center in Honolulu, a center for cultural and technical exchange between East and West.

A new foreign investment law was enacted last year, enabling foreign companies to invest independently of through joint ventures. The law provides for a top tax rate of 40%, a three-year grace period on taxes and tax-free repatriation of dividends for 10 years. Other investor rights include protection against exploration.
Mongolia's vast geologic potential offers interesting opportunities to participate in the further development of its mineral and energy resources.

A primary objective of the Mongolia's mining industry will be the development of metal processing facilities to improve Mongolia's long-term export potential. Mongolia is a leading world producer of fluorspar, used in the processing of gold, silver, copper, and lead.

Among centrally planned economies, Mongolia is a major exporter of copper and molybdenum. Molybdenum, an essential ingredient in the production of stainless steel, is in great demand. Because there are few substitutes this may the most promising area for export growth.

Production of copper and molybdenum occurs on a massive scale at the world-class Erdenet plant, in the north central region, which was created in 1975 with Soviet financial and technical aid.

As for the energy minerals, deposits of coking coal, used in making iron and steel, will be exploited as a matter of urgency. Resources at the Tavan-Tolgoyt deposit are 530 kilometers from the capital, Ulan Bator, are estimated at more than 5 billion tons. The quality of these coal resources reportedly are on par with deposits in Australia and Canada major players in the world coal market.

But Mongolia's ability to boost minerals and energy production will depend on its ability to raise financing. This, in turn, will depend on the timing and extent of the Soviet withdrawal and Mongolia's ability to expend hard currency. Other factors will include constraints on infrastructure and the division of management control at the enterprises.
On possible source of funding for mining projects is Japan. Japanese Prime Minister Kaifu and his Mongolian counterpart Dumaagyn Sodnom last March formalized a trade agreement granting Mongolia most-favored-nation status.

Mongolia has requested Japanese government support to develop such natural resources as zinc, lead, and rare metals for export. Recently, Japan has been assisting in the construction of an iron and steel metallurgical plant in Mongolia. And Japan has been investigating copper and non-ferrous metal prospects throughout the country.
Japan also has expressed interest in building a copper smelter at Erdenet, capable of producing 60,000 tons a year. The Mongolian government assigned priority during the 1991 to 1995 period to the production of copper concentrates and finished products made from copper.

Mongolia also is seeking to establish cooperative projects with China, North and South Korea, Canada, and the United States on bilateral and multilateral levels.
Though still a remote possibility Mongolian officials are considering setting up special economic zones in the resource-abundant eastern region to facilitate economic ties with neighboring Asia and the West.

Though relations between Mongolia and the United States were re-established only four years ago. President Bush in January accorded Mongolia most-favored-nation trade status, reducing tariffs on Mongolian exports to the lowest possible levels, and raising the possibility of a big increase in U.S.-Mongolian trade.

American technology now is being used in oil exploration in Mongolia. The American-based Amoco and Chevron corporations have indicated that they will pursue exploration in Mongolia once an appropriate legal regime to guide such efforts is established

Faced with the impending Soviet economic withdrawal, Mongolia intends to use its huge mineral base to attract overseas investment. How Mongolia will fare in the absence of Soviet support remains to be seen. However, the country's mining potential is great and in the years ahead, ample opportunities for developing this resource-rich land will unfold.

INVESTMENT OPPORTUNITIES IN MINING INDUSTRY

1. MINERAL OPPORTUNITIES

1.1. Gold (Au)

Gold mineralization on Mongolian territory has occurred with varying intensity during the late Precambrian, early Cambrian, Paleozoic, Mesozoic and Cenozoic time periods. However the most significant gold mineralization is associated with magnetic activity during Permian, Triassic, and Jurassic periods. Placer gold deposits were formed during the Cretaceous, Neogene, Pliocene, and Holocene time periods.

The known economically significant gold mineralizations in Mongolia occur in 3 deposit types: veins, mineralized zones, and placers. Although vein occurrences are the most widespread of all gold deposit types, the bulk of proven recoverable gold reserves are associated with mineralized zones and placer deposits.

On the basis of geological data, ten main gold metallogenic provinces have been delineated within Mongolia. However true gold potential of the western and southern regions of Mongolia is largely conjectural due to the fact that, to date, little detailed geological exploration has been conducted in these regions. Emphasis of geological exploration in these areas has only focused on placer deposits and quartz vein mineralization. Nevertheless, the number of occurrences determined based on limited data clearly suggests a high gold potential overall for these regions.

Additionally, available geologic data indicate that as yet undiscovered occurrences of gold will likely be found in the following geological formations:

(a) Gold-bearing conglomerates of Cretaceous and Tertiary age in southern and western Mongolia.

(b) Gold mineralization associated with ancient volcano-sedimentary areas in Central Mongolia.

(c) Ancient epithermal gold occurrences (island arc associations) in the Kharkhira, Ulzeet, and Southern Mongolian gold provinces.

1.2. Base Metals (Cu, Mo, Pb, Zn)

Copper-molybdenum (Cu-Mo) mineralization in Mongolia occurs primarily in three types of deposits, late Paleozoic to early Mesozoic Cu-Mo porphyries, copper-nickel (Cu-Ni) magmatic segregations associated with gabbro of unknown age, and Paleozoic to Mesozoic stratabound copper. The Cu-Mo deposits described above occur in four main base metal provinces in Mongolia, located in the Altai range, northern Mongolia, and southern Mongolia.

In addition to these Cu-Mo deposits, Mongolia also has a large number of middle to late Mesozoic lead-zinc (Pb-Zn) deposits, which occur in a variety of deposit types. The main Pb-Zn deposit types include skarns, mineralized explosive pipes, veins, and mineralized zones. The known base metal deposits were formed for the most part in the middle to late Mesozoic. The main Pb-Zn deposits occur primarily in the eastern part of the country, but also in central Mongolia and the Altai Mountains.

The northern, central, and southern metallogenic provinces of Mongolia have a high potential for a discovery of new deposits of copper, molybdenum, lead, and zinc. In the northern and southern Mongolian provinces, the potential is greater for Cu-Mo porphyries, while in central Mongolia both Pb-Zn and Cu-Mo porphyry deposits occur.

The most promising prospects for the discovery of large scale copper and polymetallic mineralization is in the Altai area of southwestern Mongolia, where three regional geologic structures intersect, the Altai metallogenic province, the Beitianshan tectonostratigraphic terrain, and a complex zone of faults.

Regionally the Altai metallogenic province includes areas of Russia (Gornii Altai), China (Altai), and Mongolia (Mongol Altai). In the Gornii Altai Republic of Russia, large Pb-Zn deposits have been discovered, whereas on the Russia-Mongolian border hydrothermal Pb-Zn deposits and volcano-clastic iron (Fe) mineralization have been identified.

In the Altai region of China, mid-Paleozoic sandstone, shales and volcanoclastic deposits of synorogenic-synvolcanic origin contain massive copper-nickel (Cu-Ni) sulfides, which indicate that at least two major synorogenic massive sulfide deposits will be discovered. Based on criteria similar to those used in the China Altai region, it is inferred that similar Cu-Ni sulfide deposits would have been formed in the adjacent Mongolian Altai area. On the basis of this, it has been predicted there should be economic deposits of Cu, Mo, Pb, Zn, and Ni in the Mongolian Altai. Copper occurrences of stratiform type were recently discovered in the northern part of the Altai area, as well as synorogenic Cu-Ni mineralization associated with gabbro bodies.

In southern Mongolia, the Altai metallogenic province borders on the Bietianshan tectono-stratigraphic terrain, and at this convergence zone both areas are in turn intersected by a Devonian-Carboniferous age fault zone extending northwest from China through Mongolia. The fault zone is approximately 850 to 900 km in length and 30-50 km in width, and, based on recent studies, is known to be tectonically active. This area of complex intersection of the three zones is known to contain Pb-Zn deposits, however there is believed to be a large potential for the occurrence of several deposits and deposit types. In particular, the complex rock types present in this area include volcano-sedimentary and sandstone-carbonate formations, small to medium sized intrusions of tonalites, leucogranites, alkalic granites, syenites, gabbro, and ultramafic rocks. Additionally, numerous crosscutting faults of different orientation provide the host environment for diverse deposit types.

1.3. Fluorite (CaF_2)

Fluorite mineralization is widespread throughout Mongolia in rocks of late Paleozoic to late Mesozoic age. The major period of formation of economically important mineralization took place during late Mesozoic to late Jurassic and early Cretaceous time periods. The fluorite mineralization occurs in two economic types, epithermal vein and metasomatic ore bodies. Late Mesozoic fluorite mineralization is associated with rare earth and lead-zinc mineralization, but not in economic quantities. Three major fluorite provinces have been defined in Mongolia, the

Northern Mongolian, Trans-Mongolian, and Southern Mongolian fluorite provinces, with the Trans-Mongolian province having the largest reserves and being the most actively mined.

1.4. Rare Earth Elements (Ta, Nb, Zr, W, Y, Sn)

Rare earth elements (REE) in Mongolia are primarily felsic and alkalic rocks of late Mesozoic, early Mesozoic, and late Paleozoic age. Known deposits of REE are subdivided on the following basis:

REE mineralization with alkalic granitoids and volcano-plutonic complexes (metasomatic zones).

Tungsten (W) veins and stockwork mineralization in granitoids.

Tin (Sn) veins and skarn mineralization in granites and carbonate rocks.

Within Mongolia six REE provinces have been identified, the Altai, Northern Mongolian, Khentii, Khangai, Southeast Mongolian, and Southern Mongolian provinces. REE occurrences are widely distributed throughout Mongolia, and available data indicate that the Altai and South Mongolian provinces are the most promising for future discoveries of Tantalum (Ta), Niobium (Nb), Zircon (Zr), Tungsten (W), Yttrium (Y), and other REE.

1.5. Uranium (U)

Soviet and Mongolian geologists began exploring for uranium in Mongolia in the 1940's. Prior to 1966, numerous uranium occurrences were discovered associated with deposits of coal. From 1967 to 1988 more systematic exploration for uranium was undertaken, and four major uranium deposits were defined in Mongolia, the Priargun, Gobi-Tamtsag, Khentii-Daur, and Northern Mongolian uranium provinces. Uranium deposits of economic value were discovered in the Dornod, Gurvanbulag, and Mardai areas of eastern Mongolia and the Kharaat area of southern Mongolia. The proven uranium resources of Mongolia in these deposits are about 62,000 metric tons, while the uranium resources of the entire country are estimated to be 1,307,000 metric tons. Uranium mining in Mongolia began in 1989 with opening of the Mardai open pit mine in eastern Mongolia. The ore is processed in the Russian Priargunsky ore dressing plant and the mine was operated as a joint Russian-Mongolian venture until 1993.

In 1998 Mongolian-Russian-American joint company was established to reopen the mine. Unfortunately, due to low market price and financial problems of the company the mine has been closed again.

1.6. Phosphorite (P_2O_5)

There is a large phosphorite-bearing basin located in the north-central region of the country. Since mid-1960s, several joint geological expeditions involving Mongolian, Russian, and Czech teams have explored 25,000 km^2 of the Khovsgol Lake region, discovering more than 30 phosphorite occurrences in the process. Estimated phosphorite reserves in the region are 2,400 megatons.

The Burenkhaan phosphorite deposit is located 370 km northwest of the Erdenet copper plant, some 30 km north of Moron and 100 km south of Khovsgol Lake. Average grade of carbonate-phosphorus anhydrite (P_2O_5) is 20%. Total reserves of deposit are 300 megatons, 192 megatons of which could be mined by open pit operations. However, development of the Khovsgol phosphorite deposit will require implementation of rigorous environmental protection procedures because of growing tourism activities in the region.

1.7. Industrial Minerals

Some deposits of industrial mineral deposits may occur in quantities suitable for export. Notable deposits include limestone, zeolite, gypsum, graphite, semi-precious stones, and sand and gravel. Limestone reserves at the Khotol plant exceed 20 megatons.

2. MAJOR MINERAL DEPOSITS OF MONGOLIA

2.1. Copper Deposits

Erdenet Copper Deposit

The Erdenet deposit is the site of Mongolia's single largest mine, which is a joint Mongol-Russian venture. The deposit is located 365 km northeast of Ulaanbaatar and 165 km southwest of the Trans-Mongolian railroad junction at the city of Darkhan. A spur rail line connects the Erdenet Mine with Salkhit station on the Trans-Mongolian railroad, near Darkhan.

The Erdenet mine has been in operation since 1978, and at present has a production capacity of approximately 20 million metric tons of ore annually, which yields approximately 354,000 metric tons of copper concentrate and 3,500 metric tons of molybdenum concentrate each year. In 1990, the Soviet Union purchased 90% of Mongolia's copper concentrate and 100% of its molybdenum concentrate. Composition of copper concentrate from Erdenet is typically as follows: 27-35% copper, selenium (50-60g/metric ton), silver (50-70 g/metric ton), tellurium (8-9 g/metric ton), and gold (0.3-0.5 g/metric ton). Composition of molybdenum concentrate from Erdenet is typically as follows: 47-54% molybdenum, rhenium (450 g/metric ton), selenium (90 g/metric ton), and tellurium (15 g/metric ton). Overall, approximately 124,000 metric tons of copper and 1,672 metric tons of molybdenum are produced annually from concentrate mined at Erdenet. A small but increasing amount of tungsten is also produced from the mine's ore.

The Erdenet Mine is located within a large porphyrite intrusive complex with associated volcanic rocks, and is considered a typical stockwork copper-molybdenum porphyry deposit. Within the larger intrusive/volcanic complex, four spatially separated ore-bearing stockwork zones have been identified. The main stockwork, which occurs on the western flank of the system, is usually called the Erdenet deposit. This stockwork, like the other three zones, is a clearly defined vertical stockwork composed of discreet stringers which are 2-5 mm in thickness and randomly oriented. The main stockwork occurs in association with 2 smaller stocks with numerous epiphyses cross-cut by many gently to steeply dipping dikes.

The main stockwork is approximately 2400 meters in length and 300 to 1300 meters in width. In the central section it extends approximately 1000 meters deep, while near the porphyry it extends approximately 600-700 meters deep. Overall the main zone of the Erdenet deposit has a surface area of about 2 km^2 or roughly 2300 x 800 m as delimited by a cutoff grade of 0.25% copper.

The principal minerals of economic importance in the oxidized/leached zone of the deposit are cuprite, delafessite, malachite, azurite, brochantite, pantellerite, turquoise, and native copper. The average grade of the oxidized/leached zone is 0.1% Cu. The zone of secondary enrichment, underlying the oxidized/leached zone, is characterized by chalcocite, bornite, and covellite with a copper content ranging from 0.65 to 1.35% and molybdenum content ranging from 0.077 to 0.3%, the average values being 0.81% and 0.17% respectively. The primary ore of the Erdenet deposit is characterized by pyrite, chalcopyrite, and molybdenite, with lesser amounts of sheelite irregularly distributed throughout the ore body. The typical ore averages 20-68 g/metric ton of tungsten, with content ranging locally up to 80-300 g/metric ton.

Estimated reserves of the main zone of the Erdenet deposit are 2,295 megatons of ore with average contents of 0.50% copper, 0.014 g/metric ton molybdenum, 1.81 g/metric ton silver, and 0.05 g/metric ton of gold. Reserves at deeper stockwork horizons are estimated to contain approximately 1.4 megatons of copper metal and 37 kilotons of molybdenum metal.

Surven Sukhait Copper Deposit

The Surven Sukhait copper deposit is located 164 km southwest of the Zuun Bayan railroad station, in the sparsely populated semi-desert region of Dornogov Aimag, in southeastern Mongolia.

The Surven Sukhait deposit is one of seven porphyry copper-molybdenum occurrences within the Tsagaan-Suvarguin district. Throughout the district, copper-molybdenum mineralization of various intensity can be discontinuously traced for a distance of about 10 km ranging in width from 0.8 to 3.0 km. Overall, the copper-molybdenum mineralization occurs within an extensive late Devonian to early Carboniferous intrusive syenite massive. Although the seven mineralized areas have been studied, the Surven-Sukhait deposit is considered to have the greatest economic potential. Copper-molybdenum stockwork mineralization in this deposit extends for approximately 1980 meters, with a width ranging from 180 to 500 meters and a maximum depth of mineralization extending to 420 meters. The stockwork zone strikes northeast and dips at an angle of 35° to 55° to the northwest.

All rock formations facially grade into each other. Stock-like bodies and dikes of the final stage of the massif formation are developed in the western part of the massif. They are represented by leucocratic aplite-like granites, granite-porphyries, and granosyenite-porphyries which have undergone varying degrees of kalifeldspathization and molybdenum-copper mineralization.

The stockwork zone is strongly fractured, consisting predominantly of quartz syenites and syenites which are intensely kaolinized, serecitized and silicified, and is cross-cut throughout with quartz-chalcopyrite-molybdenite stringers.

Vertical sections of the stockwork zone consist of an upper mixed zone of oxidized and enriched ores which are developed to a depth of 10 to 30 meters and reach a maximum depth of 100 meters along faults. Within the upper zone secondary enrichment is poorly developed, however in areas of intensive fracturing it may persist to a depth of 150 to 180 meters.

The major primary ore minerals are chalcopyrite, bornite, and molybdenite, with lesser amounts of pyrite, chalcocite, sphalerite, galena and pyrrhotite. Principal gauge minerals are quartz, feldspar, muscovite, and sericite.

Commercial ore reserves of the deposit have been estimated at 220 to 240 megatons, with marginal ore reserves estimated at 77 megatons. The commercial reserves contain 0.3%-0.7% copper and 0.001%-0.03% molybdenum, with average grades being 0.54% and 0.019% respectively. The average grades of the marginal reserves are estimated to be 0.25% copper and 0.009% molybdenum. Associated elements of possible importance in the economic reserves are 2.64 g/metric ton silver, 0.0084 g/metric ton gold, 0.39% g/metric ton rhenium , 8.3 g/metric ton selenium, 12.8 g/metric ton tellurium, and 0.1-7.0 g/metric ton gallium.

A mineral exploration license for the Surven Sukhait Copper Deposit is held by a Mongolian mining company, but exploration remains incomplete and mining of the deposit has not yet commenced.

2.2. Lead and Zinc Deposits

Tumurtiin Ovoo Zinc Deposit

The Tumurtiin Ovoo zinc deposit is located in Sukhbaatar Aimag, in eastern Mongolia, 180 km southwest of the Bayan Tumen railroad station and the city of Choibalsan. Skarn deposits form the primary mineralization in the thick sequence of Devonian sedimentary-volcanogenic rocks which have been strongly contact metamorphosed by the intrusion of a late Paleozoic granitic complex. Sequentially the upper diabase unit has been converted to hornfels and hornfels blastides, while the lower limestone and shale formations have been converted to marble, with various associated skarns and plagioclase-pyroxene hornfelses. The limestone sequence and skarns, which are primarily sphalerite, form a distinct zone which coincides with garnet-magnetite skarns in the upper portion of the unit.

A main lenticular sphalerite orebody and its numerous associated lenses define the deposit, which extends for a length of approximately 800 meters averaging 200 to 230 meters in width and 14 m in thickness. Maximum depth of the central zone of the deposit has been determined to be 480 meters. The upper 60 meters of the orebody contain oxidized material consisting primarily of sulphides, especially sphalerite. The deposit is estimated to have 7.7 megatons of ore with an average grade of 12.43% zinc and 0.024% cadmium.

A joint Chinese-Mongolian venture holds the mining license for the Tumurtiin Ovoo Zinc Deposit but have yet to begin production.

Ulaan Zinc and Lead Deposit

The Ulaan zinc and lead deposit is located in Dornod Aimag in northeast Mongolia, 110 km northwest of the town of Choibalsan and 6 km northeast of the Mardai uranium mine.
The Ulaan deposit represents an intricate fluidized-explosive structure consisting of four breccia pipes, which extend to depths of 200 to 500 meters. The main pipe containing the bulk of the mineralization is a structure with a wedge-shaped surface expression that ranges in width from 20 to120 meters, and which is a breccia consisting primarily of fragmented wallrock clasts. The clasts have either fine grained fluidized fragments or hydrothermally deposited material in their centers. Base metal mineralization has been traced to a depth of 800 m with no sign of attenuation. The ores are to a greater or lesser extent are oxidized to a depth of 30 to 35 m, and occasionally to a depth of 90 m. Thus within the deposit oxidized and semi-oxidized ores have been identified. The deposit

contains 68.1 megatons of ore estimated to contain 2.0% zinc, 1.2% lead, 53 g/metric ton silver, and 0.21 g/metric ton gold.
A Mongolian mining firm currently holds the mining license for the deposit but is seeking financial assistance from outside investors to begin development of the deposit.

2.3. Tungsten, Tin, and Molybdenum Deposits

Ondor Tsagaan Tungsten-Molybdenum Deposit

The Ondor Tsagaan tungsten deposit is located in Khentii Aimag in Northeastern Mongolia, 170 km east of the Baga Nuur railroad station and 70 km northwest of the aimag administrative center of Ondorkhaan. The deposit is located in a synclinal fold where the fold axis abruptly changes orientation from a northeast to a northwest direction. Within the deposit the major structural features are folds and northwest trending faults. The rock types include lower Devonian quartz-sericite, quartz-biotite, chert, and shales emplaced by gabbro-diabase bodies.

The deposit is elliptical in plan, being 1500 m in length and 500 to 700 m in width. The stockwork trends northwest and consists of randomly oriented quartz-wolframite stringers which range in thickness from fractions of mm to a few cm.The maximum proven depth of mineralization is 550 m. The western portion of the area is dominated by tungsten mineralization, while the eastern portion is dominated by molybdenum mineralization which becomes richer with depth. The mineralized host rock is strongly altered giving it a spotty appearance, and is locally massive, brecciated, and crosscut by numerous stringers.

The primary ores contain over fifty minerals, including wolframite, magnetite, hematite, pyrite, and chalcopyrite. The estimated reserves of the deposit are 186 megatons with an average grade of 0.17% W_2O_3, 0.018% Mo, 0.07% Li, 0.13% Rb, and 0.009% Cs.
Although an exploration license has been taken out on the deposit area, exploration is as yet incomplete and no mining has begun.

Yugodzer Tungsten Deposit

The Yugodzer tungsten deposit is located in Sukhbaatar Aimag in the extreme southeast of Mongolia, 280 km south of the Choibalsan railroad station and 150 km southeast of the aimag administrative center of Baruun Urt. The geology of the area is composed of a sandy Ordovician siltstone sequence cut by late Triassic to early Jurassic intrusions of porphyritic granites.
The tungsten mineralization is represented by two morphological types, veins and a greisen body. The tungsten bearing greisen body is located in the apical portion of a porphyritic granite stock, is crescent-shaped in cross section, and dips steeply and concordantly with the contact surface of the granites. The main area of mineralization is more than 2 km^2 in area, and approximately 1700 m in length and 100 to 120 m in width. Based on sampling using a cut-off grade of 0.5% W_2O_3, eleven lenses were outlined within the body. The largest of these, which contains 90% of the deposit's reserves, is 1400 m in length, 400 to 950 m in width, and has a thickness of 50 to 250 m. The greatest concentration of lenses occurs in the domal portion of the intrusion.

The principal economically-valuable minerals of the greisen body include wolframite, molybdenite, and beryl. The average grade of the deposit is 0.197% tungsten and 0.056% molybdenum, while higher-than-normal contents of beryllium oxide (0.08%) and bismuth (0.132%) have been noted at certain locations in the deposit. Total reserves are 21.6 megatons including 42,500 metric tons of W_2O_3, and 12,000 metric tons of MO.
As of this writing neither mineral exploration nor mining licenses have been issued for the deposit area.

2.4. Gold Deposits

Boroo Hard Rock Gold Deposit

The Boroo hard rock gold deposit is located 150 km north of Ulaanbaatar and 24 km from the railroad station at Baruun-Haraa in Southern Selenge Aimag. Gold mineralization in this deposit is associated with zones of intense hydrothermal alteration (chloritization, albitization, and beresitization) which occur at the contacts of late Permian to early Triassic leucocratic and biotite granites and lower Paleozoic Kharin Group sandy-flysch sequences.

The mineralized zones have been traced 15 to 700 m along the strike of the formation, and 150 to 300 m downdip at an angle of 10 to 20 degrees. Two horizons, a 7 to 8 m thick upper zone and a 3.5 m thick lower zone separated by a 4 m thick zone of weakly mineralized granites, constitute the principle ore horizons. Ores are oxidized to a depth of 40 m. Gold content averages 3-4 g/metric ton. Reserves of gold are approximately 30 metric tons and small amounts of silver are present.

At this writing the mining license for the deposit is held by Australian investors. Construction of a cyanide based ore processing plant is underway and production is expected to begin by the early autumn of 2001.

2.5. Silver Deposits

Asgat Silver Deposit

The Asgat deposit is located in Bayan Olgii Aimag, in the extreme northwest of Mongolia, 170 km north of the aimag administrative center of Olgii. The deposit was discovered in 1976 in a mountainous area where maximum altitudes range from 2,300 to 3,650 m above sea level.

Silver and accompanying base metal mineralization in the Asgat area is concentrated in 11 ore-bearing zones with several radiating apophyses that trend north to northeast and dip steeply to the southeast. The zones are from 1.5 to 12 km long, range in thickness from 5 to 80 m, and consist of a complex network of single branching quartz and siderite veins, quartz-siderite cemented breccias, and siderite stringers. The veins have associated strong alterations consisting of argillization and silicification. Within the ore-bearing zones individual orebodies range in thickness from 0.8 to 3.3 m and extend from 170 to 640 m along the formation strike and up to 500 m down dip.

The main ore minerals found in the Asgat deposit include tetrahedrite, chalcostibite, chalcopyrite, pyrite, arsenopyrite, bismuthitite, and native copper, silver, and bismuth. Subordinate minerals include sphalerite, galena, argentite, marcasite, melnikovite, and pyrrhotite. The main ore mineral is silver, and the principle by-products are copper, bismuth, and antimony. Both silver and silver by-products are distributed irregularly throughout the orebodies. However the average content of the major ore components is variable amongst individual orebodies within the following ranges: silver 100-450 g/metric ton, bismuth 0.03-0.09%, antimony 0.04-0.7%, and copper 0.19-1.17%. Mercury is present in minor amounts. Estimated silver reserves are approximately 10,000 metric tons.

Although a mining license has been issued for the deposit, the license holders are seeking outside investment in order to begin development of the deposit.

2.6. Rare Earth Elements and Metals

Halzan Buregtei Rare Earth Deposit

The Halzan Buregtei deposit is located in Hovd Aimag, on the left bank of the Hovd River, 50 km northeast of the aimag center of Hovd. Complex tantalum-niobium-zirconium-rare earth mineralization is spatially and genetically associated with a late Paleozoic (Carboniferous) multiple phase intrusion of alkaline granitoids.

Alkaline granitoids form the Halzan Buregtei massif which is small in size, 800 to 2,000 m in length, and is elongated in the northwest direction. It is composed of nordmarkites, alkaline granites, rare earth metal alkaline granites, and has associated dikes of various composition. The principle ore mineralization is concentrated in alkaline microcline-albite granites which form a stock-like body emplaced in nordmarkites.

Alkaline granites containing rare earth metal mineralization are usually transformed into arfvedsonite-albite-quartz metasomatites. The total surface area of rare earth metal metasomatites is 0.85 km^2, which is characterized by abundant fluorite veins. Rare earth metal mineralization is represented by evenly disseminated zircon, pyrochlore, columbite, rare earth fluorcarbonates (parasite, bastnaesite), polylithionite, and zirconium silicates (elpidite, tyttinsite), and less frequently by xenotime, monazite, thorite and ferrithorite. The average content of the ore is 0.20% Nb_2O_5; 1.5% ZrO_2, and 0.35% Y_2O_3.

Estimated resources of rare earth metals to a depth of 200 m are 600,000 metric tons of niobium oxides, 35,000 metric tons of tantalum oxides, 4,000,000 metric tons of zirconium oxides, 1,000,000 metric tons of rare earth oxides, and more than 100,000 metric tons of yttrium oxides. It is also highly probable that zircon-pyrochlore placers may have been formed near the rare earth metal bearing granites.

Although an exploration license has been taken out on the deposit area, exploration remains incomplete and mining has yet to commence.

Lugeengol Rare Earth Deposit

The Lugeengol vein-carbonate rare earth deposit is located in Dornogovi Aimag, Khatanbulag province. The deposit occurs within the contact zones of the early Jurassic nepheline and pseudoleucite syenite Lugeengol massif, which lies on the eastern flank of the South Gobi Alkaline Rock Belt.

The deposit is composed of nepheline-bearing syenites, pseudoleucite rocks accompanied by dikes of leucitephyries, nepheline syenites, and rhyolites and vein carbonates intruded into a

Permian shale-argillitic sequence interbedded with siltstones and limestones. These host rocks have been converted into biotite-feldspathic hornfels in a locally fenitized contact aureole.

Seventeen carbonate veins have been studied within a 0.2 km^2 area of the mineralization occurring between the massif and its host rocks. Metasomatically altered syenites enriched in fluorite, feldsparsericite, muscovite, hematite, and ironsulfides accompany carbonate veins within the massif. The veins are arranged in an en-echelon pattern with individual veins ranging from a few meters to 430 m in length, the predominate length range being 200 to 259 m, with thicknesses ranging from 0.2 to 1.0 m, typically being about 0.5 m thick. Two types of carbonate veins are recognized, calcite and calcite-fluorite veins, with synchysite as their major component occurring as a fine dissemination. The rare earth element oxide content of the deposit ranges from 0.22 to 3.68%, averaging 3.23%. Rare earth content on the surface is somewhat higher due to calcite leaching. The rare earths belong to the cerium subgroup and contain cerium 50.77%, lanthanum 32.96%, neodymium 9.14%, praseodymium 4.96%, and samarium 0.97%. The remainder of the rare earths are present in fractions of tenths and hundredths of a percent. Reserves are estimated about 200,000 metric tons.
A mining license has been issued for the Lugeengol rare earth deposit, however mining has yet to commence.

2.7. Fluorite Deposits

Bor Undur Fluorite Deposit

The Bor Undur deposit is located within a larger ore field in the extreme southwest of Khentii Aimag, about 80 km east of the town of Choir. The ore field is a tectonic block bounded by faults on all sides and is the largest mineralized area in Mongolia. In the core of the block there are Triassic granites cut by a system of crossing dikes and dike-like bodies which are composed of fluoritized breccias of trachyrhyolites. Permian acidic effusives occur to the north whereas late Mesozoic andesitic basalts are developed to the east. More than 20 orebodies of economic importance have been discovered within the ore field, which are typically high-angled, vein-like mineralization zones composed of host rock breccias with fluorite and quartz-fluorite cement. The ore bodies are grouped in four deposits, the Bor Undur, Adag, Bayan Ulaan, and Undur Ovoo deposits, which are spaced from 2 to 10 km apart. Ore body thicknesses range from 0.5 to 32 m, extending for 100 to 3400 m along the formation strike and 20 to 350 m down dip. The average content of major components varies within the following limits: CaF_2 28-44%, SiO_2 40-55%, $CaCO_3$ 0.8-2.2%.

The Bor Undur deposit is the largest fluorite deposit in Mongolia. It is situated in the eastern part of the ore field where 14 high angle, 65° to 85° orebodies have been discovered and explored in detail. These ore bodies extend for 150 to 2,280 m along the formation strike, 60 to 400 m down dip and average from 2 to 9 m thickness. The orebodies occur both in lower Permian acidic and late Jurassic to early Cretaceous basic effusives. Northwest and northeast trending faults constitute the most important ore-controlling structures. Identified reserves of the deposit are as follows: 12.2 megatons of ore, of which 5,200 tons contain fluorite with an average grade of 40-50%.
The Bor Undur fluorite mine is the single largest fluorite mine in Mongolia, and has been in continuous operation as a joint Mongolian-Russian venture since 1970.

Urgen Ore Field

The Urgen ore field is located adjacent to the Trans-Mongolian railroad in Dornogov Aimag, about 60 km southeast of the aimag center of Sainshand. The ore field is broken into a number of blocks by multiple faults which control fluorite mineralization. 17 metasomatic ore zones and orebodies have been discovered within a 12 km^2 area. The ore zones usually occur at contacts between limestones and granites, limestones and schists, and less frequently within granites. The orebodies extend for 50 to 520 m along the formation strike and 30 to 260 m down dip. They range from 1 to 70 m in thickness with dip angles ranging from 30° to 60° .

The ore zone known as the "Urgen ore zone" is located in the center of the ore field, and is the zone of greatest economic importance. The Urgen ore zone strikes approximately north-south and is composed of intercalated crystalline limestones, Permian granites, mica-feldspathic quartz intruded by mid Paleozoic hyperbasites, and accompanying dikes of microdiorites, diorite porphyrites, and granite-porphyry.

The ore zone includes a major calcite-quartz-fluorite ore mass which extends on the surface for 520 m along the formation strike and 30 to 260 m down dip. The width of the mass is 20 to 173 m on the surface and 17 to 113 m at depth. Individual orebodies are composed primarily of low carbonate calcite-quartz-fluorite and high carbonate quartz-calcite-fluorite ores.

The Urgen field has been worked since 1981 and has total reserves of 9.0 megatons of ore containing 4.0 megatons of Ca_2F with an average grade of 45%. Undiscovered resources at the deposit are estimated to be 1.1 megatons.

2.8. Coal Deposits

Tavan Tolgoi Coal Deposit

The Tavan Tolgoi coal deposit is unique in Mongolia for both its size, 90 km^2, and the high quality of its coal. The deposit is located in the Ulannuur coal-bearing depression in Omnogov Aimag, 560 km south of Ulaanbaatar and 90 km east of Dalanzadgad, the aimag center. The deposit occurs in a large synclinal structure modified by faults and superimposed folding. The late Permian coal-bearing sequence is up to 965 m thick in the central part of the syncline, and occurs within units of intercalated sandstone, siltstone, and conglomerates. Overall, the coal-bearing sequence includes 16 coal seams ranging from 2 to 72 m in thickness. The aggregate thickness of coal beds in the central part of the structure is 163 m, which occur at a maximum depth of 945 m.

The central 9 km^2 area of the deposit has been studied in detail to a depth of 340 m, while deeper horizons have only been subject to preliminary exploration. Other areas of the Ulannuur basin, such as the Ukha Khudag, Eastern, and Bortolgoi localities, have also been probed to a depth of 340 m. Chemical-analyses made by the Eastern Coal-Chemical Institute in Sverdlovsk, Russia indicate that coal from the Tavan Tolgoi deposits is comparable in quality to the principal types of coals exported by the U.S., Canada, and Australia.

The overall coal resources the Ulannuur basin, including the Tavan Tolgoi, Ukha Khudag, Eastern, and Bortolgoi areas are estimated to be 7.0 billion tons, which includes 4.0 billion tons of coking coals of varying quality. The overall coal reserves of the Tavan-Tolgoi deposit alone are estimated to be 5.0 billion tons, of which 2.8 billion tons are amenable to open pit mining to a depth of 340m.
At present only one small scale mine is in operation at the Tavan Tolgoi deposit, and further outside investment will be needed before large scale production can begin at Tavan Tolgoi.

Baga Nuur Coal Deposit

The Baga Nuur coal deposit is located in the Tabunsubatuin depression in Eastern Tov Aimag, 110 km east of Ulaanbaatar. The deposit is linked to the Trans-Mongolian railroad through the railroad branch line beginning at Mant Station. The mine is also accessible from the communities of Ulaanbaatar and Ondorkhaan via an improved dirt road. The coal-bearing sequence occurs in a depression that is 5 km wide and 14 km long. The sequence is 480 to 500 m thick, and comprised of intercalated sandstones, claystones, and siltstones. Two coal-bearing horizons containing 24 coal seams and interbeds are recognized within the coal-bearing sequence, and contain approximately 600 million tons of coal amenable to open-pit mining.

The Baga-Nuur coal deposit has been mined continuously since 1978, and is the source of 80% of the coal used by Ulaanbaatar's power plants.

OIL & GAS SECTOR OPPORTUNITIES

Ministry of Fuel and Energy
Ulaanbaatar 46, Baga Toiruu 6
Mongolia
Tel: +976 1 291 16

Mongol Petroleum Company
Uildverchnii, Gusamj MGT, Ulaanbaatar 37
Mongolia
Tel: +976 1 331 176
Fax: +976 1 331 176

Petroleum Authority of Mongolia
Uildverchinii str-37/81, Ulaanbaatar
Mongolia
Tel: +976 1 331 208 , 976-1-3312
Fax: +976 1 331 239
E-mail: petromon@magicnet.mn
URL: www.pam.mn/

INVESTMENT CLIMATE

- Mongolia is risk free politically and offers an open commercial environment.
- Favorable legal condition; The Petroleum Law of Mongolia is one of the top 10 petroleum laws (AAPG, Explorer, Aug. 1995, van Meurs rates)
- Open 16 blocks (each acreage approximately 10,000 sq. km) and more acreage available
- Stable politically and regulatory condition
- One of the most favorable Tax condition in the world

Exemption from:

- Corporate Income Tax
- Customs Tax
- Excise Tax
- Value Added Tax

- Mutually beneficial fiscal terms (Production Sharing Contract)

- Stability agreement for Stabilized tax environment for 10-15 years

(The Amendments to Foreign Investment Law of Mongolia, Jan 2002)

- High possibility of recourse

Recoverable petroleum resource estimated to be 4-6 billion barrels by American experts. (CNPC attributed original oil-in-place in Tamsag Basin to be approximately 1.5 billion barrels. Chinese recovery factors in analogous basins range around 30%. (Oil and Gas Journal, Oct. 29, 2001, Vol. 99-44, p. 37)

- Near oil market in North Chinese refineries.

The vast Chinese energy market is about to move to the center stage of world oil industry activity and senior oil company executives are likely to be spending the coming months signing contracts running into billions of dollars. The long-predicted boom in the region is about to burst into reality (OGJ, Oct 29, 2001, p. 38).

BIDDING INFORMATION

On 22 August 2003 the Tender Comission had its meeting and decided to award the Bidding to the Chinese company Shi Ji Yang Guang one of the four companies that applied for oil exploration operations in the Nyalga XVI Exploration area of the Central Mongolian Basin. The Tender Comission was appointed by the Order from 20 August 2003 of Chairman of the Petroleum Authority of Mongolia (PAM), Government Implementing Agency. A final negotiations between PAM and winner Shi Ji Yang Guang company will start shortly.

PIPELINE PROJECT

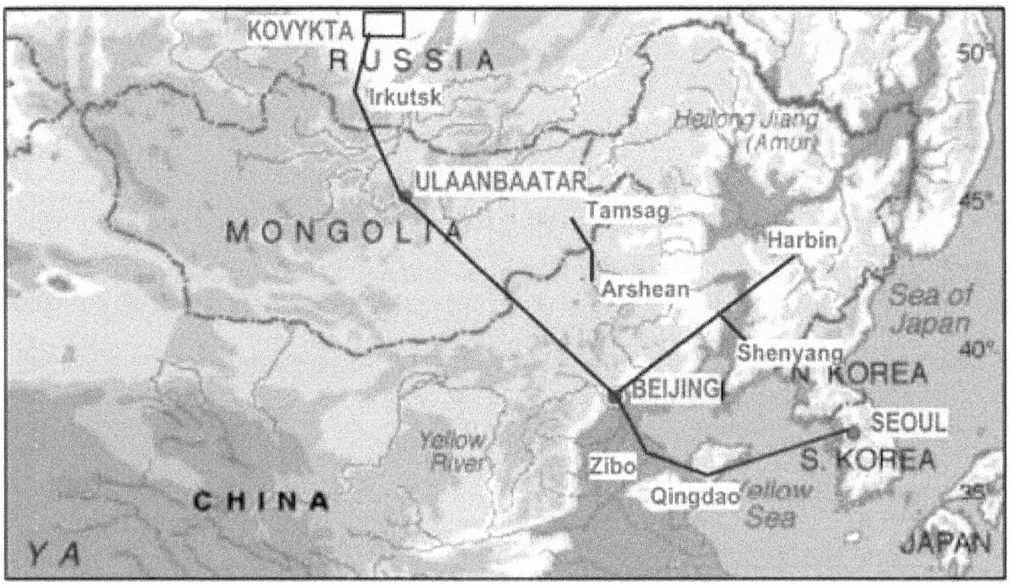

The Petroleum Authority of Mongolia has cooperation with the companies, participating parties of a pipeline project. Kovyktinskoye gas is planned to be used to supply both the Irkutsk region market, neighboring areas, and the large and growing markets of China and South Korea through a long distance pipeline. There is also possibility of supply to markets in Mongolia and Japan.

Discussion between Russia, China, South Korea, Japan and Mongolia regarding gas supplies from KOVYKTINSKOYE have been held on a number of occasions on a "five nations" multilateral basis.Kovykta is expected to be proven to be one of the largest natural gas accumulations in the world. Estimated reserves are more than one trillion cubic meters of natural and more than 40 million tons of gas liquids that are as condensate.The long-distance pipeline will be transporting 30 billion cubic meters per year of gas for regional use and for export, for a more than 25 years.

PROFESSIONAL ORGANIZATIONS

1. MINERAL PROCESSORS ASSOCIATION

President: M. Damdinsuren
Executive Director: S.Davaanyam

- Consolidate effort and initiatives of members of the Association who work for Mongolian mining companies and Research and training institutions, disseminate to the members scientific and technological information rapidly.
- To provide a cohesive management for R&D of mining companies in exploitation and flotation; contribute to processing plants development, technological reform and increase their efficiency
- To collaborate with international organizations

Address:
Room 103, Institute of Technology , Erdenet City, Mongolia
Phone: 976-1-352-73421, 73406, 976-99351418, 99139610
Fax: 976-1-352-73002, 23002
E-mail: MMPA@emc.erdnet.mn

2. MONGOLIAN GEOLOGISTS ASSOCIATION

President: S. Oyun
Vice President: G.Ankhbayar

- Develop Geological science in Mongolia, and it's promotion, implement international projects and organize symposiums and field trips, develop geological research work and industry up to international level

Address:
Room 303, 3rd floor, Delta Center building, Juulchny gudamj, 1st khoroo,
Chingeltei District, Ulaanbaatar, Mongolia
Phone: 976-11-323645, 319760
Fax: 976-11-312039
E-mail: monrud@mongol.net

3. ASSOCIATION OF MONGOLIAN GEOPHYSICISTS

President: D.Odkhuu
Vice President: L.Gankhuyag
Executive director: P.Dugaraa

- Develop long-term plan for geo-physics development in Mongolia, assist implementation of tasks

Address:
Geophysics Training Centre, Room 427,
Mongolian University of Science and Technology,
Sukhbaatar District, Ulaanbaatar, Mongolia
Phone: 976-11-324590-2214

4. MONGOLIAN SOCIETY FOR MINE SURVEYING

Chairman: D.Dondov
Deputy chairman: B.Bold

- To support activities of companies, academic institutions and professionals operating in mineral and contruction and engineering surveying harmonizing their operations;
- To participate in drafting of laws that regulate mining and surveying in the country and to submit an appeal to the Government regarding regulations that are disadvantageous for its members.
- To cooperate with similar organizations from other countries and facilitate its members' international activities.

Address:
Rooms 233A, 235, 2nd floor, Mongolian University of Science and Technology, Ulaanbaatar, Mongolia
Phone: 976-11-324590, 681444, 976-99194213, 99199447
Fax: 976-11-324590

5. MONGOLIAN METALLURGICAL ASSOCIATION

President: D.Ganbold
Executive Director: Ts.Munkhjargal

- To support the development of metallurgical production, research, technical and technology and education in Mongolia

Address:
Darkhan sum, Darkhan Uul Aimag, Mongolia
Phone: 976-01372-29266
Fax: 976-01372-29266
E-mail: metal@mongol.net
P.O.B-98, Central Post of Darkhan Uul Aimag, Mongolia

6. MONGOLIAN COAL ASSOCIATION

Executive Director: G.Tulga

- Regulate and harmonize operations and activities of coal companies and professionals; assist in implementation of government policy in coal sector; to participate in law drafting to better serve for the rights of its members; to increase production efficiency, introduce latest technologies, expand its cooperation with foreign organizations, support professional training

Address:
5th floor, MCS Plaza building,
Seouliin gudamj-4, Ulaanbaatar, Mongolia
Phone: 976-11-328582
Fax: 976-11-328582
E-mail: coalasso@yahoo.com
P.O.B-1079, Ulaanbaatar-13, Mongolia

7. MONGOLIAN DRILLING ASSOCIATION

Chairman: Ts.Dashdorj
Vice Chairman: M.Naranbat
Executive Director: J.Tseveenjav

- Formulate management and technological policies on drilling for geology, mining, hydrology, oil and gas; prepare proposals on industry regulations to submit for review by policy-makers; conduct research and provide consultancy services

Address:
Room 311, Mongolian University of Science and Technology, Ulaanbaatar, Mongolia
Phone: 976-11-324590-240, 976-99163180, 99114686, 99764013.
Fax: 976-11-312291
E-mail: btseveen2003@yahoo.com
P.O.B-13, Ulaanbaatar-20, Mongolia

MINERAL PROCESSING TECHNOLOGICAL CENTRE OF MONGOLIA

Mineral Processing Technological Centre (MPTC) was founded on May of 1991. Temporary installation of the Laboratory 's equipment and training of personnel started in 1990. The MPTC is a Technological research institute carrying out the investigations and laboratory test works and processing ore beneficiations technologies. The Centre includes the special laboratories , such as combination , mineral processing, mineralogical, chemical and hydrometallurgical laboratory and options of establishment of a pilot plant and development of the laboratories in the future .

MINERAL PROCESSING LABORATORY (MPL)

Established to provide various beneficiation tests on different types of ferrous and non-ferrous metals and industrial minerals as well as precious metal ore can be made as batch tests. Also the possibility for small mini-pilot tests is included.
The laboratory batch- test operation is the first step process development for a new ore deposit or it can support the development of existing process or pilot plant test.
The results of the batch tests will be presented in a report which will give sufficient information for process design and equipment selection as well as operating cost estimation.
The MPL comprises equipment and space to make beneficiation tests using methods like:

- flotation
- gravity separation
- magnetic and electrostatic separation
- hydrometallurgical operations

The flotation of metallic ores and industrial minerals is an essential part of mineral beneficiation .Both gravity and magnetic separation can serve as central or complementary part in processing many metal ores and industrial minerals.
Flotation cells "Denver" and "Mechanobr" conventional gravity, magnetic and electrostatic separation equipment such as;
mineral jig "Denver", multi gravity "Mozley" separator, high intensity magnetic separator from UK, high tension roll separator and electronic separator "Reading and Lismore" from Australia etc. are available in the laboratory .
To support tests and process development the MPL also includes facilities to make other kind of tests and processes in connection with beneficiation tests such as:

- grinding
- screening and classification
- grind ability
- filtration and thickening
- drying
- sample preparation

and equipment for measuring particle size, pH and temperature etc.

MINERALOGICAL LABORATORY

The laboratory conducts mineralogical investigations needed for sample studies, evaluation studies of mineral deposits planning of laboratory and later on also pilot scale tests, studies and control of process operations , assessment of the test work and forecasting of the metallurgical processing, products, recoveries and economy.
All activities of the laboratory are focused on mineralogical studies of rock, ore and soil samples, drill core samples, mine samples and process samples or fractions from laboratory , pilot scale and plant scale operations.

At present the mineralogical laboratory is equipped by polarizing microscopy ''Olympus'' from Japan and polarizing microscope"MIN-8", binocular ''MBS-9" from S.U. and facilities for sample preparation and purchasing of X-ray diffract meter and scanning electron microscope with energy dispersive spectrometer is taken into account.

CHEMICAL LABORATORY

Chemical analyses for mineralogical and mineral dressing studies are made here. The laboratory analysis elements from the batch tests metal balance calculations and quality of the products mainly by the means of atomic absorption spectrophotometer GBC from Australia.
For wet chemistry there used the titrimetric and gravimetric methods to determine the main components of mineral processing products like concentrates. Iodometric and EDTA –titrations are the most favorite methods for components like Cu,Fe and photometric and calorimetric methods are used for trace element and water analysis and determination of anionic components.

LABORATORY OF HYDROMETALLURGY

Establishment of Hydrometallurgical laboratory is now in initial stage and designed to conduct tests for leaching process simulation There are installed leaching conditioners, solvent extraction equipment and autoclave in this laboratory .

OUR ADDRESS:

Mineral Processing Technological Centre
P. O. 211137 Post 250
Ulaanbaatar, Mongolia
Telephone and fax 976-11-633898

CENTRAL GEOLOGICAL LABORATORY

Address:
Central Geological Laboratory
Songino khairkhan duureg, 18th khoroo,
Trade Union street, Ulaanbaatar - 211137
Mongolia

Mailing address:
Central Geological Laboratory
P.O.Box-55, Ulaanbaatar-211137
Mongolia

Telephone: +976-11-632904, +976-11- 632914

Fax: +976-11-632944

E-mail:
cengeolab@magicnet.mn
cengeolab@mongol.net

Web-site: www.cengeolab.com

Bank:
Trade and Development Bank
Trade street-7, Ulaanbaatar-11
Mongolia
Tel.: +976-11-312362, +976-11-327020
Факс: +976-11-325449, +976-11-328231

MAIN ACTIVITIES

- Determination of physical and mechanical properties, mineralogical and elemental composition of mineral resources;
- Production of certified reference materials for mineral resources;
- Expertise analysis, external control and professional advice for other laboratories of this special sector;
- Scientific studies and investigation, students and trainees training.

Special activities

Professional stone carving techniques are applied to produce Mongolian stone souvenirs of traditional style or
customers individual design..

Analytical objects

Typical application fields of our analytical service:

· Minig prospecting
· Exploration of deposits
· Estimation of reserves
· Control of mining processes
· Quality assessment of raw materials for industrial production
· Various kinds of mineral resources such as minerals, ores, rocks
· Soil, natural water, salt, mineral water
· Industrial wastes
· Metals and alloys
· Flammable and inflammable raw material
· Food and agriculture

BUSINESS TRAVEL TO MONGOLIA

BUSINESS TRAVEL

BUSINESS CUSTOMS

* Personal relationships in business are critical. The Mongolians like to deal with *old friends.* Exporters, importers and investors must establish and maintain close relationships with their Mongolian counterparts and relevant government agencies. Equally important, American exporters should encourage strong personal relationships between their Mongolian agents or distributors and the buyers and end-users. A web of strong personal relationships can smooth development of business in Mongolia.

* Family and school ties remain strong in Mongolia. Learn who is related to whom when establishing business connections.

* Mongolians look for cues of serious intent by how much effort—time and material—a foreign investor puts in the early phases. Initial meetings should be conducted in formal settings, in suit and tie, with an exchange of cards. Small gifts are always appreciated. Subsequent meetings can be more relaxed as circumstances permit. Lunches and dinners are always appreciated. However, expect and allow the Mongolians to be generous hosts, as this is an important part of local culture. Being a good guest and business partner requires that one partake of the festivities at the start of any business relationship. However, to keep the relationship balanced from the start, we advise businesses to host a meal(s).

* New entrants to the Mongolian market tend to see Mongolians through the prism of their neighbors. That is, one may think that Mongolians are like the Chinese or the Russians or the Koreans, etc. While historical and cultural affinities exist between Mongolia and her neighbors, Mongolians are very conscious and proud of their history and the progress of their country over the last decades. They become offended if confused with China and deeply resent being compared to other developing countries with similar commodity-dependent economies—especially those from Africa. Rather they prefer to be compared to other former East-Bloc nations as Poland, Kazakhstan, Ukraine, the Czech Republic, etc.

* Avoid letting cultural sensitivity to Mongolian norms get in the way of good judgment and commonsense. Some Mongolians will tell investors that

Mongolian customs preclude best commercial practices, insisting that an attractive deal may not go through if those practices are not ignored. We advise investors to politely but firmly cleave to sound business principles. Investors who do so will earn the respect of the Mongolians and may protect their investment, too.

TRAVEL ADVISORY

For more on international travel, travel advisories, etc.; please see travel information on the Department of State's website: http://travel.state.gov/travel/cis_pa_tw/cis/cis_973.html . The US Embassy in Ulaanbaatar also has a website: http://mongolia.usembassy.gov/ .

VISA REQUIREMENTS

Mongolian Visas

Mongolia requires a valid passport for American visitors. No visa is required for Americans visiting for less than 90 days. However, certain registration requirements may apply. For updated registration requirements please inquire from the Mongolian Immigration, Naturalization and Foreign Citizens Agency (INFCA) in Ulaanbaatar (http://immigration.gov.mn/index.php). American visitors who fail to register and stay longer than 30 days may be stopped at departure, denied exit, and fined. Americans planning to work or study in Mongolia should apply for a visa at a Mongolian Embassy or Consulate overseas. Failure to do so may result in authorities denying registration, levying a fine, and requiring that the visitor leave the country. For current information on visa/registration requirements, contact the Embassy of Mongolia in Washington, D.C. at: (202) 333-7117 or http://www.mongolianembassy.us .

Please be advised the U.S. Embassy cannot assist you with visa applications or intercede on your behalf should you have a problem with a Mongolian visa.

Residency Permits

A foreign investor must present a request issued by the Invest Mongolia Agency (IMA) to the Immigration, Naturalization and Foreign Citizens Agency (INFCA). IMA issues such requests to approved foreign investors. Permits are generally issued within a couple of days and are valid for three months to one year. Individuals may renew temporary residency permits an unlimited number of times. Each renewal will re-validate the permit for a period of three months up to one year, as requested by the investor.

For more detailed information about residency permits, contact IMA at www.investmongolia.com .

Those seeking employment in Mongolia or foreign-owned enterprises, including NGOs, must apply to the Labor Coordination Agency. Those wishing to establish an NGO must

first obtain a permit from the Ministry of Justice. After obtaining the required permits, all foreigners must then apply for residency permits at INFCA.

Travel Information

U.S. citizens transiting China to reach Mongolia can obtain a 72-hour transit visa exemption at ports of entry in Beijing and Shanghai for short stays; subject to satisfying certain requirements (see http://beijing.usembassy-china.org.cn/acs_faq.html.) However, US citizens traveling to Mongolia via China may also obtain a valid Chinese visa from an authorized Chinese diplomatic mission--even if the traveler is only transiting Beijing airport.

U.S. Companies that require travel of foreign businesspersons to the United States should be advised that security options are handled via an interagency process. Visa applicants should go to the following links.

State Department Visa Website: http://travel.state.gov/visa/index.html

United States Visas.gov: http://www.unitedstatesvisas.gov/

U.S. Embassy in Ulaanbaatar: http://mongolia.usembassy.gov/index.html

TELECOMMUNICATIONS

Mongolia has an evolving telecommunications system. In the capital of Ulaanbaatar, the Internet is available and reliable if not as fast as businesses might need. Mongolia has reliable satellite, Wi-Fi, and fiber-optic linkages to the World Wide Web; however the last mile of connection for some publicly accessible systems, especially in rural Mongolia, remains through landlines and dial-up modems. Consequently, downloads to these sites may be slow and subject to interruption.

Mongolia has numerous ISPs and Internet cafes offering a full range of services.

Most hotels, usually in *business centers,* offer regular access to the Internet. A growing number of hotels offer in-room connectivity. We advise travelers to contact their hotel in advance of travel regarding this issue.

Wireless services have become common at private venues. Usually, these private venues offer the service to customers at no charge.

In the countryside computing remains a challenge. Most provincial capitals have several Internet cafes but some linkages are by land-wire to Ulaanbaatar, which are subject to regular disruption. Firms requiring e-services in the field may have to make provision for some sort of satellite infrastructure.

Regarding phone service, Mongolia has followed a fairly regular pattern for Asia. Rather than upgrading its land-based system, Mongolia has encouraged the speedy

development of a cellular system. Ulaanbaatar and most of its surrounding municipalities are linked by four existing private cellular service providers Mobicom, Skytel, Unitel, and G-Mobile. These firms offer sales and service for handsets and other products related to their fields.

Cellular service in the countryside is available in all provincial capitals and in most county centers. Satellite-phone service is also available through Mobicom.

TRANSPORTATION

Business travelers can best enter Mongolia by plane (or train if time is less of an issue). Currently there are no direct flights from a US point of departure to Ulaanbaatar, Mongolia. One can fly from the US to Seoul/Inchon, Beijing, Tokyo, Berlin, Frankfurt, Istanbul or Moscow; and then take the last leg into Ulaanbaatar's Chinggis Khaan International Airport. Korean Airlines, Air China, Aeroflot, Turkish Airlines and Mongolian National Airlines (MIAT) maintain weekly flights. Summer schedules offer more flights than in winter, including as of summer 2014 direct flights from Paris (Hunnu Airlines) and Frankfurt (MIAT) but still flights are limited. In summer seating may be in short supply during high season (June-September). We advise booking early in the summer.

During the spring (and sometimes in summer), severe storms may cause flight cancellations but more normally delays.

Domestic air service is available to most provincial capitals through MIAT and Hunnu Airlines.

The difficulty of in-country travel is directly related to how far one wishes to travel from Ulaanbaatar. There are generally no restrictions on in-country travel, except when within 25 kilometers (15 miles) of Mongolia's international borders with China and Russia. If traveling to these areas check with a local travel company regarding required permits.

Within the capital transport options abound. Taxis, Mini-buses, buses, and electric trolleys are readily available. We suggest that first time business travelers arrange for a car and driver with a local travel firm. Costs vary with type of car and driver, but cars ranging from US limousines to Russian Jeeps are available.

Traffic and road conditions in Ulaanbaatar have become progressively worse over the last few years; and so, travelers are advised to schedule their meetings and trips with no less than a half-hour margin.

In the countryside, travel requires a reliable, off-road vehicle and a skilled driver. Jeeps are also available for hire to more remote destinations. Most of Mongolia's road network is unpaved and travel is unpredictable. Ulaanbaatar has hotels with standard amenities, but few hotels exist outside of the capital. In the countryside, there are ger camps (encampments of 15 to 40 traditional round felt tents). Each ger usually accommodates four persons. Most tourist camps have a restaurant and are usually equipped with toilets and showers with hot water.

LANGUAGE

Mongolian is the official language of Mongolia. All contracts and other legal documents must be in Mongolian if the business conducted is done in this country. Translations of contracts, laws, regulations, etc., have no force in Mongolian courts, agencies, and other government offices.

English is the *de facto* language through which most foreign investors engage with their Mongolian counterparts. Russian, Japanese, German, Korean, and Chinese are also used.

HEALTH

Medical facilities in Mongolia remain limited. Some western medicines are unavailable. Infectious diseases, such as plague and anthrax, are present at various times of the year. Serious medical problems requiring hospitalization and/or medical evacuation to the United States can cost thousands of dollars or more. Additionally, many medical transport companies will not transport people without previous arrangements and agreements have been made. All visitors are recommended to have medical evacuation insurance. Doctors and hospitals often expect immediate payment for health services. For more information, please contact the U.S. Embassy in Ulaanbaatar or the Centers for Disease Control and Prevention's international travelers hotline. Also check www.http://travel.state.gov for the latest U. S. State Department warnings and updates.

SOS operates a clinic in Ulaanbaatar. Individuals may purchase clinic 6 month to one year membership package; or can be treated on a fee for service basis without a membership. For more information contact:

SOS Medica Mongolia UB International Clinic 4a Building, Big Ring Road, 15th Micro District, 7th Khoroo, Bayanzurkh District, Ulaanbaatar, Mongolia Opening hours: 9am-6pm – Monday to Friday After hours, weekends and public holidays – Emergency call-out service Contact details: Telephone: +976-11-464325 /26/27 Clinic Manager: +976-99096175 Fax: +976-11-454537 For after hour emergencies please phone:

+976-9911-0335 (English) +976-9191-3122 (Mongolian) E-mail: admin@sosmedica.mn , marketing@sosmedica.mn

Website: http://www.sosmedica.mn

Sanitation in some restaurants is inadequate. Stomach illnesses are frequent. Bottled water and other routine precautions are advisable. Information on vaccinations and other health precautions, such as safe food and water precautions and insect bite protection, may be obtained from the Centers for Disease Control and Prevention's hotline for international travelers at 1-877-FYI-TRIP (1-877-394-8747); fax 1-888-CDC-FAXX, (1-888-232-3299), or via the CDC's Internet site at http://www.cdc.gov/travel .

LOCAL TIME, BUSINESS HOURS, AND HOLIDAYS

Mongolian Standard Time (MST) is thirteen (13) hours ahead of EST in the fall and winter months and 12 hours ahead in the spring and summer months. Mongolia does not use daylight-savings time in spring and fall. The standard 40 hour workweek is 0900-1800, Monday through Friday, with an hour for lunch. Holidays are as follows:

MONGOLIAN AND U. S. OFFICIAL HOLIDAYS

January 1 Wednesday New Year's Day US/Mon
January 20 Monday Martin Luther King's Day US
January 30-31 Thurs-Fri Lunar New Year Mon
February 17 Monday Presidents Day US
March 7 Friday International Women's Day Mon
May 26 Monday Memorial Day US
June 2 Monday Mother/Children's Day Mon
July 4 Friday Independence Day US
July 11-15 Fri-Tues Naadam Holiday Mon
September 1 Monday Labor Day US
October 13 Monday Columbus Day US
November 11 Monday Veterans Day US
November 13 Thursday Chinggis Khaan's Birthday Mon
November 27 Thursday Thanksgiving US
December 25 Friday Christmas Day US
December 29 Monday Independence Day Mon
*Note: Lunar New Year date may change according to the local astrologers' decision.

TEMPORARY ENTRY OF MATERIALS AND PERSONAL BELONGINGS

The Mongolian National Chamber of Commerce and Industry can arrange for duty free import of display items for trade shows. For more information, contact the MNCCI in Ulaanbaatar:

Tel: 976-11-327176 Fax: 976-11-324620 Email: chamber@mongolchamber.mn Web Site: www.mongolchamber.mn

MNCCI Building Mahatma Gandhi street 1st khoroo, Khan-Uul district Ulaanbaatar 17011

WEB RESOURCES

Mongolian Resources
Invest Mongolia Agency: http://www.investmongolia.com/

General Tax Authority of Mongolia: www.mta.mn
State Registration Office of Mongolia: https://burtgel.gov
General Authority for Social Insurance: www.ndaatgal.mn
Government of Mongolia: http://www.pmis.gov.mn
Intellectual Property Office: http://www.ipom.mn/
Mineral Resources and Petroleum Authority of Mongolia: http://www.mram.mn
Mongol Chamber of Commerce and Industry: http://www.mongolchamber.mn/en/
Mongolian Builders Association: http://www.buildersasso.mn
Embassy of Mongolia, Washington, DC: http://www.mongolianembassy.us
Parliament of Mongolia: www.parliament.mn
American Chamber of Commerce Mongolia: http://amcham.mn/
Business Council of Mongolia: www.bcmongolia.org/
U. S. Government Resources
Commercial Specialist: richmondmd@state.gov
U.S. Embassy, Ulaanbaatar: http://mongolia.usembassy.gov
U.S. Department of State: http://www.state.gov/
U.S. Department of Commerce: http://www.commerce.gov/
U.S. International Trade Administration: http://www.trade.gov/
U.S. Trade and Development Agency: http://www.ustda.gov
U.S. Export-Import Bank: http://www.exim.gov/
U.S. Overseas Private Investment Corporations: http://www.opic.gov

SUPPLEMENTS

US AND COUNTRY CONTACTS

A. MONGOLIAN GOVERNMENT

Ministry of Agriculture and Industry
tel: (976-1) 325-028
fax: (976-1) 323-442

Ministry of Defense
tel: (976-1) 458-755
fax: (976-1) 450-496

Ministry of External Relations
Political Department
Foreign Trade and Economic Cooperation Department
Enkh Taivny gudamj 7A
Ulaanbaatar, Mongolia
tel: (976-1) 311-311
fax: (976-1) 322-127
mongmer@magicnet.mn

Ministry of Finance
tel: (976-1) 329-070
fax: (976-1) 320-247

Ministry of Health and Social Welfare
Olympic Str.-2
Ulaanbaatar-11, Mongolia
tel: (976-1) 321-569
fax: (976-1) 327-872
mhsw@magicnet.mn

Ministry of Infrastructure Development
Government Building-2
United Nations Str-49
Ulaanbaatar 210646, Mongolia
tel: (976-1) 324-379
fax: (976-1) 311-381

Ministry of Justice
tel: (976-1) 325-225
fax: (976-1) 322-383

Ministry of Nature and Environment
tel: (976-1) 326-595
fax: (976-1) 321-401

Ministry of Science, Technology, Enlightenment and Culture
Government Building III
Ulaanbaatar, Mongolia
tel: (976-1) 327-445
fax: (976-1) 323-158
bmostec@magicnet.mn

Central Bank
The Bank of Mongolia
Commerce Str. -6
Ulaanbaatar-11, Mongolia
tel: (976-1) 322-166
fax: (976-1) 326-252
telex: BOMCB MH 79333

Civil Aviation Administration of Mongolia
Buyant-Ukhaa Airport
Ulaanbaatar-34, Mongolia
tel: (976-1) 379-888
fax: (976-1) 313-127
caamak@magicnet.mn

Coal Authority of Mongolia
Ulaanbaatar-21, Mongolia
tel: (976-1) 681-995
fax: (976-1) 681-995

Customs General Administration
Ulaanbaatar-20, Mongolia
tel: (976-1) 323-715
fax: (976-1) 329-024

Ulaanbaatar Customs Administration
PO Box 86
Ulaanbaatar-34, Mongolia
tel: (976-1) 328-473
fax: (976-1) 328-970

Foreign Investment and Foreign Trade Agency
2nd floor, Sambuu Str. 11
Ulaanbaatar 38, Mongolia
tel: (976-1) 321-438
fax: (976-1) 324-076
investboard@magicnet.mn
website: www.mol.mn

Intellectual Property Office of Mongolia
Baga toiruu-31
Ulaanbaatar-46, Mongolia
tel: (976-1) 321-323
fax: (976-1) 327-638

Minerals Resources Authority
Builders' Square 13
Ulaanbaatar 211238
tel: (976-1) 310-370
fax: (976-1) 327-307
mram@magicnet.mn

National Tourism Center of Mongolia
Ms. Haliun, General Director
Chinggis Avenue-11
Ulaanbaatar-28, Mongolia
tel: (976-1) 318-492
fax: (976-2) 318-492

National Statistical Office
Baga toiruu-44
Government Building 3
Ulaanbaatar-11, Mongolia
tel: (976-1) 320-262
fax: (976-1) 324-518

Petroleum Authority of Mongolia
PO Box 37/81
Ulaanbaatar, Mongolia
tel: (976-1) 631-176
fax: (976-1) 631-176
petromon@magicnet.mn
http://www.pam.mn

General Department of National Taxation of Mongolia
Jigjidjav Str-6
Ulaanbaatar-46, Mongolia
tel: (976-1) 321-340
fax: (976-1) 327-686

B. CHAMBERS OF COMMERCE/TRADE ASSOCIATIONS

American Mongolian Business Group
Mr. Maurice Lynch, President
Munkh-Orgil, Idesh and Lynch
International Trade Center
Baga toiruu 37 B
Suite 500/5th floor
Ulaanbaatar, Mongolia
tel: (976-1) 325-344
fax: (976-1) 325-358
mlynch@mongolialaw.com

Mongolian Association of Advocates
Ulaanbaatar-46, Mongolia
tel: (976-1) 326-861

fax: (976-1) 326-861
erdem@mtu.edu.mn

Mongolian Chamber of Commerce and Industry
Mr. S. Demberel, Chairman
Sambuu Str-11
Ulaanbaatar-38, Mongolia
tel: (976-1) 327-176
fax: (976-1) 324-620
monchamb@magicnet.mn

Mongolia Consumers' Union
Mr. Tsendbayar, Director
Room 302
Trade Unions Building
Sukhbaatar Square
Ulaanbaatar, Mongolia
tel: (976-1) 320-026

Mongolian Employers' Federation
Khudaldaanii gudamj-15
Ulaanbaatar-38, Mongolia
tel: (976-1) 325-635
fax: (976-1) 325-635
monef@magicnet.mn

Mongolian Stock Exchange
Sukhbaatar Square-14
Ulaanbaatar, Mongolia
tel: (976-1) 310-470
fax: (976-1) 325-170
msebatj@magicnet.mn

Mongolian Women Lawyers Association
PO Box 547
Ulaanbaatar 210646, Mongolia
tel: (976-1) 322-212
fax: (976-1) 322-212
mwla@magicnet.mn

C. MARKET RESEARCH FIRMS

Mongolian Advertising Association
Room 1205
Sambuu Str-11
Ulaanbaatar-38, Mongolia
tel: (976-1) 323-035
fax: (976-1) 323-035
buderdene@usa.net

Mongolian Marketing Associatioin
Mr. Dagvadorj, President (also professor at National University of Mongolia)

PO Box 20/192
Ulaanbaatar, Mongolia
tel: (976-1) 327-813
fax: (976-1) 324-385
econinst@magicnet.mn

D. BANKS

Golomt Bank
Sukhbaatar Square-3, 4th floor
Ulaanbaatar-11/20A, Mongolia
tel: (976-1) 311-530
fax: (976-1) 312-307
telex: 79247 GLMT MN
golomt@magicnet.mn

Trade And Development Bank
Khudadaalnii gudamj-7
Ulaanbaatar-11, Mongolia
tel: (976-1) 326-289
fax: (976-1) 311-618
telex: 79334 TDB MH
SWIFT Code: TDBMMNUB
TDBMGTG@magicnet.mn

Savings Bank
tel: (976-1) 312-043

E. US EMBASSY CONTACTS

US Embassy Ulaanbaatar
Big Ring Road
Ulaanbaatar
Mongolia
Tel: (976-1) 329-095
Fax: (976-1) 320-776

Mailing Address From US:
US Embassy Ulaanbaatar
4410 Ulaanbaatar Place
Department of State
Washington, DC 20521-4410

Ambassador's Office
Ambassador Alphonse F. La Porta
ambassador@usembassy.mn

DCM Mark Willis
dcm@usembassy.mn

Defense Attache Office
Maj. John Baker

Defense Attache
dao@usembassy.mn

Economic/Commercial Section
Economic/Commercial Officer Laura Byergo
econ@usembassy.mn

Commercial Assistant Allison Croft
commerce@usembassy.mn

Political Section
Political Officer Lynn Roche
pol@usembassy.mn

Consular Section
Consular Officer Tim Roche
cons@usembassy.mn

F. WASHINGTON-BASED USG MONGOLIA CONTACTS

US Department of Commerce
International Trade Administration
Mongolia Desk Officer Brenda Carter
14th And Constitution Avenue
Washington, DC 20230
Tel: (202) 482-3583
Fax: (202) 482-1576

Multilateral Development Bank Office
Tel: (2020) 482-3399
Fax: (202) 482-5179

TPCC Trade Information Center
Tel: 800-USA-Trade

US Department Of State
Office of China And Mongolia
Bureau of East Asia & Pacific Affairs
Room 4318, 2201 C Street, NW
Washington, DC 20520
Tel: (202) 647-6796
Fax: (202) 647-6820

US Department of Agriculture
International Trade Policy
Asia American Division
Foreign Agricultural Service Stop 1023
1th And Independence Ave., SW
Washington, DC 20250-1023
Tel: (202) 720-1289
Fax: (202) 690-1093
Email: deatonl@fas.usda.gov

Office of US Trade Representative
600 17th Street, NW
Washington, DC 20506

G. US BASED MULTIPLIERS
US-Mongolia Business Council
Steve Saunders, President
1015 Duke Street
Alexandria, VA 22314-3551
tel: 703/549-8444
fax: 703/549-6526
steve.saunders@us-mongolia.org

EMBASSIES, CONSULS AND HONORARY CONSULS

EMBASSIES

Bulgaria
Accredited to: Albania, Greece, Cyprus, Macedonia, Slovenia, Croatia, Yugoslavia, Bosnia-Herzegovina
Sofia 1113, ul.Frederic Jolio Curie 52, Embassy of Mongolia, Fax: 00359-2-9630745, Tel: 00359-2-9630765
E-Mail: mongemb@mbox.infotel.bg

Belgium
Accredited to: Denmark, Luxembourg, Netherlands
Ambassade de Mongolie, Avenue Besme 18, 1190, Bruxelles, Belgium, Fax: 0032-2-3443215, Tel: 0032-2-3446974
E-mail:embassymongolia@skynet.be

Canada
Consulate Genaral of Mongolia
BCE Place, Suite 1800, P.O. Box 754
181 Bay Street, Toronto, Canada M5J 2T9
Tel: (416) 865-7776; Fax: (416) 865-1515
E-mail: consulgen@mongolia.org

China
Accredited to: Australia, New Zealand, Pakistan, Brazil, Argentine
Embassy of Mongolia,No 2,Xiushui Beijie Jian Guo Men Wai Da Jie, Beijing, China, Fax: 0086-10-6532-5045, Tel: 0086-10-6532-1810
E-mail: monembbj@public3.bta.net.cn

Cuba
Accredited to: Mexico, Chile
Embajada de Mongolia, Calle 66 No 505 Esguina a 5 ta-A, Tel: 0053-7-242763, Fax: 0053-7-240639

Czech Republic
Accredit to: Slovakia, Romania

Velvyslanectvi Mongolska, Na Marne 5,Praha-6, 160000 Ceska Republika, Fax: 004202-24314827, Tel: 004202-24311199
E-mail:monemb@bohem-net.cz

DPRK
DPRK Pyongyang, Mansu-dong, Embassy of Mongolia, Fax: 00850-23817616, Tel: 00850-23817322

Egypt
Accredited to: Palestine, Jordan, Syria, Israel, Oman, Yemen, Kuwait, Emirates
Embassy of Mongolia, 33A Mohamed Mazhar street, Zamalek Cairo Egypt, Fax:0020-2-3414229, Tel : 0020-2-3409574
E-mail:monemby@intouch.com

France
Accredited to: Spain, Italy, Portugal
Ambassade de Mongolie, 5, Avenue Robert Schumann, 92100 Boulogne-Billancourt, Fax:0033-1-46053016, Tel: 0033-1-46052318
E-mail:106513.2672@Compuserve.com

Germany
Accredited to: Switzerland
1.Botschaft der Mongolei Siebengebirgsblick 4-6, 53844 Troisdorf Germany, Tel: 0049-2241-402727 Fax: 0049-2241-47781
E-mail: Mongolbot@aol.com
2. Gotlandstrasse 12, 10439 Berlin, Fax: 0049-30-4469321, Tel: 0049-30-4469320
E-mail: ganbat@metronet.de

Hungary
Accredited to: Austria, Moldova
Hungary 1022 Budapest, Bogar Utca 14/cMongol Nagykovetsege, Fax:00361-2125731, Tel: 0036-1-2125731
E-mail:mnk@mail.datanet.hu

India
Accredited to: Nepal, Bangladesh, Sri-Lanka
Embassy of Mongolia, 34,Archbishop Makarious Marg, New Delhi 110003 India, Fax:0091-11-4633240, Tel: 0091-11-4631728
E-mail:Embassy.mongolia@gems.vsnl.net.in

Japan
Embassy of Mongolia, 21-4 Kamiyama Cho Shibuya Ku, Tokyo 150, Fax:0081-33-469-2216, Tel: 0081-33-469-2088
E-mail:embmong@gol.com

Kazakhstan
Accredited to: Kyrgyzstan, Tajikstan, Turkmenistan
g.Almaty ul.Aubakerova 1/1, Embassy of Mongolia
Fax: 007-3272-293259, Tel: 007-3272-200865
E-mail:monkazel@kazmail.asdc.kz

Lao PDR
Accredited to: Cambodia, Thailand, Myanmar, Brunei

Embassy of Mongolia, Q. Wat Nak Km.3, P.O.Box 370, Ventiane Lao P.D.R, Fax:00856-21-315221, Tel: 00856-21-315220

Poland
Accredited to : Latvia, Lithuania, Estonia, Ukraine
Ambasada Mongolii 00478 Warszawa, Polska , ul.Rejtana 15 m.16, Fax:0048-22-484264
E-mail:mongamb@ikp.atm.com.pl

R.O.K
Embassy of Mongolia
33-5 Hannan-Dong, Vongsan-gu, Seoul, Korea Fax:0082-2-794-7605,Tel:0082-2-794-1350
E-mail: monemb@uriel.net

Russian Federation
Accredited to: Armenia, Belarus, Georgia, Iran, Finland
Moscow 121069, ul.Borisoglebovskaya 11, Embassy of Mongolia, Tel:077-095-290679 ; Fax:077-095-2916171
E-mail: mongolia@glas.apc.org
bayar@msk.tsi.ru
Website: http://www.icsti.su/mongol

Switzerland
Accredited to Holy See, Malta
Mission Permanente de la Mongolie Geneve 4, Chemin des Mollies 1293 Bellevue/GE, Fax:0041-22-7743201, Tel: 0041-22-7741974
E-mail:mission.mongolia@itu.ch

Turkey
Embassy of Mongolia, G.O.P. Koza Sokak-107, Ankara
Tel: 0090-312-4467977; Fax: 0090-312-4467791
E-mail: mogolelc@turnet.net.tr

Vietnam
Accredited to: Malaysia, Philippines, Singapore, Indonesia
Embassy of Mongolia, 39, Tran phu str.Hanoi, Vietnam, Fax: 0084-4-8454954, Tel: 0084-4-8453009
E-mail:mongembhanoi@hn.vnn.vn

UK
Accredited to: Iceland, Norway, Sweden
Mongolian Embassy, 7 Kensington Court, London W8 5DL, United Kingdom, Tel: 0044-171-937-0150 ; Fax:0044-171-9371117
E-mail: embmong@aol.com

USA
Accredited to: Canada
1. Embassy of Mongolia, 2833 M street, N.W. Washington, D.C.20047, USA
Fax:001-202-2989227; Tel: 001-202-333-7117
E-mail:monemb@aol.com

2. Permanent Representative of Mongolia to UN
not accredited to other countries but serves as point of contact with countries of Africa, Latin America and the Pacific

6 East 77th street, New-York, N.Y.10021 USA , Fax: 001-212-8619464
Tel: 001-212-4726517
E-mail:mngun@undp.org
Website: http://www.undp.org/missions/mongolia

CONSULS

Russia
1. Irkutsk
Irkutsk, St. Lapina-11, General Consulate of Mongolia
Tel: 007-3952-342145, 007-3952-342447
2. Ulaan-Ude
Ulaan-Ude, St.Erbanova-12, "Baikal" Hotel General Consulate of Mongolia
Tel: 007-30122-20507, Fax: 007-30122-63244
E-mail: mnc@bss.ru

China
Huh hot
Zhongguo Huhe Haote, Xincheng gu Wulanziagu 5 hao, Lou Menggu Lingshiguang
Tel: 0086-471-4953254, Fax: 0086-471-4953250

Singapore
100, St. Patrick Road, St. Patrick Garden,Singapore 424191
Fax:0065-3481753, Tel: 0065-3480745

HONORARY CONSULS OF MONGOLIA

Austria
Mr.Johannes Stiedle, Honorary Consul of Mongolia in Austria, AUHOFSTRASSE 65-67, A-113-Vienna/Austria,
Fax: 431877373336

Australia
Mr. Sean Hinton, Honorary Consul of Mongolia in Australia
112/189 Phillip street, Waterloo, NSW 2017, Australia, Tel&fax: 61- 2- 93194797,
E-Mail:sean_hinton@mckinsey.com

Denmark
Mr. Anders Jungersen, Honorary Consul of Mongolia in Denmark
UNISCRAP A / S, Genvindings Industry Fiskerihavnsgade 6, DK-2450 Kobennavn SV,
Fax: 45 33 12 03 73

Italy
Mr. Aldo Colleoni, Honorary Consul of Mongolia in Italy
Via Giulia, 10-34126 Trieste- Italy
Tel: 39 40 575422, Fax: 39 40 575431
E-mail: consmong@tin.it

Israel
Dr. Jacques Leventhal, Honorary Consul of Mongolia in Isreal
9 Frishman Street. TelAviv 63578. Isreal
Tel: 972 35 243 929, Fax:972 35 272 361
E-Mail:clascard@netvision.net.il

The Netherlands
Mr. J. G. Brummeihuis, Honorary Consul of Mongolia in the Netherlands
Notarissen De Cuserstraat 5, 1081CK Amsterdam-Buitenveldert, Postbus 71094, 1008 88 Amsterdam, Fax: 020 644 96 38

Sweden
Mrs. Anita Gerdne, Honorary Consul of Mongolia in Sweden
Gotabergsgatan 34, S-411 34 Gothenburg,
Fax: 46 31 160770

Thailand
Dr. Supong Limtanakool, Honorary Consul of Mongolia in Thailand
94 Rimklongprapa road Banksue,Bangkok 10800, Thailand, Fax: 662 259 03 59

USA
Mr.Edward T. Story, Honorary Consul of Mongolia in USA
1221 Lamar Suite 1201, Houston, Texas 77010 USA
Tel: 713-759-2922, Fax: 713-646-6666

Germany
1. Mr. Dirk Pfeil, Honorary Consul of Mongolia in Main, Germany
Eshersheimer Landstr.62-60, 60322 Frankfurt am Main
Fax: 069 153 096 66, Tel: 069 153 096 10
2. Mr. Bernd Klingsohr, Honorary Consul of Mongolia in Bavaria, Germany
Automag Bushner & Linse GmbH & Co KG Postfanch 12 01 09, 80030 Munchen, Fax: 089 510 22 02, Tel: 089 510 22 66
E-mail: Hon_consul@mongolei.de

Korea
Mr. Zeon Beyon-Kuk, Honorary Consul of Mongolia in The Republic of Korea
189-17, Onchon 1-Dong, Dongrae-Gu, Pusan, Korea, Postal Code No. 607-061, Tel: 8251 555-8182, 558-3891, Fax: 8251 555-4715

Malaysia
Mr. Datuk Syed Abdul Rahman Alhabshi, Honorary Consul of Mongolia in Malaysia
45th floor Empire Tower, City Sq. Center, 182 Jalan Tun Razak, 50400, Kuala-Lumpur, Malaysia
Tel: 03-2621933, Fax: 6032620933

FOREIGN EMBASSIES & REPRESENTATIVES OF INTERNATIONAL ORGANIZATIONS IN MONGOLIA

Foreign Embassies

Bulgaria

POB 702, Olympiin Gudamj 8, Ulaanbaatar Tel: 329721, Telex 220 BGTIS
Ambassador H.E. Mr. EDVIN SUGAREV

E-mail: posolstvo.bg@magicnet.mn

China People's Republic

C.P.O. Box 672, Zaluuchuudyn Urgun Chuluu 5, Ulaanbaatar 13, Mongolia
Tel. 320955, 323940, Fax 311943

Ambassador H.E.Mr. QI CHIJIA

Cuba

C.P.O.Box 710, Negdsen Undestnii Gudamj 5 ,Ulaanbaatar 13, Mongolia
Tel. 327709, 327708, Telex 79228

Ambassador H.E. Mr. ESTEBAN LOBAINO ROMERO

Czech Republic

C.P.O.Box 665, Diplomatic Apartments 95, Ulaanbaatar 13, Mongolia
Tel. 321886, 326661, Fax. 323791, Telex 255 OBZA MH

Ambassador H.E. Mr. JOSEF FASS (res. in Beijing)
Charge d` Affaires Mr. ZDENEK OKUNEK

E-mail: czechemb@magicnet.mn

Democratic People's Republic of Korea

C.P.O.Box 671, Negdsen Undestnii gudamj 12, Ulaanbaatar 13, Mongolia
Tel. 322795, 323458, Telex 250

Ambassador H.E. Mr. JONG JANG HYON

France

B.P.687, 13 Ulaanbaatar Mongolia Tel.312118, 99114424, Fax.324519

Ambassador H.E.Mr. JACQUES-OLIVIER MANENT

AmbaFrance@magicnet.mn

Germany

C.P.O.Box 708, Negdsen Undestnii gudamj 7, Ulaanbaatar 13, Mongolia
Tel. 323325, 323915, Fax. 323905

Ambassador H.E.Mr. JURGEN ELIAS

E-mail:uz1@magicnet.mn

Hungary

C.P.O.Box 668, Enkhtaivany gudamj 1, Ulaanbaatar, Mongolia
Tel. 323973, 320972, Fax. 311793, Telex 79322

Ambassador H.E. Mr.BELA TOROCSIK

E-mail:Hunamb@magicnet.mn

India

C.P.O. Box 691, Zaluuchuudyn Urgun Chuluu 10, 11th Micro District, Ulaanbaatar, Mongolia
Tel. 329522, 329524, Fax. 329532,

Ambassador H.E. Mr. KUSHOK BAKULA

indembmongolia@magicnet.mn

Japan

C.P.O. Box 1011, Olympiin gudamj 6, Ulaanbaatar, Mongolia
Tel. 320777, Fax. 313332

Ambassador H.E. Mr. SHINJI KUBOTA

E-mail:eojmongol@magicnet.mn

Korea

C.P.O. Box 1039, Olympiin gudamj 10, Ulaanbaatar, Mongolia
Tel. 321548, 310153, Fax. 311157

Ambassador H.E. Mr. HWANG KIL SHIN

Lao P.D.R

C.P.O. Box 1030, Ihk Toiruu 59, Ulaanbaatar 13, Mongolia
Tel. 326440, 329898, Telex 79251

Ambassador H.E.Mr. VANHEUANG VONGVICHIT

Russia

C.P.O. Box 661, Enkhtaivany gudamj A-6, Ulaanbaatar, Mongolia
Tel. 326836, 327071, Fax. 327018, Telex 251 UB

Ambassador H.E. Mr. NIKOLAI VICTOROVICH PAVLOV

Turkey

Enkh Taivny gudamj 5,Ulaanbaatar, Mongolia
Te: 313992

Ambassador H.E. Mr. VAROL OZKOCAK

E-mail:turkemb@magicnet.mn

United Kingdom

C.P.O. Box 703, Enkh taivany gudamj 30, Ulaanbaatar 13, Mongolia
Tel. 358133, 358238, Fax. 358036, Telex 79261

Ambassador H.E. Mr. JOHN CLIVE DURHAM

E-mail:britemb@magicnet.mn

USA

C.P.O. Box 1021, Ikh Toiruu 59/1, Ulaanbaatar 13, Mongolia
Tel. 329095,329606, Fax. 320776

Ambassador H.E. Mr. ALPHONSE LA PORTA

E-mail:aeub@magicnet.mn

Viet Nam

Enkhtaivany Urgun Chuluu 47, Ulaanbaatar, Mongolia
Tel. 358923, 358917, Telex 249

Ambassador H.E. Mr. VU VAN VACH

Yuqoslavia

C.P.O. Box 700, Diplomatic Apartment 95, Ulaanbaatar, Mongolia
Tel. 322380, Fax. 325597, Telex 259Yu amb

Charge d` Affaires Mr. RAIKO GRIGICH

Finland

Ministry of Foreign Affairs of Finland
P.O. Box 176, Fin-00161, Helsinki
Tel. (358-9) 134151, Fax. 13415798

Ambassador H.E. Mr. TAISTO Tolvanen

Kazakhstan

District Chingeltei, 6th MicroDistrict, Diplomatic Building 95, Apartment 11, P.O. 38, Box 291, Tel: 312240

Charge d` Affaires Mr. VALIKHAN KONURBAYEV

Representatives of International Organizations

UNDP

Resident Representative Mr.Douglas GARDNER

Mailing Address: UNDP, C.P.O. 49/207, Ulaanbaatar, Mongolia
Street Address: 7 Erhuu Street, Ulaanbaatar
Tel. 327585, 321539 Fax. 326221

E-mail: registry@undp.org.mn
Website: http://www.un-mongolia.mn

UNFPA

Resident Representative Mr.Douglas GARDNER

Mailing Address: UNFPA Representative, P.O.Box 49/207
Ulaanbaatar, Mongolia
Street Address: Enh-Taivan Street-13B Research and Training Centre of Health Management, National Institute of Medical Science Ulaanbaatar, Mongolia

WHO

Resident Representative Mr. U.H. Susantha de SILVA

WHO Representative,Post Box 663, Ulaanbaatar, Mongolia
Tel. 327870 Fax. 327870
Street Address: Government Building No.8 3rd Floor, 3 Karl Marx Street , Ulaanbaatar, Mongolia

E-mail:wrmog@magicnet.mn

IMF

Resident Representative Mr. Geoffrey OESTREICHER

Room 257, Government House, Ulaanbaatar
Tel. 329153, 323802 Fax. 312181

UNICEF

Asst.Representative Ms. Katherine HINTON

Ulaanbaatar-46, Government Building ? 2 Rooms 402-414
Tel. 312201, 312183 Fax. 327313

Mailing Address: UNICEF Assistant Representative Sukhbaatar Duureg, Ulaanbaatar-46, Mongolia

E-mail:unicef@magicnet.mn

UNCHR

Street Address: Trade Union`s Building, 2nd Floor, Room 214 Sukhbaatar Square 3, Ulaanbaatar-11, Mongolia
Mailing Address: C/o UNDP Resident Representative P.O. Box 49/207, Ulaanbaatar, Mongolia

E-mail:unchrmon@magicnet.mn

SELECTED BUSINESS CONTACTS

MAJOR NEWSPAPERS

Business Times - a weekly business paper, in Mongolian, published by the Mongolian Chamber of Commerce and Industry
Mongol Messenger - weekly English language paper published by the Mongolian news agency MONTSAME (the Mongolian national news agency)
Mongolyn Medee - (News of Mongolia) daily newspaper of the Erel Company
Odriin Sonin - (Daily News) daily newspaper
UB Post - weekly English-language newspaper published by Mongol News Group
Unoodor - (Today) independent daily newspaper published by Mongol News Group
Zuuny Medee - (Century News) daily newspaper

TELEVISION STATIONS

Channel 25, owned by the Mongol News Group
Eagle TV - independent station operated by a US-Mongolian joint venture
Mongol TV - state-owned broadcaster
RGB - independent television station in Darhan
UBS - (Ulaanbaatar Broadcasting System) citizens representative board

ADVERTISING ASSOCIATION:

Mongolian Advertising Association
Room 1205
Sambuu Str-11
Ulaanbaatar 38, Mongolia
tel: (976-1) 323-035
fax: (976-1) 323-035
buderdene@usa.net

MONGOLIA STOCK EXCHANGE MEMBERS

MEMBER

"Regulations on Membership of the MSE" regulates admission of legal entities as a member of the MSE, licensing and supervising the regular members, cancellation the license and governs any other relations between the MSE and its members.

The legal entity, interested in membership of the MSE duly applies to the MSE in accordance with the "Regulations on Membership of the MSE" and the final decision is made by the Board of Governors of the MSE.

As the end of 1999, the MSE has 42 regular members.

There was no admission in 1999.

ADMISSION FEE

1. Entrance fee	MNT 5 million.	From a new member (once).
2. Charge on trading floor	MNT 10 million.	From a regular member (once).
3. Annual fee	MNT 700 thousand.	From a regular member for use of trading floor.

SERVICE FEE OF MEMBERS

Members shall pay fee to the MSE, at 0,8% of securities trading value.

Regular members shall charge their client service fee of 1,5 - 3,0% of trading value.

The MSE enters in agreement with the every regular members evaluates activities of the members on quarterly, semi-annual and annual basis.

Delgerkhangai Trade, Ajnai Invest and Argai Best member companies were selected as the best securities trading companies and their combined volume of trading accounted about 40% of the total turnover of the MSE.

RATING OF MEMBER COMPANIES OF THE MSE

Rank	Name of the member company	1st Qtr	2nd Qtr	3rd Qtr	4th Qtr	Total
1	DELGERKHANGAI TRADE	69.1	69.09	76.36	90.91	305.46
2	ARGAI BEST	93.6	94.55	55.45	56.36	299.96
3	AJNAI INVEST	75.0	61.67	74.17	58.33	269.17
4	MERGEN SANAA	67.3	59.55	70.91	58.18	255.94
5	DARKHAN BROKER	77.9	62.80	60.42	54.17	255.29
6	BATS INVEST	50.0	56.48	87.04	61.68	255.20
7	ALTAN KHOROMSOG	69.5	62.73	67.27	53.64	253.14
8	GENDEKS	62.7	56.48	60.19	56.07	235.44
9	NIKI	44.5	54.63	74.07	60.75	233.95

10	ALTAN SAN	55.7	53.91	63.48	59.13	232.22
11	KHANSH INVEST	45.5	60.19	66.67	58.88	231.24
12	DORNOD BROKER	60.9	56.52	56.52	56.52	230.46
13	MONSEC	70.8	49.17	54.17	54.17	228.31
14	MURUN SEC	57.0	59.13	55.65	54.78	226.56
15	SANKOM	53.6	57.41	61.11	53.27	225.39
16	B.D.SEC	45.8	59.17	55.42	64.17	224.56
17	BUMBAT ALTAI	60.0	53.91	54.78	51.30	219.99
18	ZERGED	73.2	56.82	44.55	43.64	218.21
19	TOLIN SECURITIES	54.5	55.56	54.63	53.27	217.96
20	POST SECURITIES	58.2	50.00	50.00	57.01	215.21
21	MUTSA	54.5	50.93	55.56	53.27	214.26
22	LOG	50.0	56.67	50.00	57.50	214.17
23	GAN SEC	50.9	53.7	53.70	54.21	212.51
24	UNDURKHAAN INVEST	54.5	55.91	46.36	55.45	212.22
25	MARAL INVEST	50.0	51.85	56.48	53.27	211.60
26	ERDENEST	64.2	52.92	54.58	38.33	210.03
27	BULGAN INVEST	49.1	55.65	49.57	55.45	209.77
28	NOYON SUUDAL	62.1	44.17	47.50	55.00	208.77
29	TOD SEC	49.1	50.93	52.78	52.34	205.15
30	TAVAN BOGD	44.2	55.83	45.00	60.00	205.03
31	M&G TRAST	42.7	55.56	52.78	53.27	204.31
32	OCH MUNKH	59.2	50.83	45.00	46.67	201.70
33	KHAIRKHAN UNDURKHAAN	53.3	47.50	46.67	52.50	199.97
34	SANAR	55.9	42.73	48.18	51.82	198.63
35	SELBRO	49.2	39.17	51.67	55.83	195.87
36	TUMEN BULL	50.9	48.18	48.64	45.45	193.17
37	SHAND ERDENE	56.7	50.83	44.17	39.17	190.87
38	MUNKHUD	60.4	46.96	51.30	32.17	190.83
39	CHANDMANI BAYAN	42.2	44.35	52.17	50.43	189.15
40	MEGA SECURITIES	55.5	49.07	44.44	39.25	188.26
41	ORCHIL INVEST	49.2	41.25	55.42	40.83	186.70

CONTACT TO MEMBER COMPANIES

Company	Head office phone	Branch office phone	Trading floor phone	E-mail
NOYON SUUDAL	055-22548	324507	313315	

SELBRO	049-22102	311372	313327	
TUMEN BULL	310403		313356	mbroker@magicnet.com
SANAR	453218		313634	
ZERGED	366509		313346	tszerged@magicnet.mn
MERGEN SANAA	451626		311020	
B.D.SEC	047-2235	321763	313372	guys_bdsec@yahoo.com
ORCHIL INVEST	325258	065- 3549	313672	
UNDURKHAAN INVEST	684193	033- 2230	313311	undurhaan@mongolnet.mn
ALTAN KHOROMSOG	455822		313648	
DORNOD BROKER	061-3665		313285	
MURUN SEC	041-3084	328219	313676	murunsec@magicnet.mn
BULGAN BROKER	067-22746		313323	
AJNAI INVEST	053-2184	313763	313765	
DARKHAN BROKER	037-27004	328970	313339	
KHAIRKHAN UNUDURKHAAN	039-2282	684193	313497	
ERDENEST	326751	035-20731	313301	
MONSEC	051-290	321538	313526	monsec@magicnet.mn
CHANDMANI BAYAN	045-219		313656	
MUNKHUD	057-2451		310547	
BUMBAT ALTAI	043-3846		313481	
ALTAN SAN	069-2873	323472	310683	
LOG	059-3742		313747	
TAVAN BOGD	071-2093		313291	
SHAND ERDENE	063-2557	327262	313511	
ARGAI BEST	328108		313324	
OCH MUNKH	320567	073- 2444	324424	
DELGERKHANGAI	360074	313235		
NIKI	324790		310510	
GENDEKS	329657		323807	

BATS INVEST	457843		323774	
GAN SEC	327985		323871	
MEGA SECURITIES			323817	
TOLIN SECURITIES	312484		323932	
M&G TRAST	353574		323751	
MARAL INVEST	323029		323715	
MUTSA	369377		323090	
POST SECURITIES	324723		323068	
SANKOM	457991		310487	
TOD SEC	323559		323085	
KHANSH INVEST	328705		321021	
MIRAI SHOKEN	313787			

YEAR IN REVIEW

Purchased				Sold		
Securities company	Volume \thous.\	Value \MNTmln.\		Securities company	Volume \thous.\	Value \MNTmln.\
DELGERKHANGAI	3,493.5	656.0	1	DELGERKHANGAI	1,771.3	237.3
AJNAI INVEST	2,745.0	325.5	2	AJNAI INVEST	1,815.2	214.8
ZERGED	834.1	244.7	3	ZERGED	630.0	172.1
MERGENSANAA	675.1	219.7	4	MERGENSANAA	1,977.8	170.4
ARGAI BEST	1,799.6	206.4	5	ARGAI BEST	590.8	162.3
KHANSH INVEST	487.3	193.5	6	KHANSH INVEST	530.1	145.2
BATS INVEST	646.8	160.6	7	BATS INVEST	568.8	135.5
DARKHAN BROKER	1,288.7	117.8	8	DARKHAN BROKER	805.4	131.7
ALTAN SAN	566.0	104.3	9	ALTAN SAN	646.3	125.4
BIDISEK	627.6	97.4	10	BIDISEK	851.3	112.9
NIKI	972.0	85.3	11	NIKI	493.2	107.3
MURUN SEK	235.9	58.1	12	MURUN SEK	641.8	97.6
TUMEN BULL	258.7	56.0	13	TUMEN BULL	471.6	97.2
SANCOM	377.9	54.4	14	SANCOM	1,137.7	96.1
MONSEC	444.8	51.1	15	MONSEC	583.0	85.3
GENDEKS	232.4	48.2	16	GENDEKS	718.8	83.8
LOG	72.4	48.1	17	LOG	316.6	80.9
MUNKHUD	387.3	46.7	18	MUNKHUD	512.8	78.2

ORCHIL INVEST	414.4	44.8	19	ORCHIL INVEST	310.1	73.5
POST SECURITIES	428.0	44.0	20	POST SECURITIES	551.4	71.4
SANAR	435.8	40.5	21	SANAR	271.2	69.4
OCH MUNKH	432.8	39.4	22	OCH MUNKH	619.4	65.0
SELBRO	295.7	39.2	23	SELBRO	321.4	64.0
ALTAN KHOROMSOG	519.0	38.0	24	ALTAN KHOROMSOG	486.4	55.0
ERDENEST	387.8	37.1	25	ERDENEST	184.5	52.9
BULGAN BROKER	456.3	24.3	26	BULGAN BROKER	214.7	51.0
DORNOD BROKER	339.1	23.8	27	DORNOD BROKER	337.9	49.7
UNDURKHAAN INVEST	177.8	20.3	28	UNDURKHAAN INVEST	362.3	49.1
TAVAN BOGD	165.1	19.6	29	TAVAN BOGD	347.8	42.4
MARAL INVEST	155.6	17.9	30	MARAL INVEST	256.6	39.1
OTHER	1,094.2	111.6		OTHER	2,120.9	257.8
TOTAL	21,446.7	3,274.2		TOTAL	21,446.7	3,274.2

MULTILATERAL AGREEMENTS

1.	Geneva Convention for the Amelioration of the Condition of the Wounded and Sick in Armed Forces in the Field, 1949	1958
2.	Geneva Convention for the Amelioration of the Condition of Wounded, Sick and Shipwrecked Members of Armed Forces at Sea, 1949	1958
3.	Geneva Convention relative to the treatment of prisoners of war, 1949	1958
4.	Geneva Convention relative to the protection of civilian persons in time of war, 1949	1958
5.	Charter of the United Nations, 1945	1961
6.	Convention on the privileges and immunities of the United Nations, 1946	1962
7.	Constitution of the World Health Organization, 1946	1962
8.	Constitution of the United Nations Educational, Scientific and Cultural Organization, 1945	1962

9.	Convention for the Unification of Certain Rules Relating to International Carriage by Air, 1929	1962
10.	Treaty banning nuclear weapon tests in the atmosphere, in outer space and under water,1963	
11.	Convention of the World Meterological Organization, 1947	1963
12.	Convention against discrinimation in education, 1960	1964
13.	Convention for the Protection of Cultural Property in the Event of Armed Conflict, 1954	1964
14.	Convention on the Political Rights of Women, 1953	1965
15.	Convention on Transit Trade of Land-locked States, 1965	1966
16.	Vienna Convention on Diplomatic Relations,1961	1967
17.	Treaty on principles governing the activities of States in the exploration and use of outer space, including the moon and other celestial bodies, 1967	
18.	Constitution of the International Labour Organizations, 1919	1968
19.	Constitution of the United Nations Industrial Development Organization, 1966	1968
20.	Protocol for the Prohibition of the Use in War of Asphyxiating, Poisonous or Other Gases, and of Bacteriological Methods of Warfare, 1925	
21.	Slavery Convention,1926	1968
22.	Supplementary Convention on the Abolition of Slavery, the Slave Trade, and Institutions and Practices Similar to Slaver,1956	1968
23.	Treaty for the Non-Proliferation of Nuclear Weapons, 1968	1969
24.	Convention on the Prevention and Punishment of the Crime of Genocide, 1948	
25.	International Convention on the Elimination of All Forms of Racial Discrimination, 1966	1969
26.	Convention (No. 103) concerning maternity protection, 1951	1969
27.	Convention (No. 59) , fixing the minimum age for admission of children to industrial employment, 1937	1969
28.	Convention (No. 100) concerning equal remuneration for men and women workers for work of equal value, 1951	1969
29.	Convention (No. 111) concerning discrimination in respect of employment and occupation, 1958	1969
30.	Convention (No. 87) concerning freedom of association and protection of the right to organize, 1948	
31.	Agreement on the rescue of astronauts, the return of astronauts and the return of objects launched into outer space,1963	1969
32.	Convention on the privileges and immunities of the specialized agencies of the United Nations , 1947	1970
33.	Treaty on the prohibition of the emplacement of nuclear weapons and other weapons of mass destruction on the sea-bed and the ocean floor and in the subsoil thereof, 1971	1971
34.	Convention for the Suppression of unlawful seizure of aircraft, 1970	1971

35.	Montreal Convention against unlawful actions against security of civil aviation, 1971	
36.	Convention on the prohibition of the development, production and stockpiling of bacteriological (biological) and toxin weapons and on their destruction, 1972	
37.	Convention on the international liability for damage caused by space objects, 1972	1972
38.	Constitution of the Universal Postal Union, 1874	1973
39.	Statute of the International Atomic EnergyAgency, 1956	1973
40.	International Covenant on Economic, Social and Cultural Rights, 1966	1974
41.	International Covenant on Civil and Political Rights, 1966	1974
42.	Constitution of the United Nations Food and Agricultural Organization 1974	
43.	International Convention on the Suppression and Punishment of the Crime of Apartheid, 1973	1975
44.	Convention on the prevention and punishment of crimes against internationally protected persons, including diplomatic agents, 1973	1975
45.	Convention on the Representation of States in International Organizations, 1975	1976
46.	Convention (No. 122) concerning employment policy, 1964	1976
47.	Convention on the High Seas, 1958	1976
48.	Barselona Declaration recognizing the Right to a Flag of States having no Sea-coast, 1921	
49.	Convention on the prohibition of military or any other hostile use of environmental modification techniques, 1976	1978
50.	Convention on the prohibition of military or any other hostile use of environmental modification techniques, 1976	1978
51.	Convention establishing the World Intellectual Property Organization, 1967	1979
52.	Convention on the Elimination of All Forms of Discrimination against Women, 1979	1981
53.	Convention concerning the minimum age for admission to employment underground in mines, 1967	1981
54.	Convention on prohibitions or restrictions on the use of certain conventional weapons which may be deemed to be excessively injurious or to have indiscriminate effects, 1980	
55.	Convention concerning the Use of Broadcasting for the Cause of Peace, 1936	1985
56.	Convention of Paris for the Protection of Industrial Property, 1883	1985
57.	Madrid Agreement concerning the International Registration of Marks, 1891	1985
58.	Convention on registration of objects launched into outer space, 1974	1985
59.	Chicago Convention on International Civil Aviation, 1944	1986
60.	Vienna Convention on the Physical Potection of Nuclear Materials, 1979	1986
61.	International Telecommunication Convention,1865	1986
62.	Convention Against Apartheid in Sports, 1985	1987
63.	Vienna Convention on the Law of Treaties, 1969	1988
64.	Constitution of the International Civil Aviation Organization 1944	1989
65.	Vienna Convention on Consular Relations, 1963	1989
66.	Convention on the Rights of Child , 1989	1990
67.	Convention on Offences and Certain Other Acts Committed on Board Aircraft, 1963	

68.	Articles of Agreement of the Internal Monetary Fund (IMF), 1945	1991
69.	Articles of Agreement of the International Bank for Reconstruction and Development (World Bank), 1946	1991
70.	Constitution of the Asia Pacific Telecommunity, 1976	1991
71.	Supplementary Protocol to the International Covenant on Civil and Political Rights, 1966	
72.	Convention on Consent to Marriage, Minimum Age for Marriage and Regsitration of Marriages, 1962	1991
73.	New York Single Convention on Narcotic Drugs, 1961	1991
74.	Patent Cooperation Treaty, 1970	1991
75.	New York International Convention against the taking of hostages, 1979	1992
76.	United Nations Framework Convention on Climate Change, 1992	1993
77.	Rio de Janeiro Convention on Biological Diversity, 1992	1993
78.	United Nations Convention to Combat Desertification in those countries Experiencing Serious Drought and/or Desertification, particularly in Africa,1993	1993
79.	Convention on the Prohibition of the Development, Production, Stockpiling and Use of Chemical Weapons and Their Destructions 1993	1994
80.	Convention on International Trade in Endangered Species of Wild Fauna and Flora, 1973	
81.	Vienna Convention for the Protection of the Ozone Layer, 1985	1995
82.	Protocol Additional to the Geneva Convention relating to the protection of victims of armed conflicts, 1977	1995
83.	Convention on the Settlement of investment disputes between states and nationals of other states, 1965	
84.	Agreement on the Establishment of World Trade Organization, 1994	1996
85.	General Agreement on Tariff and Trade, 1994	1996
86.	Convention on the International Maritime Organization, 1948	1996
87.	Convention on Maritime Transportation, 1958	1996
88.	United Nations Convention on the Law of the Sea, 1982	1996
89.	Convention on Contract for the International Sale of Goods,1980	1997
90.	The Comprehensive Nuclear Test-Ban Treaty, 1996	1997
91.	Basel Convention on the Control of Transboundary Movement of Hazardous Wastes and Their Disposal, 1989	1997
92.	Berne Convention for the Protection of Literary and Artistic Works, 1886	1997
93.	Convention on Road Traffic, 1968	1997
94.	Convention on Road Signs and Signals, 1968	1997

BASIC TITLES FOR MONGOLIA

title	ISBN
Mongolia A "Spy" Guide	1433034239
Mongolia Air Force Handbook	1433034247
Mongolia Banking & Financial Market Handbook	1433034255
Mongolia Business and Investment Opportunities Yearbook	1433034263
Mongolia Business and Investment Opportunities Yearbook	1438733747

title	ISBN
Mongolia Business and Investment Opportunities Yearbook Volume 1 Strategic Information and Opportunities	143877740X
Mongolia Business and Investment Opportunities Yearbook Volume 1 Strategic Information and Opportunities	143877740X
Mongolia Business Intelligence Report	1433034271
Mongolia Business Law Handbook	1438770537
Mongolia Business Law Handbook	143303428X
Mongolia Business Law Handbook	1438733755
Mongolia Business Law Handbook	1438770537
Mongolia Central Bank and Financial Policy Handbook	143306247X
Mongolia Company Laws and Regulations Handbook	1433070340
Mongolia Constitution and Citizenship Laws Handbook - Strategic Information and Basic Laws	1438779488
Mongolia Constitution and Citizenship Laws Handbook - Strategic Information and Basic Laws	1438779488
Mongolia Country Study Guide	1433034298
Mongolia Country Study Guide Volume 1 Strategic Information and Developments	1438775075
Mongolia Country Study Guide Volume 1 Strategic Information and Developments	1438775075
Mongolia Customs, Trade Regulations and Procedures Handbook	1433034301
Mongolia Diplomatic Handbook	143303431X
Mongolia Ecology & Nature Protection Handbook	1433034328
Mongolia Ecology & Nature Protection Laws and Regulation Handbook	1433074435
Mongolia Economic & Development Strategy Handbook	1433034336
Mongolia Energy Policy, Laws and Regulation Handbook	143307219X
Mongolia Export-Import Trade and Business Directory	1433034344
Mongolia Foreign Policy and Government Guide	1433034352
Mongolia Foreign Policy and Government Guide	1438733763
Mongolia Free Trade and Industrial Zones Handbook	1433034360
Mongolia Immigration Laws and Regulations Handbook - Strategic Information and Basic Laws	1438783094
Mongolia Immigration Laws and Regulations Handbook - Strategic Information and Basic Laws	1438783094
Mongolia Industrial and Business Directory	1433034379
Mongolia Industrial and Business Directory	1438733771
Mongolia Internet and E-Commerce Investment and Business Guide: Regulations and Opportunities	1433034387
Mongolia Investment and Business Guide	1438768257
Mongolia Investment and Business Guide	1433034395
Mongolia Investment and Business Guide	1438768257
Mongolia Investment and Trade Laws and Regulations Handbook	1433076357
Mongolia Labor Laws and Regulations Handbook - Strategic Information and Basic Laws	1438781296
Mongolia Labor Laws and Regulations Handbook - Strategic Information and Basic Laws	1438781296

title	ISBN
Mongolia Land Ownership and Agriculture Laws Handbook	1438759584
Mongolia Land Ownership and Agriculture Laws Handbook	1438759584
Mongolia Land Ownership and Agriculture Laws Handbook	1438759584
Mongolia Mineral & Mining Sector Investment and Business Guide	1433034409
Mongolia Mineral & Mining Sector Investment and Business Guide	143873378X
Mongolia Mining Laws and Regulations Handbook	1433077892
Mongolia National Security and Defense Policy Handbook	1433034417
Mongolia National Security and Defense Policy Handbook	1438733798
Mongolia Recent Economic and Political Developments Yearbook	143306412X
Mongolia Recent Economic and Political Developments Yearbook	143306412X
Mongolia Recent Economic and Political Developments Yearbook	143306412X
Mongolia Starting Business (Incorporating) in....Guide	1433067234
Mongolia Tax Guide	1433034425
Mongolia Tax Guide	1438733801
Mongolia Taxation Laws and Regulations Handbook	1433080486
Mongolia Telecom Laws and Regulations Handbook	1433082225
Mongolia Telecommunication Industry Business Opportunities Handbook	1433034433
Mongolia Traders and Investors Handbook	1433034220
Mongolia Traders Manual: Export-Import, Trade, Investment	1433067242
Mongolia Transportation Policy and Regulations Handbook	1433067250

Burundi Business Law Handbook Volume 1 Strategic Information and Basic Laws
Cambodia Business Law Handbook Volume 1 Strategic Information and Basic Laws
Cameroon Business Law Handbook Volume 1 Strategic Information and Basic Laws
Canada Business Law Handbook Volume 1 Strategic Information and Basic Laws
Cape Verde Business Law Handbook Volume 1 Strategic Information and Basic Laws
Cayman Islands Business Law Handbook Volume 1 Strategic Information and Basic Laws
Central African Republic Business Law Handbook Volume 1 Strategic Information and Basic Laws
Chad Business Law Handbook Volume 1 Strategic Information and Basic Laws
Chile Business Law Handbook Volume 1 Strategic Information and Basic Laws
China Business Law Handbook Volume 1 Strategic Information and Basic Laws
Colombia Business Law Handbook Volume 1 Strategic Information and Basic Laws
Comoros Business Law Handbook Volume 1 Strategic Information and Basic Laws
Congo Business Law Handbook Volume 1 Strategic Information and Basic Laws
Congo, Democratic Republic Business Law Handbook Volume 1 Strategic Information and Basic Laws
Cook Islands Business Law Handbook Volume 1 Strategic Information and Basic Laws
Costa Rica Business Law Handbook Volume 1 Strategic Information and Basic Laws
Cote d'Ivoire Business Law Handbook Volume 1 Strategic Information and Basic Laws
Croatia Business Law Handbook Volume 1 Strategic Information and Basic Laws
Cuba Business Law Handbook Volume 1 Strategic Information and Basic Laws
Cyprus Business Law Handbook Volume 1 Strategic Information and Basic Laws
Czech Republic Business Law Handbook Volume 1 Strategic Information and Basic Laws
Denmark Business Law Handbook Volume 1 Strategic Information and Basic Laws
Djibouti Business Law Handbook Volume 1 Strategic Information and Basic Laws
Dominica Business Law Handbook Volume 1 Strategic Information and Basic Laws
Dominican Republic Business Law Handbook Volume 1 Strategic Information and Basic Laws
Ecuador Business Law Handbook Volume 1 Strategic Information and Basic Laws
Egypt Business Law Handbook Volume 1 Strategic Information and Basic Laws
El Salvador Business Law Handbook Volume 1 Strategic Information and Basic Laws
Equatorial Guinea Business Law Handbook Volume 1 Strategic Information and Basic Laws
Eritrea Business Law Handbook Volume 1 Strategic Information and Basic Laws
Estonia Business Law Handbook Volume 1 Strategic Information and Basic Laws
Ethiopia Business Law Handbook Volume 1 Strategic Information and Basic Laws
Falkland Islands Business Law Handbook Volume 1 Strategic Information and Basic Laws
Faroes Islands Business Law Handbook Volume 1 Strategic Information and Basic Laws
Fiji Business Law Handbook Volume 1 Strategic Information and Basic Laws
Finland Business Law Handbook Volume 1 Strategic Information and Basic Laws
France Business Law Handbook Volume 1 Strategic Information and Basic Laws
Gabon Business Law Handbook Volume 1 Strategic Information and Basic Laws
Gambia Business Law Handbook Volume 1 Strategic Information and Basic Laws
Georgia Business Law Handbook Volume 1 Strategic Information and Basic Laws
Germany Business Law Handbook Volume 1 Strategic Information and Basic Laws
Ghana Business Law Handbook Volume 1 Strategic Information and Basic Laws
Gibraltar Business Law Handbook Volume 1 Strategic Information and Basic Laws
Greece Business Law Handbook Volume 1 Strategic Information and Basic Laws
Greenland Business Law Handbook Volume 1 Strategic Information and Basic Laws
Grenada Business Law Handbook Volume 1 Strategic Information and Basic Laws
Guam Business Law Handbook Volume 1 Strategic Information and Basic Laws
Guatemala Business Law Handbook Volume 1 Strategic Information and Basic Laws
Guernsey Business Law Handbook Volume 1 Strategic Information and Basic Laws
Guinea Business Law Handbook Volume 1 Strategic Information and Basic Laws
Guinea-Bissau Business Law Handbook Volume 1 Strategic Information and Basic Laws

Guyana Business Law Handbook Volume 1 Strategic Information and Basic Laws
Haiti Business Law Handbook Volume 1 Strategic Information and Basic Laws
Honduras Business Law Handbook Volume 1 Strategic Information and Basic Laws
Hungary Business Law Handbook Volume 1 Strategic Information and Basic Laws
Iceland Business Law Handbook Volume 1 Strategic Information and Basic Laws
India Business Law Handbook Volume 1 Strategic Information and Basic Laws
Indonesia Business Law Handbook Volume 1 Strategic Information and Basic Laws
Iran Business Law Handbook Volume 1 Strategic Information and Basic Laws
Iraq Business Law Handbook Volume 1 Strategic Information and Basic Laws
Ireland Business Law Handbook Volume 1 Strategic Information and Basic Laws
Israel Business Law Handbook Volume 1 Strategic Information and Basic Laws
Italy Business Law Handbook Volume 1 Strategic Information and Basic Laws
Jamaica Business Law Handbook Volume 1 Strategic Information and Basic Laws
Japan Business Law Handbook Volume 1 Strategic Information and Basic Laws
Jersey Business Law Handbook Volume 1 Strategic Information and Basic Laws
Jordan Business Law Handbook Volume 1 Strategic Information and Basic Laws
Kazakhstan Business Law Handbook Volume 1 Strategic Information and Basic Laws
Kenya Business Law Handbook Volume 1 Strategic Information and Basic Laws
Kiribati Business Law Handbook Volume 1 Strategic Information and Basic Laws
Korea, North Business Law Handbook Volume 1 Strategic Information and Basic Laws
Korea, South Business Law Handbook Volume 1 Strategic Information and Basic Laws
Kosovo Business Law Handbook Volume 1 Strategic Information and Basic Laws
Kurdistan Business Law Handbook Volume 1 Strategic Information and Basic Laws
Kuwait Business Law Handbook Volume 1 Strategic Information and Basic Laws
Kyrgyzstan Business Law Handbook Volume 1 Strategic Information and Basic Laws
Laos Business Law Handbook Volume 1 Strategic Information and Basic Laws
Latvia Business Law Handbook Volume 1 Strategic Information and Basic Laws
Lebanon Business Law Handbook Volume 1 Strategic Information and Basic Laws
Lesotho Business Law Handbook Volume 1 Strategic Information and Basic Laws
Liberia Business Law Handbook Volume 1 Strategic Information and Basic Laws
Libya Business Law Handbook Volume 1 Strategic Information and Basic Laws
Liechtenstein Business Law Handbook Volume 1 Strategic Information and Basic Laws
Lithuania Business Law Handbook Volume 1 Strategic Information and Basic Laws
Luxembourg Business Law Handbook Volume 1 Strategic Information and Basic Laws
Macao Business Law Handbook Volume 1 Strategic Information and Basic Laws
Macedonia Business Law Handbook Volume 1 Strategic Information and Basic Laws
Madagascar Business Law Handbook Volume 1 Strategic Information and Basic Laws
Madeira Business Law Handbook Volume 1 Strategic Information and Basic Laws
Malawi Business Law Handbook Volume 1 Strategic Information and Basic Laws
Malaysia Business Law Handbook Volume 1 Strategic Information and Basic Laws
Maldives Business Law Handbook Volume 1 Strategic Information and Basic Laws
Mali Business Law Handbook Volume 1 Strategic Information and Basic Laws
Malta Business Law Handbook Volume 1 Strategic Information and Basic Laws
Man Business Law Handbook Volume 1 Strategic Information and Basic Laws
Marshall Islands Business Law Handbook Volume 1 Strategic Information and Basic Laws
Mauritania Business Law Handbook Volume 1 Strategic Information and Basic Laws
Mauritius Business Law Handbook Volume 1 Strategic Information and Basic Laws
Mayotte Business Law Handbook Volume 1 Strategic Information and Basic Laws
Mexico Business Law Handbook Volume 1 Strategic Information and Basic Laws
Micronesia Business Law Handbook Volume 1 Strategic Information and Basic Laws
Moldova Business Law Handbook Volume 1 Strategic Information and Basic Laws

Monaco Business Law Handbook Volume 1 Strategic Information and Basic Laws
Mongolia Business Law Handbook Volume 1 Strategic Information and Basic Laws
Monserrat Business Law Handbook Volume 1 Strategic Information and Basic Laws
Morocco Business Law Handbook Volume 1 Strategic Information and Basic Laws
Mozambique Business Law Handbook Volume 1 Strategic Information and Basic Laws
Myanmar Business Law Handbook Volume 1 Strategic Information and Basic Laws
Namibia Business Law Handbook Volume 1 Strategic Information and Basic Laws
Nauru Business Law Handbook Volume 1 Strategic Information and Basic Laws
Nepal Business Law Handbook Volume 1 Strategic Information and Basic Laws
Netherlands Business Law Handbook Volume 1 Strategic Information and Basic Laws
New Caledonia Business Law Handbook Volume 1 Strategic Information and Basic Laws
New Zealand Business Law Handbook Volume 1 Strategic Information and Basic Laws
Nicaragua Business Law Handbook Volume 1 Strategic Information and Basic Laws
Niger Business Law Handbook Volume 1 Strategic Information and Basic Laws
Nigeria Business Law Handbook Volume 1 Strategic Information and Basic Laws
Niue Business Law Handbook Volume 1 Strategic Information and Basic Laws
Northern Mariana Islands Business Law Handbook Volume 1 Strategic Information and Basic Laws
Norway Business Law Handbook Volume 1 Strategic Information and Basic Laws
Oman Business Law Handbook Volume 1 Strategic Information and Basic Laws
Pakistan Business Law Handbook Volume 1 Strategic Information and Basic Laws
Palau Business Law Handbook Volume 1 Strategic Information and Basic Laws
Palestine (West Bank & Gaza) Business Law Handbook Volume 1 Strategic Information and Basic Laws
Panama Business Law Handbook Volume 1 Strategic Information and Basic Laws
Papua New Guinea Business Law Handbook Volume 1 Strategic Information and Basic Laws
Paraguay Business Law Handbook Volume 1 Strategic Information and Basic Laws
Peru Business Law Handbook Volume 1 Strategic Information and Basic Laws
Philippines Business Law Handbook Volume 1 Strategic Information and Basic Laws
Pitcairn Islands Business Law Handbook Volume 1 Strategic Information and Basic Laws
Poland Business Law Handbook Volume 1 Strategic Information and Basic Laws
Polynesia French Business Law Handbook Volume 1 Strategic Information and Basic Laws
Portugal Business Law Handbook Volume 1 Strategic Information and Basic Laws
Qatar Business Law Handbook Volume 1 Strategic Information and Basic Laws
Romania Business Law Handbook Volume 1 Strategic Information and Basic Laws
Russia Business Law Handbook Volume 1 Strategic Information and Basic Laws
Rwanda Business Law Handbook Volume 1 Strategic Information and Basic Laws
Saint Kitts and Nevis Business Law Handbook Volume 1 Strategic Information and Basic Laws
Saint Lucia Business Law Handbook Volume 1 Strategic Information and Basic Laws
Saint Vincent and The Grenadines Business Law Handbook Volume 1 Strategic Information and Basic Laws
Samoa (American) A Business Law Handbook Volume 1 Strategic Information and Basic Laws
Samoa (Western) Business Law Handbook Volume 1 Strategic Information and Basic Laws
San Marino Business Law Handbook Volume 1 Strategic Information and Basic Laws
Sao Tome and Principe Business Law Handbook Volume 1 Strategic Information and Basic Laws
Saudi Arabia Business Law Handbook Volume 1 Strategic Information and Basic Laws
Scotland Business Law Handbook Volume 1 Strategic Information and Basic Laws
Senegal Business Law Handbook Volume 1 Strategic Information and Basic Laws
Serbia Business Law Handbook Volume 1 Strategic Information and Basic Laws
Seychelles Business Law Handbook Volume 1 Strategic Information and Basic Laws
Sierra Leone Business Law Handbook Volume 1 Strategic Information and Basic Laws
Singapore Business Law Handbook Volume 1 Strategic Information and Basic Laws
Slovakia Business Law Handbook Volume 1 Strategic Information and Basic Laws
Slovenia Business Law Handbook Volume 1 Strategic Information and Basic Laws

Solomon Islands Business Law Handbook Volume 1 Strategic Information and Basic Laws
Somalia Business Law Handbook Volume 1 Strategic Information and Basic Laws
South Africa Business Law Handbook Volume 1 Strategic Information and Basic Laws
Spain Business Law Handbook Volume 1 Strategic Information and Basic Laws
Sri Lanka Business Law Handbook Volume 1 Strategic Information and Basic Laws
St. Helena Business Law Handbook Volume 1 Strategic Information and Basic Laws
St. Pierre & Miquelon Business Law Handbook Volume 1 Strategic Information and Basic Laws
Sudan Business Law Handbook Volume 1 Strategic Information and Basic Laws
Sudan South Business Law Handbook Volume 1 Strategic Information and Basic Laws
Suriname Business Law Handbook Volume 1 Strategic Information and Basic Laws
Swaziland Business Law Handbook Volume 1 Strategic Information and Basic Laws
Sweden Business Law Handbook Volume 1 Strategic Information and Basic Laws
Switzerland Business Law Handbook Volume 1 Strategic Information and Basic Laws
Syria Business Law Handbook Volume 1 Strategic Information and Basic Laws
Taiwan Business Law Handbook Volume 1 Strategic Information and Basic Laws
Tajikistan Business Law Handbook Volume 1 Strategic Information and Basic Laws
Tanzania Business Law Handbook Volume 1 Strategic Information and Basic Laws
Thailand Business Law Handbook Volume 1 Strategic Information and Basic Laws
Togo Business Law Handbook Volume 1 Strategic Information and Basic Laws
Tonga Business Law Handbook Volume 1 Strategic Information and Basic Laws
Trinidad and Tobago Business Law Handbook Volume 1 Strategic Information and Basic Laws
Tunisia Business Law Handbook Volume 1 Strategic Information and Basic Laws
Turkey Business Law Handbook Volume 1 Strategic Information and Basic Laws
Turkmenistan Business Law Handbook Volume 1 Strategic Information and Basic Laws
Turks & Caicos Business Law Handbook Volume 1 Strategic Information and Basic Laws
Tuvalu Business Law Handbook Volume 1 Strategic Information and Basic Laws
Uganda Business Law Handbook Volume 1 Strategic Information and Basic Laws
Ukraine Business Law Handbook Volume 1 Strategic Information and Basic Laws
United Arab Emirates Business Law Handbook Volume 1 Strategic Information and Basic Laws
United Kingdom Business Law Handbook Volume 1 Strategic Information and Basic Laws
United States Business Law Handbook Volume 1 Strategic Information and Basic Laws
Uruguay Business Law Handbook Volume 1 Strategic Information and Basic Laws
Uzbekistan Business Law Handbook Volume 1 Strategic Information and Basic Laws
Vanuatu Business Law Handbook Volume 1 Strategic Information and Basic Laws
Vatican City Business Law Handbook Volume 1 Strategic Information and Basic Laws
Venezuela Business Law Handbook Volume 1 Strategic Information and Basic Laws
Vietnam Business Law Handbook Volume 1 Strategic Information and Basic Laws
Virgin Islands, British Business Law Handbook Volume 1 Strategic Information and Basic Laws
Wake Atoll Business Law Handbook Volume 1 Strategic Information and Basic Laws
Wallis & Futuna Business Law Handbook Volume 1 Strategic Information and Basic Laws
Western Sahara Business Law Handbook Volume 1 Strategic Information and Basic Laws
Yemen Business Law Handbook Volume 1 Strategic Information and Basic Laws
Zambia Business Law Handbook Volume 1 Strategic Information and Basic Laws
Zimbabwe Business Law Handbook Volume 1 Strategic Information and Basic Laws